WITHDRAWN

Enduring Liberalism

American Political Thought
edited by
Wilson Carey McWilliams and Lance Banning

Enduring Liberalism
American Political Thought Since the 1960s

Robert Booth Fowler

 University Press of Kansas

Published by the University Press of Kansas (Lawrence, Kansas 66049),
which was organized by the Kansas Board of Regents and is operated and
funded by Emporia State University, Fort Hays State University, Kansas
State University, Pittsburg State University, the University of Kansas, and
Wichita State University.

Library of Congress Cataloging-in-Publication Data

Fowler, Robert Booth, 1940–
    Enduring liberalism : American political thought since the 1960s /
Robert Booth Fowler.
      p.   cm. — (American political thought)
    Includes bibliographical references and index.
    ISBN 0-7006-0974-1 (alk. paper)
    1. Liberalism—United States—History—20th century. 2. Consensus
(Social sciences)—United States—History—20th century.
    3. Political science—United States—History—20th century.
    I. Title. II. Series.
    JC574.2.U6F68   1999
    320.51'3'097309045—dc21   99-27237

British Library Cataloguing in Publication Data is available.

Printed in the United States of America
10 9 8 7 6 5 4 3 2 1

For Ben

Contents

Preface

Enduring Liberalism: American Political Thought Since the 1960s has two inevitably intertwined objectives. One is to explore the political thought of both American public intellectuals and the general public since the 1960s. The other is to consider the major interpretations of American political thought. As a result, the book grapples with a significant part of the intellectual history of the United States, while also plunging into the treacherous waters of interpretation.

My argument is straightforward, but its structure is more complicated, and my interpretation is controversial. One part of my story describes how the consensus view in post–World War II American political thought collapsed among public intellectuals in the tumult of the 1960s. The consensus view held that there was wide agreement among Americans on such liberal values as individualism, individual liberty, political equality, economic opportunity, and consent of the governed.

Another part is my claim that the general public continues to be largely consensual in its political values. I maintain that there has not been a collapse of consensus among the general public since the 1960s. While the common wisdom here is just the opposite, such a view flies in the face of the substantial information we have on public attitudes about basic values.

Moreover, I contend that at the level of cultural practices since the 1960s there is more substantiation of the continuing sway of liberal norms. Indeed, American cultural practices provide plentiful evidence of an accelerating triumph of liberal values. This is notably true in much of civil society, especially the home and church, where liberal norms were rarely central in the 1950s or before. In short, the announcement of the death of liberal consensus in the United States is premature.

I insist, however, that we recognize that everything depends on the level of analysis. In the thought of public intellectuals, there is no doubt that a liberal consensus—if, indeed, there ever was one—is long gone. By "public intellectuals" I mean a certain kind of reflective participant in American public life. The most obvious examples are those whose names are familiar in the major intellectual journals of the day—people such as Robert Bellah, William Bennett, Jean Bethke Elshtain, Seymour Martin Lipset, Michael Walzer—people whose ideas, theories, and arguments are the common currency of intellectual discourse in this era. Their very publicness, their active participation on the public intellectual stage, defines them.

My compass for public intellectuals in this study, however, goes beyond the familiar names. I include many others who, while they may be less well known, are important public participants in political discourses relevant to this book, such as green political thought or the explanation of problems in the African-American family. These individuals write and sometimes speak about issues in the public realm. While not all are influential, together they have played a significant part in the broader intellectual debates this book considers.

In this world of public intellectuals, one frequently walks on shaky terrain, given the many fissures over values that open in it. There is no consensus here and no prospect of it. Pluralism is the reality in American intellectual thought. Yet in considering contemporary intellectual thinking here, I concentrate on three particular themes that attract many public intellectuals today as possible redirections for the United States. All receive close attention to give a sense of what order there is within the diverse political thought of present-day public intellectuals.

One theme is the tremendous concern for community; engagement with the environment is another; and the now fashionable interest in civil society is a third. Each reflects the considerable (if hardly universal) dissatisfaction with liberalism in theory and/or in practice among contemporary intellectuals. Each also represents a possible alternative. Each has its own varieties, often sharply contested, which in turn underscore the pluralism of intellectual thought today.

Yet all three participate in one, somewhat murky drift, which is a search for "community." This drift, however, is still unfocused, and it is complicated by fierce contests over multiple versions of the good community. Moreover, the community focus is sometimes self-conscious, sometimes not, sometimes proposed as an alternative to liberalism, sometimes as a companion of liberal values. Perhaps the most interesting political thought in the United States today comes from thinkers such as Jean Bethke Elshtain and Michael Walzer, who want us to become, if you will, communitarian liberals or liberal communitarians.

Recognition of this often inchoate concern with what I call community, however, should not for a moment obscure the fractious (and perhaps wonderful) reality of contemporary intellectual political thought. There are, for example, a host of intellectuals who are fearful of community, however conceived. Concern with community is important, but there is no sign of a firm consensus on this direction, much less on what it might mean.

In the end, I attempt to draw the evidence and the analyses together and present a view of intellectual and public thought about political values that itself is an interpretation. And, somewhat reluctantly, I offer a few of my own reactions to the world I see or, as postmoderns would have me say, the world I have created.

In chapter 1 I delineate classic interpretations of American political thought. I argue that these interpretations, which may be grand and even beautiful, are increasingly relics, artifacts of other times and other intellects. They make often-grandiose claims to explain the pattern of American political thought, but they are not really able to sustain them. Put more bluntly, the classic interpretations simply do not work anymore—if they ever did—to explain the history of American political thought. Moreover, it is often hard to tell just what they meant to explain. Most are vague about what realms of thought they consider: the views of intellectuals, the sentiments of the public, or the cultural practices of the United States.

I explore a number of past interpretations, including the analyses of Alexis de Tocqueville, Charles Beard, V. L. Parrington, Louis Hartz, and Daniel Boorstin. The consensus theories of the 1950s, especially those of Hartz and Boorstin, remain a key background against which contemporary interpretations proceed. They are routinely rejected, indeed often denounced, by advocates of the plethora of alternative conceptions of U.S. political thought that have unfolded since. Perhaps unintentionally, their critics reaffirm their continuing importance.

In chapter 2 I focus directly on consensus theory and the criticisms of it. Consensus theory was the focal point of the debates over how to interpret American political thought that raged during the later 1960s and well into the 1970s—and it continues decades later. Central to the attack on the adequacy of consensus views is the claim that such a consensus was a myth; it just didn't exist, and it certainly doesn't now.

In chapter 2 I also describe the great explosion of political pluralism among intellectuals since the 1960s. I briefly chronicle such developments as contemporary feminism, postmodernism, and conservatism. I also note the renewed vitality of liberal thinking in several forms. By this means, I underline the hollowness of any claims for a consensus in the political thought of American public intellectuals.

I caution, however, that popular opinion is quite another story. The American public is not similarly pluralist in its basic political ideas. Public opinion surveys make clear that U.S. citizens mostly hold liberal values, a situation that has not changed since the 1960s. I contend that what change there has been suggests that the public has grown even more committed to liberal values, while diversity has occurred among American intellectuals. Always I insist we must be clear about whose political thinking one is discussing and be wary of vague claims about something named American political thought.

Much of the past discourse about consensus interpretations has concentrated on the accuracy of their portrayals of American history. I consider this matter in some detail in assessing the consensus interpretation. I recognize that scholars proceeding from many points of view and employing diverse methodologies conclude that the story of our history is not a consensus story, and I agree.

Critics' main complaint is that conflict, brushed by in consensus versions of American history, has been a crucial factor in American life. They emphasize religious, ethnic and racial, or economic conflicts, among others. The larger point is that conflict has been important in American values and history, and critics often argue that a conflict interpretation of one form or another is the correct one.

Chapter 3 looks at other interpretations that seek to understand the American political tradition and American political thought.

Some softer dissents from the consensus view suggest that value conflicts that take place within a broad consensus may represent the most accurate picture. Others propose that one consensus has followed another over time, each different. Still others like to describe American political thinking in terms of dialectical engagement, often between impulses toward individualism and community.

Today's leading interpretation is the multiple-strands view, whose proponents contend that the narrative of American history is far from any consensus. Rather, the story of our political thinking concerns several strands of thought, often clashing, each reflecting a particular strand of American life and culture. Chapter 3 also explores postmodern perspectives on American political thought and culture.

Another way to consider and evaluate competing interpretations of American political thought, past and present, is to test their worth in a modest case study that assesses their effectiveness in understanding the thought of one period in some depth. I do this in chapter 3, which examines approaches to the Founding of the United States. This intensely contested arena proves a good setting for observing the elaborate diversity of interpretations of the American tradition(s) of political thought. The case study of the American Founding and its modern-day interpretations leave little doubt that nothing remotely like a consensus exists on how to read American political thought.

To get a sense of the adequacy of current interpretations, one must confront American political thinking of the past. Yet the issue of political thought in the United States must also be engaged in a contemporary context. Chapter 4 begins that task, arguing that liberal values have in fact gained dramatically in the public sphere in the current age. From one perspective, I report that many cultural commentators acknowledge this reality when they bemoan the liberal acid they see as contributing to the decay of American society and institutions. From another angle, I concentrate on two institutions and developments within them: American political parties and the American educational system. In both, I maintain, there is bountiful evidence that the march of liberalism has proceeded apace.

Studies of public opinion find the same. Liberal attitudes such as pluralism and greater emphasis on the individual have made substantial headway in the public, which the classic theorists of the

1950s had already declared to be attitudinally "liberal." Indeed, there is a far better case to be made today for the claim that present-day Americans are more firmly a part of a liberal tradition than were Americans in the past.

Moreover, I contend that even among American intellectuals, who are more diverse than the public in their political thinking, liberalism is more evident than one might suspect. Through a case study of so-called conservative intellectuals in the United States— thinkers who are, in fact, more and more "liberal" and "libertarian"—chapter 4 questions how different from the mainstream this significant "alternative" ideology within American political thought is. "Conservatism" may have grown as a political and intellectual force since the 1960s, but this does not mean it has grown as a significant alternative to liberalism. In fact, it has not, which may explain much of its growth.

It is, however, in the more personal and less public aspects of American life, those areas once called private, that the most dramatic changes have taken place since the 1960s. Here is where a revolution has occurred, in which liberal attitudes steadily erase the famous public and private distinction first identified by Tocqueville. It was always in the home, in the church, and among women that liberal values were less secure and far less triumphant than elsewhere in American life. And it is in these areas that liberalism has wrought distinct, quite remarkable, changes in the last half century. Chapter 5 examines case studies that illustrate this change. One, for example, explores women's roles today, addressing the status of the family, relevant government policies, and the perspectives of feminist thought. All reveal the influence of liberal values.

Overall, my argument is that the record of American practice and general public opinion is not a narrative about the retreat of liberalism. The reality is liberalism's increasing momentum in public and so-called private life and in public opinion, despite many interpreters' insistence to the contrary.

With this in mind, I turn next to consider the themes that many intellectuals now engage as their uneasiness rises in often unspoken acknowledgement of the growth of liberalism in American culture. In chapter 6 I discuss the most popular topic—"community." The widespread intellectual engagement with community is evident everywhere, as many intellectuals invoke it as the cure for ailments they discern in liberalism as well as assorted liberal practices and institutions.

Of course, community is a capacious term. When intellectual thought turns from general complaints about liberalism in the name of "community" to proposing ideas about community—which happens less often than one might wish—one meets the vast variety of conceptions of community. Chapter 6 considers some of the models of community. Each has its able public intellectual advocates, and each demonstrates the extent to which community is a contested concept in the diverse world of contemporary public intellectuals.

Chapter 6 also investigates some other dimensions of the community phenomenon. These include evidence from public opinion data and cultural practices in the United States that suggests that there is a far wider interest in community than just among intellectuals. It also looks at the considerable intellectual resistance to some of the community enthusiasms of this day, including reservations by some feminists and advocates of group identity.

I give attention to environmentalism as a growing dynamic in contemporary intellectual thought in chapter 7. There is no question about the tremendous popularity of environmentalism among most Americans. While the public rarely interprets environmentalism as an ideological alternative to liberalism, a growing number of intellectuals do. Chapter 7 notes the widespread criticism of liberalism and traditional Western religions that green intellectual thought presents. It observes the emerging foundations for a green political ethic, including natural rights, intrinsic natural values, religious claims, and pragmatism. I also reflect on several green images of the good society and their intellectual advocates. These images include holistic and communitarian societies that are in accord with nature, tough-minded authoritarian orders, godly creation societies, and libertarian models.

Finally, in chapters 8 and 9, I move to the much discussed topic of civil society in American thought. Today there is great interest among many public intellectuals in the human relations and institutions apart from the state—family, church, and innumerable other "private" associations. Thinkers who represent many points of view suggest that a revival of the nation's weakening civil society is integral to the resuscitation of the United States.

Chapter 8 enters the intense discourse and debate over civil society and its revival. It investigates key thinkers in the discussion such as Jean Bethke Elshtain and Alan Wolfe. It also addresses the reluctance some intellectuals, especially on the Left, have regarding civil society as the best place to make efforts to revive American society. They fear that a focus on civil society will leave society vulnerable to capture by uncontrolled capitalism.

Most public intellectual and social science discussion on how to strengthen civil society addresses the "battle over the family." So does my consideration, therefore, and I look at the discourse on marriage and divorce, two-parent and one-parent families, and the burgeoning social science literature on children from a variety of family backgrounds. In this context chapter 8 studies the family revival movement and its critics.

In chapter 9 I continue the subject of the revival of civil society as a proposed redirection in the United States. I concentrate first, and at some length, on the controversial and sensitive discussions of the African-American family. No area is more contested within African-American thought, yet none is more intimately connected with civil society concerns and debates.

In chapter 9 I also shift to another major aspect of civil society, religion and religious institutions. Both intellectual and popular attitudes toward religion reveal that many Americans place considerable hope in religion and/or religious institutions to help the United States. Yet liberal beliefs and behaviors have triumphed in much of American religion, just as they have in the family. This is just more evidence that liberalism's victory in American culture is real.

In chapter 10 I sum up my overall interpretation and gingerly offer a few reflections of my own. Intellectual thought about politics and society in the United States has indeed left consensus behind. It is now pluralistic in ways and to degrees that consensus interpreters of the 1950s could not have imagined. At the same time, I temper this conclusion by noting that there is more support for basic liberal norms among public intellectuals than many commentators realize.

Moreover, there are signs that some public intellectuals are struggling toward expressing a shared aspiration for community or, in many cases, some intersection of community and liberalism. There is no consensus on this direction, much less on a specific vision of community. Yet one sees and feels the winds of this movement, especially in the discourse today on how to revive America through civil society, environmentalism, and, most obviously, through building community itself. Only in the twenty-first century, however, will we discover whether these inclinations had any lasting force. My own hope, quiet but unashamed, is that they will.

There is no doubt that I have been tremendously helped by the kindness of so many people as I went along in my sometimes forlorn efforts to write this book. Of course, I am deeply grateful to Fred Woodward, Rebecca Knight Giusti, and others at the University Press of Kansas and to the anonymous reader who helped me do a lot more work. I want to thank the following colleagues who read one or more chapters and gave me good (and sometimes welcome) advice toward trying to do better: Charles Anderson, Kevin denDulk, John Evans, Finessa Ferrell-Smith, Jeff Hellmers, Bart Lambert, Carey McWilliams, John Meyer, Andrew Murphy, Laura Olson, David Reidinger, Alisa Rosenthal, Polly Schloesser, Kathi Sell, David Siemers, Marion Smiley, Andy Spalding, and Robert Yablon. Thanks also to my favorite detective and politician, Henry Fox. Above all, once again I thank the wonderful Alice.

Chapter One

Classic Interpretations

Contemporary struggles to interpret American political thought join a long tradition of similar efforts. Some have been brilliant and might, perhaps, induce a certain humility in present-day practitioners of this old art. In any case, there can be no avoiding past interpretations of American political thought and culture. Some are fascinating in their own right, but past interpretations must be engaged here because they are the background against which contemporary interpretations proceed—and have since the 1960s. Thus, while these classic interpretations have few devoted adherents today, they remain as the setting against which contemporary analysts argue. To understand the present-day interpretive discourse on American political thought and culture, one must know past perspectives.

My purpose in this chapter, therefore, is to explore the classic interpretations as the essential background for contemporary thinking. It is not to construct a single interpretive thread that will tie disparate perspectives tightly together. Each interpretation has its own integrity—and frequently conflicts with others. What unifies this chapter is the fact that each classic interpretation has had dialectical influence on current interpretive thinking about the United States. The chapter also displays a certain appreciation of these classic views, a recognition of their insights, and a willingness to respect their limitations as well.

There is no choice but to begin with the two great interpretations of the nineteenth century, those of Frederick Jackson Turner and, earlier, Alexis de Tocqueville. While Turner's view is distinctly dated, it has had far too much influence on his successors to be

1

slighted here. Tocqueville's analysis has had more staying power, and he remains a perceptive guide to how a certain kind of liberalism has overwhelmed all else in practice (although not in intellectual thought) in the contemporary United States. Yet Tocqueville remains so insightful—despite his current vogue—mostly dialectically. His basic analysis of American political thought and culture no longer works, a reality that, ironically, marks liberalism's all but complete triumph in practice in our time.

Next this chapter considers the world of conflict interpretations, whose model of clashing cultures, ideas, and forces enjoyed intellectual popularity in the Progressive Era a hundred years ago and for a while after. Charles Beard and Vernon L. Parrington were the renowned architects of this view. Their specific, *particular* analyses of the conflicts that they insisted divided Americans have been pretty much discredited. These men were better ideologues than historians, granting that the line between the two can be narrow. But their *general* assertion that conflict was central to the American story is far from discredited and has undergone a robust renewal in our time. Indeed, this perspective has never been more accepted—and acceptable—in American intellectual life, as we will see in chapter 3.

Finally, I grapple with the consensus interpretations of American thought and culture that were so dominant after World War II. While consensus views are now out of intellectual fashion both as a description of reality and as a normative model for a multicultural nation, consensus historians such as Louis Hartz and Daniel Boorstin were once interpretive giants of U.S. political thought. Mention of their names now can produce a somewhat embarrassed silence. More often, the reaction to consensus views is quick dismissal. They are often characterized as a serious mistake, which served the 1950s mood of conservatism.

Nineteenth-Century Interpretations

The two interpreters of the United States in the nineteenth century who stand out over all others are Alexis de Tocqueville, the famous example of the foreigner who saw more deeply, and Frederick Jackson Turner, who argued that to see America one had to turn away from Europe. Both have had their ups and downs in terms of intellectual popularity, but their reputations as classic interpreters of American culture are secure. If Tocqueville enjoys the more favorable reputation today and his analyses are still alive and still spark debate, Turner's views have become less and less influential, although Turner is not yet only a footnote. Turner, however, may have another day, since the image of the frontier remains a powerful one in the American mythos.

Alexis de Tocqueville's America

Alexis de Tocqueville's (1805–59) continuing sway over students of U.S. political and social thought is underlined every year as more and more serious studies of his work appear, especially those addressing Tocqueville and American culture and civilization.[1] Surely it is no mean feat that his *Democracy in America*, the product of his visit to the United States in the 1830s to study prisons, retains such great appeal. Indeed, Tocqueville is especially important for us to consider because his work remains the basis for many contemporary interpretations of the United States and its thought and culture in the present day.

Part of the explanation for the long life of Tocqueville's United States derives, no doubt, from *Democracy in America*'s confident analyses and predictions about the long run. Considering which of Tocqueville's predictions are still plausible is a favorite classroom game today, as it has long been. I first learned about Tocqueville by playing this game, and I have often observed it being played since. Has Russia emerged as the great alternative power to the United States? (Just now, no.) Is our country deeply threatened by an "Aristocracy of Manufacturers"? (Take a stand.) Is our culture still low-brow and practical? (What do MTV and *Married with Children* suggest?)

Another standard approach to Tocqueville, of course, has been to engage his discussion of the relationship between liberty and equality, and between the individual and the tyranny of the majority. These issues continue to be highly relevant today as they were 170 or so years ago when Tocqueville toured the United States. Indeed, the relationship between liberty and equality in America would be prominent on any short list of disputed questions of our time. How could they not be in light of debates over affirmative action, government and the economy, government decentralization, gay rights, the role of Christian conservatives, feminism and multiculturalism, and all the rest? Again and again, questions of liberty, equality, individualism, and the majority rule swirl around us and each other. Definitions and particulars change, and those changes matter, but the issues remain.

Even more broadly, however, Tocqueville's work has become a setting through which almost all contemporary questions facing the American polity and society may be pursued. For example, through Tocqueville's "profound" discussion of American loneliness, Cornel West meditates on the individual and community in the United States, noting the similarities between Tocqueville's observations and those of Emily Dickinson and Arthur Miller. If we start from Tocqueville, West suggests, we learn that "there is something about the soulcraft of a market-driven society that leads Americans inward . . . that makes it difficult to constitute healthy relations and community."[2]

Michael Sandel agrees and calls on Tocqueville to denounce "the commercial society and consumer culture." Advertising has created a new version of soul-destroying tyranny that has nothing much to do with government but is terrible in its effects. For Sandel, Tocqueville "was alive to the threat that was posed to civic virtue by materialism or the preoccupation with the pursuit of material well-being and self-interest."[3]

My interest in Tocqueville and his thought runs in a somewhat different direction. I am concerned with how he fit his discussion of various political inclinations into an overall interpretation of American political culture and its ideas. One part of Tocqueville's contribution to understanding of U.S. culture was his sense of the dialectics in American public practice. He saw a kind of consensual public ideology in the United States but observed that it operated with perplexing and sometimes disturbing tensions. Two examples he noted were Americans' commitment to individual freedom and their practice of social conformity and a widespread groupism combined with much loneliness. Tocqueville is justly famous for such perceptions of paradoxes among Americans. Yet from a contemporary perspective, perhaps Tocqueville's two-tiered interpretation of American life and thought is his most salient contribution. This aspect of his work receives attention here in part because it occupies such a significant role in all that follows.

After all, much of the story of the spread of liberal values in recent decades focuses on how the public-private distinction—Tocqueville's two tiers—has steadily eroded. The result is that Tocqueville's description of the United States in this instance is increasingly less accurate. Yet his analysis remains valuable as a guide to how important a change this is in American history, and the alarm he would feel about the consequences of such a change for social cohesion stimulates a certain attention.

Tocqueville saw an American (liberal) society with two distinct realms—one public, the other private—each closely bound to and dependent on the other. For him, these two interconnected arenas were not just integral to American culture but were also a means toward understanding it. Tocqueville's public realm included the worlds of work, property relations, money and economics, politics and the courts, and the life of the organized groups so many Americans found congenial. It was a gendered, male world. In contrast, Tocqueville identified the private sphere as the place of the home and the church, a world where women were at the center.

While the masculine realms of farming, trade, and the emerging factory, as well as politics and the courts, were important, Tocqueville insisted that this public world—or, in gender terms, men—required a healthy private sphere to function as well as to increase human happiness. Each dimension of American life complemented the other, as women did men. Yet for Tocqueville the public sphere especially needed the private sphere if the United States were to continue to be a satisfying civilization.

Church and home provided and promoted religion, and religion, Tocqueville famously argued, was the essential foundation for ethics in the United States. America was oriented toward individuals (and their families); it was enamored of expansive personal liberty in its public life; and it was a highly competitive society. Such attitudes, Tocqueville perceived, could be dangerous to the existence of an enduring social order. They could lead to destructive conflicts as egoistic men struggled to achieve their individual (or family) goals in a relatively open environment. What "men" needed as a result, Tocqueville argued, was religion to provide and justify moral beliefs that would restrain human (male) behavior.

Tocqueville judged that people required basic norms of human respect and honesty to ensure reasonably fair trade and relatively honest politics. Religion could provide these. This is why he insisted that "men cannot do without dogmatical belief" and why "it is much to be desired that such belief exist among them."[4] This is also why Tocqueville insisted "if faith be wanting in him, he (a person) must be subject and if he be free, he must believe."[5]

Of course Tocqueville's religious interest was not concerned primarily with theologies or dogmas. Rather, it concentrated on meeting the very utilitarian goal of providing a common ethical creed. While the United States today is far more religiously pluralistic than in his time, this fact might not concern Tocqueville as long as shared values were promulgated. What might concern him much more is the evident secularization present in our still religious society. Tocqueville's constant worry was, What can control the selfish American individual—or the tyrannical majority?

To be sure, Tocqueville judged that public life also provided checks, especially through civic associations and the legal system, both of which he took seriously. He admired the jury system as an arrangement through which people learned from each other and collectively reached toward the public good. What he might think today in the age of political action committees and ruthless lawyers, both of which are contemporary images for unchecked egoism, one may well imagine.

Overall, Tocqueville's mood was moderately optimistic. He was sure that free men could do without much external control, including a strong government, if they lived in a society with a vigorous private sphere directed by good women. Women's well-honed consciences would restrain men, guiding young men at home and in church, and reminding adult men throughout life of the common moral standards. This was the basis for Tocqueville's confidence that the spirit of both liberty and religion, "admirably incorporated and combined with one another," made the United States work.[6] On the other hand, if private life were to yield to public liberal values, which Tocqueville considered possible in the long run, optimism was much less merited.

Meanwhile, Tocqueville divided his two tiers by gender. He always made women the cornerstone for his entire analysis and thus for the American experiment. The United States' success was due to women, and its continued success in the future equally would depend on them.[7] Women's superiority as agents of civilization with the free men of liberal America was as obvious to him as was his conviction that only women could perform their vital role: "Morals are the work of women."[8] Women had, Tocqueville contended, a special capacity to reach into people's hearts—and that was essential in an America where men were often alone in the deepest imaginable sense, each left only with the overwhelming "solitude of his own heart."[9]

Of course, Tocqueville was far from satisfied with the behavior of women as he understood it in the United States. He realized that women were unusually free and that the American culture encouraged them to be so. He worried about this result of the culture, given the role women had to play as conservators of communal values. Thus he was uneasy at best about women who did not play the domestic role he prescribed for them and upon whom he was convinced American democracy depended. He was patriarchal and somewhat condescending in his writings on women, and he was hardly enthused about their political or economic rights. Yet he knew that women's influence was essential to everything he hoped for in the United States.[10]

Fundamental to Tocqueville's analysis was his belief that Americans were terribly vulnerable. This was true partly because so many were lonely and might sacrifice their liberty to escape their loneliness. It was also true because Americans' passion for equalities of various sorts could lead them more and more to the trap of majority tyranny, one that threatened their liberty and encouraged mediocrity in American art and learning.[11] Yet all was not lost. Indeed, matters were promising if there continued to be a sure religious faith, firmly rooted in the conscience of individuals through church and home. Tocqueville counted on this possibility and insisted that the results of a gendered America were beneficial.

In other terms, we may characterize Tocqueville's interpretation of (his) United States as a certain kind of liberal consensus view, one quite different from that of the famous consensus thinkers of the 1950s. He saw a society that loved freedom and equality in the public sphere, complemented by a traditionalist, nonliberal, matriarchal private sphere that fostered the virtues that prevented public liberalism from becoming egoistic self-destruction or democratic despotism. Liberal values were not the full story of the United States, but widespread consensus on the values appropriate for each sphere of life was.

Frederick Jackson Turner

Tocqueville's *Democracy in America* has soared in popularity in recent decades, in good part because of his perceptions about the social needs and problems of an increasingly "free"—or liberal—social order. Frederick Jackson Turner's late-nineteenth-century essay *The Significance of the Frontier in American History*,[12] however, has met a harsher fate. This classic, the basis of Turner's famed theory of the dynamics of the American experience, increasingly finds itself relegated to the status of a museum piece.[13]

Frederick Jackson Turner (1861–1932) was self-consciously a son of the (Middle) West, born in the small town of Portage, Wisconsin, widely liked all his life as "forthcoming, articulate, with genial laugh."[14] He was in love with fishing, canoeing, and camping. Turner was for decades a history professor at the University of Wisconsin–Madison, the department's leading light and an assertive participant in university affairs of all sorts.[15] Turner's brief *Significance of the Frontier in American History* is a reminder that scholarly contribution and a long list of publications have no necessary connection. Despite his reputation as an underachiever as an academic scholar, in fact, Turner wrote a number of other works, some short and some longer, although he never produced the great second book that he struggled to compose. He was widely admired as a graduate teacher, became president of the American Historical Association, and gave lessons to others about how to succeed (critics said hustle) as a professional.[16]

The Significance of the Frontier was very unconventional in academic terms. Since it is largely bereft of scholarly evidence to test or substantiate its claims, one can almost hear the complaints his work might receive today from modern tenure committees.[17] Yet the general absence of research evidence was advantageous for Turner's project. It allowed him to propound his theory apart from all the scholarly reservations and hesitations that more cautious scholars must acknowledge.

From within his frontier thesis, Turner's view at the end of the nineteenth century was that the United States had formed itself out of its own lived experiences, as its frontiers advanced, as people steadily conquered and settled the land. The availability of cheap or sometimes free land was crucial to "explain American development,"[18] since it provided opportunity and allowed people to take advantage of that opportunity, constantly creating new frontiers. For successive generations, experiencing the frontier led to a transformation of Americans into optimistic individuals, committed to opportunity, a people who were democratic and egalitarian in spirit, social life, and politics. They were sympathetic to individual families on their farms but also committed to community through a myriad of activities in the public realm.

As his career unfolded, however, Turner, as an "undeclared social scientist," became interested in far more than the frontier.[19] His main interest became sectionalism, and he emerged as an advocate of the view that sectionalism and the interaction of sections in the United States—more than the advancing frontier—constituted the largest single factor in the American story.[20] Over time, in fact, Turner developed a capacious analysis of American history and its sectional dynamics, and he by no means held that it ended with the frontier in 1890.[21]

On balance, little marred Turner's enthusiasm as he surveyed the history of the American nation, and this included most of his treatment of the ever-expanding frontier. His discussion of the frontier, however, was short on such problematics as relations between whites and Native Americans, matters of gender, or the ugliness of greed or crime, which were by no means absent on the frontier. These topics have assumed a far greater role in the "new history" of the West written in recent years.[22] And in this history, perhaps predictably as generation replaces generation, Turner's work has not fared well.[23]

The frontier, moreover, was also far less free and far less egalitarian than Turner believed. It was also less influential in American history. His conviction that the frontier experience mattered overwhelmingly led him to make breezy claims such as that "the slavery question" was no more than "an incident" in U.S. history.[24] There were also serious problems in his analytic categories, especially with his concept of "frontier." They were often too vague or too elastic to be of much use for rigorous historical investigation.[25]

Yet such objections, and the host of others that scholars have generated in the hundred years since the publication of *The Signifi-cance of the Frontier*, are not the main point here. More relevant is Turner's fear as he peered into the future. His famed contention that with the close of the nineteenth century the frontier itself was end-ing suggested the United States faced a major crisis. Since the fron-tier was the principal cause of Americans being democratic and individualistic, its closing had to pose a profound threat to the con-tinuance of the kind of America of which Turner so ardently ap-proved. The closing of the frontier had the potential to aid all sorts of corruptions of the American character. It could open the United States to European influences, or it could result in the growth of anti-democratic distinctions among people, possibilities that deeply con-cerned Turner.

While at first Turner worried about such dangers acutely, when he was ensconced at Harvard University in his later years and far from his original interest in the frontier, he stressed his hopes for the Ameri-can experiment and regularly proclaimed his continuing faith in the possibility of individualistic democracy in the United States. He ex-plicitly rejected Charles Beard as an economic determinist whose lack of confidence in the American people's capacity to control their fate he did not share. How he might have responded to suggestions that his frontier version of American history was romantic and suffered from simplicity compared with Tocqueville's we cannot know. Turner and Tocqueville, however, did have some things in common. Above all, Turner's frontier theory (but not his sectionalism) was as much a consensus interpretation as Tocqueville's. Turner's conviction was that we could speak of Americans—children of frontier values, if no longer of frontier experiences—largely as one.[26]

Turner, then, like Tocqueville, is an important representative of the early consensus interpretations of American political thought and culture. Both had a real sense that there was somehow an es-sential United States—that it related to basic American values—and it was unique in the nations and cultures of the world. While the substance of the values was far from identical, both analysts were pioneers in constructing a consensus view of the origins and substance of the American experience, and both were decidedly influential in that role.

Progressive Era Views

The Progressive Era, lasting from the late 1890s until America's entrance into World War I in 1917, was a brief period even in the United States' short history. Yet it was an exciting era and fertile intellectually, including in creative attempts to interpret American thought and culture. In particular, it was during the Progressive Era that the famous conflict narrative of U.S. history emerged. Its proponents held then, as some do now, that there has been plenty of conflict in American history and that most of the conflicts have been rooted in economic and class divisions. Indeed, their argument was and is that such conflicts are the most revealing guideposts to comprehending our history and its social and political thought. The model, in short, stressed the age-old conflict between the few and the many, between the elite and the masses, and conflict analysts invariably supported the "democratic" masses.[27]

This classic view had two great champions in the Progressive Era, Vernon L. Parrington and Charles Beard, both well known in their age, whose *specific* interpretations inevitably look less formidable today than they once did. Their *general* conflict mode of interpretation of American history, however, has undergone a tremendous revival in the second half of the twentieth century, as chapter 3 illustrates. Conflict theory is very much back in style, and in this manner Beard and Parrington live on.

Vernon L. Parrington

I begin discussion of the conflict interpretation of American political thought with Parrington. No one was more important in terms of articulating conflict theory's approach and its characteristic themes —despite Parrington's near-total disappearance from American intellectual history.[28]

Born in 1871 in Illinois, Parrington was raised in Kansas and educated in part (and very unhappily) at Harvard. He held a series

of stressful academic positions, which often ended badly; they in-
cluded a notorious time at the University of Oklahoma, which ended
in Parrington's dismissal as a professor. Perhaps he would be pleased
to know that today a plaque on Parrington Oval in the heart of the
University of Oklahoma campus apologizes for his ugly fate there.
Eventually Parrington found a secure and satisfying position at the
University of Washington. There Parrington wrote his career project,
Main Currents in American Thought, for which he won the Pulitzer
Prize in 1928 for the first two volumes. Although published after the
Progressive Era's passing, *Main Currents* was distinctly a product
of a certain Progressive Age reform mentality. Influenced by Charles
Beard's economic determinism and Turner's democratic faith, *Main
Currents* pulsed with the spirit of the populist and progressive mood
of the late nineteenth and early twentieth centuries.[29]

Parrington's *Main Currents* sweeps from the earliest Puritan
times into the 1920s, dramatically recounting American political and
literary thought. Its voice is distinctly personal and frequently passionate, yet it is never casual. Parrington had obviously read almost
everything written by any American with literary pretension. He
knew his subject, and in his long book he shares much of his knowledge with his readers, sometimes in exhausting detail and often
without providing a sense of relative importance among the numerous figures he treats.

Parrington assessed American literary notables and their work
with a much clearer telos. His approach was decidedly political,
which is why his study really focuses on American political thought
and thinkers. His purpose was to define and defend a "good" American past and rally forces for reform in his day.[30] For Parrington,
American political thought and life were about the conflict between
those seeking economic equality, decentralized democracy, and
political liberty (values he assumed could fit together snugly) and
rapacious elites and their literary sycophants in pursuit of economic
gain.

Thus Parrington admired such American revolutionaries as
Thomas Jefferson and Tom Paine. Parrington considered himself
a Jeffersonian, and he gushed over the model of agrarian democracy that he believed Jefferson favored, although he was less than
happy with Jefferson's authoritarian presidency. Like Jefferson,
Parrington's most admired Americans were likely to be agrarian

democrats in touch with a people's ethos found on the farm and field. He, like these people, was suspicious of the city, the factory, and the East. Against them lay the evil capitalists, especially those of the late nineteenth century, who participated in what Parrington famously termed "the Great Barbecue": the eating up of American resources and values by exploitative capitalists. From Alexander Hamilton to the robber barons of the late nineteenth century, all sorts of capitalists and neocapitalists personified Parrington's image of his selfish, greedy, and ruthless opponents. They were the bad side of the American experience. For Parrington, the best Americans engaged in an unending struggle against them, a struggle that was never easy in an environment in which hostile elements ruled.[31]

Parrington's European hero was Jean-Jacques Rousseau, and he also admired other French egalitarians whom he judged to be democrats. Parrington actually loved Rousseau, in fact, and he showered him with praise time and again. He thought Rousseau agreed with him that people were naturally good and well disposed to each other and shared his conviction that a society with a wide-ranging scope of liberty was both ideal and possible. There are as many interpretations of Rousseau, of course, as of any political thinker, and Parrington's is hardly strange as Rousseau interpretations go. The question here is why such a reading of Rousseau attracted Parrington. The answer appears to be fairly straightforward. Parrington wanted an egalitarian democracy as well as a free society, and to have either or both, he believed, people had to be social and social-regarding by nature. His understanding of Rousseau reassured him on just this score, and Parrington was eager to find such reassurance.

Parrington's interpretation of American history enjoyed considerable vogue in the 1920s and 1930s but fell from grace after World War II. Partly this was the result of the times, when conflict views were out of favor due to the ascendancy of the "consensus" school. Partly it was the result of a barrage of intellectual critiques that devastated Parrington's arguments and damaged his intellectual reputation. For example, Lionel Trilling and other critics ridiculed Parrington as a literary analyst. Indeed, Parrington's literary pretensions became something of a crude joke. Critics concluded that his judgments of American literary figures were unreliable at best and embarrassing at worst, far too personal and political, derived neither from independent standards of literary merit nor from any particular human insights. It was easy to show that most of the time what mattered in Parrington's assessment of an individual's literary contribution was whether the writer shared his politics.

Critics also complained that Parrington often mischaracterized the views of his subjects and repeatedly simplified all of them. Thus in Parrington's mind Benjamin Franklin somehow became an agrarian democrat, which allowed Parrington to put him in his select pantheon of American greats. Parrington obliterated complexity in Lincoln and crowned him a simple and heroic egalitarian, democrat, and opponent of capitalism. Parrington turned Thoreau into the Rousseau of his age, providing no serious argument for why Thoreau was an egalitarian democrat, much less for how he could be connected with Rousseau's distinctly community-oriented *Social Contract*. Parrington also celebrated Ralph Waldo Emerson as a pure idealist, the best and most hopeful of souls, presenting Emerson as a bland sap.[32]

Parrington's most notorious judgments were his dismissals of Henry James and William Shakespeare. Parrington faulted James as someone not concerned about anything more than the psychic trivia of human life. James was obviously no robust American democrat and egalitarian, and that was all that Parrington thought needed to be said about him. Parrington condemned Shakespeare as a social climber who cuddled up to the powers that be of his day, blithely concluding that Shakespeare was of little value. Perhaps less preposterous was Parrington's attack on Henry Adams's *Democracy*. Parrington understood that *Democracy* offered no enthusiasm, indeed no hope, for democracy. For him it followed that Adams's *Democracy* merited no further attention, a characteristic expression of Parrington's antagonism to any view that was not his own.[33]

Parrington's views now also can be painfully dated. They are distant not only from anything recognizably postmodernism but also almost as far from modernism. From this angle, Parrington has little to offer because he has a "premodern sensibility." That is to say, his critics contend, he is out of touch with the urban, industrial world, with the modern engagement with psychology, and with the sense of complexity, paradox, and irony that is present in the American value system (and much else).[34]

Those who dislike Parrington's views often have recourse to straightforward political judgments themselves, damning Parrington for having the wrong politics. A common complaint is that he had no enthusiasm for the state or for government action of virtually any type. In fact, Parrington really was a small-state Jeffersonian. Franklin Roosevelt may have overseen the development of both the Jefferson Memorial and modern liberalism, but the two are not necessarily cousins. Parrington was dead before Roosevelt's presidency and the New Deal and all that followed. That was just as well, since Parrington so deeply feared the big state—or even a moderate-sized state. To him, it was little more than a happy hunting ground for the selfish.[35]

In these times he might have become a sort of conservative. He might look to a (lost) Jeffersonian world and from that angle condemn the contemporary one. After all, Parrington's enthusiasm was for a people who chose his Jefferson, not Franklin D. Roosevelt or big government or modern liberalism. Parrington's democrats would not choose big government. More likely, Parrington would just be bewildered. Where he could turn and who would serve as his political—and literary—heroes today is unclear.

Parrington has emerged from a neglected—or negative—place only recently, through such treatments as H. Lark Hall's biography or some modestly affectionate commentaries such as Daniel Aaron's.[36] Hall in particular aggressively defends Parrington from the basic charge that haunts his memory, the claim that Parrington was a political reductionist and an aesthetic nonentity (or worse). Hall observes that despite his reputation Parrington did identify admirable sides in some thinkers with whom he disagreed. Hall rightly offers John Adams as an illustration of Parrington's ability to appreciate those who did not fit his ideal. Parrington recognized that Adams was a complex theorist who could not be dismissed as a hopeless conservative. The same applied to his reflections on John C. Calhoun. While Parrington complained that Calhoun wasted his potential by mortgaging everything he did to preserve the hateful slave system, he still admired Calhoun as a political thinker.[37]

Beyond such specific examples of Parrington's breadth, however, the question remains whether he ordinarily perceived aesthetic or political complexity among thinkers he disagreed with or, perhaps more telling, among those he applauded. It is hard to see how many contemporary readers of *Main Currents in American Thought* would share his judgments. Parrington routinely sacrificed complexity and balance to the demands of his bipolar conflict theory.

Arguments over Parrington's approach to individual authors and theorists in American political and literary history do not affect the basic matter at hand, which is his overall interpretation of American political thought. Parrington's view was that conflict was the heart of the American story—the rich few often manipulating government to their objectives against the democratic, earthy, decentralized, exploited many. His perspective has been important in the development of conflict interpretations of the United States.

Charles Beard

While Parrington's reputation sank in part because he could not distinguish the aesthetic from the political, this was hardly a concern for Charles Beard or, eventually, for his reputation. Beard was not particularly interested in anything literary, and he spent little of his professional effort on this dimension of the human experience. Beard was as great a conflict historian as was Parrington, but Beard grounded his analysis of the reality of conflict in what he saw as the brute economic facts of American life. Most famously, he explored what he claimed were the economic conflicts in American society in the late eighteenth century and how they affected the creation and adoption of the U.S. Constitution. In the process he emerged as—and has remained—the most important theorist of conflict interpretation, a view that now is experiencing a major revival in other versions than Beard's.

Charles Beard, born in 1874, was a prominent and influential historian from the Progressive Era through the New Deal and World War II. Beard published his masterwork, *An Economic Interpretation of the Constitution of the United States,* in 1913. Beard's later works, such as *Economic Origins of Jeffersonian Democracy* (1915), *The Rise of American Civilization* (1927) (the widely used textbook he wrote with his feminist wife, Mary Beard), or his later essays devoted to denouncing Franklin D. Roosevelt and his foreign policies, consistently generated controversy just as had his *Economic Interpretation.*[38]

Beard believed economic conflict was the great engine of history in the United States and had been from the nation's beginnings. He concluded that these conflicts were rooted in very human economic desires and motivations rather than determined by impersonal, or

Marxian, economic forces. Beard had an Enlightenment confidence in reason and its ability to discern this reality about history both in general and in its particular historical manifestations. In the celebrated case of Beard's views applied to the U.S. Constitution, the immediate result was a public scandal. His less than pious attitude toward the Constitution and its origins did not fit with the Progressive Era's ardent worship of the Constitution. Ironically, Beard's economic perspective was hardly new to other historians and social scientists of the period, but it did shock some in the larger public.

Beard's argument in *An Economic Interpretation* is straightforward. He maintained that the evidence established that the search for economic gain was the most important motivation driving those who crafted and then pushed through the Constitution. Beard insisted that this motivation was amply revealed in the provisions of the Constitution, as well as in the often unsavory politics surrounding its adoption. His famous conclusion was that the Constitution was "essentially an economic document" and could be adequately understood in no other way.[39]

Less well known, however, are the specifics of Beard's argument. According to him, the elite economic interest that dominated the constitutional struggle was largely composed of affluent public bond holders who sought to create a constitution that would benefit them by redeeming their bonds and upholding property interests in general, which is just what happened, the unsentimental Beard declared. While he understood that the nature of reigning economic forces varied at other times and places, what did not vary was the basis for a central fact of history—conflict—and that was the rule of economic power in history. Struggle among economic elites was also common in history, as was the contest between elites and the masses.

It followed that for Beard the U.S. Constitution was not democratic in its origins, its provisions, or the way it was ratified.[40] No wonder Beard gave little time to studying the political thought of the Founders—or that of any other dominant group. Their thought was no guide to their "real" and highly selfish motivations. For Beard, the political thought of most Founders could be best understood as little more than rationalization for their concrete economic goals.[41]

Today Beard's specific claims about the Founders do not hold up any better than do many of Parrington's literary judgments.

Beard's assertions about the economic interests and motivations of a host of actors in the creation of the Constitution as well as about the economic situations in various states at the time have mostly fallen before more accurate and more complete information. For example, economic divisions over the Constitution existed, but they did not regularly follow creditor-debtor lines. More often they involved divisions between commercial and noncommercial economic interests.[42] Moreover, we now know that much else was involved in the creation of the Constitution besides the pursuit of economic advantage, including a host of complex and conflicting political ideas and ideals. Beard's specific claims about the Constitution are now mostly a monument to the limits of reductionism in historical analysis.[43]

In the 1920s and early 1930s, Beard moved beyond strict economic interpretation and recognized cultural, scientific, and intellectual realms as he rarely had before. This was especially true in his and Mary Beard's *Rise of American Civilization*. Beard also became considerably more optimistic regarding the potential of the United States to move in the social democratic and secular directions that he considered progressive.[44] Beard's public career ended badly, however, when he returned to a sharply economic analysis of world events during the 1930s and 1940s, lambasting capitalist economic interests on the world stage and governments that he considered too much in their hands. Beard eventually became an isolationist and an obsessive FDR hater, ironically elevating one person and his personality above all else, including the imperialist economic interests Beard believed FDR served.[45]

Yet Beard's interpretation of American history and thought, which mostly swirled around conflicts between economic elites and sometimes resisting masses, remains very much alive. It is also often one element in multiple-strand analyses, which include other bases of conflict but also share Beard's conviction that there has been much more to the American story than consensus.[46] Indeed, as there has been a revival of conflict interpretations in our time, Beard, as the renowned founder of the conflict view, receives renewed attention. Today he is an icon in some contemporary interpretations of American thought and culture, which is why his work must be addressed here.

Even his specific interpretation of the Constitution, moreover, has considerable value when suitably reinscribed for contemporary times. After all, the framers did deliberately construct a document that was attractive to planters and merchants, and there were no artisans, women, or slaves present in the historic meetings at Philadelphia when the Constitution was drafted. There is no doubt that the Constitution was the product of an American elite and pleasing to American economic elites.

Henry James's Other United States

It was in the Progressive Era that serious, scholarly interpretation of American political thought and culture became an important intellectual activity, coinciding with the rise of the research university on the German model and the appearance of many more professional scholars and intellectuals. While the most prominent interpretations to emerge from these developments were conflict theories, from the first they were contested, a process of intellectual discourse and division over how to understand the United States that has hardly ceased. The most significant dissenting view of the Progressive Era did not come, however, from the academy or from the newly emergent worlds of social science. It came from Henry James, the American writer, as he looked back at the United States from abroad.

James is important because he offered a consensus theory in an age of conflict views and because his decidedly contrasting perspective developed from a certain literary sensibility. James did not proceed in conventional interpretive categories of his era, much less our own. His work reminds one of the obvious, but often unacknowledged, point that there is no one method for fashioning a creative or insightful understanding of the American story.

Expatriate Henry James (1843–1916), famous as an author of sensitive fiction of manners, morals, and cultures, presented his most formal view of the United States in *The American Scene* (1907).[47] Despite its often opaque prose, *The American Scene* is an involving essay, but it must be studied rather than merely read. In his life James swept over a large amount of American territory, and in the process he observed a great many people in the North and South—men and women, black and white, native and immigrant, just as did Tocqueville before him.

What he saw led James to insist that the United States was a distinct culture with a defining set of characteristics. James's Americans were hustlers, always scrambling to get ahead economically, and the American culture centered on money, the businessman, and economic growth.[48] Since most Americans were ensnared in this world, they received James's disdain. Above all, James disliked the fact that Americans ranked economic gain and economic development much higher than beauty. This terrible truth about Americans condemned them.[49]

James appreciated the importance of a sense of social democracy and an intensive concern for equality in the American character, and he understood that uneasiness over any formal distinctions among people followed inevitably. It was equally predictable that formal manners and courtesy did not count for much in the United States. They were often a mere "fiction" that was ignored in "the wash of gold."[50] As James put it, the United States was a "democracy of trade," necessarily resulting in the reign of "the cheap, the common, the commercial, . . . the ugly."[51] In such an atmosphere everyone could compete or partake fully in society, which was why the culture focused on people as "simply people" rather than on the "kinds of people" they were.[52]

Thus James perceived, as had Tocqueville earlier, few significant distinctions in American public life—and little patience for those that did exist. Among Americans James could find no subtle "play of mutual recognition, founded on old familiarities and heredities,"[53] nor any sympathy for the sense of tradition that was the basis for the distinctions in Britain that James so admired. America was not about "continuity, responsibility, transmission."[54] James realized that this situation encouraged the unity of American culture, since it eliminated any established class and cultural arrangements and prepared the way for a melting pot nation.

James did not address distinctions based on race, but he did note a vast number of "swarming" immigrants flowing into the United States at the turn of the century. James was, in fact, far more aware of this dramatic event than either the curiously removed Parrington or Beard. While James certainly did not welcome the immigrant tide, he expressed no fears that the immigrants would create a different culture and a worse America. He was convinced, rather, and somewhat sad about the fact, that most immigrants and their children would all too quickly integrate into the larger society and adopt its mercenary norms.[55]

James shared Tocqueville's perception that women played an unusually large role in U.S. society. Tocqueville's emphasis was more self-conscious, but James made the same observation, concluding that while businessmen ruled the public realm, women ruled the rest of life in the United States.[56] James may have placed women in an even more essential place than did Tocqueville. Tocqueville's view was that women and the family shared their influence with religion in the private sphere; for James it was women alone who counted. James granted that there was a large church membership in the United States, but he concluded that it did not mean much. Religion in America was—like so much else—a "shallow tide." To James, the American people were, after all, pretty superficial, and so of course could be counted on to miss the subtle and the "hidden." This was reflected in their religion as elsewhere, as they passed ignorantly by "the deep sea . . . of spiritual passion."[57]

Even here Tocqueville and James were close. After all, Tocqueville did not find any of James's "spiritual passion" in American religion either. Indeed, Tocqueville saw religion in the United States in the same terms that James did. That is, religion's role in the United States was largely practical; it existed primarily to provide moral restraint. The crucial difference was Tocqueville's claim that religion mattered—if only in its pragmatic effect—in the United States; on that score, James dissented. Religion, he said, was only window dressing for most Americans.

In short, from his expatriate stance, James suggested that Americans were different from each other in some ways, but nevertheless shared the same values. Granted, James offered no self-conscious theory of a common culture or a consensus interpretation. He spurned that sort of thinking, but like Tocqueville before him he insisted there were many shared characteristics in American culture. To James they were a reality not easily ignored.

As something of a consensus thinker, James illustrated the continuing appeal of consensus interpretations—even in the Progressive Era. He is important as well as a pioneer who observed the power of American cultural consensus even in the face of an enormously ethnically diverse nation in an age which in that way was similar to ours.

Consensus Theory in the 1950s

The onset of the Great Depression in the 1930s and the divisions that followed at first provided many political intellectuals a congenial setting that confirmed the plausibility of conflict analysis of American life and thought. The age of Franklin Roosevelt and the New Deal, the years of World War II, and especially the first decades after that war, however, eventually worked in the opposite direction. In particular, the cold war proved to be a most uncongenial time for conflict theory as an interpretation of the United States, especially in its by then somewhat faded Progressive Era expressions.

After World War II it was consensus theory, not conflict theory, that again became the mainstream approach to understanding American thought. During the 1940s and 1950s and through the middle 1960s, the consensus outlook never totally pervaded intellectual understanding of our political and social thinking, but it was the standard interpretation. To its promoters and many others, it made sense because it seemed to fit the empirical facts of the era. This is why consensus theory became the primary interpretation of the time, even as it was a child of that time.[58]

To study consensus interpretations in the 1940s through the early 1960s is essential because so much of today's interpretive debate builds from an attack on consensus theory. Postwar consensus analyses came in a variety of forms, although their core proposition was that Americans had long shared many common perspectives and that political thought in the United States reflected that consensus well. In short, there was an American value consensus that substantially defined the nation (in many versions it was also unique, and thus the United States was an "exception" in comparison to other places and cultures).

There was less agreement on the content of the consensus (which no theorist ever defined as unanimity of intellectual or popular opinion) than on the fact of consensus itself. Most accounts considered the consensus to turn around agreement on liberal values, meaning on the worth of the individual, assorted individual liberties, consent of the governed, and private property and capitalism.

A good number of the most prominent intellectuals in the postwar decades advanced consensus interpretations. It was no out-of-the-way perspective, attracting only minor figures. Richard Hofstadter (1916–70), perhaps the most influential postwar historian of the United States and a longtime professor at Columbia University, first presented his version in *The American Political Tradition* (1948), which remains an enormously stimulating and controversial achievement.[59]

Richard Hofstadter

Hofstadter's book was a set of brilliant essays on commanding figures in American politics throughout our history who, in Hofstadter's hands, became ordinary mortals at best. Hofstadter did not self-consciously develop a full-scale consensus theory in *The American Political Tradition*. This was not his way. Yet Hofstadter's American story was largely an account of the growth, development, and protection of capitalism, an account of the political system's service to capitalism, and a report on how the shared values in the United States served capitalism. Hofstadter did not deny that there were other norms than the liberal capitalist values of property, a certain view of freedom, and the acquisition of wealth among Americans, but he considered other norms comparatively unimportant. On this (consensus) all else really rested, and it was far more important than other, superficial divisions that some commentators had singled out in their accounts of U.S. history.

His analysis was a case in point, Hofstadter later remarked, of what became an often forgotten truth: that consensus interpretations originated from diverse political perspectives.[60] Hofstadter himself was a left-leaning, former neo-Marxist when he wrote *The American Political Tradition*, and he was hardly a celebrant of U.S. history or many of the representatives of the "American political tradition." He also showed that—despite some misinformed charges then and since—there never was anything inherently "conservative" about consensus theory. Telling a story and endorsing it have no necessary connection.

By the 1970s, however, Hofstadter had cooled on the plausibility of consensus interpretations. His magnificent *Progressive Historians* is a meditation on consensus theory. A chastened Hofstadter decided that consensus interpretations suffered from their virtue, which was their clean and all too clear lines of interpretation.

Hofstadter now identified himself as among those who happily appreciated "the rediscovery of complexity in American history."[61] He had learned that consensus history had ignored great swaths of conflict in the American story, including conflicts rooted in cultural, ethnic, religious, and racial divisions. Hofstadter had rediscovered conflict as an integral part of American history and regretted that he had not perceived its importance earlier, although he did not embrace Progressive Era conflict theories either. They dwelled far too exclusively on economic conflict.[62]

Hofstadter never fully rejected the consensus approach. He had lost his enthusiasm for it by the 1960s, but he refused to say that it was an entirely false step or to repudiate his own contribution to it. Consensus theory provided its insights into the United States and its thought, which were to be valued as long as it did not simultaneously blot out the history and influence of the many conflicts in our story. It followed, too, that Hofstadter was not interested in swinging over to conventional conflict theories. They concentrated too exclusively on economic conflicts and in their way also denied historical complexity.[63]

Reinhold Niebuhr

A second important postwar consensus thinker was Reinhold Niebuhr (1892–1971), a public intellectual, leading theologian, and much quoted social theorist in debates of the postwar decades even into the Vietnam era.[64] As a young Christian pastor and then theology professor on the Left in the 1930s and 1940s, Niebuhr wrote a number of challenging books, especially *Moral Man and Immoral Society* (1932)[65] and *The Children of Light and the Children of Darkness* (1945).[66] It was only after World War II, however, that a notably less radical Niebuhr made exploration of U.S. culture and ideology a priority, most memorably in *The Irony of American History* (1952).[67]

In his argument about the postwar United States, Niebuhr was concerned with what he judged were the ironies America faced given its ideological and geographic "innocence." He argued that the United States had clung too long to a belief in liberal perfectionism (as "children of light" in the City on a Hill) and now found itself inescapably intertwined with a world that refuted its treasured illusions. Niebuhr wanted the United States to learn to live the Christian teaching that no individuals and no peoples were innocent or without sin, and that it was both foolish and sinful to believe differently. Ironically, in the postwar situation, Americans, who too often fancied themselves innocent, faced a Communist enemy that made even bolder claims for the purity of its worldview. Both badly needed a grasp on reality.

In his meditations on postwar America and its international situation, Niebuhr took for granted that there was an American consensus on crucial liberal values and attitudes. He spent much less time trying to defend this claim, which was then hardly controversial, than he did complaining about the liberal political vision's sad naïveté and overconfidence in its benevolence at home and abroad. Yet Niebuhr also recognized as another irony that the consensus perspective had, in fact, helped to produce a great nation, successful in many ways, especially politically and economically.

In due time the pendulum swung, and Niebuhr's analysis has suffered, as have so many others of the consensus outlook. Niebuhr's interpretation now faces relentless objections from critics who charge that he was seduced by the United States of the 1950s and painted a portrait of the nation that was far too simplistic and far too favorable. The skeptic and ironist of his age has been transformed into an apologist for the ruling elites of his time, one irony that Niebuhr would not appreciate.

Intellectuals such as Hofstadter and Niebuhr were significant figures, but they adopted a consensus view during only one period in their long and multisided careers. Even in the 1950s, moreover, they were lesser deities in the consensus pantheon compared with its two most famous or notorious figures, Louis Hartz and Daniel Boorstin.

Louis Hartz

Louis Hartz (1919–86) was a Harvard professor of government, originally from Nebraska, whose dramatic lectures were as direct and engaging as his writing was mannered.[68] Hartz's masterwork was *The Liberal Tradition in America* (1955), which was enormously influential despite its style.[69] His work continues to be a starting point for all sorts of intellectual discussions about American culture in a wide variety of disciplines, especially for critics of consensus interpretations of American political thought or culture. While chapter 4 notes that Hartz has received praise from a few contemporary analysts sympathetic to his perspective on the Founders, by now his ideas have undergone several decades of determined assault. There is, however, no dispute over the fact that Hartz commanded the heights of interpretation of American thought and culture for several decades until the late 1960s, when the New Left that had originally agreed with him (as we shall see) turned against all consensus views—and the ideas of Hartz and other consensus theorists began their steep descent in popularity.

Hartz developed his argument first in *The Liberal Tradition in America* and then later, in collaboration with others, in *The Founding of New Societies* (1964), where his model was applied to a good portion of the rest of the globe.[70] Hartz's famous argument was that "liberal" values had long governed the view of most American intellectuals and the culture as a whole. Liberal values included the celebration of the individual and individual liberties, consent of the governed, and private property. For Hartz, these were *the* norms of the nation in the 1950s and in the past.[71]

Hartz used the British philosopher John Locke as the appropriate sign for the American consensus. We had a Lockean consensus, often "irrational" Lockean, in Hartz's analysis. He meant Locke and "Lockeanism" symbolically and, despite a common misunderstanding, did not pretend that his symbolic Locke could be neatly equated with the real Locke or with all of Locke's ideas. More generally, Hartz called on a vast array of American political thinkers to illustrate his consensus thesis, again not suggesting that his use of them fully represented their often complex thought. They were merely invoked to illustrate Hartz's overall argument, which was his constant project. The result was that his characterizations of specific American thinkers was sometimes bewildering and at other times brilliant.[72]

Hartz went far beyond claiming there had long been a consensus among U.S. political thinkers to claiming there was such a consensus in the American culture as a whole. He never offered empirical data on the beliefs of the broader public to sustain his hypothesis, but others did try to test the accuracy of Hartz's assertions. Their findings supported his claims that there was a good deal of agreement within the American public in the first decades after World War II on general political principles.[73]

Hartz offered no empirical data, in part because he styled himself as a grand theorist who was beyond what he considered dubiously informative public opinion studies. The same attitude partly explained why Hartz's work, despite the numerous names scattered across its pages, was not really about individual American thinkers.

As a grand theorist he sought the fundamental patterns of American culture, which he was confident neither surveys nor detailed discussions of particular theorists could establish. What mattered were the deep patterns (in a subsequent age they came to be termed *deep structures*) of American culture, nowhere very consciously articulated.[74]

It was Hartz's view, which reflected his neo-Marxian side, that America's longtime ideological consensus originated in the nation's social and especially economic roots, which he suggested were relatively classless. Hartz did not mean that there were no economic divisions among Americans in colonial days. His point, rather, was that, unlike Europe, America had no elaborate and sharply unequal class system. Following Tocqueville, Hartz contended that in this sense people were "born equal" (comparatively, anyway) in the United States and saw themselves as such. In practice, Hartz famously argued, this prevented the development of different ideologies, since he assumed that different classes were the origin of different ideologies. Not having sharply differentiated classes, the United States had only one ideology. Thus, for example, nothing like European conservatism flowered in the United States to oppose the reigning liberalism. Conservatism's absence was to be expected, since the United States had no aristocratic class, in a European sense, that could produce a conservative ideology. As a result, American conservatives either were supporters of the liberal status quo or sought some other version of liberal values than was in power. There were few signs of any European conservatives devoted to hierarchical community and accenting human sinfulness. American "conservatives" were really part of the liberal consensus.

Similarly, there was little evidence in the late nineteenth and early twentieth centuries of serious intellectual interest in socialist or Marxist ideology or of a strong socialist movement among the U.S. population. Once again, Hartz's explanation was that there was no class, no self-conscious working class in this instance, to create such a world. What American workers wanted, he argued, was to get ahead, to succeed as participants in the liberal world. American intellectuals, moreover, found it hard to escape the hold of liberalism on their thought. The intellectual mainstream did not choose socialism as an alternative.[75]

At the same time, Hartz believed that once the basic structure ("born equal") was in place in the colonies, the ideas and culture it generated took over. They may have started as superstructure, but soon enough they rendered everything else superstructure. The founding of the colonies led to the birth of a liberal tradition that by the nineteenth century ruled Americans quite regardless of their individual social or economic or other conditions. A Hegelian Mind ruled and overrode any and all social realities.

It was just this fact that was responsible for Hartz's famous unease (Richard Hofstadter later called it Hartz's "exasperation,"[76] John Diggins, his "quarrel" [77]) with the "irrational" Lockeanism he discovered as America's ruling ideology. Our tight consensus screened out anything that did not speak its language and thus was a potent mechanism for distorting Americans' perception of their national situation. Consensus promoted "liberal tolerance," but as a monolithic mind-set that just did not see or hear outside its framework. At worst, the consensus crushed anything that stood in its way at home: dissident ideas or people or movements. When consensus faced the outside world, moreover, it could not understand different nations or cultures. It reacted to assertive alternative perspectives and nations either by withdrawal or by all-out attack. Both responses were, Hartz insisted, versions of the same dangerous incomprehension of global pluralism.[78]

Among the most famous of Hartz's specific moments in consensus interpretation were his readings of the American Revolution, the Civil War, and the New Deal. Each illustrated his overall perspective. For Hartz, the American Revolution was a relatively tame affair, primarily a dispute among those who held the same Lockean liberal values. Since there was little at stake in terms of fundamental values, the quarrel between the colonies and Britain was mostly a matter of differing emphases and opinions on how to realize Lockean liberalism.[79]

The bloody American Civil War was in good part the same thing. To be sure, it was a major war, but Hartz contended that for many of the participants, Southern as well as Northern, it was no struggle between liberalism and some other ideology. Indeed, what impressed Hartz most was how much free men in the North and South shared the same political and social beliefs. While there were exceptions to this reality among some Southern intellectuals, the South's defeat eliminated them and reinforced liberal consensus in the United States. Always Hartz's theory was that nothing stood— or could stand—in the way of the march of the liberal consensus.

This is why he assured his critics that, as with the Civil War, he did not ignore conflicts but put them in perspective, showed their depth but identified their transitory and, in ideological terms, narrow nature.[80]

Hartz also claimed that the growth of the peacetime state beginning with the New Deal did not contradict American exceptionalism among the great industrialized nations. The U.S. government had expanded, but liberal values (or the defense of liberal values) were integral to every major step along the way. Each expansion was an example of government acting to save liberalism, as was the New Deal specifically. By this view, the New Deal succeeded because its advocates portrayed it as it was, liberalism in action and far from socialism.[81]

No one who reads Hartz could confuse him with an admirer of the consensus liberalism he describes, although he was a liberal as he understood that term. It was Hartz's judgment that consensus liberalism was in its very consensus a denial of the liberal principles of freedom and individualism and was unsuited for a diverse world. Yet he rejected pessimism about the situation. A major reason for hope was that the world had grown smaller in the modern age. As it continued to do so, the United States would have to engage other cultures and other ideologies. Hartz appreciated that this could lead to missteps and worse, but he hoped it would lead to tolerance, a more open society, and the decline of consensus that was essential for both the freedom promised by liberalism and the international cooperation vital in a dangerous age. It was this hope that defined Hartz's intellectual goals, ones that should not be confused by an image of him as "some splendid exotic bird, cruelly forced to live on the coarse and indigestible flora of America."[82] Yet Hartz fully realized that the change he sought would come slowly—and by the untimely end of his career in the 1970s, he could discern only modest progress.[83]

Daniel Boorstin

It is not easy to think of two interpreters of American culture in the postwar era—or any other—less alike than Louis Hartz and Daniel Boorstin. Of the two, Boorstin (1914–) was in some ways, especially in his curiously intellectual anti-intellectualism, "the more characteristically American."[84] He certainly was happier with American culture than was Hartz, and this may be partly why some contemporaries assess his interpretation as much inferior to Hartz's. It is now quite common for Boorstin's classic interpretation of the United States to be dismissed as foolishly antitheoretical, without substantive insight, and something of a mindless celebration of the status quo. One thing everyone understands, however, is that Boorstin shared with Hartz a place at the head table of consensus analysis in the post–World War II years.[85]

Daniel J. Boorstin articulated his version of the consensus view most famously in *The Genius of American Politics* (1953), and most of the argument over his perspective centers on this work.[86] Yet this essay was only one part of what became a running argument by Boorstin over his long academic career and his service as the librarian of Congress. For example, Boorstin also pursued his case for consensus in his sprightly histories of the United States, *The Americans: The National Experience* (1965) and *The Americans: The Democratic Experience* (1974).[87]

In more recent years Boorstin has devoted himself to a far larger stage than the American political tradition or even American history, publishing his best-selling works on world historical figures from many areas of learning and art. In 1992, for example, he published *The Creators*, which reveals him as much more interested in Michelangelo or the French impressionists than in the American Puritans or the development of American technology.[88] Boorstin can rightly boast that he has had several careers and now has left behind his role as analyst of American culture. But his work as an interpreter of American culture endures—and so do the critiques of it.

Boorstin's argument was that the American political tradition had three interwoven aspects that had benefited the nation. One was a basic "givenness," the foundational assumptions that the first colonists and their successors took for granted and that others after them formulated and reformulated; these were the basic American ways of thinking and living. We may call this Boorstin's understanding of the American consensus. These values and practices had a tendency to operate synergistically over time, and they have endured together throughout our history. This is what Boorstin calls America's "seamlessness."

Finally, Boorstin classes the American practice of pragmatic adjustment as equally central. Pragmatic adaptation, he maintains, gives consensus its continuing strength. It ensures consistent revision of givenness and seamlessness, guaranteeing a flexibility that allows the growth he thinks is essential in the U.S. experience. Indeed, the presence of pragmatic adaptation is a major reason that Boorstin has viewed the history of the United States so favorably. Americans have demonstrated the proper flexibility and ability to change over time as situations have demanded.

It is silly, he suggests, to try to define the United States through any enduring and unchanging set of values—or anything else. Thus Boorstin rejected any effort to connect him with a particular substantive consensus such as the "liberal tradition" that Hartz proposed. For Boorstin, the American story is about an evolving givenness and seamlessness that, in practice, is always changing and adapting through interactions with American experience. This is the reality, and Boorstin concludes it has worked.[89]

Boorstin's image of the United States as an ever-changing pragmatic society can lead his readers to underestimate the significance of the preformational and seamless sides of his description. Michael E. Meagher, in particular, is skeptical when Boorstin is portrayed as little more than a celebrant of pragmatic adaptation. Meagher recognizes several "personalities" in Boorstin's work and challenges readers to explore whether Boorstin holds consistent values or believes the American experience contains enduring values. Too much emphasis on Boorstin's view of the United States as simply a story of pragmatic adaptation may be wrong.[90]

Boorstin considers the Puritan colonial experience a crucial area in which to test his views. According to his reading, the Puritans came to America with one set of values—highly idealistic religious values—but they steadily modified them over time to accord with the experience and the demands of living in America. Values were always present, but so was their refashioning in line with experience.[91] Boorstin also uses the American Revolution to make his point. For him, it was a "revolution without dogma,"[92] and he reads the Declaration of Independence as mainly "a document of imperial legal relations."[93] In short, the Revolution and the Declaration of Independence were not about ideological conflict in American history. They reflect, instead, practical men arguing over practical issues within an evolving consensus. To Boorstin this explains why the American Revolution generated no significant or memorable political thought: it just was not about great ideological issues.[94]

Like Hartz, Boorstin knows that his interpretation of America faces its most obvious challenge in the brute fact of the terrible American Civil War, a conflict that easily dwarfed the Revolution by every conceivable measure. Yet, like Hartz, Boorstin is not fazed by this fact. He grants the obvious, that the Civil War involved conflict, but insists that nothing fundamental was at stake for its participants—a claim he argues is supported by the quick healing of the wounds of the war. Boorstin's Civil War was nothing much more than a sectional dispute that got out of hand, although obnoxious and dangerous zealots such as the abolitionists tried to make it much more.[95]

Boorstin's America has often displayed openness to change, an eagerness for the new, and the willingness to compromise that practical life requires. Ideological differences have popped up sometimes, but they have been "overshadowed by the need to get together."[96] In the process this civilization has met Boorstin's test. As it has been "revised again and again,"[97] Americans have developed "new ways of holding men together—less and less by creed or belief, by tradition or by place, more and more by common . . . experiences."[98] In short, Americans are creators, and the United States is their continuing, impressive creation. They have been just the kind of people Boorstin most respects: people engaged in a never-ending experience of creation and re-creation, never fixed and always dynamic.[99]

It has followed that the givenness, seamlessness, and pragmatic flexibility that resulted in a nonideological society have had "nothing in the line of a theory that can be exported to the other peoples of the world."[100] After all, "the genius of American politics" is just its nonideological, adaptable character so well suited to the specific milieu of the United States. This necessarily means that we have no set of political or social ideals appropriate for others. Insofar as our culture embodies an evolving givenness and seamlessness whose origins are in America's particular experience, they are unique to the United States and hardly exportable.

Boorstin realizes that his critics have dismissed him as a smug apologist for the United States. In fact, he has shown little of the ambivalence that Louis Hartz felt about the American experiment. Yet Boorstin has insisted that he is far from guilty of smugness. It is ideologues who are smug, always, as they try to translate truths they do not doubt into practice, inevitably at the expense of others: "No one is more smug than the Crusader."[101] They are also dangerous. After all, Boorstin believes, there is no way to make "a perfect world." We would be wiser to use our efforts to "preserve and improve free institutions where they now exist"—in the United States and elsewhere—rather than spend time fruitlessly running all over the world trying to make it "better."[102]

Over his career, however, Boorstin has proved he can be critical of pragmatic liberalism. *The Genius of American Politics* betrayed few reservations, but in his later histories, especially *The Americans: The Democratic Experience*, a chord of doubt can be heard in the chorus of celebration. Boorstin sometimes wonders, as Tocqueville had —and as many wonder now—whether our democratic culture is increasingly vapid and homogeneous, even in its multicultures. Boorstin laments that the United States has lost some of the cultural differences (which, unlike ideological differences, he welcomes) and begun to mass-produce everything, from "the regions to the seasons."[103] More and more decline grips our lives as they become ever "thinner"[104] in a "prefabricated, packaged, predictable" world.[105] In such a situation, Americans experience a sad "befogging of all distinctions" and a kind of "desperate quest" to break out of the pack.[106]

These later doubts, however, do not dim Boorstin's hopes. The United States might not have turned out to be deep in one sense or another, but it is still open and creative in its evolving responses to changing environments. While this culture cannot be exported, it remains one for which Boorstin has felt no need to make apologies.

Conclusion

The days and years of Daniel Boorstin's consensus analysis and of all the other consensus thinkers are now long gone. Yet no more than Tocqueville or Beard are the 1950s interpreters of U.S. political thought forgotten. As chapters 2 and 3 indicate, their interpretations remain the basis for the fashioning of contemporary and, indeed, all post-1960s interpretations. The process generally operates dialectically in the contested realm of interpretation of American political thought and culture. That is, the rejection of these past views, and the reasons for their rejection, have been the crucial first step toward the construction of alternative views in the present day. This dynamic is what makes knowledge of past interpretations so enormously important. To grapple with contemporary interpretations, therefore, there is no substitute for understanding their predecessors. For contemporary views are in constant dialogue with them. They have not let this past go, and there is little sign that they will do so soon.

Chapter Two

The Fall of Consensus

The 1950s and early 1960s were the great age of consensus historians such as Louis Hartz and Daniel Boorstin. They were also the point at which social scientist Daniel Bell famously proclaimed "the end of ideology."[1] While Bell understood there were diverse ideologies in the world, he did indeed think ideological conflict had greatly declined in the United States. This perspective led to plenty of debate among American political intellectuals at the time.[2] Yet Bell's conclusion was a commonly shared opinion among public intellectuals in the age of Dwight Eisenhower and John Kennedy.[3]

By the late 1960s, however, consensus views of American thought and culture were under severe attack. By the 1990s they were pretty much dead. This collapse of consensus interpretations of American culture and thought constitutes an important and fascinating part of this study. Its examination is crucial because it was the first step toward the interpretive diversity of our contemporary era. The next several chapters address some of the intriguing dimensions of the history of ill-fated consensus thought.

Four developments in particular have undermined consensus claims since the 1960s. The first in historical terms was the era of the 1960s itself, especially the civil rights and Vietnam conflicts that marked that decade. The intense disputes surrounding these events dealt a devastating blow to those who had serenely assumed the United States was a consensual society. A second factor, and a companion of the first, was the intellectual assault on the claim that consensus was the story of America. It also began in the 1960s and since then has continued unabated. Another was the tremendous burst of intellectual diversity and political pluralism that swept into American intellectual life beginning in the 1960s. Now, decades later, it flourishes as vibrantly as ever. This diversity has powerfully undermined all consensus claims.

In chapter 3 I will look at the final development, the broad critique of the historical accuracy of consensus views and the attempt to formulate alternatives that also began in the 1960s and continues today. What distinguishes the present chapter from chapter 3 is that here the focus will be on the debate over the value and plausibility of a consensus view since the 1960s. Chapter 3 addresses the debate over the accuracy of consensus interpretations applied to the full course of American history and explores alternative interpretations of our thought and history.

In contrast to the superficial calm of the previous postwar years, the dramatic events of the 1960s were a potent acid that eroded the consensus worlds of Hartz, Boorstin, and the rest. By the later 1960s it was a standard—and reasonable—position to conclude that there was no basic value consensus in the United States. The furies of cultural and political clashes over civil rights and Vietnam had spilled into the streets, and the word *consensus* could no longer describe the United States. The widespread realization that the arrival of considerable public conflict in the United States was utterly unpredicted by consensus theorists only fortified this conclusion. It was no wonder most public intellectuals quickly moved on from consensus views. Suddenly consensus interpretations were badly out of date and out of fashion.

The immediate consequence was an intense attack on consensus theories, an assault that accelerated the descent of the consensus interpretations into their graves. These critiques, which became standard in the 1960s, have never ceased. Before long they metamorphosed into an interpretive orthodoxy—or antiorthodoxy—that may be as tight as or tighter than the hold of the consensus outlook in the 1950s. Its central tenet is the claim that a consensus does not exist in the United States and never has. A frequent corollary is that 1950s consensus advocates were political conservatives devoted to the defense of an elitist, inegalitarian past that was not worth preserving.

The 1960s (and Later) Attacks on Consensus

This chapter explores these critiques that concentrate on the failure of consensus models as a means of interpretation of American thought and culture since the 1960s. The critiques have taken two directions, although each often circles around the other. One faults consensus theory for being a poor empirical description of American thought and life since the 1960s. The other denounces consensus theory on moral grounds. Exponents of the latter perspective sometimes concede that consensus interpretations were plausible or at least a partially accurate description of the United States until the 1960s. Yet they loathe this reality and have sought to destroy any signs of consensus in the United States, celebrating every indication of its demise.

Garry Wills's *Nixon Agonistes* (1970) is a classic example of this genre.[4] Wills was delighted by the collapse of consensus in the 1960s, since he bemoaned the consensus that he judged had been too characteristic of our past. He was happy at the forces destroying consensus in the 1960s, although he carefully disclaimed being a member of the New Left, which he felt confused an ethic of personal authenticity with a serious, systematic political and social outlook. For Wills, the essence of the old liberal consensus was the conviction that "selfishness is a *duty* with us," and that on this and other matters the only problematic divisions had been on "matters of emphasis."[5]

In other words, Wills's Americans had been—and still were, to a distressing extent—captives of a liberal market ideology. They held tightly to the idea of individual self-reliance, and they liked environments where market competition was the rule as it was in American politics and economic life. The individual and the market were the ideological twins of Americans, Wills claimed, despite the fact that they existed much less often in practice than they were invoked in theory.

Of course the special sheen of *Nixon Agonistes* came from Wills's skillful use as his master metaphor the life of Richard Nixon before and during his presidency that began in 1969. Wills recounted Nixon's life journey—as understood by Wills—in fascinating and telling detail, creating in Nixon the very epitome of the dying but undesirable American consensus. Wills's Nixon embodied the reigning ideology in every bone of his body and every action of his life—which was exactly why Wills loathed him so much.

The New Left history that poured from the presses in the later 1960s and the 1970s was another expression of this critique. Examples abound, but two of the most well known were Barton Bernstein's *Toward a New Past* and Staughton Lynd's *Intellectual Origins of Ameri-*

can Radicalism.[6] These works and others argued, contrary to Wills, that the true historical record of the United States showed that there had been no consensus in American history or culture, just as there was none now. In the hands of these "new" historians, often social historians of "ordinary" people, U.S. history teemed with pluralisms of every conceivable variety—economic, ethnic, regional, racial, gender, religious. Thus it contained innumerable "dissenting" histories, which were far too often missing in consensus history. New Left historians joined with Wills, however, in their shared distaste for consensus as a normative ideal, especially if the consensus was anything remotely like modern liberalism. Instead, they were given to lauding a wide range of (if also carefully selected) alternative Americas and Americans. They were, in fact, the founders of the contemporary multicultural ideal for the United States.

A third critical expression, best represented by C. Wright Mills (1916–62) and Herbert Marcuse (1898–1979), had the greatest impact in 1960s disillusionment with consensus theory. Mills had a major influence in Left intellectual circles especially in the late 1950s and early 1960s. The motorcycle-riding sociologist and social critic was a romantic hero to many,[7] a figure who sadly and yet fittingly died far too young. While Mills was not self-consciously a consensus theorist in his meditations on the United States, his conclusions reinforced this perspective as he angrily denounced an America he judged dangerously conformist.

Mills's most famous work, of course, was *The Power Elite.*[8] It was his effort to expose the three-sided group of the rich, military leaders, and top politicians whom he charged ruled the United States, making a mockery of the idea that America was a democracy. In this setting the image Mills drew of the American population was not flattering. Americans were a mass lured into an unthinking acceptance of an elitist system, one that blatantly denied Mills's support of participatory democracy.[9] This negative image was nothing new for Mills. It followed from his earlier attack on the middle classes in *White Collar,*[10] where he derided these Americans as compliant, unreflective sheep.

Mills drifted steadily to the Left in the course of his intellectual career, eventually becoming something of a Marxist. He was always clear that Americans were not identical in terms of class or power. In his most theoretical work, *The Sociological Imagination,*[11] a demolition of ordinary social science, he revisited the idea that there was a single ideology in the United States. He argued in the familiar "end of ideology" language of the time that the old ideological frameworks were exhausted, and he complained that there was no effort by social science intellectuals to reach toward a new vision beyond their numbing obsession with "facts" and low-level empirical theory. Put another way, Mills saw a Boorstin-like unselfconscious consensus at work. Mills fiercely protested this reality, believing it denied most people democratic equality and benefited only his notorious power elite at home and abroad.

Herbert Marcuse was the most influential intellectual in the United States in the 1960s and early 1970s, as well as the most important philosopher of the New Left. Marcuse obtained near-heroic status among some in those years, and his remarkable work in the context of American thought, *One-Dimensional Man*,[12] was present in many a (then) young radical's hand.

Marcuse's analysis of the United States was closer to Mills's in some ways than to that of many New Left historians. This was because Marcuse had no doubt that the United States in the 1960s and earlier was a consensus society. He did not use that term, a product of a world he wished to repudiate. Yet he argued in *One-Dimensional Man* that the central truth about America was its one-dimensionality, its lack of diverse perspectives, traditions, and cultures. The essence of this one-dimensionality that dominated the United States was our repressive liberalism. He insisted that liberal ideology and the technocapitalism that enforced it everywhere in American culture ostensibly lauded the individual, while actually denying people's deepest needs. For Marcuse, moreover, this domination by repressive liberalism was as strong among intellectuals (or, had been until the 1960s) as among the rest of the population.

In fact, Marcuse's analysis made the hold of consensus on the United States far tighter than the consensus of either Louis Hartz or Daniel Boorstin. Marcuse saw one-dimensionality completely ruling the American people and their culture, whereas Hartz and Boorstin concentrated on political or, at most, general public values, not all of life. This was exactly why Marcuse so hailed the emergence of the New Left. It was an intellectual and political movement that, however inchoate, burst the terribly stifling bonds of "repressive tolerance" and brought into intellectual life and American culture desperately needed new ideas and fresh possibilities. The 1960s student movement might seem ideologically confused and organizationally ragtag to others, but Marcuse saluted it as a destroyer of consensus and a great potential force for human liberation.[13]

Of course, Marcuse shared with Mills and New Left historians the utter disgust felt by all 1960s rebels for any version of the consensus view of American thought. Marcuse was also critical of the consensus he perceived in the USSR (although not in countries he perceived as revolutionary, such as Maoist China). But he was especially critical of the liberal consensus of the United States, and the intensity of his feeling revealed that he had expected more from this country, his adopted homeland.

What began modestly in the 1960s became by the 1970s and thereafter a tidal wave. The ranks of critics of consensus interpretations swelled as they made what soon became the standard twin objections to consensus theory: that it was false now as in the past in the United States, and that it was thoroughly morally objectionable as well. Over the next decades feminist, African-American, Native American, Latino, gay, and lesbian voices joined with earlier scholars who denied the historical validity of consensus interpretations and still others who fashioned alternative interpretations for the story of the United States and its thought. More and more, the "consensus" view became that the United States was overwhelmingly a multiracial and multicultural nation in fact and in values, and it was inconceivable that anyone could think—or could have ever thought—otherwise.

One of the most effective voices presenting this analysis was John Higham, a much-respected historian of U.S. immigration. Although no member of the New Left, Higham shared the sense that consensus history was terribly flawed by its "moral complacency," often parading in "the guise of neutrality."[14] He did not deny the consensus interpretation's "substantial" contributions to understanding America, but he disapproved of its "amorality" and its disinterest in "critical judgment."[15] Equally unattractive was the resulting history's lifelessness. Consensus history was not just "false"; it was also "vacuous," "bland," and limited by "a certain tameness."[16]

The most important reason for the collapse of consensus theories, after the initial flurry of attacks, was the argument that the United States was now very diverse—and maybe always had been. It contained many narratives, not just one. The straightforward claim often was that complex and diverse American policies and politics in the last quarter of the twentieth century showed how silly consensus views were—and few disagreed.[17] But, more than anything else, it was the extraordinary burst of creative intellectual diversity in political and social ideas after 1970 that doomed consensus theories. The presence of real intellectual diversity mocked consensus claims and rendered them implausible.

The Burst of Diversity

One careful study of elite intellectuals in the late 1960s found considerable agreement among them and with the larger American public also. This was true in their shared (if general) liberal values, but also on a number of policy questions, including policies on race and race relations and Vietnam, where opposition to U.S. involvement was strong, although mostly for pragmatic reasons.[18]

Yet by the 1970s, agreement among political intellectuals had faded, and there are few obvious signs of its return. Moreover, many public intellectuals by the 1970s, and certainly thereafter, celebrated the arrival of this pluralism and were delighted that consensus views had met their demise. Confidence was high that the nation was much better for the denouement of consensus, which signaled that the United States had become a much freer and more open society. Of course, there were conflicts, but how could they be addressed if they lay half disguised under the smothering cover of an alleged consensus? The ethic that increasingly governed modern America was freedom, which led to the possibility of individuals and groups achieving some of what they sought ("fulfillment") in a less structured and constrained nation.[19]

This optimism was not universally shared. Most political intellectuals welcomed the demise of consensus, but not all judged the results as entirely happy. Indeed, the intellectual mood of the 1970s could be described, for example, as one of considerable malaise. A mood of pessimism, uncertainty, and skepticism pervaded the thinking of many American intellectuals regarding the contemporary situation in the United States, as well as its future.

There was, as David McConnell argues, plenty of engagement with the metaphor of failure. Vietnam, Watergate, and the situation of minorities trapped in deteriorating inner cities clouded the sky. By the 1990s the feeling persisted in the face of the problems of making racial and ethnic pluralism work, the troubled status of the family, and the inability of the state to vanquish crime, illegitimacy, poor schools, and the rest. Meanwhile, the conviction that there is no common faith or ideology—or consensus—that could somehow respond to the problems at hand and bring healing continues to be taken for granted.[20]

Some public intellectuals have been explicit critics of the new pluralistic world. Daniel Bell was one in the 1970s in his *Cultural Contradictions of Capitalism.*[21] Bell argued that the successes of capitalism had generated an intellectual and artistic class—"the new class"—that lacks any commitment to Western institutions and values and, indeed, seeks to undermine the very order that gives them their privileged place in society. Bell continued to argue that no societal consensus had emerged, nor was there an incipient consensus among "new class" intellectuals, except a temperamental hostility to the American economic, political, and social order.

Such critical readings of the situation, however, grew more muted as the 1980s and 1990s unfolded. They faded into the pluralism and thickness of a varied American intellectual life. This diversity increasingly overwhelmed all else, including those who self-consciously sought some (no longer existent) centrist position, as Alan Wolfe complains in his thoughtful book *Marginalized in the Middle.*[22] The idea of consensus became a mirage in intellectual America.

To understand this event, we need a sense of the pluralism of intellectual, political, and social thought that characterizes contemporary American political intellectuals. To this diversity this chapter now turns, providing a glimpse of the contemporary intellectual scene in several of its many expressions.

The Left

A legacy of the 1960s was the creation of a larger and more respectable Left in American intellectual life. Its period of greatest growth expressed as Marxism, other forms of socialism, and anarchism came in the 1960s and 1970s. Tight ideological lines were less common than mixtures of Marxist, neo-Marxist, anarchist, or "economic democracy" ideas.[23]

Some concentrated on leftist historical studies, as did Jerome Weinstein in *The Corporate Ideal in the Liberal State: 1900–1918*, to mention one example among many.[24] Others developed philosophical arguments, as did Robert Paul Wolff in *The Poverty of Liberalism*. Wolff exposed what he saw as the manifest philosophical limitations of liberal freedom—a concept less about choice than oppression—and reflected on the failures of the United States, which had little authentic individualism or desperately needed community.[25]

Others, and more so over time, focused on an egalitarian and participatory community as the ideal. Carole Pateman did so in her influential book *Participation and Democratic Theory*, which gained a major hearing among intellectuals on the Left.[26] Pateman delineated what she argued was a participatory and egalitarian tradition in Western thought, although, unfortunately for her, she selected Yugoslavia as the latest instantiation of that tradition. Later, 1980s versions of this ideal included such works as Joshua Cohen and Joel Rogers's *On Democracy*.[27] There, once again, a kind of egalitarian, participatory model of community received warm treatment—as it did with others such as Arthur Stein and Harry Boyte, who wrote enthusiastic reports on the success of local participatory communities.[28]

Noam Chomsky, the brilliant scholar of linguistics, whose political activism over the past three decades has marked him as a very public and unapologetic Left intellectual, has expressed a rather different spirit. A militant advocate of economic and socialist democracy, Chomsky is especially known for his fierce denunciations of the United States. He contends the United States is controlled by a capitalist elite who exploit the masses, manipulate them by "manufacturing consent," and ruthlessly oppress much of the world for greedy capitalist ends.

Chomsky is not known for his temperate political language—in person or on the written page. Nor does he wish to be. His critics describe him as a fossil from the 1960s, but others welcome the continuing presence of such an angry Left political intellectual in a time in which Chomsky's charges of elite conspiracies and blatant oppressions have subsided in much of the American Left. What is certain is that Chomsky on "class warfare" or the American "culture of terrorism" remains a potent draw today, long after he first began making his political arguments public.[29]

After the collapse of the USSR and its satellite nations, there was a notable dilution of Marxist language on the Left and a steady decline in such 1970s intellectual concerns as Marxist structuralism. But it did not follow that the collapse of Soviet Russia and its satellites somehow required a similar end of Marxist thought. After all, few American intellectuals sympathetic to Marxism believed the Soviet Union was a representative of true Marxism. Nevertheless, the intellectual Left today is far less interested in Marxism than it was twenty years ago, even as Marxism remains a lively part of American intellectual discourse. This is apparent from discussions in the *Nation*, the leading journal of the American intellectual Left, as well as a host of other Left intellectual journals, including the *Progressive*, *In These Times*, and the *Utne Reader*.

The most frequent theme in Left intellectual political thought today is the promotion of democracy—often understood to imply or to require the end of capitalism and the arrival of a radical, people's democracy at home and abroad. From another angle, there is no common element at all, only what Todd Gitlin has described as "the exhaustion of commonality."[30] Indeed, Gitlin argues that even the idea that there should be agreement on a single outlook, program, or strategy has faded for much of the Left. It bothers Gitlin that more often today it is conservatives who defend the vision of a holistic United States.[31] He complains that left-leaning racial, feminist, sexual, and ethnic groups are busy fighting for "the crown of thorns" in the world of Left identity politics. He is discouraged about a Left wandering in such a racial, ethnic, and gender sectarian nightmare.[32]

Gitlin insists that the Left today must unite and avoid the divisions of identity politics. It must also skirt the trendy (and anticommunal) "postmodern nihilism" that he also believes contributes to Left factionalism.[33] He realizes the goal of a united Left is not going to be easy to achieve, but he maintains it is the only route for a Left seeking social impact. To do so, it will have to get back in touch with issues that affect the broader national population and move away from issues on the margin, of interest only to small, sectarian factions.[34]

Feminism

While the fortunes of the Left in American intellectual life have been to some extent affected by the status of world Communism, radical thought after 1970 continued to occupy an important place in the American intellectual life. Although it lacked a base within the population at large, that was not the case in intellectual and academic circles. This was particularly true of the most important offspring of the 1960s Left, feminism and feminist thought, which by now play a crucial role in American intellectual life.[35] Indeed, the changes that feminism has brought to the American intellectual world since the 1960s are astounding. Feminism provides a major explanation for why consensus interpretations seem hopelessly outdated today.

There is no quick way to give an idea of the richness of feminist political and social thought since the 1960s. There have been many attempts to do so. Some proceed in analytic terms, distinguishing liberal feminism, Marxist feminism, radical feminism, and the like.[36] Others are chronological, identifying phases or waves of feminist theory since the 1960s.[37] My discussion will follow this second approach, although much feminist thought is too complex, and sometimes too original, to group in any simple category.

The first phase of feminist thought, which emerged in the 1960s and 1970s, emphasized the theme of women's oppression, usually but not always explained its causes as socially constructed, and was sympathetic to an ideal of gender equality, often gender androgyny. Among the most prominent voices were those of the National Organization for Women in its early liberal, equal rights years, Kate Millett, and even Shulamith Firestone, although she built her analysis on biological differences between men and women.[38] Since then there have been many proponents of liberal feminism, even though this outlook now lacks cachet in academic women's studies circles. Liberal feminist thinkers are often fully aware that their feminist critics complain they are too oriented to the individual and to individual rights. Liberal feminists reply that praising individual women and the right to freedom and equality for all women need not lead one to deny the social side of life or the reality of human interdependence. They also note the obvious fact that only liberal feminism has a significant following in the nation as a whole.[39]

A second phase came in the 1980s, and its legacy too has definitely continued. It shifted attention to women in contrast to (oppressing) men. Its advocates saw women as different from men, whether by nature or embedded culture. These feminists had little interest in androgyny and much more enthusiasm for women as women. This outlook often was essentialist, holding that there was some essence to women as women—with which they were deeply sympathetic. Sometimes this approach has been semimystical, as in Susan Griffin's poetic *Woman and Nature*.[40] At other times psychological studies have led the way, especially the work of theorists and social scientists such as Carol Gilligan and Jean Baker Miller, which discerns distinctions between men and women, sometimes identifying women as more caring or more intuitive and less linear in their thinking than men are.[41]

In more recent feminist thought there has been stress on how to move men—as well as some women—toward traits such as care and less inclination to make essentialist claims about gender differences. For instance, Joan Tronto, in her widely discussed *Moral Boundaries: A Political Argument for an Ethic of Care*,[42] gives serious attention to working through some of the issues of "a care perspective" for and by all people.[43]

At the same time, there continues to be an active strain of "difference" feminism that insists on a distinction between men and women and identifies its important social and political implications. Mary Daly has long been one of the most famous exponents of this view, training her fire especially on patriarchal religious worlds. Susan Brownmiller achieved at least equal fame in her use of rape as the symbol of historic male aggressiveness practicing domination over women.[44] More controversial in recent years, perhaps, have been Andrea Dworkin and Catharine A. MacKinnon, who have addressed pornography as a prime example of male patriarchy. They are severely critical of men, their lives, the (male) legal order, and other social institutions that they believe serve men and not women.[45]

Another part of the "difference" tradition has been self-conscious lesbian feminism, sometimes directed toward separatism, sometimes not. A pioneer here was Jill Johnston, whose point of view is evident from the title of one of her works, *Lesbian Nation: The Feminist Solution*. Perhaps the most influential author in this voice has been Adrienne Rich, who has written in several genres. She has articulated a complex vision of lesbian and "difference" feminism that is less formal philosophy and more renowned poetry.[46] But much more is happening in lesbian feminism, including a good deal of work in a postmodern genre that is decidedly political.[47]

Most recently feminist thought has continued to take many paths. The resulting landscape is too complex and diverse to characterize swiftly, but feminist thinkers share a determination to alter the way people think and live politically, to demand "revisioning the political."[48] The paths include Betty Friedan's argument that women must not be reduced to a single interpretive theory, required to make either-or choices in their lives, or face denial of their freedom. For her, there was a need to argue less about abstract concepts and goals and more about the practical means to help women, especially the many women who work and have children and husbands in often difficult life situations.[49] There has also been a rise of self-conscious feminist thinking from a "minority" point of view, above all through the postmodern writings of African-American feminists such as bell hooks.[50]

There has also been increased attention to what we might call philosophical issues. Nancy Hartsock, for example, has been active in this area, working from an outlook sympathetic to both Marxism and postmodernism.[51] Among the issues feminist philosophers have explored are the "essentialist" and "difference" controversies regarding women and men, as well as whether there is a philosophical case for a more "practical feminism," to borrow Marion Smiley's term. This view resists universal truth claims about the genders because they dissolve the individual woman and her experiences into intellectual categories that may mean little to her, or to anyone else, in real life.[52] Others address this idea also in an effort to show that both pragmatism and feminism have much to learn from each other and together can contribute to human emancipation.[53]

There have also been a good many attempts to connect with the world outside feminism, an effort that is easier to endorse than to carry out. Jean Bethke Elshtain's work and its controversial reception within feminist circles demonstrate both points. Elshtain has tried to fashion her own views and endeavored to apply them in policy terms. She describes herself as a social feminist, concerned with building a more public and communal setting for women in the real world, who is also unsympathetic toward large parts of both liberal feminism and academic feminism. But her work has hardly escaped controversy.[54] There have also been discourses on the situation of women—and feminism—in the current environment, such as Susan Faludi's best-seller *Backlash*.[55] These reports link feminist perspectives and the actual events of historical and feminist life, invariably voicing a particular vision of the feminist ideal and of current realities.

Conservatism

Chapter 4 explores American conservative intellectuals' thought today in some detail and asks whether it is really just an offshoot of liberalism. Here, however, my point is to note that conservative political thought has played a significant part—albeit one less commonly recognized than feminism—in expanding the diversity of American intellectual life since the 1960s. Moreover, conservative thought itself has appeared in strikingly varied expressions.[56] The rise of the conservative movement in American political life, beginning with the Barry Goldwater phenomenon in 1964 and continuing to the role of the Christian Coalition and Focus on the Family in the 1990s, paralleled the major growth of conservative thought—and of various types of conservative thought. Indeed, the flourishing of conservative thought may deserve equal billing with feminism as the most important intellectual development in the United States since 1970. That it has involved different intellectuals and taken place in different sectors of society than feminism only underlines the pluralism in American political thinking today.

There is little disagreement over the main contours of the conservative intellectual renaissance in the United States. Russell Kirk was the leading voice for a traditionalist (or social or cultural) conservatism, an outlook that affirms God, the nation, local traditions, and a shared moral community above all else.[57] Milton Friedman has made popular the libertarian stream of conservative thought, which almost every contemporary conservative shares to some extent, through such best-selling books as *Capitalism and Freedom* and *Free to Choose* (the latter with Rose Friedman).[58] Friedman insists he is not actually a conservative, since he is no Kirkian traditionalist, a stance that more uncompromising libertarians adhere to even more resolutely. In more recent years, Charles Murray has promoted the libertarian position in both policy and political theory terms. His succinct manifesto, *What It Means to Be a Libertarian*, has achieved considerable influence.[59]

At the same time, others who represent the mainstream of the American conservative movement practice a "hybrid" version that now is the official ideology of American conservatism.[60] Its defenders combine libertarian, pro-market, and antistatist themes with an emphasis on the values of family, religion, and social and moral order (sometimes providing for their state enforcement). This perspective does not necessarily meet a logician's test for consistency, but it reflects the compromise present in practical thought in the post-1960s conservative renaissance.

The 1980s and 1990s, of course, also saw the rise of Christian conservatism and active efforts to promote this viewpoint intellectually. Christian conservatism is by no means a latter-day equivalent of Kirkian social conservatism. It is more insistent on its foundation in religious truth and on its morality, and it has less Burkean respect for established institutions or for localism than does Kirkian social conservatism.

Christian conservatism is well known in its largely religiously conservative Protestant expressions—the Christian Right—but its most sophisticated intellectual defender is Richard John Neuhaus, now a Roman Catholic priest. In its measured way, Neuhaus's monthly journal, *First Things*, presents a political and social vision derived from (his understanding of) Christian truth that constitutes a case for a form of Christian conservatism that has gained considerable attention.

In some other versions Christian conservative thought is also, perhaps surprisingly, far more enthusiastic about the market than Burkean traditionalists ever have been or could be.[61] This reality brings home how quite different branches of conservatism have united in their antipathy to the state. To be sure, there is no perfect consistency here, as social conservatives campaign for state control of abortion and many market conservatives support a large defense budget. But the mood of overall hostility toward the state is pervasive among American conservative intellectuals today, and this belief more than anything else joins them together.

Finally, the 1970s and 1980s saw the appearance of the "neoconservatives," some of whom were once radicals and many of whom were former liberals. Neoconservatives were frequently concerned with the fate of Israel, the defeat of Communism, and the reconstitution of a more public-regarding and communal society at home. Their intellectual contributions had substantial impact within and without conservative intellectual circles. Irving Kristol is perhaps the preeminent neoconservative voice.[62] Even though few have been eager to embrace the label, many others, such as Jeane Kirkpatrick and Norman Podhoretz, have been animated by a tough stance toward the Communism that threatened all they treasure.[63]

Kristol insisted that it was also time to defend American political—and economic—institutions from attacks from the 1960s Left and their successors who were well established in academia, foundations, and other intellectual centers as the century waned. Neoconservative defense of capitalism for its roles in generating great prosperity for society as well as in preserving political freedoms was especially controversial. This did not bother Kristol, although he specified what he judged to be proper limits of neoconservative enthusiasm for capitalism, which lacked a spiritual dimension and contributed to our overly bureaucratized society.

Kristol and other neoconservatives were quite annoyed, however, that U.S. capitalist leaders did not fight for American institutions and values, leaving them vulnerable to hostile "new class" intellectual elites.[64] At the same time, Kristol was insistent that capitalism or any other American tradition could be supported only if it met the demands of the public good and empirical reality—as neoconservatives felt basic American institutions did. There was to be no mystical or romantic defense of anything. Neoconservatives saw themselves as realists at home as well as abroad.

The movement won few plaudits from the rest of the conservative movement, although during the Reagan years neoconservatives worked in a sometimes tense cooperation with more conventional so-called paleoconservatives. Many conservatives view neoconservatives as latecomers to the cause and suspect that they are too enamored of government to be true conservatives. In the late 1990s, as Communism was in eclipse, Israel and the Middle East were edging toward peace, and some of the neoconservative pro-family agenda was broadly accepted, neoconservative energy and influence declined. But its role in the post-Vietnam intellectual revival of conservative thought and politics was and continues to be substantial.

The Postmodern Revolution

The revival of conservative thought has involved fractious dispute on some issues, such as state regulation of "private" moral behavior. Intellectual conservatism, however, has no division of opinion on the rise of a postmodern disposition in modern intellectual life. Conservative intellectuals continue to agree, as do many on the Left, that there is such a thing as truth. Of course, there is sharp disagreement on its content, the means to reach it, and even its very conception, but not on the existence of truth itself.

The postmodern perspective that sprang to the forefront of American intellectual life in the 1980s and thereafter, however, does not agree. After all, much of postmodernism is about moving beyond the notion of truth itself. For postmodern thinkers, who did not really exist in American intellectual life until the 1970s, the only "truth" that matters is that individuals and cultures construct their own reality and truth. People may claim or believe their "truth" has some independent status, but there is never anything to the claim. Truth is always a human construction. This postmodern claim is a radical one in the context of the American tradition, where political and social values have almost always rested on such (sometimes "self-evident") truths as natural rights, nature, God, or even America's destiny.

As the postmodern perspective swept into literature, history, and cultural and artistic life, pluralism necessarily expanded sharply. So did fierce conflict over whether there was truth and whether it was possible to proceed "without foundations." Some religious thinkers also weighed in exploring the idea of "spirituality without truth," as postmodern controversies have spread everywhere in American intellectual life.[65]

The impact has been quite direct on political and social thinking. There is no single political outlook that is integral to postmodern thinking. After all, a perspective that passes beyond foundationalism and conceives the universe through very open lenses is likely to yield a host of political visions. While among postmoderns Friedrich Nietzsche has emerged as something of a hero, so has the American John Dewey, and in their differing temperaments and politics these two nicely reflect the range of postmodern thought. Yet there is no doubt that most postmoderns are highly critical of the United States and its political and cultural order. This stance, in turn, has led the movement to draw the ire of those who resent the perspective and critique "the literary critics, philosophers, and self-styled post-modern thinkers who have made the very name 'America' a symbol for that which is grotesque, obscene, monstrous, . . . the symbol of oppression."[66]

Among the more recognizable directions of postmodern social and political thinking are skeptical and ironist political thought, identity theory, and social constructionism. The prominent philosopher Richard Rorty has been a contentious advocate of a skeptical, ironist political vision that, in his hands, is sympathetic to a liberal, constitutional democracy. He proceeds from the premise that we are creatures, captives really, of inherently contingent language and cannot know any truth that purports to transcend the historically specific place of its claimant. Given this situation, what we need is more individual self-creation, less cruelty toward each other, and more human solidarity. We also need to turn away from philosophy, theory, or metaphysics. Such a program, Rorty appreciates, may not seem very dramatic, but it is down-to-earth, a politics that can help make individual and collective lives better in a world without God or any other truth.[67]

Political theorist Michael Shapiro well illustrates this kind of postmodern political sensibility, although in a self-consciously deconstructive context. Shapiro is in synch with many of the leading European and American voices of deconstruction, while at the same time pursuing his own creative path. Whether exploring political theory through text or photography, Shapiro dismisses worlds of certainty as outdated and challenges conventional perceptions—and politics—including the liberal skepticism of those like Richard Rorty.[68]

It is Johns Hopkins professor William Connolly, however, who is perhaps the most well known postmodern political theorist, although hardly the most radical. Connolly has written numerous books that reflect a postmodern inclination. While his book approaching Augustine in this spirit was an embarrassment,[69] Connolly succeeds in advancing a nuanced, reflective version of a postmodern politics. The politics he constructs turns out to be a kind of left-leaning postmodern liberalism. Affirming that "nothing is fundamental," challenging all set interpretations of contemporary life, including one's "own projections," Connolly urges a liberalism that breaks from the "cramped and defensive" United States and flows from a far more explorative "pluralist imagination."[70] In this pluralism the animating ethic will be an "ethos of critical representativeness" that "supports . . . boundary crossings," an increased sense of contingency and openness to new ways of living and of organizing life, altogether "a more fluid and mobile pluralism."[71] The result, he hopes, will be more people willing "to loosen, challenge, or interrupt sedimented presumptions about identity, . . . gender, morality, nationality, diversity, civilization."[72]

Postmodernism has had tremendous influence in literary studies, and Stanley Fish may be the best-known literary critic who has systematically tackled relevant issues in political thought in *There Is No Such Thing as Free Speech . . . and It's a Good Thing Too*—a title that might remind a reader of Herbert Marcuse's work on the same theme of a quarter century ago.[73] To be sure, a postmodern such as Fish has a different outlook than Marcuse in important ways. Fish does not accept Marcuse's foundational truth that was an alchemy of Frankfurt school criticism, Marxian history, and neo-Freudian "human needs." He offers no independent truth or foundation for his values or arguments. He insists that each person creates his or her own meanings shaped by individual experience, and thus no one should pretend that what they understand somehow has independent or universal status as truth. Truth is what different persons and communities believe to be truth.

The connection with Marcuse's outlook is real, however, in the content of Fish's familiar (but skillfully presented) complaints against liberalism. Thus Fish objects to liberalism's usual defense of free speech (as Marcuse objected to liberal tolerance) because it gives the impression that there is such a thing as truly free speech whose consequences are neutral. Fish denies this, asserting that speech is always conditioned by the circumstances from which it comes and the assumptions it makes. All speech favors some people and some interests over others. For Fish (as for Marcuse) the issue is who benefits and who loses in each conception of free speech (or tolerance).

Fish's argument today is far from the exclusive perception of a certain postmodernism. For instance, in the conservative magazine *Chronicles* Kenneth Craycroft Jr. shares his suspicion of liberal free speech doctrine.[74] Craycroft maintains conservatives have no business lining up with liberals and praising free speech as if it were a divine enactment. Conservatives, he argues, should support liberal free speech only when it promotes conservative values and should oppose liberal free speech when it does not. It is no universal truth, but a liberal value that may and sometimes does retard conservative objectives. Like Marcuse and Fish, Craycroft's conservatism historicizes liberal (although not all) values and in the process, perhaps unintentionally, reflects the postmodern temper of the age.

Postmodernism has also had major influence on feminist thought, but its political influence has spread out in almost all other conceivable directions as well.[75] For example, it has been integral to the development of the politics of identity, which involves the defense of (selected) groups in modern society, commonly gender, race, and sometimes class or ethnic groups. It rejects any politics that claims there are general truths, and it is decidedly skeptical of any politics whose telos is a single community (not to speak of a single consensus). Such an analysis includes ardent support for multiculturalism, with its understanding that there is really no truth and that every truth constructed by every (or at least every approved) group deserves appreciation.[76]

Postmodernism has been influential in legal thought, especially in critical legal studies. This movement is multidimensional, but all sides reject a worshipful view of law and the legal order. In a disenchanted and left-leaning political mood, it seeks to deconstruct the roles of law and the legal system in society and to expose those they do and do not serve in the social order. The most widely read postmodern venture in critical legal studies is Patricia Williams's *Alchemy of Race and Rights: Diary of a Law Professor*.[77] Through her semidiary format, Williams attacks the idea that there is any cognitive truth. This critique is part of her project to undermine conventional legal thought and legalism and to promote instead (once again) a politics that honors difference or pluralism. In the process Williams displays a familiar postmodern sensibility. She celebrates "the ambivalent, multivalent way of seeing, . . . a fluid positioning that sees back and forth" crossing all boundaries, although as she translates this stance, what she offers is a quite familiar Left politics.[78]

Postmodernism has often proved to be a fertile ground for those who defend constructionism, the idea that human action creates the intellectual and cultural frameworks and human institutions of life, no matter how often people attribute such creations to God or nature or other forces. This perception leads many post-modern intellectuals to the settings in which ideas originate and the recognition that ideas or values obtain their limited validity from their fit with a given context, although they have no validity across all contexts.[79] Such "contextualism" is for them an important illustration of what postmodernism involves: that political societies, social categories (such as race or gender), and just about everything else are best understood as creations of human artifice in specific times and places.[80]

A radical politics that concentrates on debunking and "deconstructing" such categories as God or nature is also routine within postmodernism. So can be a certain enthusiasm for redoing the world. After all, if much of the world is a human construction, it may be able to be reshaped by human hands—reconstructed, one may say. While the prevailing mood is far from utopian, postmodern intellectuals are often change-oriented (although what is sought by way of reconstruction of course differs among thinkers).[81]

And yet not every radical American political intellectual has welcomed postmodernism. Sheldon Wolin, a longtime intellectual voice for a Left democratic politics, has denounced it, arguing that it is a shame to see so many able intellectuals wasting their time on word games, demonstrating their cleverness rather than committing themselves to the realization of social democracy, community, and, yes, the realization of truth.[82]

In this context the postmodern taste for deconstructing "modernity" on the road to assorted postmodern perspectives is fascinating. The process inevitably involves its own fallible constructions, since it often treats "the human condition in recent centuries as a coherent and integrated whole."[83] Whether we are really in such a new age is highly debatable in part because it depends on characteristic postmodern constructions: of a past called modernity and a present called postmodernism.[84]

Yet there is little question even from some skeptical observers that postmodernism has had a significant effect in opening American intellectual thought to a whole range of new ideas—and thus greatly increasing diversity in this form. The paradox, perhaps, is that just as postmodernism opens space for new approaches and fresh interpretations of older paradigms, it undermines the "truth" value of such perspectives. This situation bothers some

American political intellectuals but few committed postmoderns, who suggest we have to move beyond foundational claims in politics as elsewhere.

Community

The community movement in American intellectual thought is more linear in its politics and far wider in its reach than is postmodernism. Since chapter 6 concentrates on community as a mode of American political thought since the 1960s, this is not the place to dwell on the topic.[85] Yet it is necessary to acknowledge here the importance of this direction in public intellectual life. The community critique of American culture and liberal thought flourishes handsomely today, as does the business of proposing and defending assorted ideals of community.

Such community critiques and community ideals were missing from the consensus interpretations of American political thought in the 1950s. The idea of community was hardly on the mind of a consensus theorist such as Louis Hartz. His discussion of consensus must not be confused with the contemporary calls for community that emanate from so many American public intellectuals, not least because Hartz disliked the idea of consensus and displayed no interest in community. At one level, such social theorists as Berkeley's Robert Bellah and Harvard's Michael Sandel have called for an expansion of community in the United States to combat our disturbingly centrifugal, fractured, and disoriented society. Even if, as Bellah and his associates contend, there is a language in American society that reflects an enduring yearning for community, they know that American culture is a long way from realizing community in its public life.[86]

At another, less sweeping level there has been considerable exploration of "republican" themes among American public intellectuals.[87] This focus addresses ideas of the common good and community in American history, especially at the time of the Revolution, the Constitution, and the early nation, as well as the possibilities of their revival now. The breadth of interest in this republican, common-good tradition in American life has been extraordinary. It is a powerful sign of the desire for community among many public intellectuals in recent years.

Another dimension of the concern with community is the effort to integrate community ideas with the main aspects of the Western liberal tradition *and* with current human practice. Those sympathetic to this approach have led the way in organizing and publishing symposia on the nature of community, community's theoretical and analytical dimensions, and how community can be translated into specific policies and practices. Its advocates believe that the current interest in community in American intellectual life is worth little if there are no bridges between theory and practice to help realize community in day-to-day life.[88]

The Flourishing of Liberal Ideas

To appreciate the growth of diversity in American thought, it is not enough to observe feminism, conservatism, postmodernism, the entrancement with community—or any of the other plausible candidates for attention in our contemporary political intellectual life. Each of these orientations conceives of itself in good part as a revolt against liberalism or particular understandings of liberalism. Yet a significant feature of the post-1960s pluralist intellectual development in the United States has been the spirited reinvigoration of liberal thought itself. Liberalism's renewed vigor has propelled it in several important directions that constitute a fascinating element of the diverse political thinking in the United States today.

At the heart of the rebirth of liberal thought since the 1960s has been the courage to do liberal theory, rather than only tell its history or cautiously reflect on the ideas of others. This development occurred most brilliantly in John Rawls's controversial book *A Theory of Justice* (1971), which undertook a highly theoretical and influential defense of liberalism.[89]

The amount of debate and discussion that Rawls's work has promoted in the last thirty years is truly amazing. Rawls's neo-Kantian efforts to ground and order liberal values have especially engaged philosophers, political theorists, and legal intellectuals. Rawls's influence has undoubtedly cooled as other approaches to liberalism, especially pragmatism, have bloomed, but few would dispute that he constructed the most important argument for and about liberal political philosophy in the last half century at least. In specific milieus, such as some legal intellectual circles, Rawls remains as significant as ever. Moreover, his *Political Liberalism*, published in 1993, has sustained interest in his argument for liberalism, especially since Rawls now self-consciously situates his liberalism in contextually liberal settings rather than choosing to present it as a neo-Kantian universal.[90]

Michael Walzer's defense of his own brand of Left-liberalism has propelled him to a central role as a public intellectual in the past three decades. I discuss his thought in some detail in chapter 8, but his importance must be noted here. Walzer's classic, elegant attempts to fashion a liberalism that is sensitive to a range of values, including community, equality, pluralism, liberty, and an appreciation, perhaps above all else, of the complicated and textured reality in which actual people dwell, have resulted in a great many admirers. Perhaps Walzer's *Spheres of Justice* (1983) has had the greatest impact, but more recent books have also merited attention, such as *On Toleration* and *Thick and Thin: Moral Argument at Home and Abroad*.[91]

Oftentimes the mood of this liberal thought accords with what Kenneth Grasso expresses well when he asserts that "the task today" is "to save liberty—and liberalism . . . from modernist liberalism."[92] What counts as modernist liberalism varies, of course, but many theorists accept the idea that something has gone wrong with much liberal theory and practice, and thus liberalism must dress in new clothes. It is in this familiar, critical spirit that the new liberalisms have appeared.

The revival of liberal thought is also evident in frankly polemical liberal argument, unashamed and unapologetic in its liberal sympathies and boldly critical of alternative views or temporizing defenses of liberalism. Stephen Holmes is the master of this controversial and disputatious approach, demonstrated in his free-wielding *Anatomy of Antiliberalism*.[93] Holmes cuts a wide swath and seems impervious to critics who fault him for his broad and occasionally superficial analyses. Among the figures he has cheerfully cut down are Roberto Unger, whose work he presents as mostly booming, buzzing confusion; Alisdair MacIntyre, the darling of many contemporary community-oriented theorists; Leo Strauss and what Holmes considers to be his obscurantist cult; and the late Christopher Lasch, whom Holmes indicts, along with a host of others, for a "vague and milky communitarianism."[94]

Some of the other interesting strands of recent liberal thought proceed with the postmodern assumption (though not its sensibility) that skepticism of foundationalism must be integral to liberal theory in the contemporary age. One example is the late Judith Shklar's version of liberalism. Over the course of her fruitful career, this Harvard political theorist traveled from her original skeptical liberalism to a "liberalism of fear," a journey that Bernard Yack has recounted.[95] Shklar tried to provide some psychological realism to modern liberalism, underlining how important fear and cruelty are in politics and how vital their reduction must be to a satisfactory political society. Her outlook left behind cheery emphases on "progress" and triumphant rationality, as well as a romantic faith in people. But she held on to Enlightenment liberal values, while acknowledging the influence of psychological, historical, and cultural factors in human choices. Along the way, Shklar rejected postmodernism as an outlook that made epistemological and metaphysical skepticism (which she had long held to be the only possible human stance) the gateway to a politics of nihilism. She scorned nihilism in politics and elsewhere, as well as those who adhered to it.[96]

At the same time, however, Shklar attempted to move her skeptical and "realistic" liberalism toward having an impact on public policy and thus in its way toward pragmatism. For example, in *Faces of Injustice*,[97] she characteristically dismissed the traditional grand models of justice. Based on foundational claims that cannot be sustained, making sharp distinctions that do not fit the actual world, and paying little attention to people's sense of the injustices they experience, grand theories were not the road to take. Moreover, Shklar complained, classic theories of justice viewed too many of people's perceived injustices as misfortunes, about which they could do little.[98]

Shklar advocated approaching justice, instead, from the perspective of injustice, a direction that connected the subject with people's ordinary feelings and experiences. This approach and Shklar's meditations hardly clear up the conceptual and practical problems connected with injustice, not to mention justice. But Shklar contended they did allow her to reach her main objective. She was able to affirm people and their ordinary sense of victimhood—of injustice. They also permitted her to urge, as she did elsewhere, that the real goals of politics should be reducing "suffering" and the injustice tied to it in actual lives, not the pursuit of abstract theories of justice.[99]

Along the way, Shklar offers numerous skeptical liberal touches. She joins Montaigne in critiquing talk of "justice"; Plato and Aristotle receive criticism as elitists in their discussions of justice; and religion is—of course—brushed aside because Shklar believes it focuses on "eternal salvation" rather than on Shklar-approved, this-worldly victims of injustice.[100]

In fact, Shklar's earnest concerns (such as suffering and cruelty) and her policy directions (combating injustice) are at least as vague and philosophically insecure as most justice claims. The larger point for her, however, is that as a skeptical liberal she struggled to formulate a practical liberalism in an age without liberal certainties. In this sense, she has been one of the most important contributors to new liberal thinking.

Another stream of contemporary liberalism is known for its commitment to liberal democracy of the most "deliberate" or rational sort. This is presented, for example, by Amy Gutmann and Dennis Thompson in their book *Democracy and Disagreement*.[101] Concerned with achieving a more satisfactory democracy than its current forms, these intellectuals argue for a liberal democracy that provides genuine reciprocity, publicity, and accountability in a setting where liberal values reign but genuine opposition also exists. Children of the Enlightenment, they genuinely seek a world where people truly are prepared to reason together. While skeptics doubt that their ideal is congruent with real politics, they tackle concrete issues to illustrate their project.

Pragmatic liberalism has been another robust current of liberal thought. It has gained force in recent decades as postmodern skepticism challenged the validity of sure foundations for politics, ethics, and everything else. While not explicitly identifying with pragmatism, Thomas Spragens's classic *Irony of Liberal Reason* argues that the kind of liberalism America needs now must avoid the abstract conceptual rationalism characteristic of most liberal thought in the past as well as many other social and political traditions. People now require a liberal pragmatic reason that concentrates on problem solving within given social and intellectual contexts and is chastened from failed past pursuits of abstract claims and universal visions.[102]

Charles Anderson's self-conscious essay in pragmatism, *Pragmatic Liberalism*, undertakes to move political intellectuals away from grand justifications for standard liberal principles such as reason, liberty, individualism, and pluralist democracy, which principles he also supports.[103] Pragmatic liberalism, Anderson maintains, must deal with the practice of societies and governments that people are involved in—which means, in the West, with liberal society and government. There is no sense in proceeding on any other, alternative plane. To operate in specific historical and cultural contexts, Anderson suggests, people must employ pragmatic reason as their companion. They must employ deliberative argument that takes into account the facts, practices, and values of their environment. For Anderson, this orientation leads toward the development of a political judgment properly focused on practice and sympathetic toward present practice, although not to be conflated with it.[104]

In fact, Anderson insists, such an approach will help both to construct a strong pragmatic liberal political theory and to support existing pragmatic liberal societies. And, of course, for Anderson as for Spragens, such political judgment will free us from sterile exercises in abstract theorizing or from discussing politics or society in global or universal terms. Thus, for its admirers, pragmatic liberalism suits our times, when many people are without foundations but want to skirt hopeless nihilism or pointless subjectivism.

Attitudes in the Broader Public

The apparent collapse of consensus and the rise of dynamic and determined multiple perspectives among American political intellectuals since 1970 is a phenomenon of historic importance. To be sure, a few voices argue that there is much less intellectual dissent from liberal values than appears. Bruce Douglass urges, for example, that "few (if any) of those who present themselves as opponents of liberalism are prepared to call into question its basic orientation toward public affairs." "Predictably, too," he says, "the alternatives held out by critics have much more the character of amendments (even refinements) than new departures."[105] Yet, while this claim has its value, as chapter 6 suggests, by casting skepticism on how serious many "communitarians" are about community, it has its limitations as well. The fact is there is no consensus favoring liberalism among contemporary American intellectuals. Quite the contrary. Diversity is alive and well in American intellectual life, and it is more and more the reality.

When one turns from the thought of public intellectuals, however, to the views of the American public since the 1960s, this situation alters. Substantial differences of opinion on basic (and liberal) political values do not exist within the American public. Seymour Martin Lipset confirms the situation in his recent work, *American Exceptionalism*.[106] Lipset argues that comparisons with Western European countries and Japan show that the considerable agreement on a set of liberal values distinguishes the United States from these other nations. Lipset draws on numerous surveys that identify the norms of liberty, equality of respect and opportunity, individualism, populism, and moderate laissez-faire as key liberal norms. He understands that considerable agreement on these norms does not preclude the existence of abundant conflict among Americans, conflict over policies to realize principles, conflict that can become intensely moralistic.[107]

Lipset is intrigued by the argument that public opinion has broken into segments, multicultures, as some insist, but he cannot find such a phenomenon. Thus in his study of African-American opinion he finds that most blacks consider the United States a land of opportunity and favor both equality of opportunity and a merit reward system, as do most other Americans. Lipset does observe, however, as others do, that African Americans are far more sympathetic to the state. Its purpose should be to realize the equal opportunity they judge is woefully lacking,[108] a judgment that was on display in many African Americans' reaction to the first O. J. Simpson verdict.

Lipset suggests that there have been two shifts in public opinion and behavior over the last half century, the acceptance of a much more active state since the Depression of the 1930s and the emphasis on group rights and opportunities since the 1960s. Yet he does not think these shifts have fundamentally altered the American value structure as reflected in public opinion. This is especially true, he argues, if one compares the United States with other nations.[109] In short, Lipset argues that there is broad consensus on American values, a conclusion that he maintains is inescapable if one studies the data.

The numerous studies of U.S. public opinion since the 1960s do reveal plenty of disagreements on assorted policy questions, over who is perceived to be the beneficiary or victim of this or that policy, and over candidates, parties, and elections. But such divisions are much scarcer when it comes to basic values. This is so even though the authors of such studies rarely have the same objectives, follow the same methods, or ask the same questions.

It is essential to look at some of this literature because too often discourse on American political culture and political thought substitutes declarations about popular beliefs for serious data. Page and Shapiro, in their *Rational Public*, for example, find that there has been tremendous stability in public attitudes over the past half century. Their work, which defends the general political competence and good sense of the public, reports wide public agreement even on most policy issues. Changes in sentiment do occur sometimes as a result of events or elite or media presentation of events, but these changes generally also demonstrate considerable popular sense. And when changes have come, as in the movement toward social liberalism in the 1960s, the population tends to shift modestly and in similar directions.

Page and Shapiro, in short, cannot find a population splintered into multicultural or multi-ideological pieces. Indeed, even in areas of distinct disagreement, such as between African Americans and the rest of the population over the role of government, dissenting opinion drifts toward the perspectives of the larger public. Convergence is the main story about disagreements, rarely greater conflict.[110]

While this somewhat benign view of the general public's rationality does not fit with the commanding role of elites in some other public opinion studies,[111] most accounts replicate the finding of substantial consensus on general political values in the American public. Thus sociologists Jerome Kluegel and Eliot Smith conclude (with regret) from their study of public opinion, including that of African Americans, that most Americans have supported the U.S. political and social system over recent decades.[112] They also report that most citizens support the liberal ideology that underlies it. Americans are egalitarians in just the sense Lipset finds; they believe everyone should count equally in moral terms but they oppose economic equality of results, affirm the importance of equality of opportunity, and honor the value of individual effort. As another account based on even more recent data puts it, the public attitude toward equality remains "still a distinctively individual-centered conception."[113] Kluegel and Smith, among others, have found that much of the dispute over equality in the United States is not concerned with basic conceptions of equality. It is concerned with how well the system lives up to the widely shared values, with a good many blacks especially convinced it is not working as it should.[114]

This situation is reflected as well in other surveys, which demonstrate both the strong support in the black community for affirmative action and other state measures to assist African Americans and less alienation from standard American values than some intellectuals might expect. As one recent survey maintains, dissatisfaction at the chances blacks have in the real world increases as class level of blacks rises. Poor African Americans retain more hope; relatively successful blacks are more likely to raise questions about the system. What many surveys also report, however, is the evidence of social conservatism among African Americans, such as their religiosity, strong support for prayer in the schools, and a lack of sympathy for welfare recipients who do not get into the workforce after a reasonable time.[115]

William Mayer's detailed exploration of U.S. public sentiment examines the period since 1960, exactly when intellectual political thought splintered in so many directions. Mayer concentrates on public opinion changes during recent decades, especially on social and cultural issues—changes in tolerance, racial attitudes, women's liberation, and sexual attitudes. He finds that most of what changes took place occurred from the middle 1960s to the middle 1970s, a conclusion that is in line with other studies. More important for my purposes, Mayer understands that liberalism is the context for what change has occurred, and he underlines its continuing hold among the public. Indeed, he suggests that this explains why changes that have taken place, such as those in sexual morality, are elite induced and, in most cases, have peaked in their public approval. The American public is stable in its liberal values; it is the elites who are more likely to change from the mainstream.[116]

Another side to the matter of public opinion is attitudes toward political and economic values and systems in the United States. Here again, students have noted considerable popular consensus. Herbert McClosky and John Zaller argue that the data show an "ethos" at work here that includes approval of both democracy (in its American hybrid form) and capitalism (in its modified practice in the United States) among the citizenry.[117] Of course, they acknowledge, there have been and are plenty of disagreements within this context. Unchecked capitalism draws objections; so does an expanding government, even when it expands under democratic demand; and there are conflicts between democracy and capitalism within the United States, for example, over the proper role of unions or the legitimate role of government regulation of business. But these amount to much less than they seem. Such disagreements occur in "a relatively restricted segment of the ideological spectrum."[118] For McClosky and Zaller, the basic picture in American political and economic life is consensus—and vigorous disputation on everything within it.

This is not to say that Americans are satisfied with how their institutions work; this is hardly the case, as chapter 4 makes clear. What is now widely known is that disenchantment with many institutions of the American political system is widespread. This is only to be expected, indeed it is confirming, of a society that is more and more absorbed into liberalism, especially liberal individualism and a coincident distrust of institutions.

At the same time, there is strong commitment to the value of democracy. In the United States, where people's life satisfaction often is high, where most citizens have great pride in their country, think the nation is the best place to live, and believe that its best days lie ahead, there is almost unanimous affirmation of democracy (seen as the American ideal of government) as the best form of government.[119] Even more pessimistic readings that concentrate on popular dissatisfaction reaffirm that the American democratic system continues to receive broad approval and that only a very small minority offer "low system support."[120]

Reaction to how American democracy works in practice is another matter. Chapter 4 considers this theme at some length, but even on this issue a majority is supportive, just as a majority endorses the United States' mixed capitalist economic system. Jack Dennis has done a particularly creative job of exploring what democracy means for Americans. He identifies "populism" as one aspect of democracy on which there is much agreement. But Dennis notes that there is also considerable warmth toward democracy defined in "liberal" terms, meaning democracy in terms of rational decision making on behalf of self-interest. He finds that people also conceive of democracy as being about self-interested individuals acting for both their own good and the common good. Finally, Dennis says the public identifies with a third dimension of democracy, what he calls its pluralist side, democracy conceived in terms of interest groups and political parties pursuing their goals. This is the least popular conception of democracy and the most criticized, as we all know. Dennis argues, however, that all three aspects—populism, liberalism, and pluralism—are part of the overall picture of the "democracy" that is widely accepted in the American value system.[121]

Granted, there is a question of whether public opinion studies are the best way to measure basic political beliefs in the broader public. Critics sometimes assert that there is no better evidence of such studies' severe limitations than their failure to pick up the diversity of basic norms among Americans in this age. Others suggest that the problem with such studies is not their accuracy but the significance of what they report. From this angle, the agreement that the studies report means little. The supposedly shared values are so vague and general that they have scant significance in practical terms. On the other hand, the plentiful disagreements over policies and candidates in American politics, as well as over how to realize specific liberal and democratic values in practice, have enormous practical significance. The issue sometimes becomes what matters more, an alleged vague general consensus or the real and quite specific divisions that exist in practice?[122]

Conclusion

A straightforward reading of public opinion studies lends little support to the idea that most Americans differ significantly on basic political norms. This conclusion is reinforced, moreover, by some qualitative studies as well, including Alan Wolfe's recent, widely discussed *One Nation, After All,* which receives serious consideration in chapter 10.[123] Of course, this description is not accurate for all citizens. Nor does it mean that every group believes it gets the treatment it deserves, nor suggest that it should be easy to resolve policy disputes.

The core of a value consensus remains, however, standing in obvious contrast to the political diversity that may be the reality among American intellectuals today. Granted, both these conclusions may be more apparent than real. The consensus views of the mass public may be so general as to be meaningless or may even hide serious cleavages beneath their generality. And much of contemporary intellectual pluralism may be just variations within liberalism. After all, there is no tight or fully shared definition of liberalism. It is a cluster concept with no self-evident meaning, and maybe it should be spoken of only as liberalisms. Both these possibilities will be addressed in this book, but for now public consensus and intellectual diversity describe the contemporary United States. This conclusion leads us back to the past, a vital arena in the ongoing argument over how to interpret American thought and culture. Was there ever a consensus in American culture or among political intellectuals before the 1960s? Consensus thinkers argued that there was, but few have agreed since, and many have attempted to reconceptualize the history of American political thought in other ways. To this story this book now turns.

Chapter Three

The Broader Critique and Alternative Perspectives

After 1970, critics of consensus theory agreed that no consensus interpretation illuminated the contemporary United States. Considering that matter settled, they turned more and more to the whole of U.S. history, and their critique broadened as they insisted consensus interpretations were as false for the American past as they were for the present. Soon consensus interpretations came to be seen as artifacts of the 1950s, historical curiosities rather than valid descriptions of the American past. This was the broader critique that after 1970 doomed the consensus theory to the proverbial dustbin as another failed moment in interpretation. The only consensus now was that consensus views of the American story were illusions.

This chapter examines this broader critique and in the process considers some of the objections that critics have made to consensus interpretations of the American past. It goes on to explore the alternative interpretations of U.S. history that have sprouted in the last thirty years. What emerges is an essay in the dialectics of interpretation of American political thought and culture in the contemporary age.

The Broader Critique and Hartz and Boorstin

Louis Hartz and Daniel Boorstin and their interpretations of American thought fell far from favor by the 1970s. They have hardly experienced a revival, although they and their work receive an occasional nod of respect. Instead, they have encountered a barrage of often-angry criticisms that makes the dissents Turner or Parrington or Beard faced before them look both genial and modest. The most common objection, of course, has been that the consensus interpretations left out the conflict, or too much of the conflict, in U.S. history. How could Boorstin have ignored the War over the Bank in his discussions of the Jacksonian era? How could he have slighted the bitter sectional disputes in pre–Civil War history? How could Hartz have finessed such conflicts as ongoing political party divisions, personality disputes among crucial political leaders, disputes over federalism, and many more?

Moreover, critics complain that when consensus theorists deigned to acknowledge conflicts such as the Civil War that they could not avoid, they played them down, often portraying them as unconnected with disputes over basic values. This annoys critics who suggest that if this approach is accurate, then whether or not we had a consensus on basic values does not matter. If a consensus on political values, for example, did not prevent the enormously bloody Civil War, how important could such a consensus be?

Critics also charge that the values supposedly composing the consensus were so abstract that they had little meaning. What did such oft-used but vague words such as *liberty* or *capitalism* mean? For some consensus thinkers they could and did mean almost everything and therefore nothing. Questions also arose over the level of analysis used in consensus interpretations. Who shared the supposed consensus? Did political thinkers, intellectuals, white males, or Americans in general? Often there was no answer. In short, the complaint was and is that the sweeping discussions of many consensus thinkers had a breezy way of ignoring real questions about levels of analysis, key concepts, specific periods, or individual thinkers. They painted dramatic pictures but proved hard to pin down when anything specific was under consideration.

The central issue, though, was and is an empirical one. How accurate were the claims of consensus interpreters, at whatever level of analysis? And on that matter, their critics insist, the classic consensus interpreters failed.[1] Sometimes the argument asserts that consensus history is flat-out wrong. For example, Karen Orren maintains in her *Belated Feudalism* that consensus claims that feudalism disappeared early before the liberal tidal wave are false.[2] She notes that a crucial feature of feudalism, the law of master and servant, was long present in the United States. For most of our history the

master ruled and the worker was bound to him in economic relations (and, often, much more)—and the courts systematically upheld
and enforced this relationship. Challenges really only began in the
late nineteenth century. It was not until the New Deal, Orren argues,
that collective bargaining brought down this central precept of
feudalism.

More critiques have addressed the evidence that consensus
views suppressed the reality of conflict in U.S. history. Several major
kinds of conflict have received particular attention. One, of course,
has been conflict based in class and economic divisions. New Left
historians and others of diverse political persuasions since maintain
that consensus analysis looked away from the substantial economic
conflict in U.S. history—sometimes before the Civil War, but notably so after it, whether in the late nineteenth century or in the New
Deal and beyond. They claim that the story of labor and capital in
the United States is full of conflict, sometimes quite violent, but who
would know that from reading Hartz or Boorstin?[3]

Some regret the reality of conflict they perceive; others regret
the conflict less than who won (conservative forces) most of the conflicts. What they agree on, however, is the insight of conflict theory,
which we know was once the reigning Progressive interpretation of
U.S. economic life. Standard views now take seriously economic
conflicts in our past in a kind of straightforward neo-Progressive or,
sometimes, neo-Marxian way. Some historians in the spirit of Marxist
Antonio Gramsci, moreover, have pushed beyond the obvious evidence of economic conflict and looked into deeper, putative structures of American life and the American order. Aileen Kraditor, for
example, identified conflict in deep class and structural terms that
went beyond famous particular clashes between capital and labor.[4]

The significance of economic conflict is contested. Seymour
Martin Lipset, for example, continues to be impressed by the lack
of a substantial socialist movement in the United States. He maintains that talk of this or that incident of labor strife in the United
States cannot easily explain away this revealing, overall picture that
greatly reduced potential class conflicts. For him the absence of significant socialism in the United States shows that the class tension
behind much economic conflict was modest.[5] From quite a different
perspective, Gabriel Kolko, among others, has argued that there was
more consensus between labor and capital in the American experi-

ence than many other radicals believe, especially in the late nineteenth and early twentieth centuries. Then capitalist elites self-consciously used the government to calm economic life and thereby stabilize labor and capitalist relations in the nation.[6]

Others have concentrated on the plentiful evidence of racial and ethnic conflict in American history. They maintain no responsible person could downplay the great conflict over slavery and our subsequent racial upheavals and divisions. They ask how one can discuss the history of the United States without considering the struggles between Native Americans and whites. They ask about the history of Latinos in the United States and the experiences of Asian Americans. They record other painful conflicts that involved immigrant groups in the nineteenth century and that continue today, struggles among groups and between them and the dominant culture. Given our diverse, and often clashing, racial, ethnic, and religious cultures, they conclude that it is incredible that anyone could ever have blithely talked of consensus. And who would want to, some ask. To do so would be to deny the history of many in the American rainbow, or worse.[7]

Many enemies of consensus interpretations who stress class, ethnic, racial, religious, or gender conflicts contend that consensus analysis was really little more than disguised celebration of the winners in U.S. history. They observe that when Boorstin serenely ignored conflict and concentrated on the dominant elements in American life, he was not merely avoiding the reality of conflict. He was also hiding the defeat of those who lost in those conflicts. A standard claim is that consensus theory is really a conservative political perspective devoted to winners.[8]

In this spirit, Gary Nash, one of the most self-confident contemporary historians, has labeled the consensus view a winners' history and hardly the history of most Americans. Thus "the overarching themes achieved in older histories derived from studying mostly the experiences of only one group of people in American society. . . . The contribution of the social historian is precisely to show that . . . overarching themes and grand syntheses promulgated by past historians will not hold up when we . . . start investigating the history of all people."[9]

There has also been a fair amount of discussion of violence in the American experience. While violence is hardly the only form that conflict can take, critics of consensus views contend that there can be no denial of its major role in American history. It has been common, in fact, something the reader of consensus history would never know. More and more there has come to be a sense that consensus theorists had an astonishing blindness at best about violence in U.S. history. At worst, the consensus view is equated with a conservatism that dared not acknowledge how it used violence to crush insurgent groups in American life.[10]

From still another side, critics object that conflicts between the United States and other parts of the world also often disappeared in consensus interpretations. They maintain these conflicts have been a crucial part of American history—and frequently have produced additional turmoil at home. They ask who but consensus interpreters of the World War II generation could somehow have sailed past America's wars and the conflicts generated within the United States by the War of 1812, the Mexican War, the Indian Wars, and World War I—not to speak of Vietnam.[11]

All these perspectives insist that conflict in U.S. history has been much more important than the consensus thinkers claimed. Even the most temperate critics at least conclude that what we need is "a renewed appreciation of conflict in our history."[12] Each has his or her particular emphasis, but together they have sharply judged the disappearance of America's sometimes terrible conflicts in post–World War II consensus history. No wonder that as the decades rolled on after 1970, consensus interpretations increasingly faded from circulation. The tales they told had been judged false.

A great strength of consensus theory, however, was its interest in comparative analysis. It routinely situated American consensus in explicit or implied comparison with other parts of the world (especially Western Europe) and argued that the United States stands as a cultural or ideological exception among nations. This outlook was integral to Tocqueville and James and, of course, to the thinking of Hartz, Niebuhr, and Boorstin in the 1950s. The most famous example was Hartz's memorable discussion (building on Walter Sombart) of the absence of a vibrant socialist movement in the United States. His comparative analysis pointed out that in this instance the United States was an exception in the Western world, one that begged for an explanation that consensus thinkers were eager to provide.

Yet over time the interest in comparative analysis became another stumbling block for consensus theories. Comparison with other cultures, especially European ones, did underline the relative absence of labor and other economic conflicts in the United States, but it also highlighted all sorts of other conflicts—racial and ethnic, for example—that were more common in American history. Comparative analysis undermined the claim that conflict was very modest in U.S. history when a more inclusive understanding of conflict was used.

Softer Dissents/Other Alternatives

As we have seen, much of the dissent from consensus theory proceeds from a reading of American history that emphasizes the reality of conflict. This is now the orthodox view. The salient issue now is what kinds of conflict have been most prevalent or most important, not whether there has been much conflict. In short, conflict theory is back in the saddle in interpreting American history, as it was in the Progressive Era.

To be sure, today's conflict interpretations try to avoid grand theory. Postmodernism has had its impact. The interest in sweeping theories, especially in the discipline of history, is now out of fashion. Beard or some modern Beard has not replaced Hartz. The most common approach is to dismiss both the consensus interpretation and any alternative broad theory, while at the same time noting the reality of conflict in American history and, sometimes, in American political thought.

Yet over the years since 1970 there have been plenty of approaches to political thought and culture that have proposed broad alternative interpretations to discredited consensus theories. Some stop short of simply dismissing consensus views out of hand. They are the gentler critiques of consensus theory, even as they are also efforts to reformulate a general interpretation of American thought or life.

There is, for example, the "conflict within the consensus" view, which Bernard Sternsher and, more recently, David Greenstone have argued.[13] This perspective claims there has been a considerable consensus on liberal values in the American experience, but it contends that conflict has been abundant also. It resolves their mutual relations by maintaining that most of the conflict in U.S. history has taken place within a shared value consensus. Sometimes there have been conflicts over how to understand the shared values; at other times, conflicts have arisen over how to translate shared norms into policy. While these conflicts have been real, the "conflict within the consensus" view always returns to argue that the presence of consensus has also been real. Thus sharply divided elections and divisive policy votes in Congress do not deny broadly shared values. Rather, our consensus sharply circumscribes our conflicts, and they can only be understood in light of that consensus.

In this spirit, Seymour Martin Lipset's *First New Nation* declares that there was much agreement on the importance of the individual and on citizen equality in the American colonies and the independent states that succeeded them. Yet that still left a great deal of room for the famous disputes (such as those over the Constitution) during the Founding of the United States, since these were really conflicts within the consensus.[14]

In his book *The Lincoln Persuasion*, the late David Greenstone grants that American political thought has involved a liberal consensus and rejects contemporary efforts to dismiss the fact of this consensus. Not surprisingly, Greenstone's "genus liberalism" is a very capacious entity. But Greenstone carefully argues that it is easy to draw unwarranted significance about what the existence of a single "genus liberalism" implies. Influenced in part by the later Wittgenstein, he holds that in a linguistic world where individual words and concepts have multiple meanings, liberalism can be more as well as less than one might assume.

Specifically, Greenstone maintains that his close study of American political thought demonstrates that there have been two often conflicting versions of genus liberalism, "humanist liberalism" and "reform liberalism." His humanist liberalism focuses on the realization of individual preferences, as exemplified in the politics and political ideas of Thomas Jefferson, Stephen Douglas, and the great creator of the political party, Martin Van Buren. His reform liberalism, on the other hand, is concerned to advance the moral development of all individuals. All kinds of reformers have embodied its spirit, including the abolitionists, about whom Greenstone writes at some length.

Greenstone crowns Abraham Lincoln the great hero of liberalism and the United States in the nineteenth century because Lincoln
skillfully combined both varieties of genus liberalism. Lincoln was
a reform liberal who promoted the end of slavery so all Americans
could develop freely. Yet he proceeded within well-established
humanist liberal channels, including the existent political system,
which Greenstone interprets as designed for the realization of individual preferences.[15]

Of course, not all voices speak directly of a conflict within consensus interpretation. This is hardly to be expected in the current
situation. Alan Dawley characterizes American political experience
as "change-within-continuity" and argues that since the Progressive
Era the nation has modified its liberal norms but has not abandoned
liberalism. Instead, the United States has moved to expand the
amount of equality within liberalism. Although America has hardly
achieved the broad substantive equality Dawley favors, it now has
"liberalism with a social face."[16]

I call a second alternative interpretation the "successive approach." Its advocates accept a consensus view of American political
thought—recognizing that consensus hardly means unanimity—but
deny that there has been a single liberal consensus over the course
of American history. Proponents argue that there have been several
(often just two) expressions of consensus, each dominant in a different historical period. They insist that this situation, combined with
nonconsensus transition periods, tells a story that conventional,
single-minded consensus analysis has missed.

This account often incorporates research from the past fifteen
or twenty years that contends a liberal consensus did exist but not
for the entire course of the American experience. Thus analysts such
as Richard Matthews and Dan Rodgers maintain that there were
ideas and practices in the colonial period that were far from liberal.[17]
Feudal, republican, and religious communal ideas, for example, were
widespread. They may have been on their way out by the time of
the Constitution, but there is a lot of American history before 1787.
Through this lens, the problem with consensus theory is its time line.
Its claims are too ambitious, but they may have some plausibility
for part of the national experience.

Another example of this approach is expressed by the republi-
canism-to-liberalism thesis, which will receive considerable atten-

tion later in this chapter. Yet another stresses the nation's movement from its original norms, rooted in Protestant religion, eventually supplemented by a commitment to democracy and capitalism, to a far more "cosmopolitan" culture and value system. In the hands of intellectual and cultural historian Robert Crunden, this interpretation concludes that by now the United States has lost any intrinsic ideas and badly needs new ones.[18]

Robert Wiebe's *Self-Rule: A Cultural History of American Democracy* is a well-developed illustration of another sort.[19] Wiebe has proposed a wide range of interpretations over his distinguished career, but here he concentrates on the value of democracy (and not on all political values or explicit claims regarding consensus). He believes democracy has been central to the American political value system and to its political practice. Democracy in nineteenth-century America, Wiebe argues, meant active citizen participation, majority rule, and personal and political independence directed toward a contested common good. A vigorous, contentious, and yet communal democracy was the rule in theory and practice. This is the version of democracy Wiebe admires even as he concludes it has had its day. Wiebe's United States is a different kind of democracy now, one that no longer treasures the idea of a common good; it accents individuals more and democratic participation less. The goal of personal fulfillment has carried the day, and the state has expanded to assist this objective. In other terms, in the situation Wiebe describes, one kind of consensus has replaced another. In the process, he laments, the better American democracy has disappeared.

Yet another successive approach may be encountered in Paul Leinberger and Bruce Tucker's lively book *The New Individualists*.[20] Their argument holds that in recent decades there have been distinct changes in dominant values from one generation to the next, changes that can result in a variety of confusing perspectives. Leinberger and Tucker see Americans today in a generational phase in which the emphasis is on diverse voices. People no longer adhere to either the "organizational man" model of the 1950s or the freewheeling expressive individualism of the 1960s. This generation has fashioned something that is a combination of both and yet duplicates neither. Networks and niches are the story of people's lives. No overall community exists, but radical individualism is just as dead. Community relations are real but complex and many-sided, often far more multi-leveled than people recognize.

Does this constitute a new consensus in practice and theory? Leinberger and Tucker do not think so. They describe a situation that incorporates so much diversity in its partial individualism and community orientation that it makes little sense to employ the word *consensus*. Certainly, the point of *The New Individualists* is that there is—and has been—no enduring consensus. Generations bring changes in values, but even as each new view becomes ascendant, aspects of the old remain. For Leinberger and Tucker, "consensus" is too simple and static a view of the patterns of American thought and culture.

Nonetheless, all of these examples do involve interpretations of American culture and/or thought that stress shared values among Americans. Some concentrate on conflict within consensus, others on wide agreement on different values in different eras. While they all avoid the old consensus claims, their lingering affinity with the consensus tradition is no figment of the Hartzian imagination.

A third approach, more explicit in its critique of consensus, involves a dialectical engagement. It rejects claims that consensus has dominated American life or thought but acknowledges that liberal values have had a substantial presence in the American story. As its advocates see things, the problem with consensus theory is that it mistakes a part for the whole and, in particular, does not perceive the dialectical conflict between liberal values and their alternatives. The story of American thought in these interpreters' hands is an argument between liberalism and its opponents.

In one version or another this interpretation of American thought has been quite popular since 1970. Michael Kammen, for example, has made a career of pointing out the dialectical and paradoxical sides of American history and political attitudes. In this spirit he rarely draws neat lines, but he has a sense of how complicated and frequently ironic American beliefs and practices have been. Referring to Americans as the "people of paradox," he advances a genial, postmodern history that urges us to resist the use of easy generalizations or rigid lines.[21]

Thus, in his *Historical Perspectives on American Culture*, Kammen avoids suggesting that we may speak of any consensus in the United

States.[22] Yet he considers it obvious that the United States has a "different" or "distinctive" culture, although he also contends that its distinctiveness has diminished over time in world comparative terms.[23] Ours remains, however, a culture full of paradoxes and also one of far greater texture than Hartz realized. In Kammen's view, Hartz left out too much of the American narrative—and its dialectics—when he built his house of consensus. Moreover, ever the nondoctrinaire postmodern, Kammen argues that Hartz did not sufficiently appreciate that even when political ideologies are shared, interpretations of their meaning will differ. This, too, has constituted a good part of the American story, and with it has come, Kammen notes, plenty of conflict.[24]

Above all, Kammen urges us to have some perspective on the American experiment. We have had our conflicts within the American political tradition and abundant frontal challenges to our tradition as well. We have common traditions, many separate ones, and innumerable expressions of paradox. The reality is and has been dynamic and fascinating, and no simplistic consensus interpretation could possibly sum it up.[25]

Theda Skocpol, in her intriguing discussion of American culture, political thought, and social welfare policy since the Civil War, makes a similar point. The study of policy has taught her that things are far too complicated and variable for anything as "holistic and essentialistic" as consensus (she likes the term *national values*) theories.[26] Her view assumes that recent scholarship "undermines any essential, timeless, and holistic notion of 'American liberal values' and points to coexisting ideals of religion, republican virtue, as well as feminine ideals."[27]

Perhaps the most common dialectical approach emphasizes the repeated clashes between communal and individualistic tendencies in U.S. history. The masterwork on community in American political and social thought is Wilson Carey McWilliams's *Idea of Fraternity in America*, which argues for the competing and sometimes dialectical presence of communal visions and liberal individualism in the American tradition.[28] Robert Bellah and his team later made a similar case for white middle-class citizens, among whom a second language of community is often in tension with the first language of liberal individualism.[29] For Bellah and his coauthors this has been true throughout our political experience, although they focus on contemporary Americans. McWilliams does not address popular opinion in quite the same way; he is a cultural analyst, not a sociologist. Yet both these assessments head in the same direction: community is part of the American story and a part that is often in dialectical opposition to the liberal mainstream.

The influential Michael Sandel is more concerned with addressing the problem of our missing community today than with forging an overall interpretation of the history of American political thought. Yet he, too, accepts something like the dialectical mode in his historical constructions in *Democracy's Discontent: America in Search of a Public Philosophy*.[30] For Sandel, much of the nation's historical experience has been a contest between two traditions: (1) the civic republican tradition, with its emphasis on liberty and self-government directed toward the common good and toward encouraging personal character that respects duty, commitment, and human connections, not just selfish (and lonely) objectives; and (2) the liberal tradition, with its interest in individual rights and a free ("unencumbered") self, and its rejection of a larger good. Sandel skillfully illustrates the existence of this dialectic through our intellectual and political history. He goes on, however, to suggest its explanatory power has now greatly declined. According to Sandel, the last half century has witnessed the end of the dialectic. A self-interested and self-focused liberalism has won the day.

Multiple Strands in the Age of Multiculturalism

Early on the argument was made that to grasp the American political tradition we must skirt broad interpretations, no matter how elegant they might appear. For example, when Richard Hofstadter moved away from his own consensus stance, he insisted that complexity must govern interpretation and that grand interpretations were mostly hot air. Hofstadter first made the case when he faulted Progressive thinkers such as Charles Beard for their "conflict" understanding of the groups who fought over the ratification of the Constitution, but he eventually applied it to all sweeping interpretations.[31]

Some have developed a perspective similar to Hofstadter's and applied it in their own way in considering U.S. political thought, fashioning interpretations that recognize a multitude of ideas and factors at work and refusing to settle for glib images of a neat consensus.[32] A much-discussed example is the work of Linda Kerber, a leading historian of the Founding, who argues that we can now appreciate that consensus history was no more than one guide to "masculine identity." By focusing on individualism and the gospel of self-reliance, it left out women; further, it confused a certain male identity with that of all people, many males as well as all women.[33] Kerber's claims about the tradition of women's thought in the United States are, in turn, controversial,[34] but her larger message is that consensus claims overlook the textured reality of American thought or life.

Some have grown more confident in recent years, however, that honoring complexity and crafting a more schematic interpretation of American thought may be simultaneously achievable. They insist that the American political tradition exists and that it is a series of discernible streams or "strands." Proponents of this approach often have a distinct affection for the multiculturalism they perceive in contemporary America and a special fondness for celebrating the goal of mutual respect among Americans as the means to a better society in a multicultural world.[35]

In any case, advocates of the multiple-strands approach reject consensus theory outright. At best, they consider it an embarrassing simplification of U.S. history. Yet multiple-strand thinkers do attempt a broader analysis of American culture and thought that goes beyond what is revealed by study of a particular time, place, and subject. Much of this more ambitious new theorizing has come from intellectuals not associated with history as a formal academic discipline, which is not surprising, since most contemporary historians shy away from anything so bold—or foolish.

Yale political theorist Rogers Smith has argued exhaustively for the multiple-strands approach as the only way to proceed, and his lengthy *Civic Ideals: Conflicting Visions of Citizenship in U.S. History* has propelled him to the intellectual leadership of this outlook. He makes his case largely through legal materials concerned with defining citizenship, making the debatable assumption that this is a particularly valuable means toward comprehending the United States.

Along the way, Smith displays little patience with previous attempts to understand the American tradition. He holds the consensus perspective in particular to be hopeless at best and positively immoral at worst. After all, he charges, consensus interpreters failed to account for significant parts of the American story, including the ideas and often the practices of groups that have not been on top—African Americans, women, and others, who make our national narrative much more variegated than consensus theory told us. Thus Smith sharply condemns Tocqueville for confusing America with white men only and Hartz for ignoring Native Americans and Japanese and Chinese immigrants.[36]

Smith is especially interested in identifying strands in the American experience that represent "inequalitarian ideologies."[37] He concentrates on racism and sexism, insisting they are integral to any history of America. He declares that they may not be finessed as some minor offshoot of liberalism gone sour or anything of the sort. These "ascriptive" ideologies have had tremendous effects. "White Christian male" elements dominant in America have systematically employed them to put others into subordinate positions.[38] Smith also identifies with Progressive Era conflict theory and its suspicion of dominant American ideology, arguing that he shows "how American civic life has in a staggering variety of ways been designed to further . . . corporate economic interests usually controlled by white men."[39]

In short, Smith believes that "America has been centrally constituted by inequalitarian ideologies"[40] that remain part of the multicultural reality, companions of liberalism, although logically distinct from it.[41] He illustrates his claims by citing evidence from the historical experience of the United States. His first prominently published effort drew on evidence from the period from 1870 to 1920, which he took to sustain his interpretation.[42] Since then he has extended his treatment to much of American history. Thus he reports that colonial citizenship ignored Native Americans, African Americans, and women; the Revolution and Declaration of Independence denied that all Americans were equal; the age of Jackson was really the "High Noon of the White Republic"; and so on.[43]

Smith is by no means hostile to liberal democratic values, despite what one might suspect. He has no use for ascriptive and other inequalities, but he affirms liberal values. He judges that they are compatible with egalitarian treatment of all people and especially philosophically contrary to distinctions based on ascriptive criteria such as race.[44] Smith is not particularly negative about liberalism's record over time in the United States either. Thus he concludes that liberal democracy has often played a benevolent role in American history. In short, in Smith's hands there are no polemical denunciations of liberalism in theory or in practice, and none should be expected, since it has been no terrible evil.

Nonetheless, Smith is ambivalent about liberalism, in light of what he discerns as its drawbacks, which do have a pernicious effect on society. As he understands it, liberalism lacks philosophical coherence as well as practical internal standards to deal with value conflicts when they arise. Moreover, it does not do well at justifying its principles, providing meaning for people, or reinforcing individual communities that do provide positive meaning, such as religion. For Smith, liberalism serves more often as a dissolving acid than as a building block for living societies.[45]

Smith's own program is not mysterious. He favors the creation of a strong national state to enforce equal citizenship and equal rights for all persons and groups. His goal is a community devoted to this "dominant national purpose."[46] Like John Dewey, whom he so admires, Smith's affinity for a powerful central government as the means to realize his egalitarianism is as intense as his interest in individual liberty is modest.[47]

A much angrier voice within the multiple-strands approach is Jacqueline Stevens, as she has demonstrated in all-out assaults on competing interpretations—and interpreters.[48] An explicit constructivist, although she displays no skepticism about her own political persuasion, Stevens rejects traditional consensus views as part of the "racist, sexist, and Hartzian ideas." She insist no one should take them seriously except as deserving targets for denunciation.[49]

She is no more complimentary about some multiple-strands approaches, specifically lambasting Rogers Smith. For Stevens, Smith is a hapless analyst. His errors include a failure to acknowledge the host of feminists and historians of color who discovered "difference" in American life and thought long before he did; omission of thinkers Stevens considers key to grasping American political culture, W. E. B. Du Bois, but also Emma Goldman, C. Wright

Mills, and Angela Davis, among others; and a method that Stevens asserts explains his inability to perceive the "deeper logic" of American liberalism. For Stevens, the racism, sexism, and other evils she identifies as parts of the American story are integral to liberalism and America's liberal culture. Liberalism's logic certainly does not exclude these evils, and liberal intellectuals like Smith must come to grips with this ugly fact.

In a mellower mood, Richard Ellis offers a multiple-strands analysis that accepts the considerable conflict within the American tradition.[50] Yet he also realizes that the interpretive task leads in no simple, single direction. The American political tradition encompasses many contending views and sometimes contentious interpreters. Yet Ellis maintains that it is possible to provide a broad analysis. To do so, though, we must appreciate that any claims to straightforward consensus in American thought are illusory. Ellis concedes such views have a certain plausibility due to the uniformities in the American vocabulary of politics, but the meanings of concepts such as the individual have often been very different.

Another example Ellis offers is the misleading but widespread American agreement on the norm of self-government. Ellis encourages his readers to be skeptical and ask with him, what have been the implications of the "consensus" on this idea? To him, the quarrels between the Federalists and the Anti-Federalists or the Democrats and the Whigs over the meaning of self-government suggest the limits of the significance of consensus here.[51]

Ellis also applies his skepticism to the alleged antiauthoritarianism of the American political tradition. Again, to say we have had "consensus" on this ideal is misleading. According to Ellis, antiauthoritarianism has manifested itself in two directions, one quite individualistic and another directed toward social equality. Each direction, he says, has had sharply contrasting effects on American society.[52] In short, Ellis argues that superficial conceptual analysis dooms most consensus theory.

While one of Ellis's great strengths is that he does not deny the existence of a common (if differently understood) American political vocabulary, he also insists that other vocabularies have received short shrift in consensus treatments. For example, Ellis is impressed with the evidence of a secondary language emphasizing community in the American experience. He notes as well the variety of community ideals: community in republican, puritan, and Progressive Era modes, among others.[53]

Ellis is most interesting when he calls on his readers to consider the norm of hierarchy in the American experience. Arguing that hierarchy has been a factor that can hardly be ignored, he offers a rich collection of examples, observing how much colonial thought embodied hierarchy, as did pre–Civil War Southern planters and later capitalist entrepreneurs, and as do many social conservatives in our own age.[54]

Ellis also wants us to take seriously what we might consider minor traditions in U.S. political thought and culture. They may not be main paths, yet they are too important to be swept away in the name of a fictional consensus. Thus Ellis is intrigued by the outlook he labels "hermitude." Henry David Thoreau best illustrated hermitude, which Ellis does not consider just another form of American individualism.[55] He also meditates on something he calls "Fatalism," which he links with the experience of slavery and slaves.[56] While this strand is perhaps a stretched effort to find room for enslaved Americans and their ideas within his analysis, it demonstrates Ellis's commitment to diverse perspectives in the American story.

At this juncture in U.S. intellectual life, in fact, multiple-strand approaches have many proponents. Indeed, this interpretation has become the central route taken by those who still dare to conceptualize American political thought or culture beyond the timidity of much of professional history in this age. One may, in fact, claim that the multiple-strand approach is a kind of reverse consensus today, so hegemonic is it in the interpretive realms of American political thought and culture.[57] Each version has its own insights, of course, and many of them are fascinating as interpreters make their way through a daunting and controversial national history.

Thus Theodore Lowi, an eager political theorist of the big picture, has discovered a host of American political traditions: several familiar varieties of liberalism, republicanism (a kind of communitarianism that he dislikes, since he judges it threatens privacy), several types of conservatism (Lowi most fears conservatism that has an affection for a moral rather than a pluralistic state), and a tradition of Left radicalism, among others. Lowi has his own strand to offer as well, which he argues should entail a pragmatic, nonideological, and nonmoralistic liberalism.[58]

While Lowi is nothing if not hostile to the contemporary Republican Party and its ideas, he maintains that the Reagan revolution of the 1980s did help to reveal the many sides of American political thought. It also assisted in undermining the idea of the liberal "unidimensional polity" that never made sense in the United States, despite the claims of Hartz and other liberal consensus interpreters.[59] Lowi, however, has reached this outlook only reluctantly. While he is no enthusiast for liberalism in any form, he concludes there is no alternative. "The republic is too important to be entrusted to liberalism. But what else is there?"[60]

Toward Postmodern Corrections

As postmodern thinking has swept across parts of the American intellectual landscape in the last several decades, previous arguments over the nature of American political culture and its main patterns of political thought have come to grief. From a postmodern perspective the issue is not who has the facts straight about the political thought of one period or another. No one does, since there is no definite reality out there that a "correct" interpretation can somehow capture. Thus the problem with consensus thinking is not that it is wrong about "reality," but that consensus theory and its alternatives proceed as if there were somehow a text to the American culture or thought that awaits the interpreter able enough to find it.

Postmodernists should not quickly be conflated with multiculturalists or multiple-strand students of American political culture. While postmodern historians recognize that there will inevitably be multiple and conflicting historical perspectives, often they are most comfortable with history understood as a series of small narratives rather than one or several large stories. Moreover, the number of postmodern approaches to the history of American political thought and culture is so far quite modest compared with the burgeoning multicultural and multiple-strand studies.[61]

Postmoderns reject essentialist ontology and insist that while interpretation is necessary, indeed inescapable, all authors necessarily proceed from what they see and experience. Thus no one can "find" the true American political thought or culture; each interpreter constructs his or her own. As historian Joyce Appleby suggests, it follows that no one can expect agreement on any single historical interpretation of the United States. That would be impossible in this postmodern age, when people's interpretations will necessarily differ. But in a statement of optimism Appleby believes that the contested understandings, one may say readings, of the United States should greatly assist us in the search for the best possible sense of what the nation has been about.[62]

Two significant—and different—postmodern interpreters of the American journey are Thomas Dumm and Anne Norton, both scholars at elite eastern colleges.[63] Dumm is a tough-minded analyst of what he calls the "united states." He denies all claims that American culture has involved a consensus, maintaining that only those who choose to ignore the systematic suppression of alternative perspectives that are so much of American history could make such a preposterous suggestion. Moreover, Dumm insists that while the United States does have some strands of democracy and liberalism, it has not brought them together. As a result, both have developed in a sad, truncated fashion. Democracy has not emerged as a lively, vibrant, real rule by the people but mostly as demands for various forms of equality. Liberalism has become little more than the right to drop out of public citizenship and live a private, epicurean existence, a lifestyle that draws Dumm's decided disapproval.

For Dumm, this situation is evident in the failures of American political and cultural life, in our racial situation and other arenas, but also in the realm of intellectual discourse. Here Dumm plows straight ahead and takes on such luminaries of the liberal intellectual elite as Judith Shklar and Michael Walzer, faulting both for the contradictions he believes undermine their thought. Walzer tries to smooth over his tendency to resist taking a real stand by endorsing a host of not always compatible values with little success, while Shklar denounces cruelty and yet fails to see the cruelty her version of liberalism inevitably imposes on those of other views and lives.

Dumm's work is no conventional interpretation or argument. In a postmodern framework it should not be. For example, he shares a number of highly personal, even intimate, observations with his readers but does so in a curiously impersonal way; he is at great pains to apologize to his readers for being a straight, white man; and he delights in sexual references and assertions, which suggest his interest in sex, but it is not clear what else. Dumm's long-run objectives are not entirely clear either, beyond his zest in skewering his opponents, his nation, and its culture, and applying the insights of twentieth-century postmodern thinkers to the inviting target of the "united states."

Yet Dumm is by no means only a critic. His project is far too hard-edged for that. He does want radical changes. Although their contours are hardly obvious, Dumm seems to be reaching for a nation that is more open to the kinds of voices—racial, sexual, gendered, class—he believes have been denied their equal place in an America that should be more genuinely diverse, democratic, egalitarian, and free. How these goals might be achieved, much less achieved together, he does not discuss in any detail. One vital step for Dumm, however, is to accept that much of the American "consensus" has been realized only by repressing the alternative perspectives that have always been present. In that act of self-consciousness alone, Dumm seems to think, we would make a significant start toward acknowledging and even fashioning a real "united states."

Anne Norton's approach to the postmodern exploration of American life and thought is a good deal gentler than Dumm's. While she hardly gushes with enthusiasm at what she recounts, she is less concerned to ridicule or denounce the American experience than are some other postmoderns. Perhaps she even looks on it with a distanced affection. Certainly, she has led the way in the entire postmodern interpretive enterprise in regard to the United States. Her most important work is *Republic of Signs,* a project that illustrates another postmodern engagement with the American tradition.[64]

Norton does not undertake to report essential truths derived from close study of American history or intellectual traditions, nor—to her it is inconceivable—to study the United States through the findings of public opinion surveys. For her, these approaches are forms of empiricism futilely searching for an essentialist reality. Nor is Norton especially interested in comparing the U.S. experience with that of other nations. Norton advises students of American culture to concentrate instead on how Americans construct and reconstruct, create and re-create themselves. Through this process, she suggests, one can learn what Americans are about, although not in any essentialist sense.

Norton does not find Americans' constructions exactly inspiring. Moreover, she concludes Americans rarely understand how little their lives reflect the liberal democratic ideology of the nation. Instead, Americans' constructions reveal their obsessions with things, popular culture, and shopping. Indeed, their pursuit of clothes and fashions is the most telling sign of their efforts to make and remake themselves. Norton does not think Americans have to remain such shallow, unfocused materialists. Nothing is permanent in her postmodern world, but her outlook is hardly hopeful.

As with some other postmodern observers, Norton's work is sprinkled with aphorisms, clever lines, and reports on fortuitous conversations with friends and colleagues. This offends those who insist on a far more testable and intersubjective empirical standard of scholarship. But Norton shows no concern with such a methodology. After all, her claim is that the goal is insight into America and American culture, and she appears confident that she meets the test.[65]

Case Study: The Founding Era

No era of American history has attracted as much attention since the 1960s as the Founding period, encompassing the American Revolution, the development of the Constitution, and the establishment of the new nation. Tremendous intellectual energy has been spent trying to understand the Founding's meaning and mobilizing it as evidence for one or another interpretation of American thought or culture. The Founding period is often the ultimate prize in contemporary debates about the American past. Thus examining the lively intellectual conversation on the Founding provides an excellent opportunity to explore further critiques of consensus theory and the alternatives that have emerged to it.

Most of this discussion—perhaps *argument* is a better word— begins from the proposition that the old consensus thinkers' understandings of the Founding era are now hopeless. For example, Hartz's view that "liberal" values were the underpinnings of both the revolutionaries and the makers of the Constitution has long since drowned in torrents of criticism. So has Boorstin's belief that the

Founding period and its struggles had little to do with ideology, much less with conflicting ideologies.

The most influential alternative conception today is the claim that "republicanism" was the reigning political idea of the Founding era. Influenced by formidable works of the 1970s, especially Gordon Wood's *Creation of the American Republic,*[66] J. G. A. Pocock's *Machiavellian Moment,*[67] and Bernard Bailyn's earlier *Ideological Origins of the American Revolution,*[68] the republican thesis spread rapidly in the 1970s and 1980s. Each interpreter, of course, has his or her own variations in emphasis. Pocock concentrates on the history of American republican ideas, Bailyn addresses republican liberty at the Revolution, and Wood investigates the same terrain as Bailyn but with a greater emphasis on democratic themes. Wood also formulated what became the two-period thesis: that republicanism flourished in the Revolutionary era but sharply declined in the age of the American Constitution and thereafter.

The standard republican view is that free, white Americans in the late eighteenth century stressed the importance of reaching toward a common good and thought that community values were essential for a good life. They respected the individual and individual liberties such as private property and English political freedoms, but within a communal context. They never favored the largely unconstrained liberty in any sphere of life that some consensus thinkers had often associated with liberalism or the Founding era.[69] Instead, they emphasized the danger of "corruption" stemming from excessive individual self-interest and greed both inside and outside of government. This was their constant, at times obsessive, fear, and the reason for their great suspicion of government and government leaders and other elites. They had power and could become destructively corrupt. It followed that "eternal vigilance" was essential for the preservation of both liberty and community.[70]

Some analysts want to replace the old liberal consensus view with a new republican consensus interpretation for the late eighteenth century. Others think that would be going too far in ignoring multiple trends. All agree, however, in trying to discern when republicanism began to lose sway in the United States. One view is that the Revolution was made in the name of republicanism but the Constitution, while also written by republicans, involved an abandonment of the ideal.[71]

The argument is usually put in terms of when republicanism began to lose its influence to liberal values, or, as Richard Ellis puts it, over when Americans went from being born liberal (as in Hartz) to becoming liberal. Many are not sure.[72] Was it at the time of the Constitution, or, as Lance Banning and other students of the period have suggested, was it later?[73] Some labor historians, such as Sean Wilentz in his *Chants Democratic: New York City and the Rise of the American Working Class,* argue that there is evidence of strong republican sentiment in the labor movement well into the nineteenth century.[74] Others suggest that republican impulses were common at least until the Civil War,[75] even in the vigilante rule in San Francisco after the gold rush, or argue that the Confederacy embodied republicanism, especially in its antipolitical mood and its dislike of political parties and interest groups.[76]

For some analysts, such as Paul Rahe in his massive *Republics Ancient and Modern,* the Founders were liberal in many ways, including their concern with the individual and private property, but at the same time they also had a certain republican side, seeking self-government in a community of virtue.[77] Still others argue that while there was a strong desire for republican values, it always coexisted uneasily with the liberal orientation of a growing America. Thus republican sentiment was indeed present in the Founding era, but by then it was a kind of nostalgia that could not and did not overcome the force of a blossoming liberal market economy and its associated values.[78]

Thus there are many readings of the role of republicanism at the time of the Founding. Among them are studies by scholars interested primarily in particular topics such as the specific republican virtues admired in the Founding age.[79] For example, there is Melvin Yazawa's exploration of the complex attitudes about the family in colonial times, one of which derived from a republican dislike of dependence on family rather than the (republican) community.[80]

Some of this literature is excellent, and most of it underlines the contemporary arrival of the republican hypothesis as *the* alternative conception of American political thinking in the late eighteenth century.[81] So does evidence that a motivation for much of "the republican revival" is the search by contemporary intellectuals for a historical tradition of thought that might fit with the attempt to revive "community" in the present-day United States.[82]

Other Themes, Other Views

There are also a host of other understandings of the Founding era. Indeed, there are so many views, some made with substantial flair and plentiful data, that a considerable secondary literature has now grown up that explores the primary interpretive literature. There are arguments that economic conflict is the real story—or, at least, a central one—of the Founding. In his contemporary study of the "urban crucible," Gary Nash puts class conflict in the center of American urban life toward the end of the eighteenth century.[83] Marc Egnal and Joseph Ernst insist that changes in the economy of the eighteenth century explain why large planters in the South and ordinary merchants and middlemen in the North turned to revolution.[84] Most famously, Joyce Appleby identifies the movement toward capitalism and capitalist values as the most significant development in this period. She reaffirms in her way, as do the others, Charles Beard's claim that economic conflict and economic movements in the Founding era proved far more important than either liberal or republican analysts usually have granted—or wanted to grant.[85]

Among the more vigorous dissents from the standard interpretations of the Founding are those that maintain religious beliefs were crucial. This view urges a reacquaintance with the prominent place of religious ideas in late eighteenth-century America and a distancing from both republican and liberal interpretations of the Founding, which are often the product of secular historians and intellectuals.[86] John Diggins, for instance, insists that evidence for the republican thesis in the 1770s and 1780s is scant, while Christian and especially Calvinist Christian ideas exercised great influence.[87]

Ruth Bloch contends that there were many dimensions to the Christian influence on the thought of the age—some encouraged individualism, others communitarianism, while most were overlapping in their effect. Yet what cannot be avoided, she declares, is the influence of Christianity itself. Others note that many of the Founders had a commitment to Christianity and to Christian natural law. Ellis Sandoz, for example, maintains that the liberty of the Revolution was believed to be sacred and rooted in God's truths; it was not simply about free exercise of human will.[88] Yale religious historian Jon Butler has also detailed religion's considerable influence in the Revolutionary era. For him, as for Bloch, religion had political implications;

it was authority-oriented, accepting of coercion, and ready to defend itself through a variety of means, including politics.[89] On the other hand, Patricia Bonomi, who has concentrated on dissenting Protestant traditions in the age of the American Revolution, concluded that authority was not a central value, but republican, if not necessarily democratic, concerns were, including congregationalism, majority rule government, and voluntary associations.[90]

Others point to the impact of the Great Awakening on many aspects of revolutionary thought, including the belief in the supremacy of religious values over political loyalties and the idea that disobedience to tyrants is legitimate in service to God. Indeed, some identify the Great Awakening as the key to the American Revolution.[91] Still others have studied the preachers of the Revolution and note the attempt by many of them to turn it into a contest between saints and sinners, with salvation at stake.[92]

Barry Alan Shain makes a particularly vigorous case for the role of religion in analysis of the Founding. In the process, he faults what he calls the "myth of American individualism" in accounts of American colonial life and the Founding era. While he is more sympathetic with emphasis on republicanism in those years, he declares it fails too as an accurate description. For Shain, colonial North America was a series of agricultural communities in which Protestant religion and Protestant values ruled. It may be right to talk of community in our past, but one must understand that the relevant community was almost always formed around a variety of Protestantism.[93]

Shain makes a good case for the importance of religion through the Revolutionary period and beyond in U.S. history. Whether his evidence, however, is as good as his claim is broad is unclear. His discussions of the influence of Protestantism do not really address women or slaves, and he tends to conflate the sermons of selected New England Protestant clergy with the outlook of most Americans. New England divines did matter, but so did Thomas Jefferson and the Declaration of Independence, among other aspects of the American tradition. Perhaps some analysts overcompensate for the past neglect of religion, yet they are right to point out that religion must now be taken seriously in the endeavor to understand the ideas of the U.S. Founders, and no one has made that case more clearly than Shain.

In recent years the wheel has turned somewhat, and there has been a revival of sorts that emphasizes Locke and even something

Hartz might recognize as Lockeanism as an integral part of the Revolutionary period in American thought. Steven Dworetz, for example, makes a determined argument that Lockean liberal themes were significant in the age of the Founders, a view he has not held alone.[94] While no one, including Dworetz, explicitly affirms Hartz's full theory, few analysts now believe that there was little but republicanism in late eighteenth-century America. Robert Webking, for instance, maintains that the Revolution in particular concerned liberty and individual rights much more than some ideal of republican community.[95]

Pulitzer Prize–winning historian Jack Rakove insists that the entire (and now big) business of understanding the Founding moment of the United States is problematic and difficult by any standard. The "original meanings" of the Constitution are not obvious and require a close analysis, not rhetorical claims that are often grounded in our present-day politics. Rakove warns that even with a subtle grasp of the relevant historical setting, the leading actors, especially James Madison, and the political and intellectual forces at play in the construction of the Constitution, no one can be sure of its original meanings.[96]

Others agree, and thus many interpreters of the Founding now think that the best thing to do is to appreciate the many different elements present in the thought of that historic era. Some students, including Pauline Maier, make this conclusion integral to their understanding. While respecting the work of Wood and the republicans, Maier insists that there was great intellectual diversity and social conflict in this period and that the Constitution and early new nation hardly revealed a consensus on republicanism or on anything else.[97] James Kloppenberg agrees as he expertly weaves a view of late eighteenth-century American political thought that combines Christian, republican, and liberal dimensions. For him, it is as impossible to disentangle these dimensions from each other as it is to state confidently which was the most important.[98]

Historian Forrest McDonald, in his justly admired *Novus Ordo Seclorum,* also makes the case for the thesis that the set of influences was broad. For McDonald, all the major contenders in the contest for the intellectual heart of the Revolution and the Founding were factors that counted, but so did the Scottish Enlightenment and European legal traditions. Equally important, McDonald urges recognition of the impact of homegrown experiences, events, and leaders, such as George Washington.

Donald Lutz makes another trenchant case, underlining the presence of Scottish and English political ideas, as well as others grounded in the Bible, English common law, classical Greece, and the Enlightenment.[99] For thinkers such as Lutz and McDonald to appreciate the American journey to nationhood is to look at all these factors and respect each on its own terms. There is no way one can reduce the story to a single image or an overall consensus.[100]

On the other hand, there are those who, while recognizing the diverse patterns of thought in colonial America and the early national period, continue to insist that one or another strand was decidedly the most important. No one has written a more sophisticated account of constitutional thought than political scientist Michael Lienesch. He judges that republican ideas were the most influential, while granting that thinkers' republican inclinations were often mixed with other outlooks. Thus Lienesch contends that Federalists (and not just Anti-Federalists) addressed the Constitution as republicans, but that they also defended the Constitution in terms of such nonrepublican goals as a strong national government, economic growth, and the value of a distinctly private life. Nothing was simple.[101]

Joyce Appleby's widely discussed, and controversial, interpretation also comfortably reflects the presence of many elements in American thought of the age, even as she makes her famous argument that the market-based influences were the most significant, at least by the 1790s.[102] Then there are those such as Jerome Huyler, who suggest that the intellectual complexity in the Founders' political thought fits nicely with the views of the old consensus exemplar, John Locke. Huyler's Locke, though, is neither a liberal nor a republican. He is a thinker like the Founders, with many subtle dimensions and with sympathy for a complex set of values: equality, individualism, and social interaction and cooperation.[103]

Finally, there is no doubt that in retrospect it is embarrassing that 1950s consensus theorists offered no discussion of women thinkers or of women in general. Their apparent assumption was that men shaped the ruling views and women shared them. In more recent analyses of the Founding era, some interpreters argue that while women shared the dominant republican ethos and were integral participants in the republican community, they did so in only one particular role. They were to serve as "republican mothers," supporting the (male) public community and instilling the republican ethos in their children.[104]

Among the best voices for this interpretation are Linda Kerber and Mary Beth Norton. Kerber, in her *Women of the Republic: Intellect and Ideology in Revolutionary America*, emphasizes how widely it was understood that the "republican motherhood" role was intended only for women at home. There was no place for women in public life, even to pursue the goals of republican motherhood, although some women did enter the public realm during the Revolutionary War. True republican mothers taught their sons the republican virtues and sent them forth alone into the public sphere. This explains why, after the special circumstances of the Revolutionary War, there was no "women's liberation."[105] In her later writing Kerber notes that (male) intellectuals attempted to shore up this conclusion, arguing that women were weak and necessarily dependent on the men in their lives, and thus unsuited for service as independent republican citizens.[106]

Norton's *Liberty's Daughters: The Revolutionary Experience of American Women, 1750–1800* demonstrates how the Revolution inevitably changed many women's lives—disrupting some, leading others to greater public participation. While recognizing the constraining aspects of republican ideology for women, Norton believes that in the context of the Revolution, "republican motherhood" enhanced women's roles by making their moral leadership essential to the entire public welfare.[107]

The "republican motherhood" perspective is an example of what one might term feminist history devoted to "filling in the gaps," in this instance the omission of women from the Founding narrative of the United States.[108] There are other feminist interpretations, though, that dissent from the republican motherhood thesis. For example, Pauline Schloesser contends that Mercy Otis Warren, the principal female Anti-Federalist voice in the debates over the Constitution, was motivated by more than the ideology of republican motherhood. For Warren, active opposition to the Constitution was essential, as it was for many male republicans, because the Constitution abandoned the republican ideal. Assuming a permanently self-interested human being, the authors of the Constitution crafted a document that gave up trying to build a virtuous community of devoted citizens and turned to the lesser and, to Warren, demeaning goal of simply trying to restrain and balance men's selfish interests. For Warren, a document based on such nonrepublican pessimism deserved defeat.

Schloesser is convinced that Warren was angry about the situation because she perceived negative implications for women. While Warren had no full-scale notion of women as equal participants in the male public community, such ideas lurked in her mind and led her to reject the Constitution, which relegated women to the apolitical role of domesticity. Schloesser insists that Warren's complaint revealed her desire for women to go beyond conventional republican motherhood. It was a sign that beneath at least one woman's quiet affirmations of republicanism lay inclinations that were in tension with the limited republican motherhood ideal.[109]

Mark Kann addresses the thought and attitudes of men in the Founding period in the different mood that the gender-sensitive contemporary analysis of American social and political attitudes has fostered.[110] His orientation, like Schloesser's, breaks with traditional liberal—and republican—interpretations. For Kann, the Founders had a particular "grammar of manhood" that included the importance of strong and lawful leadership by the "better" people, republican values concentrating on developing in all citizens the common good, and liberal features accepting self-interest, if incorporated and disciplined within the family.

Deeply concerned with disorder in society, Kann's Founders sought to get men to reform themselves, to become self-controlled men who lived modestly and practiced civility. They favored this ideal in conjunction with a defense of liberty, of course, the goal being a man who embodied ordered liberty. They expected such a man would live out this ideal in one place, ensconced in his family and working his land. He would also participate in the republican fraternity of men in civic life and in other public and social communities. Essential to this understanding, Kann suggests, was disapproval of men who were not attached to the land and/or to families. The danger of unattached male youths, especially, was always real, since they could abandon ordered liberty in an irresponsible quest for sex or other excitement at the expense of social order.

Kann thinks that the Founding era's grammar of manhood held that women's important roles should not be carried out in public and must not interfere with male fraternity. Women were to teach men how to become civilized, a task in which fathers were to assist mothers. For Kann, this definition of women's place is everywhere in the writings of the Founders, and he finds it puzzling that so few other analysts of the republican mind address women's situation in the republican scheme of things.[111]

This approach, of course, could lead one on to the question of people of color—slave and free—and women of color in particular. They are the focus of a growing interest that by no means leads to a single conclusion regarding political thought and the Founders. But the point is clear: arguments over the Founding illustrate the struggle today over how to interpret American thought and culture. They also underline the crucial truth that there is nothing like an interpretive consensus today.

Conclusion

This chapter has argued that an important reason for the collapse of consensus theory after 1970 has been the findings of new historical and social analyses of American history. These analyses agree that consensus interpretations rarely grapple with the actual American past in all its complex, pluralistic, and often conflictual reality. There have been too many conflicts, intellectual and otherwise, and there is now too much evidence of multiculturalism in the United States, for any neat consensus view to be credible.

Over time, criticism of consensus metamorphosed more and more into alternative interpretations of American political thought and practice. None of them allows us to proclaim a new "answer" that somehow resolves the problems of interpretation of the American story. There is no such answer, although there are a host of advocates of one interpretation or another.

I have applied the current interpretive discourse to the Founding period to illustrate as concretely as possible what the arguments look like in a crucial period of American history. The goal was to give some flesh to the bones of abstract interpretations. Yet all the interpretive pluralism and the search for alternatives to consensus have not attracted everyone. There remain perspectives that are sympathetic to (or derivative of) the Hartzian liberal consensus interpretation. In one work of this type, *American Politics: The Promise of Disharmony*, Samuel Huntington advances his own argument but is well aware that Hartzian consensus theory has had a significant impact on it.[112]

Huntington contends that there has been and remains something of a liberal value consensus in the United States, but rarely have its values been fully realized in practice. American history may be divided into three kinds of eras: periods when this gap was accepted, others when it was ignored, and still others when citizens acted to make theory and practice coincide. The last were the times when substantial conflict broke out.

Huntington's understanding of the American "creed" or values includes familiar liberal norms: individualism, democratic constitutionalism, and assorted varieties of liberty and equality. Eras when Americans sought to realize these values more fully in practice Huntington calls ages of "creedal passion," the periods in which reform energies generated changes in American life. Huntington presents his list of these times of conflict, but anyone can construct their own predictable list, including the Revolution, the Civil War, the Progressive Era, and, of course, the 1960s.

For Huntington, such periods of conflict have been integral to the American story. They have helped foster a living culture, one that practices its values. In a post-1960s mood, however, Huntington soberly notes that there is no way that American ideals can be fully realized, a fact that both intellectuals and reformers must understand. Thus idealism has its danger as well as its promise. Huntington observes that cynicism was the current cultural motif, but he expected that in time cynicism would be replaced by other moments of "creedal passion." Meanwhile, the reality of the United States would likely continue: considerable consensus on values and a mixed record concerning their practice.

Ironically, such a Lockean and even neo-Hartzian perspective only underlines the interpretive diversity about American political thought and culture that reigns today. This is contested territory as American political intellectuals try to illuminate the United States as it enters a new millennium. Yet the larger question is what the evidence suggests, not what the interpreters argue. To that task—

the task of establishing what one can learn by exploring intellectual thought, public attitudes, and social practices regarding the basic values of the American political and social order—this book now turns. After all, interpretations are important, indeed inescapable, sometimes do provide insights, and often are fun to contemplate as well. But we all have to explore the evidence ourselves and construct our own interpretation from there.

Chapter Four

Liberalism in the Public Sphere

If most political intellectuals today share a consensus about American political thought and culture, it is that there is no consensus at all. A reigning view is that America is a multicultural society in belief and increasingly in practice, a situation exemplified as well by the wide diversity of perspectives among intellectuals. This assumption is no fantasy. We have seen its basis in the burst of diverse political outlooks that have sprung up since the 1960s, the rejection of consensus interpretations of American political thought, and the considerable number of new interpretations of American thought and life now current in the intellectual landscape.

Yet it is time, perhaps past time, to take a searching look at this orthodoxy fashioned in the years since 1970. In this chapter I start to do so by concentrating on the evidence regarding liberal values in U.S. *public* life, by which I mean the shared worlds of politics, economics, and culture in which all Americans are involved to at least some extent. By liberal values I mean above all individualism— the concern with and focus on the individual person and his or her rights, wishes, and self-expression in public life. I also include a commitment to (rough) political equality and equality of economic opportunity as expressions of liberal individualism and support for U.S. political institutions and a limited market or capitalist economy.

I argue that far from fading away, or becoming one factor among many, liberal values have in fact become even more central to American public life since 1965. I make my argument by drawing on a range of evidence. I examine public opinion studies and broader public practices which suggest that liberal values have gained considerable ground with the American citizenry over the past forty

100

years. I explore intellectual opinion, including some prominent cultural analyses of the United States, to suggest that liberal attitudes have proved to have more staying power than might be expected. I conclude by considering one important example of the supposedly expanding pluralism among political intellectuals in our age, the rise of conservative thought. I argue that this example induces caution about claims that commitment to liberal norms has slipped away in the "burst of diversity" among American public intellectuals.

Public Opinion in the Public Square

The strength of liberal values in the public sphere cannot be doubted. Study after study confirms how widespread these values have been since the 1960s. They also establish that this liberal outlook has grown in key areas. While there is no complete endorsement of public liberalism—there are other views and languages—liberalism is the reigning political norm for the bulk of the U.S. population.

A host of social scientists have reported findings that sustain such conclusions. They have established the overwhelming evidence that liberal values are well ensconced among the public at large, at least as much as they have ever been since systematic public opinion studies began in the 1940s. One of the most prominent students of U.S. public opinion sums up the data by reporting that concern for individual rights and liberties is pervasive among Americans in all aspects of their lives, public and private, although there has also been a rise in thinking in terms of group rights and liberties.[1]

The expansion of liberal individualism in recent years is reflected in the public's sharp post-1960s shift to anti-institutionalism. People are what count, and institutions, which may restrict or interfere with individuals, receive little respect. Especially relevant here is current public discontent with government and political institutions, although there is also support for aspects of the welfare state. Numerous studies of public opinion confirm this antigovernment and antipolitics phenomenon—and its increase over the past three decades—if any of us need confirmation of so widespread and obvious a public sentiment. While citizens tend to be satisfied with their own lives and have a positive sense of their own capacities, they give much lower marks to political institutions—and politicians.

This reaction has changed dramatically since the 1960s—from one of high trust and institutional approval among the large majority of citizens to the present situation where few political institutions receive as much as 50 percent approval. Distrust of government is now a well-established fact characterizing as much as 75 percent of the American public, and there is even greater distrust of interest groups and their activities.[2]

Consider the public's dislike of Congress. It is so intense that Congress sometimes seems to have become a "public enemy" in the nation. Part of the reason it is so unpopular has to do with the fact that life in Congress is highly public, making members of Congress a convenient target for contemporary liberal individualism's anti-institutionalism.[3] Institutional distrust also tars business. Capitalism, private property, the profit motive, and individual economic advancement all garner approval from the public, but distrust for the institution of business, especially big business, is real.[4]

This alienation from institutions, especially government, has become a major research agenda for some social science scholars, who by now have endlessly confirmed the lack of trust in government and government institutions. One contemporary study of "why people don't trust government" lays much of the blame on the news media and its negative portrayals of political institutions and their mixed success in meeting the inevitable challenges of a pluralistic and contentious contemporary United States. These social scientists disagree, perhaps predictably, with citizen opinion by claiming that the distrust is not based in actual failure by government institutions, public employees, or politicians.[5]

Seymour Martin Lipset and Earl Raab's recent, fascinating study of American Jews confirms that in this subgroup as in others individualistic and anti-institutional values are now everywhere in evidence. Lipset and Raab worry that the consequences of these attitudes may hurt the Jewish religion, break down the age-old traditions and connections that have bound Jews together, and threaten the very existence of the Jewish people. Jews may become a victim of American individualism, but these social scientists do not think reversing the situation will be easy. The disintegrative force of liberal individualism, they appreciate, is now too powerful for that.[6]

One study of the past fifty years of American public opinion reports a dramatic expansion of liberal attitudes toward civil rights, civil liberties, and women's rights in public and private, especially since the 1960s. Its authors understand that this development is connected with events of recent years that have expanded people's vision and has been encouraged by American elites, intellectuals, and the media, with a tremendous impact on an enormous number of Americans. The effect has been a great increase of political, economic, and other life opportunities for many people, perhaps even the majority of the public.[7]

Another important study that has charted public opinion changes over the decades since the 1960s provides abundant evidence of a liberalization of attitudes among the U.S. public toward racial and some other minorities in their public roles as citizens, employees, and consumers. Once again, one especially notes the tremendous change in attitudes regarding women as free and equal citizens and participants in economic and other parts of public life. This study concludes that it is in these increasingly inclusive attitudes that the real change—the real growth of liberalism—is occurring.[8]

Yet as Harvard's Sidney Verba and his social science associates confirm, this liberal kind of equality does not imply public support for radical economic redistribution. For example, disagreements over welfare policy are frequent in the United States. But that fact does not mean there is disagreement over the larger liberal values surrounding national and state welfare policy: the goals of individual independence, equality of opportunity, *and* opposition to substantive economic equality.[9] Other social scientists with very different political leanings have found (to their disappointment) similar results in the population at large. Equal opportunity has high approval, but income equality or any other radical economic arrangements that would challenge liberal, merit conceptions of economic justice do not.[10]

Some social theorists now argue that affluence in the West is encouraging a decline of ideological approaches to life—in economics, politics, and religion—and their replacement by more individualistic and freedom-oriented lifestyles. Much substantive data confirms this development in the years since the 1960s, and it reinforces others' findings that there has been a dramatic growth of the public's belief in individualism, as well as an expanding acceptance of multiple lifestyles.

The point is that individual freedom in every aspect of life, including the public, has taken center stage. People want it, expect it, demand it. More and more, the evidence suggests that public opinion is impatient with anything that interferes with the ethic of post-1960s liberalism. This includes the conventions and sometimes even the laws of public society, public institutions, work, and the worth of sacrifice and service as human goods.[11]

Perhaps the most important aspect of public liberalism in the United States today is the commitment to civil liberties (such as free speech and free press) for all and a concomitant sense of generous tolerance.[12] The considerable empirical information about public sentiment on these matters confirms that Americans are committed to civil liberties and tolerance to a much greater degree than some skeptics would have imagined three decades ago.[13]

Social scientists routinely argue over many aspects of the evidence relevant to these attitudes. They disagree over whether elites and the general public are equally tolerant (most find elites more so); on what may best explain the growth of tolerance—rising education and socioeconomic status or psychological factors such as strong self-esteem and high trust of others or the spread of liberal values in the culture; on whether citizen approval of tolerance really means anything in specific cases and instances; and on whether reflection by citizens increases their sympathy for civil liberties and expands their tolerance. What is not at issue, however, is that tolerance has become much admired by the American public, if sometimes more in word than in practice.

The technical social science literature that addresses attitudes toward tolerance is considerable. The first wave of studies, mostly from the early 1960s, noted a frequent lack of tolerance for outsider groups and concluded that informed elites were really the exception in their considerable tolerance.[14] Later studies found that intolerant attitudes might be even greater than had at first been thought. These studies allowed respondents to identify groups they disliked rather than asking about selected groups. The new procedure may have uncovered a range of intolerance that the old, more focused questions did not tap.[15] The subject is a complex one that has attracted nuanced social science analyses.[16]

More recently, methodological disputes have continued to bubble, but the many signs of change regarding tolerance have proved real. While this is not an uncontested claim, broad public opinion surveys report far more tolerance and even acceptance of public roles for major groups that in the 1960s many citizens held unequal or actively stigmatized, especially women and African Americans. This finding supports the view that tolerance in general has increased substantially over the past thirty years.[17]

In considering public opinion and public liberalism, it is natural to wonder whether all the major subgroups in the U.S. population, and especially the largest minority group, African Americans, share liberal values. After all, it is almost a cliché in some circles to suggest that African Americans are the main exception to claims about "American beliefs." The question is, What do the data show? Just how much are African Americans separate in their political and social attitudes compared with other Americans?

There is, fortunately, no shortage of information or reflective data analysis about the views of African Americans, and little of this information supports any claim that a vast gulf exists between whites and blacks in terms of liberal values and the public realm. Jennifer Hochschild's recent work reports (with an air of disappointment) that "the American dream" is overwhelmingly affirmed among blacks. She is referring to standard liberal values, including political equality and equal opportunity for each person. She finds commitment weakest among the most affluent and educated portions of the African-American community, not among the least advantaged blacks, quite contrary to what some observers have assumed would be true. Even among the affluent and educated, however, liberal norms are rarely repudiated in principle; it is their feasibility in the contemporary United States that is challenged. A crucial determinant is the degree to which African Americans accept the liberal individualist assumption that their failure to achieve goals is in good part their own fault. The more a person thinks such failure is not his or her fault, the more that confidence in "the American dream" recedes.[18]

Others confirm this analysis in different terms and observe that African Americans differ mostly in their assessments of how well the American system is working (for them). Thus there appear to be ample data that most African Americans do not reject liberal values—or the American political system.[19]

Yet Nathan Glazer warns that we must be skeptical of the abundant data confirming that blacks and whites share (liberal) political and social values. Glazer wonders whether survey research has been able to tap many blacks' fundamental attitudes. In any case, he also suggests that it is vital to take account of the wide differences between the two races in how they understand such racial issues as affirmative action and how they assess who benefits from the American system. Glazer's point here is the old one that haunts all such discussions. What is the significance of putative theoretical agreement if the realities of practical disagreement create racial, cultural, or policy divisions?[20]

At another, but definitely related, level is the attempt to compare blacks and whites through the lens of statistics rather than through their declared opinions and attitudes. Glazer's worries certainly justify such an effort. The trouble is, however, that this approach does not resolve much of anything either. One mostly encounters conflicting readings of similar income, family pattern, crime, or socioeconomic data. For some observers, large parts of the black community are falling into tragic chaos and slipping far away from mainstream, liberal America. For other commentators, the situation of African Americans is comparable to that of whites except for the black "underclass," which they argue is, at 10 to 20 percent of the whole, smaller than alarmists proclaim.[21]

Intellectual Views

The spread of public liberalism measured by citizen attitudes is apparent, but the views of public intellectuals and writers who address political values have been far less clear. Yet even here there are signs of a vigorous public liberalism among thinkers who represent a wide range of outlooks. Even among those who assert that they are not in sympathy with the Western or American liberal traditions, the reality is often more complex.

After all, American political thought—indeed, much of American politics beginning with and subsequent to the 1960s—has been about liberation and liberation themes. Today *freedom* is more than ever the key word in every American political dictionary. Intellectual support for feminism, for freedom in work and political life, and for individual self-expression in the arts, in sexuality, and everywhere else is vibrant testimony to intellectual approbation of liberal values whether or not their advocates protest they are liberals.

Often these advocates also support guaranteeing equal respect for different peoples and groups in the liberal fashion, by granting them equal freedom and rights and the whole panoply of liberal freedoms. The list of intellectual advocates here too is, of course, endless, and the degree of intellectual commitment not in doubt.[22]

Nor can there be much doubt about the widespread intellectual enthusiasm for "diversity" as a value in the post-1960s public cultures of the United States. Whether the argument is put in terms of accepting the realities that lie ahead for a heterogeneous America, or focuses on being fair to the diverse peoples already here, or is a serious defense of the deontological good of diversity (what we might call *deontological multiculturalism*), this stance reaffirms the longtime liberal principle of the worth of pluralism. John Stuart Mill would be proud. Once again, although diversity's most assertive proponents are often ambivalent about "liberalism" or the "American liberal tradition," their norm is unmistakably an expression of liberalism.[23]

Moreover, where the norm of multiculturalism is most firmly agreed on, for example, within African-American thought, diverse points of view abound—and are expanding. William Banks, the foremost commentator on African-American thought today, observes that contemporary black intellectuals are far more individualistic and pluralistic than they were in the 1960s. Moreover, he notes that they are becoming steadily more so, despite angry exchanges within the black intellectual community over pressures to conform.[24]

In philosophical terms—maybe metaphysical terms—the engagement with liberalism is also apparent in the postmodern mood so prominent in contemporary political and social thought in the United States. Modern liberalism is more and more a child of Millian liberalism, built on the premise (one quite inconceivable to classic liberals such as Locke, Jefferson, or Wollstonecraft) that there is no absolute grounding for values whether in religion or any other certain foundation. Much of contemporary liberalism's individualism and inclusivity assumes there are no clear—or comprehensive—social or ethical boundaries or communities. Such a view fits perfectly with such postmodern currents as deconstruction, which challenges foundations; contextualism, which stresses the impossibility of meaning outside a given historical and social setting; and constructionism, which insists that meaning is a matter of human interpretation and thus human creation. It fits as well with the revival of pragmatism in a variety of guises, a revival that is an effort to find a way to develop or declare values or "practices" without resort to absolutes.[25]

Yet there is no intellectual consensus on liberalism as it touches the public realm. One cannot casually ignore the torrent of intellectual attacks on liberal values at work in the public realm since the 1960s. After all, many of the thinkers who announce the triumph of liberalism in American public life are also fierce critics of liberalism. The most common procedure is simply to dissent from liberalism, whether in its philosophical assumptions about the priority of the individual or in its commitment to individual rights in practice or both. Consider, as two examples, the arguments of Elizabeth Fox-Genovese and Robert Bellah and his associates.

Feminist intellectual Elizabeth Fox-Genovese takes for granted the reign of liberal values in the United States. While comfortable with broad political and social theory, she is much concerned with the policy implication of public liberalism, with its attention to individual rights and interests. The contemporary situation disturbs her, particularly because she thinks feminism and liberalism are deeply intertwined in the present day, and not to feminism's advantage. For her, much of American feminism has turned out to be warmed-over liberalism, focusing on expanding individual women's rights and choices, with too little attention given to any social or communal perspectives. And, of course, the evidence of liberalism's influence in feminist circles accents its disturbing general strength in the culture.

She has something else in mind. She wants a feminism that raises more social questions, one whose policy implications she carefully spells out in such areas as abortion policy, women's economic rights, and other quite practical matters. Her larger goal, though, goes beyond developing merely a more social feminism. Fox-Genovese is a community-oriented radical who is sharply critical of both American feminism and American society. For her, the good society is a thoroughgoing community in many ways, one that would crown the common good, not individual self-interest. From this angle, Fox-Genovese genuinely challenges liberalism itself and not just liberal feminism.[26]

While Fox-Genovese develops her critique of public liberalism's obsession with individual liberty and rights in a series of thoughtful essays, sociologist Robert Bellah and his collaborators combine their research and analysis toward quite similar ends.[27] In their *Habits of the Heart* they subtly show how concentration on the self is pervasive in American public as well as private life. Their interviews reveal Americans as increasingly concerned with their own goals, with personal liberty, and with self-development and "self-actualization" rather than any broader goals or duties. They also note the current American fascination with self-creation, the idea that individuals should fashion their lives as they want, creating and re-creating themselves from their choices of jobs, politics, histories, clothes, and even names.[28]

Of course, the Bellah group maintains that there is a second American language, the language of community, which once was far more influential but still exists. Like others, they especially emphasize the colonial and Founding eras as moments in American history when the language of community was central, but the fact remains that the second language has lost out, at least for now. Liberal values are triumphant, and Bellah and his associates plainly regret it.[29]

Critics of liberalism frequently single out capitalism (put often today as "the market") as the main culprit. Yet however the argument is formulated, it is impossible not to hear the steady drumbeat of intellectual assaults on liberal values and institutions that has gone on for the past thirty years.[30] The fact is that there are many intellectual traditions and individual theorists today whose political thinking systematically challenges the liberal tradition in contemporary America.

The most widespread critiques today take place under the banner of community, although some are less radical than they may first appear. Consider, for example, Amitai Etzioni, the active social scientist advocate of community.[31] Closely connected with critiques of American individualistic liberalism and no zealous enthusiast of the liberal consensus interpretation of U.S. thought and culture, Etzioni consistently proposes what he envisions as a practical communitarianism.

Etzioni's self-conscious and determined modus operandi, like Fox-Genovese's, is to address specific issues and policies. Predictably, he is therefore suspicious of grand theories or sweeping critiques. He wants to concentrate on making change now, and so focuses on concrete policies (for example, regarding education) and how they can be redesigned to encourage greater community. In the process he and his collaborators have produced a number of works meant in good part to provide the specific connections with policy that few works of political theory ever provide—perhaps ever could provide.

But Etzioni's political instincts are not particularly radical. He designs his policy proposals to embody a livable reconciliation between the best of both liberalism and communitarianism. And he has worked hard to encourage other intellectuals and scholars to engage in discourse on how to draw together the best of liberalism and community. There is no doubt he has played a useful and decidedly constructive role in this valuable task. More determined and more thoroughgoing community-oriented thinkers, however, are less impressed. They judge this putative strength of Etzioni a limitation, the limitation of the lukewarm.[32] Thus Bruce Frohnen dismisses much of Etzioni's earnest talk of community as amounting to nothing substantial.[33]

Many community-oriented thinkers, while critics of "liberals" and "liberalism," are part of the tradition they fault, as I argue in chapter 6. The briefest of examinations reveals that many intellectual affirmations of community are actually little more than dressed-up complaints about selected aspects of liberal society. Such advocates of community today often suggest suspiciously tepid communal obligations in their understandings of community. *Community* continues to be a word of considerable intellectual fashion, but commitment to a serious and therefore demanding public community is a much rarer (and riskier) thing. The not always acknowledged reason is quite straightforward. Community could threaten the individual, or the whole constellation of public liberal values, whose appeal remains strong amid much of the chitchat about community in American intellectual circles.[34]

Confirming Practices

There is also bountiful evidence of the triumph of liberalism in the practices of American public institutions in recent decades. In this age of citizen "entitlement," the individual and his or her rights and "needs" have often overwhelmed all else in one institution after another. Every public institution, moreover, has moved toward accommodating or promoting the liberal value of diversity in its contemporary definitions. At the same time, there are signs of marked disengagement by many citizens, in some cases resulting in serious damage to public institutions. Developments in the political party and school systems in recent years illustrate the situation well.

Numerous studies confirm that Americans have turned away from political parties in the decades since the 1960s, their alienation sped along by events such as Watergate and the practiced cynicism of the media and entertainment industries. Throughout U.S. history most voters have had a strong allegiance to one party or another. We know that today that is gone, and for the bulk of Americans allegiance to a party is weak at best. There has been a correspondingly dramatic rise in the number of Americans who declare themselves independents (which is not the same thing, let us grant, as those who vote independently). Being "independent" is now the approved citizen ideal in the culture. It represents the triumph in practice of a liberal ideal of the public individual, and it fits nicely with popular suspicion toward political parties.[35]

Serious studies of what being a political "independent" means in terms of citizen attitudes, such as the work done by political scientist Jack Dennis, establish that there are, in fact, all kinds of independents. They also observe that independents may not be automatically conflated with those who are unattached to the political system. Yet Dennis and other social scientists recognize that a significant factor in the rise of independents is widespread public antipartyism. There has been a decline in psychological feelings of attachment to parties, an increase in the belief that parties should be less important in the political system, and an increase in a sense of personal political independence—all leading into our current "period of partisan decay."[36] In that light, the emergence of Ross Perot and his critique of the conventional party system in the 1992 and 1996 presidential elections were predictable and have been yet another factor damaging the standard political parties.[37]

By now a variety of alternative parties have sprung up in this antipartyism environment. Perot's creation, the Reform Party, is the most obvious, but there are others, including the Libertarian Party, which is slowly gaining national strength. The Green Party and other allied parties are also more and more visible. None have broken the back of the established two-party system. Yet there is no shortage of data suggesting that since public opinion of the conventional parties is poor, citizens are open to alternatives. We may soon see a dramatic change.[38]

Directions in American schooling are equally illuminating as indicators of the advance of liberal values in our public life. American education has always had a crucial local—and thus pluralistic—dimension in its organization, financing, and curriculum. While the "shopping mall" high school predated the 1960s, its steadily increasing impact since then, both in practice and as a principle of American secondary education, is also a prime example of the presence of liberal norms in contemporary U.S. education. This ideal of the high school as an endless series of educational options and programs to fit almost every imaginable student interest amounts to liberal diversity and market preference in action.

Equally evident have been the recent attempts to gear education to individual students, above all else. Although this model is rarely realized in practice, it is another indicator of the ardent belief in liberal individualism. The recent fad of "outcome-based education," insisting that education must be directed to diverse and individual learning styles and differing individual rates of progress, perfectly exemplifies this liberal norm.[39]

Multicultural education has undergone a rapid rise in popularity within the educational establishment as well as in many public—and private—school systems. Multiculturalism is no self-evident expression of liberal individualism, but in its earnest celebration of diversity, it reflects belief in liberal pluralism. At its best, multiculturalism is a celebration of the diversity of human ideas, practice, and choices, that is to say, of liberalism itself.[40]

Yet another illustration of the connection between American education and liberal values may be found in the controversial rise of the school choice movement.[41] To be sure, the picture is not simple. For example, many education school professors and some teachers disapprove of any form of competition in education, whether among schools or among students for grades or by achievement. John Dewey still has more than a few advocates in America's educational system. But the existence and growth of the school choice movement represents a counterenergy. The movement claims it seeks to give students and parents more individual liberty by providing greater choice among public schools as well as government aid to allow parents who wish to enroll their children in nonpublic schools. Its leading edge has been the effort to generate greater school choice for poor Americans, although critics suspect the school choice movement's interest in the poor is modest. While advocates of choice, fueled by a sense of crisis about public education, are often pessimistic about the performance of public schools, they are invariably optimistic regarding what school choice may accomplish.[42] Whether this optimism has any empirical basis depends so far only on how one reads the result of the Milwaukee school choice experiment, the one slim source we have today.[43]

One consequence of the choice movement to this point is the expansion of charter *public* schools—special schools that are able to bypass some of the ordinary administrative and union work rules— in a number of localities. Charter schools now often complement the traditional options of public schools, parochial schools, and other private schools. Joining magnet schools and alternative public schools for the alienated or "troubled," these charter schools have increased the choices in some school districts—and predictably set up some competition among schools.[44]

These developments represent an effort to attain the benefits of expanded individual freedom and competitive market liberalism in school systems. If change here has sometimes not been rapid, it is because the relevant established institutions—both the school systems and their unions—usually stand determinedly opposed for reasons of both ideology and self-interest. Another reason for the resistance, however, is the fact that the public school system has stood for so long as the one element in our diverse culture that provides some basis for national unity and a shared democratic citizenship. Indeed, support for conventional public schools has intensified in some circles just because the culture appears more and more infused with liberal individualism and group diversity.

One may well wonder if many public schools are a unifying force any longer. Some social scientists argue that Roman Catholic schools do better today in achieving effective learning across race and class than do public schools. One reason is that public schools are increasingly segregated socially and economically.[45]

One question is what impact the more numerous state-financed choices in education will have on this pattern of separatism. No one knows for sure.

It is not clear whether an effective choice program must include alternatives to the public schools or whether it could be achieved by giving students greater choices through magnet schools and other alternative schools within the public system. Nor is it obvious that publicly supported choice arrangements that include nonpublic schools "work" in terms of basic education. We have too little evidence to measure as yet.[46]

There are many other practical issues surrounding school choice. The public schools, however, still represent a democratic faith for many U.S. citizens, and that belief blocks the spread of school choice. It does so in part because it reflects other sides to America's liberalism: commitment to equal opportunity for all individuals, a conviction that education is essential for individual success, and assurance that education can be the answer for everyone. This is the liberal hope that helps explain why the battles over school choice are so fierce. Many Americans think a lot is at stake: their children and their future, but also the American liberal faith and its future.

The infusion of more individualism, pluralism, and choice into the public schools and the political party system suggests how much different facets of liberalism have made their way into U.S. public institutions. Perhaps they have speeded these institutions' decline—or unraveling—as well, although liberalism's defenders insist that this suggestion has the situation reversed. What seems certain, however, is that the political party and the public school as public institutions are good indicators of the muscular power of liberalism today. Its growing impact on practice in public spaces demonstrates that the spread of liberal values encompasses much more than changing public attitudes.

A Case Study: Conservative Thought Since the 1960s

Yet another way to ponder public liberalism is to explore its impact in a domain that self-confidently proclaims its opposition to "liberalism." My choice here is to look at American "conservatism." This choice makes sense because of conservatism's current prominence, because conservative thought counts now in American intellectual discourse, and because conservative intellectuals self-consciously distinguish themselves from liberals and liberalism. My conclusion is that most of present-day conservative thought is just another expression of American liberal political thinking. Thoughtful efforts to grasp the conservative intellectual situation abound, including George Nash's classic *Conservative Intellectual Movement* or David Frum's equally sympathetic but quite different contemporary perspective, *Dead Right*.[47] Each book offers its own analysis, as I do in suggesting that one method of comprehending contemporary conservative thought is to note four main directions it takes.[48] A first might be market conservatism or libertarianism. Within this view itself, of course, there are diverse thinkers and theories, but they disagree mostly on just where the outer limits of liberty must be. What is not at issue are such liberal norms as the celebration of as much individual liberty as possible, robust admiration for private property, and a reflexive distaste for government.

Milton Friedman, without doubt, has been the most influential spokesman for this view since the 1960s.[49] It is significant, however, that Friedman has been reluctant to accept the label of conservative. He resists, although others of a similar disposition have accepted that label comfortably enough. Friedman's uneasiness comes from his accurate perception that he is a classic nineteenth-century liberal in his conviction that a largely free market with a small government is best for the free individual, and thus is not really a "conservative" in any classic European sense.

The many who share his outlook often choose to declare themselves libertarians or libertarian conservatives. There is, in fact, little doubt that libertarian themes increasingly course through American conservatism. In this context Charles Murray has played a significant role. His social science–based exposé of the Great Society welfare program failures in the 1960s has brought him an enormous influence in conservative circles. While his analysis is continually contested from outside conservative intellectual circles, Murray provides many conservative intellectuals and politicians with empirical specifics on the failures of government policies that they previously lacked. Most recently, Murray has emerged as something of a political theorist of libertarian conservatism. In this role his influence is also considerable as he formulates a libertarianism that combines practical sense and theoretical plausibility.[50]

Another strain of contemporary conseryatism is social conservatism or moral traditionalism. This outlook has, in fact, long been part of post-1960s conservative inclinations. Its most important American exponent, Russell Kirk, is one of the key founders of contemporary American conservatism.[51] It was Kirk's view, which others share, that conservatism must follow the tradition of Edmund Burke. For Kirk, that meant conservatism must focus on the preservation of "settled things" (not necessarily to be confused with the status quo) and the encouragement of community in local institutions and contexts.

In Kirk's case, as in most others, social conservatism has involved an appreciation of religion and "conservative" social values, from love of family to respect for honesty, sexual discipline, and modesty. It has also shown distaste for big government and its frequently "failed" national policies, including the lamentable condition of American public education. Social conservatives often also express a distinct coolness toward capitalism and radical individualism unless they are restrained within the context of local communities and traditional values. The danger of both is well recognized in this branch of conservatism.

In recent years some social conservatives have sometimes joined with those influenced by the political theories of Leo Strauss and Eric Voegelin. Strauss stressed the traditions represented in a particular reading of the Greek classics and Voegelin those affirmed by a unique interpretation of Christianity.[52] Most of those who are impressed with Strauss or Voegelin are more self-consciously philosophical than social conservatives such as Kirk—sometimes much more so than Kirk welcomed.

Whether those affected by the work of Strauss or Voegelin are conservatives at all is debatable. They do, however, commonly share social conservatism's belief that truth exists and that community under truth is a central good of human life. Often they have attacked excessive American individualism and egalitarianism and the subjectivist and hedonistic directions of American culture as manifested in rock music, the movies, or trash TV. Like other social conservatives, however, they rarely repudiate the usefulness of U.S. society, institutions, or historic values. Most fashion their own combination of the traditional, the contemporary, and the "postliberal."[53]

The most influential example of a cultural critique in the Leo Strauss tradition is Allan Bloom's 1980s best-seller, *The Closing of the American Mind.* Its blistering exposé of typical college students is famous: obsessed with empty sex and corrupting rock and roll, intolerant in their tolerance, utterly empty of any serious tradition of thought or morality. Yet Bloom's work never proposes abandoning the American liberal order. A liberal culture is essential as a setting that will tolerate the few who choose to pursue truth, a truth that may have little indeed to do with liberal values but much to do with the classical tradition of Plato and Aristotle.[54]

The new voices of the Christian Right are yet another side to social conservatism. They embody an intense moralism, which includes a dedication to biblical sexual mores, opposition to abortion, and a determination to "clean up" the often licentious and violent entertainment media. Their goals are integral to what Christian conservatives such as Pat Robertson and the Christian Coalition judge is essential if "one nation under God" is not to disappear entirely in the United States. They insist that government must treat religion in general and Christians and their values in particular with the respect they deserve if the United States is to survive as an integral and moral society.[55]

Even within the ranks of social conservatives, however, not all replicate the stance of Christian conservatism. There are disagreements over what traditions matter and uneasiness over the militant, radical energy of the Christian Right movement. Moreover, while Christian conservatives share with other conservatives sympathy for individual liberty if it is rooted within the American culture, institutions, and traditions, they worry many libertarian conservatives, from whose perspective there is good reason for concern. Despite Christian conservatives' sympathy with the traditions of the United States (which are often liberal), at least some of their deepest political foundations are theocratic in a fashion that is distinctly not in the liberal tradition.

An interesting case is provided by Roman Catholic social conservatives who concentrate on liberal failure to achieve community in either theory or practice and who argue that the United States—

as a liberal society—can benefit from Roman Catholic insights if it is to endure as a moral and social order. Philosophically, this view is less libertarian even than that held by many Christian Right conservatives. Culturally also, it is a long way from the worlds of Protestant fundamentalist, evangelical, or Pentecostal religious traditions. Yet social conservatives of these varying religious backgrounds all fear unraveling of social bonds that so conflicts with their religion of communal love and forgiveness.[56]

J. Budziszewski, a University of Texas political theorist, presents another, controversial view. As an orthodox or "conservative" Christian, Budziszewski reflects considerable ambivalence toward "official" U.S. conservatism. As he writes, American conservatism is often in conflict with (his) Christian faith. This is not just a matter of much of American conservatism's frank sacralizing of the good of individual liberty but also its habit of proclaiming the United States a divinely chosen nation where government should enforce God's values. Such notions do not originate in Christianity, Budziszewski maintains. Christianity transcends any nation, any government, and any political ideology.

This is why Budziszewski is no obvious American conservative; perhaps, as he protests, he is no conservative at all. Yet his perspective is very much a part of the debate among Christian conservatives today. The issue is whether and how tightly American conservatism and Christianity fit together, if they do so at all.[57]

Many of these Christian perspectives are infertile ground for the considerable libertarian side of the conservative movement today. While they all refuse to celebrate government and all favor great amounts of human freedom, Christian conservatives' commitment to God and to community based on transcendent, not national, norms distinguishes them sharply. This is not always apparent in particular shared practical causes, but its reality always hangs ominously in the background.

One other variety of social conservatism I would call "policy conservatism." It is not part of any self-conscious traditionalist perspective or Christian conservative outlook; its social conservatism appears in its practitioners' consistent concern to address vexing policy problems by the preservation or enhancement of communal and moral bonds. For conservative social scientist James Q. Wilson this approach is essential for efforts to tackle social decay expressed in crime;[58] for William Kelso it is urgent if we want to address welfare and the breakdown of community that frequently creates the need for welfare;[59] for William Bennett it is the practical way to renew declining local communities.[60]

Thus today, as is apparent to all, the American conservative movement—intellectually and politically—reflects no single orientation. It is composed of many strands, somewhat jumbled together in sometimes uncomfortable proximity and open to the charge that it lacks intellectual coherence. In more formal terms this reality is the "hybrid" conservatism that is the ordinary ideological and practical fare of American conservatives. Such essays as publisher Frank Meyer's "Recrudescent Conservatism"[61] or, more recently, Republican leader Dick Armey's "Freedom's Choice"[62] make its case.

In most instances, hybrid conservatism represents an effort to combine libertarian norms with social conservative values, a problematic but hardly impossible mix. Although the particular mixture varies from thinker to thinker, there is a consistent emphasis on the importance of religion, family, and local communities, wide personal and political freedoms, a weak state, and a vibrant and largely unencumbered economic marketplace. This hybrid view may not always be philosophically neat, but it has become accepted in conservative circles.

In some ways this perspective accords well with another stream of conservatism, neoconservatism. Standard conservative thinkers ("paleoconservatives") and neoconservatives dwell in a relationship that can be tense. There are disputes over the role of the state (neoconservatives are less than libertarian) and personal histories (neoconservatives are often former liberal Democrats or leftists). Yet both these versions of conservatism support a United States that they understand as "liberal" in many aspects. Much of their "conservatism" is support for the preservation of liberal freedoms *and* of the truths and conditions—not always liberal—that surround and protect American values and institutions. These include commitment to community and a republican or public good perspective, as well as virtues such as self-respect and hard work that they judge are integral to the survival of the American society they hope to preserve.

Neoconservatism came into being as a post-1960s phenomenon, a reaction to the New Left and its post-1970 intellectual apologists in defense of the United States and in opposition to the world Com-

munist movement.[63] Proponents thus saw themselves as conservatives against altering the basic institutions and values of the United
States as they understood them, and for the Western liberal Enlightenment tradition in their intellectual and political commitments.[64]

Among the most important voices of neoconservatism were
Jeane Kirkpatrick, who zealously defended a tough, neorealist U.S.
policy of anti-Communism in international affairs,[65] and Norman
Podhoretz, who turned the American Jewish Committee's journal
Commentary into an organ of the movement and wrote some of the
ablest neoconservative pieces. He often argued in favor of an assertive anti-Communist foreign policy aimed at protecting both
America and Israel. Podhoretz broke intellectual taboos, daring after
the fact to defend the Vietnam War (if not its failed management),
brilliantly detailing the overwhelming ambition for success that
grips U.S. intellectual circles, and exploring the hostility of many
intellectuals toward anyone who rejects their widely shared political and intellectual canons.[66]

But it was Irving Kristol who did the most to promote neoconservatism as a self-conscious intellectual movement. He was
unusual in willingly accepting the neoconservative label that others
shied away from. His *Two Cheers for Capitalism* was probably the
most significant essay in the modest but unmistakable neoconservative defense of the U.S. economic system and its tremendous
productivity.[67] Kristol also affirmed traditional U.S. cultural norms
and firmly aligned neoconservatism with general cultural conservatism, a cause taken up later by William Bennett. In the 1980s
Kristol presented his overall perspective in his *Reflections of a Neoconservative;* in a more reflective mood in the 1990s, he wrote *Neoconservatism: The Autobiography of an Ideal.*[68] While his critics always
claimed that Kristol was not much of an original thinker, he was
certainly important as a spokesman for neoconservatism, which he,
more than anyone else, fashioned and helped become a serious factor in American intellectual, political, and conservative circles.

Some observers contend that neoconservatism is now in steep
decline. If true, this fate may be a sign of its success. After all,
American liberal values, not a largely dead Marxism or a New Left
that is increasingly ancient history, have carried the day. Because
liberal market and democratic norms are ascendant, the defensive
stance of neoconservatism may seem a bit irrelevant. Thus neo-

conservatism's success may have sped its eclipse as a self-conscious movement.[69]

In any case, exploration of conservative thought since 1970 suggests that this alternative perspective and its intellectual advocates mostly (but not entirely) share liberal principles and concentrate on conserving the liberal institutions, practices, and values of the United States. Its disposition can sometimes be highly change-oriented— as is true among some members of its Christian conservative and libertarian wings—but often conservatism defends established translations of liberal values against those who would expand the number and definition of liberal rights. "Conservative thought" in the United States, in short, is a significant factor in American intellectual life, but it provides scant ground for arguing against the existence of a broad ideological consensus.

The mainstream that most American conservatism upholds intimately involves an affirmation of familiar American liberal values. It is best characterized as a conservative liberalism focused on preserving or advancing (and the difference between preservation and advancement explains much of the variety within conservatism) liberal norms in U.S. institutions, practices, and policies. Many Christian conservatives, on the other hand, speak in a different voice, despite their frequent alliance in ordinary politics with other conservatives. They are often caught between trying to affirm the conservative version of American liberalism and a radical disposition pushing them on to try to transform the United States to serve their understandings of the Christian gospel.

Of course, there are other readings of American conservatism today. One interesting version from outside its ranks comes from Theodore Lowi in his trenchant book *The End of the Republican Era*.[70] Lowi enumerates familiar types of conservative thinking in the contemporary United States, including neoconservatism, Old Right traditionalism, populist conservatism, New Right Christian conservatism, and the substantial part of American conservatism that wishes to reach a liberal "concordance" with nineteenth-century market liberalism (an effort he judges is not succeeding and is not likely to).

Lowi's analysis certainly recognizes the importance of conservative thought and its diverse expressions, which are prime illustrations of the degree of intellectual pluralism ascendant in the nation today.[71]

He also dismisses the old Hartzian consensus claim that there has been no serious conservative tradition in the American past. This is simply wrong, he argues, and therefore so are consensus claims that U.S. history may be described as a "liberal tradition."[72]

The species of contemporary conservatism that most worries Lowi is the Christian Right.[73] Like many other public intellectuals outside the movement, Lowi finds it deeply threatening. He denies that the Christian Right embodies much in the way of liberal values, insisting that it has "rejected democracy, political pluralism, and the equality of all interests."[74] Indeed, Lowi charges that what the Christian Right is actually about is "a still deeper urge *to found a moral republic in which basic values are so homogenized that democracy can take place without risk of morally bad actors.*"[75]

Conclusion

Since 1970, liberal values have been the mainstay of public life in the United States; they may well be more prevalent today than they were in the supposed heyday of consensus. This liberal framework is broadly evident in public attitudes, in institutional practice, and in more intellectual perspectives than one might predict. There is, however, no need to exaggerate here at any level of analysis. Consensus theorists made that mistake. Their error was not that they took a part for the whole, but that they took the largest part for the whole. Moreover, one should keep in mind that more than a few interpreters of American political thought or culture would reject the argument of this chapter. Some of them are distinctly sympathetic to liberal values (unlike many other students of the subject).[76]

Two particular reservations merit some attention. One derives from that perpetual but real problem that haunts the effort to think about any body of thought even when a good deal of it shares a common language. Specifically, the issue is whether "liberalism" and "liberal values" are far too inclusive conceptually to be of substantive use in analysis of American thought and culture. Put another way, what does the widespread existence of "liberalism" or "liberal values" in American public life mean? Is liberalism just another term for virtually everything in the United States, or is it a reality that counts in the life and thought of the nation?

This chapter began with a modest effort to define some boundaries for the public "liberal" world and has tried to keep them in mind throughout the discussion. But it is hard to avoid what some will contend is "loose" usage in any consideration of "liberalism" or "liberal values." One way out of this dilemma would be to insist on essentialist definitions for these concepts. Yet by its nature, liberalism, with its emphasis on freedom and the individual, is open to many understandings—and it always has been. It is not a tight philosophical system—nor has it ever been. It cannot be so without imposing an artificial narrowness that denies the very concept and its associated values.

Even if we can agree on the general outlines of public liberalism, another major problematic inevitably confronts us. Do claims about how widespread public liberalism is ultimately help us comprehend American life? This is the crucial question. Conflict abounds in public life among citizens and intellectuals, within politics, and over public policies. Even if much or most of it takes place in a liberal framework employing a liberal vocabulary, the conflict still occurs. The case study of conservatism underlines the point. American conservatives are mostly part of "the liberal tradition," but they are in frequent and intense public conflict with their opponents— and, indeed, with each other. How much does it illuminate anything to say, "They are all liberals"?

Chapter Five

Liberalism in the Private Realm

The spread of liberal values in the public realms of the United States—despite growing intellectual and other diversity—suggests how much liberalism now flourishes in America. The next step in our project, however, is to explore the condition of liberal values in traditionally noncongenial settings, above all in the home, in the church, and in other contexts where women have been historically central. The question is, How much have liberal values come to bear in the "private" worlds where they did not reign before recent decades? To answer this question is the second major aspect of—and challenge for—my argument that liberalism is more powerful than ever in American culture.

Perhaps the greatest transformation of American life since the 1950s has been the importation—and triumph—of liberal values in what were once called the private spheres of American life. Perhaps ironically, public intellectuals have widely hailed this change. Much of the general public has affirmed it as well, if sometimes uneasily. No development has been more important in American life, none more historic, none more far-reaching in its consequences.

Drawing on public opinion studies, popular practice, and intellectual thought, this chapter presents the evidence for this notable infusion of liberalism in the private realms of American life. What I address here is the rise of the ethos of the near sacredness of individual choice, the view that increasingly governs how we live most intimately. It is the belief that our personal and private lives should be a matter of individual choice.[1] This outlook treasures a commitment to moral and metaphysical individualism and to individualism in practice. It often implicitly (and sometimes explicitly) rejects moral or metaphysical absolutes—as well as human or institutional authorities—that might override individual choices, and affirms the doctrine of a host of equal human rights for all.

Neat conceptual divisions between the public and private realms is suspect in our age. We have all learned how little the "private" is really private both conceptually and in our own lives. Yet frayed though it is, such a distinction can have important, if somewhat artificial, uses. It can point us to somewhat different dimensions of human life and action, as long as it does not become an icon of analysis or a rigid claim about reality. This is why, in a suitably skeptical mood, I employ it for analytical purposes.

By *public* I mean activities that involve direct human interaction with the larger social order. The public world involves a person's work, broad social networks, and political roles. When I refer to the *private* sphere, I mean a person's family, one's more personal and intimate relationships, and one's central beliefs, which are often spiritual or religious, and the institutions connected with them. It is this latter category that contains the areas where liberalism has spread so impressively in recent decades.

One way to approach my contention that liberalism has swept into the private realm is to contrast today's situation with that perceived by classic interpreters of America. In many cases—as feminist and other critics have correctly pointed out—classic interpretations, such as that of Louis Hartz, simply took for granted that liberal values (which Hartz saw as often nonliberal in practice) did not apply in nonpublic dimensions of life. At the least, Hartz was silent on the more private aspects of Americans' existence. He scarcely spoke of family, marriage, religion, or friends. In the process he quietly affirmed the reality and the importance of a crucial distinction between the public and the private. Yet this dimension of his work and that of most of his peers was rarely noted at the time.

What now seems obvious is that the picture Hartz drew fostered an image of American liberal society that was and is eerily incomplete. Hartz's apparent conclusion was straightforward. It was that such private life and its values were not relevant to comprehending "the liberal tradition in America."[2] But this conclusion seems strange in retrospect. How could such major dimensions of life and the inevitable human thought about them just disappear in the analysis of some of the consensus theorists of the 1940s and 1950s?

This is even more puzzling because the same era strongly upheld a cult of domesticity, religion, and private life. Adding to the mystery was the fact that this neglect was hardly characteristic of all liberal thought in the West, despite some claims to that effect in our own day. One thinks at once of John Locke's famous discussion of the family in his chapter "On Paternal Power" in the *Second Treatise*, or John Stuart Mill's now far more famous considerations on the family in *On the Subjection of Women*.

Yet in the tradition of interpretation of American political thought Hartz's analysis was standard stuff, and until recently was widely endorsed. The originator of this analysis of the United States was not Hartz, however, nor anyone else in the twentieth century. It was Alexis de Tocqueville, who in his *Democracy in America* explicitly contended that there was a separation of liberalism from private life in the United States. We know Tocqueville's position was that liberal values reigned in the public realm, while in private life—above all in the family and other personal relationships—they did not. Indeed, as chapter 1 emphasizes, Tocqueville's special contribution was his argument that there should and must be a separation between these two worlds. Only in a private home and church, separated from the public world, could a secure foundation for the necessary moral limits on human selfishness be learned.[3]

In pursuing the modern-day involvement of liberalism in what I call the private realm, I want to explore two arenas in which liberalism's contemporary success is striking. Women's lives and feminism direct us to the massive changes in the family and women's existence that began in the 1960s and continue in the United States, a liberal revolution whose accomplishment would have stunned both Alexis de Tocqueville and Louis Hartz. A second example is the widespread transformation of American religion into a home for liberal individualism, which has occurred to a startling extent, one much greater than anyone imagined even a half century ago.

The Transformation of Practice

American women pursue remarkably diverse lives today. This reality, however, does not alter the fact that a revolution has taken place regarding women's existence since the 1960s in the United

States, a revolution toward liberal feminism in practice. Although fierce disagreements continue over women's situation today, in comparative terms change is what stands out. Consideration of women's situation in three areas—employment, abortion, and marriage and the family—underlines the fact that change is the story, and this pattern of change etches again the transforming effects of liberalism on "private" life.

Today the overwhelming majority of adult women, including the majority of women with children still living at home, are employed outside the home, most of them in full-time positions. This was hardly true for the majority of nonfarm women in 1960 or before. In 1960 the civilian labor force was almost 70 million strong, but only 23 million workers were women; moreover, fewer than one-third of all married women were in the workforce. By the 1990s women constituted nearly one-half of the civilian labor force. Well more than 60 percent of women over the age of twenty were in the workforce, considerably more if only women below retirement age are counted.[4]

What this suggests for our time is historic. It means that many adult women have experienced a tremendous shift from a life led largely in the home to one spent in good part outside the home at work for pay. Most younger women know that they will work outside their homes for much of their lives, except for their years of retirement and, perhaps, for a short time when their children are young. This is a major reversal of the practice of most nonfarm women in history. It is the change, moreover, that more than any other marks the end of the old private-public distinction or, in other terms, the nearly complete penetration of liberal values into the old private world.

Second, consider abortion policy. While restrictive abortion policies were already easing in some states in the 1960s and early 1970s, the *Roe v. Wade* decision of 1973 pointedly accelerated the change. It brought the liberal concept of rights—the right to an abortion—to the lives of women (and men) in a dramatic, memorable way. "Choice" and "rights" became the triumphant and irresistible language—and reality—in as private a place as most people can imagine, a woman's body. The number of abortions rapidly expanded after 1973 until it reached its current steady state of about 1.5 million individual choices to exercise the liberal right to "reproductive freedom." And, despite considerable popular uneasiness over abortion, study after study shows robust public support for the idea that every pregnant woman has the right to choose to have an abortion.[5]

As with the life of women in the workforce, so too the legitimization of women's choice about abortion greatly bolstered women's status as full citizens in the United States and full participants in liberalism and liberal individualism. The results may be saluted or deplored, and obviously they are fiercely contested, but they have been significant. They represent profound change in modern America.

Other changes regarding marriage and the family have been closely connected to these developments. Women (and men) now marry less often than they did thirty or forty years ago; both genders marry later; and, of course, American couples get divorced far more frequently. Currently about one in two marriages ends in divorce, with the divorce rate remaining at twice what it was in the 1960s, and much higher than in earlier periods in American history.[6] Moreover, there is no sign that there are more happy marriages now than in the past, a matter divorce statistics cannot address. Like information on the age at which people marry and the rate of marriage, however, the divorce statistics have implications for the practical possibilities for a life outside of marriage. In an age of the triumph of liberalism, it is hardly a surprise that people marry later than they once did, or that the proportion of the population that gets married is smaller, while divorce is more frequent. Choices and choice—the expansion of liberalism into the practice of individual lives—make these effects likely, if not inevitable. While critics bewail divorce, the fact is that it is another form of freedom in the liberal mode, which some Americans welcome and most support, as we will see in chapter 8.

The Advance of Liberalism and Public Opinion

If women's lives now increasingly reflect the sway of such liberal norms as choice and individual independence, public opinion is strongly supportive. In public attitudes as in practice, liberal values have swept to the fore in Americans' personal existence. This is why *women's liberation* may more accurately describe the liberal revolution than does the term *feminism*. The phrase *women's liberation*, however, does obscure the extent to which, as Barbara Ehrenreich has pointed out, "men's liberation" has also been much involved at least in practice.[7] But the strength of this movement, whatever its best name, is no fantasy generated by an "elite" cadre of feminist activists, as some conservatives charge. Nor is its hold on the American public deniable even as the term *feminist* is distinctly unpopular with the general public. Nor is there much to the claim from another side that feminism's enemies are now ascendant almost everywhere. These kinds of statements are mostly political rhetoric.

Attitude studies show the situation clearly. There is now overwhelming support for equal rights for women over a broad range of issues: equal pay for equal work, equal economic opportunity, equal political participation (including running for office), abortion rights, and divorce. The shift in public opinion on these matters since the 1950s and 1960s is both wide and deep. This is unusual because U.S. public opinion tends to be quite stable over time on matters of basic values and on most public policies.[8] The truth is that the greatest single shift in U.S. public opinion in the second half of the twentieth century has been the revolution of attitudes—among both women and men—regarding women's equal rights. In my terms, this expansion of liberal values to include equal rights for women, dismantling much of the gendered public-private distinction, is robust evidence of the energy of liberal universalism.[9]

Closely connected to these attitudes is public opinion regarding individual freedom in general, opinion that is ardently supportive. Some intellectuals may denounce what they feel are freedom's contemporary excesses: selfishness, greed, incivility, waste, and narcissism. But such criticisms only underline the reality that public opinion studies show. There is great support for individual liberty in principle and expanding approval of equal liberty for almost every individual and group.

Studies also report shifts in public opinion that are relevant here, such as greater approval of extensive sexual freedom, most notably regarding sexual intercourse outside marriage, a stance that first took hold in the late 1960s and 1970s; greater tolerance of gays (although there is less acceptance of gay sexual practices); and increased acceptance of divorce. While these attitude shifts are much more prevalent in elite educational, media, and artistic circles in the United

States than in the population at large, liberalization among the mass public is also marked.[10]

Popular support for the family (however individuals define it) also remains high, and in this context studies of public attitudes toward men, liberalism, and the family are quite revealing. There is considerable evidence of popular criticism of men who are seen as too selfishly irresponsible—or too independent—to stand by family life. Explanations for this damaging male selfishness (the not nice word for one expression of liberal individualism) vary, but only at first glance. Compare, for example, the analysis of "conservative" George Gilder with that of "radical" Barbara Ehrenreich.[11] They agree that many men are adrift in a culture that no longer has a private sphere—or any substitute for it—that restrains self-interest. Men are awash in a sea of freedom, which they rarely want to give up. Thus they fear commitments and resist the demands of duty when they do commit. They too have become exemplars of liberal individualism in their personal lives.

The Intellectual Shift

Alongside historic changes in public attitudes in the United States there has been an amazing change over the last half century in intellectual opinions about how life should be led and what values should matter in the "private" side of life. There is no better way to illustrate this movement toward favoring the incorporation of liberal norms in private life than to examine intellectual attitudes concerning women. Here, practice and public opinion find a resonant echo in reigning intellectual sentiment. All three have moved together toward supporting the feminist revolution—however incomplete—in innumerable women's lives and the private parts of American life. Several features merit specific discussion here: the rise of "rights" language and the insistence on equal rights between the genders; the interest in the liberal contract model for family relations; and the willingness to call on the state to enforce liberal values in personal life.

Of these three features, the most important has been the historic explosion of "rights" language regarding women and the home. Nothing better illustrates the victory of John Locke and Mary Wollstonecraft than to see Tocqueville's home of women, religion, and community reconceptualized into a realm of rights-bearing equals—as it is now framed in much of American political thought.

Disputes are plentiful among feminist intellectuals over the proper grounding of rights—whether they are natural, socially constructed, or best understood as legal conveniences—*and*, given their importance now, over whether they are the proper model for the ideal society. But rights today are a core theme in feminism—equal rights (however grounded) for women in the home and elsewhere in private and public life. This is clear in the feminist defense of a woman's right to abortion, which remains perhaps the central substantive and emotive issue in the women's movement. It is equally apparent in politics, in education, or in the struggle for equal pay and for equal opportunity in the workplace. It is also clear in feminist support for liberalized (although not necessarily no-fault) divorce laws. Also relevant are feminist arguments that stress concern for the equality of specific groups of women, such as bell hooks's advocacy for African-American women.[12]

What unites all these positions is a belief in women's rights, however defined and justified, but especially the right to freedom, to choice, the supreme liberal right as refined by John Locke and others since. Many modern feminists have agreed that the right to exercise choice must trump all else, and in practice this is often what happens. Despite attempts by feminist intellectuals such as Catharine MacKinnon or Mary Daly, theorists who offer alternative, radical perspectives, most feminism is largely about extending equal rights, especially the right to choice, to women in the private and public spheres of life. In other words, most feminism in practice turns out to be a form of liberalism.

This is true about a good deal of lesbian feminism as well. Granted, some lesbian feminists emphasize lesbian-based communal goals, and there can be considerable tension between that ideal and commitment to individual rights. On the other hand, lesbian thought tends to rest firmly on familiar liberal claims for individual rights. This includes, of course, the right to practice one's sexual orientation. Considerations of community usually end up secondary to such liberal individualism. While the large role assigned to liberal premises is not always acknowledged, there is nothing astonishing about it. One has to search in American politics to find voices that seriously rank community over individual freedom.[13]

Consider the popular aspect of feminist thought that employs the contract model of human life. As articulated by political theorist Susan Okin, for example, it insists that human relations should be (in effect) Lockean.[14] They should be voluntary arrangements among equals who may form and end their relationships only by mutual consent, whether marriage, family, or any other social connections. This contract model is deeply and sometimes self-consciously liberal in outlook, as Okin knows. It conceptualizes people in private (and public) life as beings who must be treated as free and equal individuals, able to make and remake choices that accord with their sense of self, purpose, and freedom.

Liberal understandings also pervade much of the feminist-influenced helping professions, as others have noted.[15] Despite well-intentioned rhetoric about community or family therapy, many therapies make individual happiness their central goal in all relationships. The assumption is that the road to this goal requires focusing on the individual and on individual freedom and independence. The pleasant hope is that free and independent individuals will achieve better relationships. In another form, we have the famous Ann Landers question to dissatisfied married folk: "Are you better off with or without him or her?" This question is a perfect illustration of the modern liberal message. The individual is what matters: his or her personal rights, judgment, equality, and freedom.

Another side of feminist thought involves reliance on government action. This is such an orthodox feminist assumption that it is unquestioned and taken for granted. The state is to promote affirmative action to achieve substantive gender equality; it is to protect the right to an abortion; it is to ensure an abundance of day care; it is to provide welfare when needed and also the means to escape welfare dependency. For some feminist intellectuals, the state is to regulate what is printed (pornography) or even said (college speech codes). Government is never embraced as an end in itself, and one would not expect it to be in such a liberal-influenced movement. Yet what is striking is how few feminist theorists fear government and question whether it might prove to be more a threat to women's freedom than an aid to it.[16]

One more dimension of feminist thought that is relevant here is the much-emphasized claim that "the personal is political." The point is that private life is not exclusively private but has—and always has had—enormous public and political implications; at the same time, public life deeply affects the private spheres of life. This claim is routinely declared to be an obvious empirical fact, although some feminist intellectuals suggest that it is necessarily a constructed social claim, often advanced for its universalistic and egalitarian implications.

The idea that "the personal is political," of course, challenges any outlook that employs a public-private distinction, which is exactly what it means to do. The consequence is deeply liberal in implication, underlining liberalism's general triumph in this arena. The idea that the personal is political is in effect a reification of liberal universalism, the idea that one size or value fits all. It is liberal universalism at work, breaking down all distinctions and sweeping all reality into its fold.

There are, however, other streams of feminist thought than those that, whatever their intentions, are so explicitly liberal.[17] For example, there is "difference" or "gender" feminism, a perspective that has particularly flourished in the years since Carol Gilligan's In a Different Voice (1982) so greatly stimulated its growth.[18] Difference feminism emphasizes contrasts between men and women, sometimes maintaining that they are genetic, sometimes that they are social constructions. Its proponents often argue that women are more communal and caring toward others than are men and that men are more individualistic and self-focused (to put the distinction more mildly than it is often expressed).

While critics have noted for some time that serious empirical evidence for the perspective of difference feminism is thin, for us the real issue lies elsewhere.[19] It is whether difference feminism, as an alternative to mainstream feminism, supports the thesis that much of feminist thought is not liberal. After all, in difference or gender feminism, the individual and individual rights would seem to matter less than the female gender as a whole. Moreover, in Gilligan's understanding, women tend to avoid universal claims and think in a relational and contextual perspective, which might seem more Burkean than Lockean. On the other hand, many other group (or identity) theorists' arguments appear to be a straightforward transposition to groups of standard liberal categories—rights and freedoms—classically ascribed to the liberal individual. They are often little more than a group form of liberal thinking, believed quite sincerely to be something more radical.[20]

However one reads difference feminism, though, most feminist thought remains rights-oriented and liberal. To be sure, some liberal feminists—for example, Naomi Wolf in *Fire with Fire*[21] or Christine Sommers in *Who Stole Feminism?*[22]—believe they represent a dissenting view in American feminist thought and practice. They portray an intellectual world, especially the academic arena of women's studies, that is deeply hostile to liberal values, and where liberal feminists are disliked outsiders. The validity of their portrait no doubt varies by time and place. But it is essential that we not confuse the feminist outlooks and thought experiments in women's studies departments or journals such as *Signs* with mainstream feminism even in universities, where most women professors are feminists but not connected with women's studies. Feminism in American intellectual life—to the continuing scorn of genuinely radical feminists—remains very much in the thrall of liberalism.

The idea that liberal feminism is triumphant is frequently affirmed by alternate feminist voices. Two self-declared feminist writers, Katha Pollitt and Elizabeth Fox-Genovese, exemplify this point. Pollitt has argued in the *Nation* and elsewhere that she is repelled by the rights talk regarding women that is so common in our day. To her, it is both appalling and sad because it focuses, in my terms, on women as private individuals. Pollitt has something else altogether in mind. For her, rights (women's rights included) merit encouragement, but only when they are understood as the rights of *public* citizens who must be seriously involved in collective self-governance. Rights about political participation—social rights—are the kind of rights she welcomes, while selfish, individual, or private rights (liberal rights, in her mind) are no ideals. They stand in the way of a reconceptualization of our culture toward a participatory and community-based perspective, which goal, Pollitt concludes, casts her as an opponent of much of liberalism.[23]

Fox-Genovese agrees, but she is much more explicitly critical of feminism as a whole. She notes that a majority of women do not feel much kinship with the feminist movement, although they often support some of its broader goals. The lack of identification with feminism occurs, she argues, because most women care very much about marriage and motherhood, vocations that play a far too modest role in the feminist movement. Fox-Genovese is no reactionary who wants to require women to be stay-at-home moms, and she has no doubt that most women agree with her. Yet she points out that most women want marriage and children and that they face a sometimes-daily struggle to balance their work life, marriage, and role as mothers. What modern feminism must do, Fox-Genovese urges, is to acknowledge this situation and abjure crusades for objectives that are tangential to the lives of most women.[24]

From Fox-Genovese's perspective, feminism is obsessed with giving women rights equal to those of men (and sometimes more). Feminist thought, meanwhile, is trapped in an ethic in which individualism, the individual liberty to do whatever one wants, and a self-directed individualistic outlook supersede all else. Fox-Genovese sternly admonishes her fellow feminists to own up to these unpleasant realities and understand "feminism's complicity in and acceptance of individualism."[25] She boldly cites feminist thought on abortion and affirmative action as cases in point, contending that individual rights and the gospel of free choice, especially in the "reproductive freedom" movement, denote feminism's membership in the world of liberal individualism. While Fox-Genovese is quick to defend the opportunity for an abortion for women, she "emphatically" rejects the view that people have "an absolute right to the disposition" of their bodies.[26]

Fox-Genovese also argues that no one should give much credence to the many vague affirmations of community that abound among feminist theorists. The much more favored goal is "liberation," which often clashes with ideas of community. She contends that the standard assumption is that individuals—and women, in particular—have individual rights that must and do precede any community claims. She knows many theorists are happy that they do, given the historical record of most communities' oppression of women.[27]

Even where there is authentic support for community in feminist thought, Fox-Genovese doesn't think it amounts to much. At best, it is community subjectively defined, community at the behest of every individual thinker. In other terms, Fox-Genovese maintains that feminism, like liberalism, has no theory of the good. It focuses on individuals and rights, not community or the good. No view, however sincere, she contends, is seriously committed to community until its proponents are prepared to contemplate placing "the claims of society—the collectivity—as prior to the individual."[28] Fox-Genovese insists she is willing to do so but notes that hers is a lonely stance in a modern American feminism that supports a "unilateral right to personal autonomy, sexual freedom, and divorce."[29]

Her preferred alternative is quite a different image of the good life for women and men in both private and public spheres. It involves the achievement of a community-oriented society, much less burdened by rights talk and far-fetched assertions about the sovereignty of individuals, their freedom, even their bodies. This is an objective that Fox-Genovese does not expect to see soon. Given her analysis of liberalism's influence on feminist thought, she could hardly be sanguine about any quick changes.

Example One: The Family and the Feminist
Debate over the Family

The family, of course, is deeply involved in this liberal revolution that has so affected women (and men), which is why the family has undergone such a dramatic metamorphosis in recent decades. This transformation has been both a cause and an effect of the feminist revolution—part of a complex of factors no one fully comprehends now. But there is no doubt that changes in the family must be considered in tandem with the feminist revolution as a prime illustration of liberal change in the "private" sphere.

Consider that there are many more one-parent families (usually a mother and her children) today than there were in 1960. One in four children born since 1980 now lives in a one-parent household, and the figure is much higher in the African-American community, where single parents head about two-thirds of all households.[30] This situation reflects not only the pervasiveness of divorce in our society but also the steep rise in the number of women who have one or more children outside of marriage. It also reflects the equally steep jump in the number of men who do not take responsibility for their sexual behavior and its results. Today almost 30 percent of all births are to unmarried women, which represents a fourfold increase since 1965.

These sobering developments have many causes, of course, but the growth since the 1960s of a notably more individualistic ethic among Americans is one of them. Indeed, there can scarcely be any doubt that, as Michael Sandel neatly puts it, the search for "the unencumbered self" is present today everywhere in people's private lives.[31] In such an atmosphere, it is only natural that "no-fault" divorce laws have come into practice and that there is a shaky context for a secure and enduring "family."

There is no setting in which these developments have spawned more debate than in feminist intellectual circles. The debate is never about a patriarchal conception of the family. Feminists unite in opposition to patriarchy and the patriarchal family, a judgment shared by almost all public intellectuals today who engage the family question. It is the value of family as a social arrangement that is under debate. Definitions of what a family is and what it should be differ, but the feminist argument over the family is about more than definitions. There are bigger stakes here, and this fact is universally understood.

Three discernible feminist critiques of family are common. Each makes a different point, although none is incompatible with the others. Feminist separatists make one argument. They hold that the conventional family is too much a male world, although female separatist conceptions of family are often affirmed, as is the case in much lesbian writing.[32] This outlook is far from the center of feminist intellectual critiques of the family, but it lingers in the background and underlines the broader feminist uneasiness about or outright hostility toward the family. After all, for many feminist theorists of all sexual orientations the story of women past and present is an account of women's oppression and exploitation within the family. They do not propose to have this reality forgotten.

A more common feminist intellectual critique proceeds with a somewhat tempered ambivalence toward the family, although one that sometimes glides over into hostility. Its approach is familiarly American due to its pragmatic orientation. Barbara Ehrenreich, social theorist and columnist, and Linda Gordon, a leading feminist historian, illustrate this approach. Ehrenreich is characteristic because she does not repudiate the family altogether but persistently observes that women do not flourish in family situations. She argues that for women "home is the most dangerous place to be" given the spousal abuse and other oppressive conditions experienced by many wives and mothers. For her, the situation is serious, and action is

badly needed to relieve it. Since she is a state socialist, it is not surprising that she calls for government intervention to force gender
equality, provide for child welfare, and protect women from violence
in the family.[33]

Linda Gordon has made quite similar arguments, but her orientation is more historical, rooted in research specifically on women
and the family. She paints a grim picture of the historical record, and
she means her readers to understand it as exactly that. She insists
that U.S. history shows that oppression of women in the family has
often been painfully real, and no one should approach any contemporary discussion of family without acknowledging this fact.[34]

In many of these considerations the focus is on freedom and
equality for women, especially in the family. While the values defended are familiar ones in the American liberal political tradition,
the tone of the discussions is usually American radical. The realization of these values is taken to require radical change in the
American family. That apart, there is a noticeable disinterest in
these discussions in civil society. Often the family emerges as a set
of limitations or threats to women—and it is sometimes left at that.
Even the family, however defined and critiqued, frequently gets little
attention in terms of its role in civil society. Attention focuses elsewhere, on women's independence, freedom, and equality, not on
civil society. A frequent assumption, however, is that all will benefit from the adoption of this agenda: women, children, and men.

A third critical approach to the family by feminist intellectuals
is the most philosophically self-conscious. Its practitioners are often
devoted to reflection on the nature of the good community, and they
routinely describe themselves as change-oriented, often radical, although the credibility of this claim is not always obvious. While they
certainly do not agree on what a good community might be, they
do share in common criticism of the contemporary celebration of
family as a model for the good community. They maintain that given
historical experience, to envision family as a model for community
makes no sense, unless one wants to endorse a patriarchal community that has done great harm to women. Moreover, things are not
so different today that women should adopt the family idea as a
potential conception of the good community.[35]

More sympathetic feminist considerations of the family have
become common in recent years. They have been contested, of

course, especially in some feminist academic circles,[36] yet they are part of the current intellectual landscape. One approach concentrates on the fact that most women want a "family life" and need help in realizing their goal without bad consequences. Its advocates avoid discussing the family as an abstract good or bad and instead emphasize practical policies and advice. Betty Friedan's famous *Second Stage* took exactly this route. Friedan neither lauded nor castigated the family and deliberately set herself against any thinking that pitted women's equality against the family. Instead, she tried to figure out specific ways to assist women in family life. It was in this cause that she became an active proponent for the creation of an elaborate and inexpensive day care system.[37]

Sylvia Hewlett argues much more explicitly for the value of the conventional (and nonpatriarchal) contemporary family. Her main projects have been rallying support for working mothers and for the family itself, which she believes is beleaguered.[38] Along with Jean Bethke Elshtain and others, Hewlett casts doubt on how committed many fellow feminists are to women in the family. The University of Chicago's Elshtain joins her in defending the world of the nonpatriarchal family and the lives of ordinary men and women, which are lived in the context of family. She faults feminists who are hostile to the family. Some are liberal feminists whom she thinks would reduce rich and often fulfilling family lives to antiseptic relations founded on liberal contracts among equals. Others are radical feminists who she concludes hate families, or men, or both.[39]

Elshtain also takes issue with the concept that "the personal is the political" in private life, including the family. What this slogan amounts to, she believes, is a dangerous call to interpret the entire world in terms of power politics. Its emergence is a sad triumph of the pessimistic reductionism of Thomas Hobbes applied to every dimension of women's lives, including the family, childbirth, childrearing, and definitely women's bodies. There is little to existence in this conception except contest and conflict over power. Beneath such a formulation Elshtain detects signs of covert hostility to women in their family roles, roles that do not mostly concern power: women as mothers, child bearers, wives, indeed women themselves.[40]

Christine Hoff Sommers, who also describes herself as a feminist, offers a yet broader critique. For her, as she writes in *Who Stole Feminism?* the issue is not solely a matter of what she contends is the pervasive and relentless hostility toward the family among radical feminists. It is also a matter of some radical feminists' antagonism toward men, whom they frequently label as inherent oppressors and rapists. Sommers maintains that the implications of this judgment for the family are disastrous. After all, few would want to form a family with such evil people. The depressing reality, Sommers remarks, is that too much of feminism, which once aimed to help women, has been seized by extremists who care little for ordinary women and their struggles in or out of the family.[41]

These arguments over the family—the critiques of the family and the critiques of the critiques—take for granted that the family and with it the full realm of the personal or private have changed greatly since the 1960s—and changed in discernible directions. Consideration of these changes in American life and the developments in feminist intellectual thought requires us to acknowledge the vast, if incomplete, interjection of liberal norms into a world once considered (somewhat inaccurately) nonliberal. It supports the argument that liberalism has gained tremendous influence in American culture over the past four decades and hardly appears to be weakening. Even more, it suggests that liberalism is now rolling through the culture to a degree even recently unimagined.

A Second Example: Religion, Liberalism, and the Private Sphere

In the American liberal order, religion and liberalism have grown closely together until, despite the din of current controversies, they may now be as close as ever. Our social order has provided religion in general, as well as most specific religions, with large amounts of freedom. Conflicts have occurred, and continue to do so, but religious liberty is extensive and deep in the United States by almost any measure. To a large extent, this freedom is a gift of our liberal society, with its respect for the individual, for the right to (religious) liberty, and for a tolerant pluralism in religion as in much else.

On the other hand, throughout American history religion has played its role, too, by helping our liberal and pluralist society maintain some semblance of moral restraint and moral direction. This role is especially important in societies such as ours where there is both so much celebration of the individual and of individual self-esteem and a tattered or nonexistent public philosophy. Perhaps this is one reason that religion is still robust in the United States. It was Tocqueville, as we know, who first remarked on American religion's contribution in providing moral standards for society. Religion's role as a force for social integration, which is intricately tied to common moral values, remains evident today despite the fact that American religion is far more diverse than it was when Tocqueville traveled America.[42]

I describe the actual relationship between religion and liberalism in the United States as an "unconventional partnership." It reflects the fact that religion and government, private and public, have implicitly and sometimes explicitly agreed to form a sort of partnership. These are its terms: While religions in the United States often have values that conflict with the culture, they will not seriously challenge it. In return, the state will cede religion great liberty and often-considerable material support (as with the tax-exempt status of its nonprofit facilities).[43]

According to this perspective, religion is part of the "private" world and concerns personal beliefs and practices, the private religious association (church, synagogue, or mosque), and the home. This is hardly inclusive of all of religion today, involved as it often is in politics, for example, but it does describe the essence of religion for most Americans. Religion in the United States has mostly not been public or corporate in a larger national sense. In terms of religious culture Americans are largely Protestant, and American Protestantism has focused primarily on the individual in relation to God, the individual as interpreter of the Bible, and the home and church as the center of religious learning and life. Religion in the United States is mostly private, and changes in religion reflect changes in the private world.

A lot has happened in American religion over the past few decades, although none of it is really new. One important development is an acceleration of religion's continuing permeation by liberal values, a phenomenon that again affirms liberalism's success in the private world since the 1960s. Three developments in particular, each continuing today and underlining the liberal energy in religion in the United States, call for reflection: the spread of individual authority in religion (the expansion of religious individualism), the increase in religious diversity, and the expansion of market dimensions in American religion.

The evidence for the steady shifting of religious authority to the individual since the 1960s is overwhelming. Phillip Hammond has ably argued that recent decades have brought a third great religious disestablishment to the United States. The first disestablishment involved ending government-established churches in the colonies and did not end until the 1830s. The second involved the slow decline of the longtime, unofficial Protestant hegemony over the culture. This disestablishment took place over the second half of the twentieth century. As Hammond describes it, the third disestablishment involves the widespread shift to individual, personalized spirituality in our own age. This involves what Robert Bellah describes as "Sheilaism," the adoption of a subjective spirituality by individuals tailored to each person's values and needs. This third disestablishment ushers in a spirituality in which individual choices about faith and belief are what matter, not duties or rules, and certainly not dogmas or traditions established by others in the past.[44]

In effect, the argument is that individuals themselves have disestablished churches and church authority in the United States largely as a result of a marked increase in people's sense of individual autonomy since 1960. People who participate in organized religion now do so mostly on a truly voluntary basis, not from a sense of communal duty. One common result has been a substantial drop in participation in the churches that once constituted the religious mainline in America—the Episcopal, United Church of Christ, Evangelical Lutheran, and Presbyterian churches—even as the U.S. population has grown enormously. This is no accident. The mainline is exactly the realm in American organized religion where there has been the greatest acceptance of individual determination of spiritual values.

Wade Clark Roof's scholarship on the spiritual lives of the now-aging baby boomers is equally persuasive in its similar findings that religious individualism has increased greatly in American life over the last generation. The phenomenon of so many people going their own way in their spiritual journeys fascinates Roof, who notes that many Americans now acknowledge no religious authority but themselves. Moreover, his research shows that even when people worship in a traditional institutional setting their own spiritual insights and judgments are what ultimately matter to them. Some observers may wonder if this was not always the case. Roof insists that this phenomenon is considerably more widespread today, and thus religion is ever more privatized.[45]

No wonder Roof has found almost no limit to the kinds of spiritual or religious practice embraced by those who have come to adulthood since the 1960s. What exists is a vast and luxuriant spiritual pluralism that reflects more than the emergence of still more new religious groups. The fact of pluralism in American spiritual life now means that everyone has, in a real sense, their own religion—and few have many regrets about it. Roof judges, moreover, that it is the baby boomers who have set the current tone in American religion and have spread their spiritual culture far beyond their generation to the population in general.[46]

These findings are well accepted today and are confirmed by almost any survey of particular religious groups in the United States. American Jews, for example, have moved in exactly the same direction, according to data on their declining religious practice and rising intermarriage rates.[47] The same is true of American Roman Catholics, even among those who are committed to their church. This is perhaps best symbolized by Roman Catholics' enduring affection for their pope, an affection they couple with approval of individual conscience, not church authority, as supreme in religious affairs.[48]

Everywhere change is substantial. The sharp growth of interest in "community" in religious groups, including the spectacular growth of small Bible and faith-sharing groups within American religious denominations, supports this finding. So does the vitality of all sorts of parachurch groups from Promise Keepers to women-church. These groups are testimony to the individualism and lack of community that characterize many American religious settings and the arrival of more communal alternatives. They are, however, familiar in their loose and voluntary nature. The product of a reaction to liberal individualism, in practice they ask little sacrifice of liberal individualism.[49]

Another important example of liberalism's spread within American religion is the great expansion of pluralism *within* organized religion. This is quite separate from the fact that in American religion today many people consider themselves virtually a church of one. The pluralism at issue here manifests itself in several ways. One example is the continuing spread of diversity among Protestants, black and white, and especially the growth of conservative Protestant churches, particularly varieties of Baptists and independent evangelical and fundamentalist churches that either reject outright any denominational connections or maintain only casual ones. While this reflects the traditional congregational heritage of much American religion, in the present age reinforcement for this tradition exists in the cultural belief that everybody and every group should be sovereign. Another example is the rise of an increasingly pluralistic Roman Catholic Church, which a common Mass and struggling bishops barely hold together.[50]

A third example, and the most obvious, is the increasing presence of religious people other than the traditional Protestants, Catholics, and Jews. Catholic numbers—at least on the books—are holding steady or are even rising to constitute about 25 percent of the American population. They will likely continue at this level as a result of heavy immigration of Roman Catholics, especially Hispanic Catholics, and the high birthrate among Roman Catholic immigrants.[51] Jewish numbers have fallen precipitously in the last thirty years, and Jewish people now make up less than 2 percent of the U.S. population. The Protestant decline, however, has been more spectacular. Over its history, the United States has been an overwhelmingly Protestant country, yet it is no longer in terms of people's self-identification. Although the majority of Americans still declare themselves to be Protestants, that percentage is now well below 60. And plenty of other groups are expanding, such as Black Muslims, other Muslims, Buddhists, New Age adherents of Wicca, worshipers of other female deities, and other nontraditional (in the United States) religions. The variety is now truly limitless, and there is no reason to expect it to decline. Just as significant may be the growth, to perhaps 10 percent of the population, of those for whom "secular" is the best description of their (non-)religious perspective. They were hardly as common or as open before the 1960s.[52]

All of this religious pluralism testifies to the success of liberal religious tolerance and freedom even as it has eaten into the once widely shared religious consensus in the nation.[53] It has also allowed more and more groups the liberty to flourish on their own spiritual paths. There are many ways to describe the effects of this religious liberalism, but each proceeds from the reality that diversity well beyond our past experience is central to the contemporary story of American religion.

A final example of the triumph of liberalism in religion follows directly from the others already considered. It is the intensification of the competitive and market aspects of U.S. religion.[54] As some sociologists have argued, competition in "our religious economy" characterized the thirteen colonies and the early new nation as established churches and new groups each struggled to bring their form of Protestantism to Americans. It has endured between Protestants and Catholics for a century or more. And it has flared into existence with every new or newly arrived religious group in the United States.

This has not been the only pattern, since some groups, such as the modern Presbyterians and liberal Lutherans, have succeeded in ecumenical endeavors, bringing once competitive branches of Protestantism into unity. But market analysts of religion declare that such events are not signs of strength. They maintain that ecumenical victories lead soon enough to denominational decline, measured quite concretely by the numbers of members and by per capita giving.[55] On the other hand, those who enter the competition (not always openly, of course) among religious groups and between religious groups and other elements in the larger culture expand numbers and support. This is why a zest for evangelistic competition increasingly describes dynamic, growing religious communities. It is simply a practical necessity in a liberal world (of religion) where nothing is assumed, all is open, and the choices are nearly limitless.

As religion in the United States increasingly exemplifies these characteristics of liberalism, however, it faces a diminishing public role—especially in the government and public schools. Religion has become more and more exclusively a private affair, of the family, the church, the bedside, and the individual conscience.[56] This development may seem puzzling, even illogical. In part the situation reflects the simple fact that Christianity no longer has a near monopoly over all other religions in the United States. One way to deal with diverse and sometimes conflicting religions has become to send or take them all home. But other factors are also at work. Secularism grows steadily in American culture, and thus it should come as no surprise that the current situation partly reflects hostility toward any religion, especially within some elite sectors of society.[57]

Yet religion is also obviously entwined in public life today, and is indeed often directly involved in politics. Roman Catholic bishops, officials of the Nation of Islam, and Christian Coalition activists, among others, make this reality transparent. The resistance to this public role suggests the limits imposed by liberalism. As it finds itself more and more exclusively relegated to the private sides of life, religion might one day become a real alternative to liberal culture. Today, however, this possibility appears unlikely, since most American religion offers no serious and effective alternative set of values to those of the overall culture.

The most prominent exception may be the conservative Christian political movement, especially as manifested in Focus on the Family and, perhaps, the Christian Coalition. It both celebrates the family and private life and is determined to enter public life to regulate sexual and reproductive practices. Although this mix of agendas tends to be complex, confused, or both, the religious Right has become a substantial force in American religion and politics, and it is not to be confused with the pieties of conventional liberalism.

As a whole, however, organized religion in the United States resonates with liberal values and liberal culture. Most of American religion is no "enemy" to liberal values. Indeed, it represents a convincing case study of liberalism's contemporary reach, conquering religion as it has the home to a degree hardly predicted in the stormy 1960s.

Conclusion

Interpreters have drawn all sorts of startling conclusions from the advance of liberal values in the "private" aspects of American life. Sometimes they are happy about this development, but often they are not. Among the more popular analyses is the thesis that too much individualism is damaging all social structures, as is all too evident today in the United States. According to this view, such liberal individualism both reflects and encourages the painful decline in trust among the American people. One properly wonders whether we can have a collective social, political, and economic life without trust.[58]

Despite the arguments of this chapter, the thesis that liberalism has come to influence the private lives of most Americans to an unprecedented degree since the 1960s is far from self-evident. Skeptics abound. Some feminist intellectuals, for example, reject this analysis, maintaining it is not plausible given the still modest progress toward broadening women's freedom.[59] Some go further and insist that in the home (and much of the rest of the nonpublic world) patriarchy is far from dead, obviously challenging any notion of liberalism's triumph there. These contentions often dwell on power and power relations in family and organized religious life, holding that women have too little power in these key institutions of civil society.

Such a stress on power and who has it and who does not reveals the usually very liberal basis for these critiques. Indeed, intense concern with power characterizes liberal thinking in every age. Power has long been routinely feared in the liberal tradition. After all, power can limit freedom and curtail individual autonomy.[60] Thus determination to be on guard regarding power is constant, recalling the classic liberal warning: "Eternal vigilance is the price of liberty."

From other, much more conservative views, there is also skepticism about the alleged advance of liberal values into the family setting. Without regret, some conservatives have dared to contend that the family is inevitably patriarchal and always will be. Thus, they insist, despite all the intellectual chatter, there has been no essential change in family relations in recent decades.[61] Others contend that feminism has not been liberating in practice because feminist goals have led to more and more government action, resulting in less human freedom rather than more.[62] As we know, there is abundant resistance to government interference in the so-called private sphere because many citizens judge that government intrusion into their private lives reduces their liberty.

While it is true that the American family and the church have hardly dissolved in some disintegrating liberal acid, it is equally true they have become far more liberal institutions than they were before the 1960s. The situation of children illustrates this point, and with it this chapter's case ends. American children now have dramatically more personal liberty than at any time in this century, maybe more than children have had at any point in human history. There are benefits to this development, but other results are also noteworthy. Kids today are "freer" of their families than they were in 1960, but that also means they are left more to the care of others or themselves. They have more choices than ever in our "shopping mall" schools, but the end results are at best controversial. Their freedom, moreover, is associated with higher rates of youth violent crime, suicide, and drug abuse. Parents, schools, and society in general hardly have these developments in hand, despite enormous expenditures and tiresome cries of alarm. In practice, we are experiencing children's liberation, if often quite unintentionally. However one may evaluate the consequences, they suggest there is no end yet of the liberal transformation in the "private" sectors of life.

What remains a puzzle to the end, though, is the relation between liberal theory and practice in the transformation that this chapter recounts. One may identify liberal theory's expanding reach since the 1960s as a cause of the penetration of liberal practice into family and religious life; or one may argue that liberal practice has preceded and driven the theory due to the changing roles for women and the altered nature of families and religion in our era; or one may contend that these factors have worked synergistically. Which answer, if any, is best is elusive. What is clear is that intellectual thought, cultural practice, and public opinion have moved in the same direction. The shift has been toward liberal individualism to a degree that is historic in its sweep and that has meant liberal norms and practices have come to dominate in the "private" realms of American life.

Chapter Six

Community as a Point of Redirection

There is no doubt that "community" is the favored goal of many intellectuals seeking a redirection in the United States and in American political thought today. It is a word issued frequently from many intellectuals' lips, and it is ubiquitous on the printed page. Many proclaim community or increased community in one form or another as the answer to almost everything: crime, unwanted pregnancy, divorce, corruption, citizen apathy, greed, the environmental crisis. The pervasiveness of the call for community (or more or strengthened community) is an explicit declaration that something has gone wrong in much of the political and social culture of the United States. Almost always the culprit is identified as liberalism or too much liberalism. It is also, of course, another sign of the pluralism in an American thought today that is hardly a robotlike ratification of liberal values.

This chapter explores this favorite point of redirection for many American intellectuals. First it offers a working definition of the concept of community. Next it examines some influential visions of community proposed by public intellectuals today. Finally, it enters a broader discourse on community by probing critics' concerns about the current enthusiasm for community. For there are critics, although they must be distinguished from those whose unhappiness about the absence of "community" in the United States is really a complaint that their version of community is not ascendant.

An obvious but essential way to start is to take a look at contemporary ideas of community, but that is possible only after we establish a somewhat formal definition. Fortunately, many of the current invocations of community reflect widely shared understandings of the concept, however much nuances may vary. To indicate that agreement and avoid the sometimes astonishing application of the word *community* to almost every ideal proposed in American thought, I offer a working definition. My goal is to provide at least some analytical clarity.[1]

Community here will refer to a strong, self-conscious sharing relationship among people, whatever the setting (small groups or nation-states) and whatever the groups (those formed ascriptively by birth, such as racial groups, or those whose members choose each other). The word *strong* is vital to the definition. Community involves people who have a robust or often intense commitment to each other. A casual, not to say accidental, gathering of people is no community. Individuals whose paths routinely cross every week, every day, or even every hour do not necessarily constitute a community either. Self-consciousness is similarly essential. For a community to exist, its members must possess a sense of their mutual bonds. Thus a legal entity is not a community unless it is really united—self-consciously so.[2]

The Broad Appeal

The depth of appeal of this common enough understanding of community among public intellectuals in the United States is remarkable. Perhaps Harvard's Michael Sandel is currently the best example of a prominent voice calling for increased community in the United States and an important critic of contemporary liberalism on behalf of that cause. His recent, best-selling work, *Democracy's Discontent: America in Search of a Public Philosophy*, devoted to this cause, has received wide national attention.[3] Sandel begins his argument with a historical analysis, contending that throughout U.S. history and especially over the past sixty years liberal individualism, individual rights, an "unencumbered" model of the human person, and a system of government concerned more with procedures than with the common good have overwhelmed any national adherence to the value of community.

According to Sandel, the result has been extensive and unnecessary human unhappiness among the American people. This unhappiness, he claims, follows predictably from the evident deterioration of local and civic community in the United States. It is inevitable because people want community, which helps them realize themselves as fulfilled, happy human beings. Simultaneously there has been a sad decline of citizenship as people have turned away from an alienating public realm; this too, Sandel insists, has damaged both individuals and the nation.

Sandel claims that national economic policies are a major factor in the kinds of citizenship we have encouraged. He specifically blames the New Deal and its romance with Keynesian economics for speeding the nation on its way toward having a population of citizens far more devoted to individual consumerism than to civic involvement and concern for the common good. This model of citizenship, he believes, is now totally in control. People care mostly about consumerism and dreams of economic growth, which means that materialism rules, a materialism that has corrupted other realms of American life as well.

It is in light of these developments that Sandel makes his famous argument for the recovery of a republican character for the American nation and among our citizens. What this means for him is that there is a profound need to facilitate a social order that makes the common good its first objective and people's particular material and selfish wants a distinct second. To do so, Sandel maintains, we must address issues focusing on how to foster this kind of character in citizens. Sandel is not particularly naive. He understands that under the present circumstances the creation of the kind of public-spirited people he favors will not be easy. A republican character will not suddenly blossom after a course or two in high school or at the local college or technical institute. The best way to teach such character, he is convinced, is through experiences that lead people to become "situated beings," persons who have connections, responsibilities, and duties—in short, community—in their lives.[4] But Sandel's advice to create community in order to create community is obviously of somewhat limited value.

Readers of Sandel discover that, in fact, he—like many others—is not sure how to fashion his ideal of character or community. One reason is exactly his appreciation that reaching the goals he yearns for promises to be a challenging, complex, even tortuous, affair. Sandel possesses a certain modesty or mildness—perhaps to his credit—that infuses most of what he says. His historical analysis is sweeping, and he has his moments of romantic fancy (such as his near adoration of

Robert F. Kennedy), but the particular analyses he offers on contemporary issues are more reflective and cautious than bold or confident. This has become obvious in Sandel's occasional columns in the *New Republic,* where he has taken the opportunity to grapple with contemporary issues. There his grand objective of achieving a republican community fades before thoughtful, nuanced analyses that are likely to send few marching anywhere.[5]

Sandel's voice for community—and his critique of the price of contemporary and historical liberalism—is hardly a lonely one. A host of fellow public intellectuals share much of his vision, although few equal his eloquence in any setting. From a much more philosophical perspective, for example, Alasdair MacIntyre urges adherence to the value of community. MacIntyre is steeped in ancient Greek philosophy and Christian values and experience, and he draws on both to suggest what community might look like if it unfolds as he would wish. For MacIntyre, real community must accord above all with practices that relate to shared human experience. There is no point in thinking about it as an abstraction because communities will always be about shared experiences. Community—more properly, communities—are journeys and involve changing practices as we learn from each other and what the past has to teach us. Thus, although the past can provide no answer about community or potential communities, it can offer some practical wisdom derived from past practice of communities. This is wisdom that only fools would ignore, including the understanding that community is integral to the human experience.[6]

One more example illustrates the widespread interest in community among public intellectuals today. Consider the mature perspectives of a longtime proponent of community, sociologist Philip Selznick.[7] For him community would be a democracy devoted to the common good and infused with a shared and sharing spirit. As something of a realist, Selznick is acutely conscious of the dangers and complexities of a communal democracy, a consciousness that he reveals often and which is by no means always evident among some others. Thus Selznick recognizes the necessity of a governing norm of civility in a communal democracy; for encouraging what he describes as moral competence for community living (which includes learning to bear with the complexity of moral existence); for developing a historical awareness so valuable for any community's sense of itself; and for teaching individuals how to be community-oriented, self-respecting, and self-preserving.

The beauty of Selznick's considerations on community democracy is that he sees issues and challenges in terms that are not easily reduced to formulas, slogans, or empty praises of "community." In this he sets a high standard for all proponents of the community ideal. Yet Selznick holds out hope in the possibility of realizing public community, a hope that in his case trumps the pessimism of critics and his own sense of "realism."

As these three examples attest, the chorus of intellectual voices calling for community is both diverse and extensive. It is also routinely optimistic about the chances for creating community, despite sometimes sophisticated analyses and occasionally authentic skepticism. It is clear that characteristic American optimism abounds even among those who present themselves as the most sober and reflective advocates of community such as social theorist Amy Gutmann. She is convinced that it is possible to have both genuine democracy involving substantive citizen participation and concern for the common good if citizens are successfully taught to be part of an authentic "deliberative democracy." In her happy view, the result can be the growth of a democratic public philosophy as well as individual and communal autonomy.[8]

The setting for the calls for community is a universe of almost endless complaints about liberalism. These complaints are often central to public intellectuals' discourse on the revival of community in the United States. Many community-oriented public intellectuals normally define their visions of community through these critiques—to the extent they go beyond the fuzzy affirmations that too often characterize contemporary invocations of "community."[9]

The Common Complaints

Among the common complaints about liberalism, the most important is that contemporary liberalism is too individualistic in principle and in practice. Critics bemoan the consequences, viewed in almost any light by an almost infinite set of measures. In this context, for example, they recall Tocqueville's worry about the potential for lonely individualism in the United States and contend that his fear has become reality. So many individuals are now "shut up in the solitude of their own heart."[10]

In their book *Habits of the Heart*, sociologist Robert Bellah and his associates cite considerable evidence confirming this analysis: many Americans, for example, so value individual autonomy that they fail at intimate relationships, especially marriage, which require compromise of their egoism. They report that many marriage counselors also stress the importance of autonomy so much that they unintentionally undermine marriages and the institution of marriage, while supposedly endeavoring to save them.[11]

The Bellah team identifies the process of growing up in the United States as another of the costs of American individualism. Youths maturing in the United States quickly learn the importance of becoming one's own individual person, and they are encouraged to believe that they can create themselves as individuals quite apart from their families and backgrounds. Many people try to repeat the process and "re-create" themselves—sometimes over and over—in their later lives, too. Each attempt is a statement of the conviction that individualism and individual choice are more important than anything else.[12]

Whatever community we do encounter in the United States, the Bellah group suggests, is superficial. At most it is no more than a series of "lifestyle enclaves," which ask little serious commitment from their denizens, who freely move in and out as they individually wish. Other critics make the same point and dismiss most contemporary expressions of community as shallow and hardly meriting the name of community.[13] The fashionable phrase is "thin communities," meaning that the commitment and sharing involved amount to precious little. The desire, not the duty, of an individual "member" is what counts. Any sense of the whole disappears into a remote background.[14]

Bellah and his associates, however, do have hope as well as complaint about America's liberal society. Their intensive study of a white middle-class United States reveals, they argue, that beneath the liberal language of individualism lies a second language of community struggling to express itself. For them, this finding is good news in a society where they believe community is far too submerged in theory and practice. The challenge people face, they suggest, is how to help the language of community—that is, people's semihidden affection for community—emerge to take a much larger place in America's collective life.[15]

In *The Good Society*, Bellah and associates consider the outlines of what an escape from the pernicious individualism of present-day society might look like.[16] They do so in the context of their continuing critique of liberalism and especially liberal institutions, including business, the courts, the schools, and organized religion. The problem is, however, that what they have in mind does not amount to anything specific. Their complaints continue to abound, but beyond affirming their desire for a public and highly participatory community, there is little else, including little about how to accomplish their ideal.

Providing such guidance would be hard, of course, perhaps even impossible today. After all, what the Bellah group really wants is a radical transformation of the American individual and American society toward a communal order concentrating on the civic and common good. What that might look like and how to get there are hardly obvious. What Bellah and his team are not vague about is their sense of urgency. The United States is headed down a disastrous path away from community, and it desperately needs a sharp change in direction.

From all sides, the idea that individualism crowds out most else receives (negative) reinforcement. Daniel Kemmis's emphasis is on the rootlessness of people in the United States. Like Tocqueville, Kemmis notes how people today often choose a restless individualism over a sense of "place," and thus fail to make community possible.[17] David Wells observes that in this world, in which the individual supersedes all else, the essential place to be is before the TV. For many people it has become their only friend and their (inauthentic) community.[18]

A closely related phenomenon is the cult of self-esteem. Although it has swept through educational and pop psychology circles in the United States, the self-esteem movement frequently provokes skepticism from many community-oriented intellectuals. This is especially the case when self-esteem or the lack of self-esteem is used to explain virtually everything, while the depressing statistics on youth educational failure, crime, and suicide do not go away. Some critics consider the focus on self-esteem a problem because it is just another depressing sign of an obsessive concentration on individuals and individualism in our time. Self-esteem is fine in its place, but critics insist that it is no substitute for the community we also need, which excessive self-esteem can easily impede.[19]

For others, the problem is mostly about citizens who are without a moral or religious anchor rather than America's romance with individualism and individuals, although the two are regularly linked. In this mode a standard claim is that of J. Budziszewski, who maintains that the United States is in serious shape, since it increasingly denies the reality that every viable community must ultimately rest on religious truth. For him, there are really two community stories in the United States today. One centers on the liberal "community," which is bereft of any serious and shared truth. He suspects that this is the (thin) kind of community that many public intellectuals calling for more community really have in mind. The second is what he favors, a quite different conception of community whose denominating characteristic is a grounding in shared adherence to higher law.

Budziszewski insists that his community can proceed from more than one religious foundation, but he also knows that no successful community can try to be, as any "liberal" community does, all things to all people. One must choose which of the two models of community is correct and not fool oneself that such a choice can be finessed: "There is no other way."[20] Community without sure grounding is like liberalism without grounding. It is neither true nor in the long run practical.

For many left-leaning political intellectuals, on the other hand, it is America's adherence to liberal capitalism that poses the greatest impediment to the flowering of community. In the decade or two after the 1960s, direct attacks on capitalism as a system impeding community (among other goals) were common in American intellectual life. The worldwide decline of Marxism and the collapse of the former Soviet Union and its satellites in Eastern Europe, however, have led to less interest in this direct confrontational approach. Support for a more participatory democracy that would achieve control over capitalist enterprises or capitalism as a system has become the normal, toned-down substitute approach today. Its bottom line is no different, however: capitalism is the problem, and its control is the best single means to much greater human community.[21]

Robert Bellah and his team of scholars, for example, are among those convinced that what they call "neocapitalism" frustrates the flowering of community in American society. At one point they had predicted we might soon see the emergence of either an egalitarian democracy that was much more of a community (as they hoped) or a state where bureaucrats ruled (as they feared). Now they acknowledge that liberalism and neocapitalism have proved far more robust than they had expected—to the detriment of the growth of community.[22]

Varieties of Community as Redirection

At times the only commonalities in the community movement appear to be the vague appeals for more "community" and the barrage of criticisms of liberal values and/or liberal society. Yet this is not the full picture. Some in the community movement are committed to considering what the specific dimensions of a good community might look like. This development represents a welcome maturing of the discourse on community, although on this subject there is still much to be done.

At present, there are several main visions of community, which this chapter addresses, but there is considerably more evidence of the centrality of community in contemporary intellectual thought. Thus community is an integral feature both in environmental thought and in many conceptions of civil society, as the next several chapters indicate. The engagement with community must be understood less as one redirection than as many redirections. A great focus on the community idea is found everywhere in political thought today. *Community* is the watchword of the hour—and often it is less an expression of an alternate consensus than a yearning for rediscovery of consensus.

Inclusive Community

I describe one important approach to community today as "inclusive community." Its advocates concentrate on reaching out to, caring for, and including all people, building an inclusive brotherhood and sisterhood that has deep and loving roots. Its proponents sometimes have a specific policy agenda and sometimes pursue their vision through a historical lens. They rarely prepare detailed models of community. For them, community is first and last about a spirit of human caring and inclusivity, and everything else must follow from that vision.

Amitai Etzioni has espoused this inclusive orientation in his crusade for the "new communitarianism" both in his writing and as an organizer of others who share "community" outlooks. Etzioni is no partisan of a particular outline of the one, best community so much as he is devoted to bringing together enthusiasts for community of all sorts to discuss the policy and institutional dynamics needed to edge the United States closer to community. His works in the 1990s, such as *The New Golden Rule: Community and Morality in a Democratic Society, Rights and the Common Good: The Communitarian Perspective,* and *Communitarian Thinking: New Essays,* demonstrate his impressive commitment.[23]

Etzioni also well illustrates inclusive communitarians' episodic interest in "policy applications" as part of the process of moving forward.[24] He has ideas about public education and the family as effective communities, support for national service for youth, a rejuvenated political system with publicly financed elections, improved debates among candidates, and reducing the role of political action committees in the political system—but he is careful to propose no exact blueprints.[25]

Joan Tronto, another inclusive community thinker, is interested in developing a public philosophy—and a corresponding society—directed to a community built on the principle of an "ethics of care." This is no abstract or sentimental goal for Tronto, although she also is not in business of offering detailed blueprints for the ideal community. Rather, hers is an orientation and an ethics which, she argues, must bring all people within the embrace of a community of care. As a philosopher, Tronto makes a vigorous case for her vision of community, confident that it can be justified and satisfied with its ethic of care.[26]

Wilson Carey McWilliams's *Idea of Fraternity in America* remains the premier post-1960s expression of an inclusive model of community. McWilliams proceeds by reflecting on U.S. historical experience as he considers both theory and practice in his often elegant and frequently detailed discussions of "fraternity" in our historical and literary journey. His goal is not to propose specific models of community or detailed policies that would somehow get people closer to a desirable community. It is to take his readers through their nation's history and show them where inclusive community and its advocates have enriched their society—and where other less desirable stories may also be encountered.

McWilliams believes that fraternity (community) "is a perennial need" of human beings. We all want it, and a good community will necessarily include us all. This conviction allows him to be unusually free of the angst that darkens some other arguments on this topic.[27] For McWilliams, fraternity is natural to us, and pessimism about its future makes no sense. McWilliams is no naive optimist, and he does not expect a quick revival of the fraternity that he judges is so lacking in the United States. To think otherwise, he believes, he would have to ignore the influence of the liberal tradition, which, as McWilliams mournfully notes, has aimed "to discard fraternity as a . . . norm in everyday political and social life."[28] Unfortunately, today we are experiencing something of a reenactment of the eighteenth-century liberal Enlightenment, which understood people "imperfectly," "fraternal relations" among them "little or not at all."[29]

McWilliams recognizes that fraternity was a lot more robust among seventeenth-century Puritans or in the thought of Thomas Jefferson than it is now. Yet his confidence that a spirit of community is not lost forever is grounded firmly in his understanding of an American history that has sometimes involved community and the unending need for human solidarity. After all, we cannot lose part of ourselves forever.[30]

McWilliams, like Michael Sandel, is no conservative, and yet he has little enthusiasm for much of modern "liberal progress." This includes the New Deal, which set an unfortunate example for the decades that have followed. For McWilliams, the New Deal did not increase community in the United States. It was more about controlling the economic and national environment and the relationship between masses and leadership in the American system than it was about fostering an inclusive fraternity. The decades since then have seen the same unfortunate pattern repeated.[31]

Community as a National Democracy

Another approach that has attracted public intellectuals seeking community focuses on realizing a national democratic community. According to this view, real community is primarily about a national self-government devoted to the common good and a citizenry united in support of this kind of state. It is not primarily concerned with "care" or "fraternity" or with creating small-group communities or participatory democracy. Some public intellectuals attracted to this vision do stress the importance of instantiating a democratic public philosophy in and for the nation as a whole. They trust that this public philosophy will help citizens unite in serious pursuit of the shared, national public good, which is their image of community.

Michael Lind emerged in the 1990s as the most assertive proponent of a national conception of community. In a series of books and articles, he argues assertively for a "new nationalism" for the United States.[32] Lind has in mind the fostering of a new spirit of national purpose—democratic national purpose—that will involve unashamed use of the central government to promote the sense of national community and whatever public policies that advance what may be the common good.

Moving toward this goal has led Lind to abandon his former allegiance to political conservatism—"up from conservatism" is his label for his political journey.[33] He recognizes now that most of American conservatism is really libertarian and quite hostile to the national state. There is little sense in contemporary conservatism of much beyond a certain flag-waving patriotism that adds up to the kind of collective national community that Lind believes is so important. There are exceptions, without doubt, in conservative circles, but Lind has no interest in such projects as Christian nationalism or the effusions of the fiery Patrick Buchanan.

Lind's frank support for a national community is interesting and has provoked discussion in the community movement, but his inclination toward a Hamiltonian perspective causes uneasiness among some who are sympathetic toward a national democratic perspective.[34] One issue is how much democracy, and of what kind, actually figures into Lind's picture. Equally problematic is Lind's unapologetic endorsement of nationalism. Talk of nationalism stirs discomfort among many public intellectuals, but Lind considers them timorous souls dreaming about kinds of community that are unlikely to transform the nation and its citizenry.

Barbara Ehrenreich, a columnist for the left-leaning *Nation*, takes quite another approach in search of a democratic national community. She does not see herself as a nationalist in Lind's sense, nor does she warm to rallying other nationalist energies for her cause. But she is interested neither in celebrations of little, hand-holding communities nor in vapid intellectual affirmations of "community." She is convinced that community must be a national democratic experience, however, and she is fond of emphasizing that hard choices will be necessary to reach such an objective. Tough-mindedness will be needed, something she knows is often in short supply in discussions about the glories of "community."

Thus this active writer, who is also a columnist for *Time* magazine, favors what she calls "a tough-minded" communitarianism, one that faces the structural problems that stand in the way of community and avoids pleasant, escapist dreams about community "coziness." What this means for Ehrenreich is that it will be impossible to move toward community without challenging capitalism and establishing government management of the economy, including tight regulation of corporations and corporate behavior. For Ehrenreich, unchecked capitalism is the principal structure preventing the development of community in the United States.[35]

Community as Participatory Democracy

Other public intellectuals continue to define community largely in terms of the practice of participatory democracy, although they often also address broader conceptions of community and democracy. Those for whom community is above all participatory democracy represent a strong voice in the contemporary discourse on community, one on which the influence of the 1960s remains potent.

Like other approaches, the participatory model has its theorists and its practitioners, who are the "builders of the dawn."[36] Naturally, there are many variations—and inevitable disagreements—in the movement, but it is united in its self-definition, affirming the value of local democratic participation, mutual interdependence, and devotion to the common good as central to its community vision.[37]

There is also a distinct egalitarian side to many participatory communitarians, including a sympathy for economic equality and an ill-disguised antagonism toward capitalism. Sometimes their argument is the practical claim that a thoroughgoing egalitarianism is necessary to realize a living participatory democracy and a vibrant community. Sometimes it is a philosophical argument for the equal moral worth of all persons. Following both arguments, many participatory communitarians insist that community cannot exist without abolishing or severely restricting capitalism.[38]

Some who share sympathy for a participatory community are increasingly interested in issues of land use and land development that they believe embody some of the practical challenges and possibilities confronting their hopes for community. From this direction have come attacks on affluent homogeneous residential communities that deliberately isolate themselves from other people. Their critics judge these so-called gated communities to be elitist and dangerously nonpublic arrangements. They offer a bad model of community because they appear to be more about building a "fortress" than creating a genuine, interactive, and egalitarian community.[39]

The history of the participatory model goes back at least to the "polis state," Athens in the fifth century B.C.E.[40] What can be gleaned from that history is very much a matter of debate. Derek Phillips's recent feisty book, *Looking Backward,* has sparked considerable controversy on this subject. He suggests that much less community existed in the past than some present-day enthusiasts imagine. He also insists that most of what community did exist was highly authoritarian and often downright despotic, as the few imposed on the many for the sake of the few.

In particular, Phillips scoffs at the idea that the colonial and Revolutionary eras in the United States were especially communal, despite the frequent claim of contemporary "republican" and communitarian analysts. He asserts that classical Greece and the Middle Ages were no great eras of community either. The conflicts, as well as the oppression surrounding historical communities, too often disappear in alternative, more romantic analyses, Phillips observes, because their authors choose to praise a vision of community that exists in their minds rather than in historical experience."[41]

Alan Ehrenhalt's *Lost City* has sparked controversy on just this point.[42] Ehrenhalt's fond description of Chicago and its suburbs in the 1950s endorses the idea that the United States was decidedly more community-oriented in that era than it is today. While Ehrenhalt denies indulging in nostalgia, the reader of Derek Phillips will wonder. Certainly Ehrenhalt's conclusions are didactic. Using the 1950s as his base of comparison, he blasts contemporary Americans as "hyperindividualists" who have opted for a "worship of choice" above everything else.[43]

Phillips is hardly the first intellectual to remark that much of the community movement today is nostalgic for a past that may never have existed. But nostalgia is far from the entire story here. The question that matters is really a normative one. Whatever the past, should the United States move toward greater community today, and, if so, what would that mean? Of course, historical experience is relevant here, but those communitarians who consider themselves well grounded in the contemporary empirical world deny that community must be only a nostalgic dream. Some of their arguments are sophisticated and plausible.[44] Some are sadly in error.[45]

Among the host of public intellectuals attracted to participatory democracy as community in recent decades, two receive some attention here. Sheldon Wolin and John Dryzek are two very different voices, but each is an influential spokesperson for his variant on the common ideal. Over the past four decades Wolin, more than anyone else, has been an untiring and passionate advocate of participatory democracy as community. At Berkeley and at Princeton, Wolin argued for a vastly more egalitarian, participatory, and public life for Americans and for America. His classic study of the history of political theory, a splendid work on the subject, complemented his accounts of "the Berkeley rebellion" of the 1960s, both somewhat indirect meditations on his ideal.[46] Wolin's numerous public lectures over the years—famous efforts to advance the same goal—were invariably electric in their intensity and passionate in their conviction.

Wolin demonstrated little interest in the specifics of a participatory community. He offered little policy advice either. His main interest was arguing the moral worth of the participatory community ideal and attacking the moral failures of liberalism, liberal individualism, and capitalism. These attacks were predictable, if rarely rivaled in their sharpness. But sometimes Wolin's critiques have been controversial within his left-leaning intellectual world. This was especially true of his dismissal of postmodern theorists. For Wolin, they are false allies who repeatedly turn out to be elitists and rarely make much effort to repress their manifest contempt for the average person's grasp of the contemporary world. Wolin has also argued that many postmodern intellectuals do little for the cause of democratic community—or anything else. About all they have to offer is a politically enervating skepticism.[47]

The work of John Dryzek is as coolly analytical as Wolin's has been passionately inspired. It also illustrates how some recent participatory democrats have avoided being retreads of past perspectives. Dryzek's case for so-called discourse democracy tries to move the participatory ideal from the realms of faith and nostalgia toward a rational objective argued for in lucid reason. For the postmodern Dryzek this objective is possible only if communitarians abandon claims about objective reason, natural laws, or other so-called truths. The answer does not lie in illusory absolute truths; that itself is part of the argument for participatory community. A good participatory community must function by employing an Aristotelian practical reason, interactive discussion, and an openness to "relentless critique," which is exactly what is needed in the contemporary world to overcome the impractical and the foolish.[48]

In his tightly analytical manner Dryzek has thought through how participatory democracy could best function in practice in a postmodern world. The results have garnered considerable favorable attention. Among the good reasons for this response is the fact that Dryzek's effort has put the need to employ practical wisdom and argue seriously and rationally for participatory community on the agenda. For him, emotional or nostalgic or grand affirmations will not do.[49]

Communities as Small Groups

In the last decade or two, much of the action regarding community has followed a different road than that marked out by advocates of national community or participatory democracy. Those visions retain disciples, but their accent on public citizens fits less and less the direction of American culture, in which ideals involving citizenship are no longer much in fashion.

As numerous social scientists have reported, the most common community-oriented activities in the United States today involve participation in small groups in civil society. Few of these groups are political, and few have any connection with the broader public life of the nation. As the sociologist Robert Wuthnow observes, much of this interest in small-group community is manifested in volunteer groups, self-help groups, religious gatherings, and the myriad of other small groups that are part of many people's day-to-day lives. Whatever their form, these groups are the ordinary practical expression of today's impulse toward community in the United States.[50]

There is a therapeutic purpose to many of these small communities, whatever their formal telos. Their real subject is their members' lives, joys, and struggles, shared as community. This is obvious—and intentional—in the support groups that exist for almost every imaginable condition or problem or experience past, present, or future and to which millions of people in the United States belong. Estimates now place 40 percent of Americans in one or more such groups. Moreover, the number of such small-group communities and the size of their membership continue to expand, covering everything from alcohol abuse to quilt making and a great deal in between. They are everywhere, offering more and more opportunities for people to share their interests, feelings, hopes, and disappointments.[51]

Some participatory community advocates who recognize what is happening argue that whole neighborhoods can replicate the value that individuals receive from their small-group participation. They propose, for example, that inner-city neighborhoods could benefit enormously from the creation of small communities—especially among their youth. The context is the belief that community is a basic need for all human beings and the realization that the family community is in tatters in inner cities. The fear is that more and more inner-city youths will find the community they require in gangs. Detailed suggestions for building youth communities often follow, complete with a recognition that success in neighborhood small-group communities will require serious commitment, leadership, and genuine regard for youth.[52]

Of course most small-group communities are not primary communities. They are not the community of family or of job, and they are rarely at the core of people's lives. In some cases they are quite far from it. Ann Swidler perceptively notes that most of these communities also pose no serious challenge to unchecked individual liberty.[53] They are about community, but easy or thin community. People can and do come and go in these "communities," and often the communities themselves come and go. Yet these thin communities should not be taken lightly. They obviously matter a great deal to many of their members, and they signal the desire for community in the contemporary United States.

Spiritual Models of Community

The renewed interest in spiritual communities is another popular expression of the search for community today. This phenomenon is now widely evident in mainstream American religion. Two-thirds of all small groups in the United States, in fact, are connected to a church or synagogue. Many are Bible study groups, but others meet for prayer, religious devotions, or a meal and fellowship, and often include a personal-spiritual dimension.[54]

The growth of spiritual communities, however, takes place in many other settings as well, ones that are less traditional but of increasing importance, such as groups involved in the worship of nature and/or goddesses.[55] This development is no great surprise. The freedom some U.S. citizens experience fails to provide meaning or morality, not to mention community, which concerns spiritual communities address. Thus spiritual communities are flourishing everywhere in almost every conceivable form in America, exactly what one might expect in our liberal culture.

At the same time, many of these communities are loose, allow easy access and departure, and constitute only one part of the pluralistic lives of most of their members. These factors make most of these groups predictable expressions of community in a largely liberal and individualistic culture because they do not threaten to provide "too much" community. Moreover, they often also propound an image of a comforting God (or goddess) who loves, supports, forgives, and does not obsess over sin or sinners. In this way, too, spiritual communities commonly mark the low demands of most communities in liberal America.[56]

Some social scientists and intellectuals are fascinated by the question of the putative effects of spiritual community on the larger soci-

ety. This interest is in the venerable tradition of Tocqueville's assertion that religion was integral to a viable community in the United
States. One obvious example of the same sentiment today is found in
Richard John Neuhaus's argument in his book *The Naked Public Square*
as well as in his journal, *First Things*.[57] In both Neuhaus maintains that
religion has played an immense part in structuring—and sustaining—
the values of American democracy, especially respect for every person and for the common good of the whole community. This is why
he laments the persistent efforts of some intellectuals to drive all religion from public life. The result, he charges, will be an empty public
square, open only to selfish, secular interests that have little regard
for American democracy or its values.

Kenneth Grasso and Robert Hunt also recognize this danger.[58]
Catholic allies in the same cause as Neuhaus, they describe the
American public community as a shambles today in good part because it is no longer grounded in spiritual (read Catholic Christian)
values. While they oppose establishment of religion in any form,
their goal is a "stable consensus" on values connected with "transcendent moral and political truth."[59] Liberal efforts to substitute
"neutrality" and proceduralism, they assure their readers, will not
work. The United States has become a nation of such moral pluralism and relativism that the public square has degenerated into "a
very dangerous place."[60]

At quite another level, there is interest in the more local and
individual benefits that small-group spiritual communities might
generate. Thus there are storytellers who offer inspiring tales of
grassroots spiritual communities, communities that can make a difference, as Mary Ann Hinsdale and her colleagues report in *It
Comes from the People*.[61] Their story is about the town of Ivanhoe,
Virginia, and people there who lived biblical community in humble
locations under trying circumstances. For Hinsdale and her coauthors the lessons about local community and a growing faith are
the most important one could learn. They are lessons embedded
in the experience of real people struggling toward a tangible, godly
community.

Kathleen Norris's more personal meditations, reflecting on her
own spiritual journey, are yet another expression of a similar disposition. Her considerations on life in *Dakota*, and with Benedictines
in a monastery, have brought her acclaim as a spiritual guide. For

her, the mystical spiritual journey she has undertaken is intrinsically about community in complicated and many-layered ways—community with God, with oneself, with others, and with nature. It is also about a kind of healing that grants wholeness the chance it rarely has in the pressured world most people know today.[62]

Everywhere, it seems, there are spiritual conceptions of community, indications of the search for community among intellectuals and others in the United States. Yet there are also voices of doubt—even from within. Glenn Tinder's essays, especially *Community: Reflection on a Tragic Ideal*, are the most poignant and compelling illustrations.[63] For Tinder, spiritually grounded community is at once something religious people like himself must seek and an objective that will forever escape their reach. Moreover, he warns, efforts to achieve community, no matter what kind, often become unspeakably costly, even in human lives. This situation is doubly sad, he laments, because the costs are incurred in a cause that will inevitably fail. Such ironies abound for Tinder, although they do not lessen his certitude that humans should strive for community, nor his influence among public intellectuals concerned with community. He is a key, if pessimistic, friend of the movement, another example of a public intellectual meditating on spiritual community in American political thought and life.

Communities of Tradition

Attention to communities that adhere to one or another tradition is less frequent in intellectual discourse on community as a redirection in the United States. Yet there is much interest in versions of this conception of community too, especially in some branches of American conservatism. One variety concentrates on traditional communities in civil society such as the family, the neighborhood, and the place of worship as the fitting places to encourage community in a society that has nearly drowned in too much liberal individualism. This is the most common form of traditionalist community endorsed as often on the stump as in the study.

Traditional communitarians agree that we face a serious crisis of community in the United States, but community as they normally understand it is a slow-growing entity, proceeding organically from whatever exists according to the somewhat mysterious dynamics of human social life. As traditionalist communitarian Russell Kirk described that process, community unfolds naturally over time, and government planning—or a supposedly rational market—cannot simply create a community.[64] For many traditionalists, this is why they want to work with local communities that already exist, however weak or attenuated they may be. At least they provide a place to start.

This persuasion separates traditionalists from those who also have an affection for the local and traditional but are committed to state action to fight sprawl, enforce historic preservation, and altogether use government to regulate land use to sustain or rebuild community.[65] For traditionalist community advocates such efforts are misbegotten from the start. Their focus is properly local, often on the neighborhood, but they operate with a serious misunderstanding of community. Traditionalists insist that human will cannot create community and that government certainly cannot. The best individuals and groups can do to nourish community is to provide it with good support and then step back.

Nourish is an appropriate verb for this context, since traditionalists hold that community involves organic relationships, not those crafted by human artifice. No one has articulated this judgment more effectively than sociologist Robert Nisbet, whose observations on community were complicated, reflecting the complexity that community so embodied. Nisbet had no interest in routine "conservative" or Burkean affirmations of community; the subject was both more important and more intriguing than that. In his work, community was both mysterious and rational, strong and vulnerable, organic and yet able to be supported. It was important to study community, as Nisbet did, even as it was also beyond the busy energies of typical sociological reformers.[66]

Conclusion

Public intellectuals who explore the alternative of community in the United States are not all believers. There are skeptics and critics, too. Some are sober, carefully weighing and considering the issues in an intentionally reflective approach. This describes, for example, the meditations of political theorist Stephen Macedo.[67] In the face of contemporary community enthusiasms, he steps back and suggests praising the liberal virtues, including commitment to rational ethical analysis in public life. Macedo hopes for what he calls a "liberal settlement" on public issues if we are rational and honor moderation, individual respect, and democratic equality among all citizens. In such a liberal order, people will not be treated as creatures of obsessive self-interest, nor will they be misunderstood as persons who operate solely by moral principles. What is needed is balance in assessing human beings—complicated as we are—just as thoughtful balance is needed in public life.

Macedo favors a kind of liberal community, which he interprets as a public world that is open; shares a basic morality, commitment to rationality, and thoughtfulness; and shows concern for human sympathy and justice. What he does not want is any community that undertakes to transform life into an intense or radical experience of mutual sharing. For Macedo, reflective balance, measured rationality, and acceptance of the complexities of liberal politics—and liberal community—are a far better alternative than the follies of radical communitarianism.

Many skeptics are quite explicit in their fears that uncritical enthusiasts for community overlook its tendency to impose excessive human costs on its participants. They concentrate on the record of oppression that they assert the inauguration of serious community has historically brought with it. Often enough, as Peter Berger famously reminded his readers, the attempt to reach community has failed despite a huge effort, leaving as its legacy terrible and hideous human costs—"pyramids of sacrifice."[68] Even when community is not about great experiments, critics' fears linger. They contend that building even the smallest community may and often does require considerable sacrifice of personal freedom and must be viewed with caution. This concern, one should add, can annoy communitarians. To many, it seems needless and almost bizarrely out of context. No one denies that some attempts at community have gone tragically wrong and resulted in ghastly oppression, but that can happen with any ideal—and has.

The question is, Why is there such great fear? Why should it be assumed that moving toward community will *likely* result in unacceptable authoritarianism? After all, few public intellectuals enlisted in the community effort seek such an outcome. They stoutly insist that they oppose any reckless "majoritarianism," much less "authoritarianism," and can observe dryly that in contemporary America too much communitarianism is hardly our problem.[69] More than a few, moreover, believe that the potential of community to increase freedom among people now overwhelmed and oppressed by liberalism or liberal capitalism gets far too little attention.

Other critics concentrate on what they understand as the vapid and utopian nature of many "community" ideas. Historian Wilfred McClay writes of the Bellah community ideal that its proponents "envision strong personal morality without the taint of discipline or intolerance, strong communal and civic values without insularity or particularism, strong commitments without sanctions against those who disdain them."[70] For McClay and others, "community" often turns out to be an ideal that is just a "wish list," amounting to little more than "insubstantial word combinations, wholly without plausible historical precedent."[71]

The subject of community also is much debated in public intellectual discourse on the "politics of identity." Frank opposition to some forms of community is now a fact of life among identity theorists—even as they support the idea of ethnic, racial, or gender communities. Iris Marion Young warns that naive enthusiasm for a national community can result in a substantial loss of group identity. She is particularly concerned for groups now struggling to achieve their identity after a long time in the shadow of white male hegemony in the United States. For her, community sounds nice, but if it involves some kind of national consensus it will in practice lead to a loss of freedom for struggling groups.[72]

Whereas Linda Nicholson is uncomfortable about unrestrained claims of group identity because they sometimes imply a denial of the broader human community, she is quick to argue that identity movements have been a democratizing force, bringing neglected peoples into the human community. For her, the goal is to have both a general community and the preservation of the particular, identity-defined communities.[73]

Identity politics gained considerable public attention in the middle 1990s through the voice of Lani Guinier, who was nominated by President Clinton for a post in the U.S. Department of Justice. Before and after her nomination, she defended the idea of group difference, especially regarding her fellow African Americans. She desires a political system that would require representation of minorities and would grant a veto to minority groups. One is reminded, inevitably, of John C. Calhoun's similar proposal to protect Southern whites in the years before the Civil War—although mention of this historical analogy is not frequent in the identity literature.[74]

On the one hand, identity politics is commonly highly pro-community, since it favors awakening or enhancing or protecting community among particular identity groupings. At the same time, however, it sometimes does disappoint more inclusive community theorists who worry that what identity communities promise is mostly division, not community, from a larger perspective. And the disappointment is especially acute because the idea of identity politics often comes from those whom many in the community movement wish were allies.

Some feminist intellectuals flatly reject the community ideal because of their perceptions of the experience of women in communities of the past. They well understand how popular "community" is in the present day and generally respect the reasons that it has become a rallying cry for many intellectuals. Yet they insist that feminists must be wary, carefully examining any idea of community for its potential dangers for women. Historically, they argue, oppression of women is often integral to the story of "community."[75]

Shelby Steele is a controversial public intellectual who rejects both identity politics and the politics of community. As a dissident African-American intellectual, Steele dislikes the "politics of diversity," and specifically the white and black intellectuals who spend much time obsessing about African Americans as an identity group. This is a bad idea, Steele maintains. It hurts blacks by encouraging them to dwell on themselves as racial group members—and members of a victimized group at that—with no discernible practical benefit. What African Americans must do, he contends, is get busy working and achieving as best they can—as many have, Steele points out to those who collapse the differences among African Americans. This is not an easy path, and he does not suggest it is, but he believes groupthink denial of what is necessary for individual progress is no answer.[76]

To this argument plucked from the liberal tradition Steele adds a few pieties in the spirit of the age. Thus he declares that he, too, favors some kind of national settlement over group tensions and conflicts even as he worries that identity politics is already eroding a once-shared political and social philosophy in the United States.[77] In the end Steele's conviction is that people, whatever their "group," must consider themselves individuals above all else, must act that way, and should develop the kind of personal "character" that will make these goals a reality. The group is never superior to the individual in Steele's liberal world.[78]

Many public intellectuals suggest that the goal regarding community must be to fashion a kind of balance that although it may stir few hearts, fits with the modern world. Few theorists of community can match Donald Moon's meditations on balancing group aspirations and identities with the need for public community. Moon understands the paradoxes involved in trying to instill a greater sense of public community while retaining liberal freedoms and substantial diversity. He maintains that the best we can do to promote community is to encourage a cluster of shared norms that are requisite for collective political life. He doubts that there is a serious possibility of any greater community in the United States given the freedom and diversity in the nation.

Moon and public intellectuals like him who may be realistic in their analysis of the possibilities of community in the United States attract few accolades from those seeking greater community today. They offer a thin theory of community, and the movement toward community as a redirection in American thought and practice wants something more.[79]

This chapter has concentrated instead on some of the many ideals of community in intellectual circulation today—from community as an inclusive, national goal to community as participatory democracy, to spiritual communities. Differences aside, there can be no mistaking the fact that the movement toward community among public intellectuals flows on in an ever broadening stream, deeper than any other in our age.

Does this mark the arrival of a new consensus in intellectual thought in the United States? No. If there is a primary focus to the contemporary discourse, it is on dialogue between community and liberal values, or the status of "community" within liberalism. In fact, it would be a mistake to interpret the vibrant and growing concern for community and communities as a full-scale revolt against liberal values. It is far from that at present. Nor should the abundant complaints about liberalism or about the United States as a liberal society from within the community movement be equated with a wholesale repudiation of liberalism. Indeed, perhaps the best way to read the community redirection in American political thought is as an effort to salvage liberalism by reinforcing its now somewhat tattered community side.[80] In this way, perhaps, it underlines the continuing vitality of liberalism in the American political tradition.

Yet this description is not the full story either, for there is also something of a revolt against liberal values, and not just liberal practice, in the United States. And while no new consensus has emerged as a result, there are hints of a possible resolution, one in which community of some sort will have a central place. Whether the outcome will fit with an American public that shows little inclination to repudiate liberal values or support community in some form beyond the family and thin civil society groups remains to be seen.

There is some sense within the community movement that the auguries are increasingly favorable for change. Sadly, a good part of this perception builds from the spreading conviction that social decay has markedly worsened since the 1960s.[81] While social scientists debate how broad and pervasive the decay is and what date or era should be used as a baseline to compare the present situation with the past, the widespread conviction that the decay is real as community erodes in the family, neighborhood, church, and nation is inescapable.[82]

Thus the door opens wider for (revival of?) enhanced community in the United States, although in what form or forms is for now a mystery. For its public intellectual advocates, who are diverse but legion, the nation's entrance through the door toward community cannot come too soon.

Chapter Seven

Environmentalism as a Point of Redirection

Community may be the mantra of much of contemporary political and social thought, but there is a good case for environmentalism as the most important new source of social and political ideas addressing the future of the United States—and the globe. Interest in and sympathy for environmentalism has increased dramatically throughout American culture in recent years, even among public intellectuals, where it has joined civil society and community as central concerns. At the same time, there has been a parallel growth in the recognition that a serious ecological perspective entails crafting a philosophy of environmentalism, including a metaphysics, an ontology, an ethics, and a political theory. Many public intellectuals are now fashioning green political theories in particular, and there will be more as political thinking in the United States becomes more ecologically conscious. Thus while the voices of participants in the environmentalist discourse may be less familiar today than those in the community or civil society discourses, time will likely alter this situation. In fact, it may happen soon if continuing environmental crises conspire to move more public intellectuals toward the concerns explored in contemporary ecological thought.[1]

This chapter considers the movement toward environmentalism; the critiques of liberalism and liberal society that are so prevalent among green intellectuals; several of the more popular environmental ethics and their justifications in current environmental intellectual discourse; and green political and social thought, and the main images of the good ecological society that public intellectuals now articulate.

The Movement Toward Environmentalism

The shift toward interest in and support for environmentalism has
come from many directions,[2] and public support for environmentalism is now well established in the United States. Survey after
survey indicates that few, if any, issues are more widely and endur-
ingly popular with the American public. This sentiment, moreover,
extends well beyond abstract and rather pious affirmations of concern for the environment. Majorities regularly declare their willingness to pay more taxes, change lifestyles, and accept considerable
state interference to protect and promote the natural environment.[3]

A few demographic points deserve notice. Some of the poor and
some members of minority groups rank the environment lower on
their value priority list than do other Americans. So do Protestant
fundamentalists. The most "pro-environment" Americans are secular
citizens specifically and white, middle-class people generally. These
findings, however, are merely slight variations on a theme. Almost
all U.S. citizens vigorously claim to support environmentalism.[4]

Yet widespread green sentiments may mean less than they appear to. After all, the public continues to support liberal individualism in many ways, indeed in more ways than ever, and it definitely
endorses capitalist and market economic values, as Richard Ellis and
Fred Thompson have noted in their study of the larger public as
distinguished from devoted greens in environmental groups. The
latter favor a sharp redirection in values away from competitive
individualism, economic growth, limited government, and progress
defined in environmentally negative economic terms. These green
values reveal a far more communal or even collective orientation
(around the goal of environmentalism) and definitely conflict with
strong liberal individualism and capitalism. Yet the American public does not endorse them. It wants both environmentalism and liberal values, and suspects it can somehow have both.[5]

The rise of public intellectuals' interest in environmental thought
in the last two decades is clear enough, although it is sad that those
with an explicitly ecological perspective who have come to the fore
are still outside the ranks of the fashionable in the profession of
political theory. The first major voices relevant to green political and
social thought burst forth in the 1960s and 1970s. These classics include, of course, Rachel Carson's *Silent Spring*, although it was not

mainly a work directed toward political or social thought but one that was an enormous stimulus to broader environmental thought by others.[6] Others, such as Barry Commoner's book *The Closing Circle* and Jonathan Schell's *Fate of the Earth*, along with a steady stream of books predicting disastrous population crises, were among the most dramatic in sounding the alarm about impending ecological catastrophe and encouraging related political and social theory.[7]

Their survivalist message is often echoed today.[8] In this tradition, decline is forecast as imminent and all but inevitable. Sometimes this reading of the future derives from a sincere analysis of the signs of future times, but at others it seems designed largely to frighten readers into moving toward a new and radically more ecological society.[9]

The subject of what has been labeled ecopessimism is fascinating. The phenomenon is widespread in American intellectual life. It starts from the premise that global ecocatastrophes are so severe that existence as we know it in the United States and the West will soon end. Such notions have been heard often before. They are recognizable, in fact, as part of a long-existent subtext in Western thought that is consumed with the view that "the decline of the West" is at hand. Its contemporary exponents do not, however, recognize any such affinity.[10] The issues they are concerned with are quite different. They pose the serious, even haunting, questions of whether we are prepared to face the seriousness of our environmental problems and whether we have the will to address them.

In the late 1960s Garrett Hardin offered what was perhaps the first contemporary example of serious environmental social analysis. His argument, which has proved influential, was that we are moving beyond the planet's carrying capacity, forcing the human race into the "tragedy of the commons."[11] Hardin used this famous metaphor to attempt to show that the choices of self-regarding, rational individuals can lead to ecological disaster—and were doing so in our situation of increasing population. In the terms of Hardin's example, the commons (the planet) is a shared grassland on which any herdsman can feed his cattle. In this setting, he argues, each individual's interest is to obtain as much grass as possible, yet doing so guarantees disaster for the community as a whole. As the population of people and cattle expands, the commons will be destroyed by overgrazing.

Hardin concludes that the environmental problem is a human and ethical problem brought on by self-regarding people who often have too much freedom to pursue their (short-run) rational self-interest. It is not caused by some mysterious evil force or government or corporation. Nor are its origins technological. It is caused by too many people with too much freedom to act on their selfish interests. Free, rational people are destroying the environment.

The 1980s saw a burst of efforts by intellectuals to grapple with the environment. Some were sober expressions from social and natural scientists, such as Herman Daly and John Cobb's *For the Common Good*, which undertook to save the planet while also ensuring a viable economic life for human beings.[12] Others argued the case for the rights of nature, while still others fashioned new ecological ethics, gaining insight from the essays of Aldo Leopold, one of the founders of environmentalism.[13] Some called for radical ecocentrism, while others advanced ecological anarchism.[14] Yet others, most prominently Julian Simon and Herman Kahn, ridiculed predictions of incipient environmental collapse and sought to undercut the various radical political and social changes advocated by green intellectuals.[15]

The 1990s saw even more engagement with ecological dilemmas and the social and political thought that followed. The notion that an environmentalist redirection is urgently necessary has steadily spread. Evidence of the breadth of this movement includes not only the flood of books making the green case but also the arrival of skeptical works on what is now perceived—correctly—to be the formidable environmental movement toward change. For example, Wilfred Beckerman's *Through Green-Colored Glasses*, published by the libertarian Cato Institute, challenges the highly statist assumptions of the green movement.[16] Such books in turn regularly meet opposition, such as Paul and Anne Ehrlich's *Betrayal of Science and Reason*.[17]

Greg Easterbrook's explicitly subtitled argument, "The Coming Age of Environmental Optimism" is an example of a gentler critical genre than Beckerman's.[18] But, like Beckerman, Easterbrook casts his eye on many green policy objectives and finds them grounded in a fear of change (suggesting environmentalism is a kind of conservatism), naïveté about the time change takes, and an almost willful dismissal of the ecological progress already made. He also notes many environmentalists' considerable romanticism about the past, the primitive, and nature in general.

Public intellectuals sympathetic to environmentalism have been in far greater supply, of course. Some hope that the redirection toward environmentalism may provide the opportunity to cross increasingly rigid, even ossified, boundaries in American political thought and bring some unity in a very fractured intellectual world. At its most optimistic this aspiration can declare that "the ecology movement alone . . . has serious potential for crossing the identity trenches."[19]

Bob Pepperman Taylor has been impressive in modeling this hope in his historical works on American political theory and environmentalism. His book *Our Limits Transgressed: Environmental Political Thought in America* interprets green thought—and its several traditions—over the course of U.S. history. Pepperman suggests that conventional analysis and boundaries will not really work with this body of thought. He describes a journey that had both more nuance and more coherence than is frequently present in earlier accounts.[20] His most recent study, *America's Bachelor Uncle: Thoreau and the American Polity*, continues his effort to discern the political side of American environmentalism and break free from conventional categories. For Taylor, the environmentalist hero Henry David Thoreau was much more politically oriented than others have realized. The portrait of Thoreau as radical individualist misses Thoreau's intense concern with civic responsibility and the public good. Implicit—and sometimes explicit—in Taylor's Thoreau is Taylor's own commitment to a mature and responsible political environmentalism that fits no neat category.[21]

An area that has seen much interesting intellectual green thought in the 1990s has been ecofeminism. Its beginning is earlier, but its recent burst into prominence merits notice here. Carolyn Merchant's *Death of Nature* (1980) was a pioneering work, but many other arguments have followed.[22] Books such as Joni Seager's *Earth Follies: Coming to Feminist Terms with the Environmental Crisis* are becoming more and more common.[23]

The 1990s also saw the full-scale emergence of religious intellectuals in the movement toward an ecological redirection.[24] Lynn White launched the effort in the late 1960s with his critique of aspects of Western religious traditions that, he charged, share much of the blame for our environmental difficulties. White complained that the West had often used the Bible and Christianity to justify horrible exploitation of nature.[25] Since then, of course, a host of Christian thinkers have insisted that Christianity does not support any such exploitation even as they have helped fashion an explicitly green Christianity.[26] H. Paul Santmire has been among the most eloquent of the liberal Protestants. More and more evangelical Protestant voices have also become engaged, and the "evangelical entry into the environmental debate" is now a well-established fact.[27]

Thus, there is now no shortage of interest among intellectuals in environmentalism as the basis for a serious redirection in American thought and culture. Many organizations are also working toward this same end, and these groups are now familiar as the practical embodiment of the considerable popular and intellectual support for an ecological political agenda. They include the Sierra Club, the Wilderness Society, Greenpeace, the Nature Conservancy, and many more, including dozens of wildlife, hunting and fishing, bicycling, hiking, and camping groups. Mostly well established, the organizations are integral to the story of American environmentalism, a movement that is now so much a part of our landscape that it is generating its own laudatory histories of itself.[28]

Plenty of American religious groups also are involved in supporting an environmental redirection. They include the environmental arms of many organizations such as the National Council of Churches' Eco-Justice group, the environmental organizations of mainline Protestant denominations, largely evangelical groups such as Au Sable, the Evangelical Environmental Network, the Christian Environmental Council, the Christian Environmental Association, and the Christian Society of the Green Cross.[29]

Altogether the broad range of support behind an environmental redirection is unmistakable. This is not to say that there is a single animating vision of what such redirection should look like in specific social, economic, or political terms. Yet interest in ecological matters in the culture has now become intense enough that some observers ask whether it serves as a kind of faith for many adherents, as perhaps it must if it is to lead to any profound redirection in human life and thought.

Michael Barkun has explored one aspect of this possibility in a controversial analysis. He notes strands of apocalyptic thinking that are present in much of contemporary ecopolitical thought. The standard focus on overwhelming ecological crisis, the sometimes obsessive engagement with end times analysis, and the constant theme of human failure recall the category of sin in Western religious faiths—and perhaps this is not entirely an accident.[30]

The Critique

Green intellectuals are often predictably relentless critics of liberalism in theory and practice in the United States today. In a sense, these blistering complaints from those who want to refocus on an ecological agenda are ironic. After all, many of the great voices of past liberal social and political thought on both sides of the Atlantic constitute a tradition that made "nature" a normative standard. This was as true of John Locke as of Thomas Jefferson, of Mary Wollstonecraft as of Ralph Waldo Emerson. These liberals relied on diverse definitions of nature and its ethical postulates; there is at least as much diversity among present-day ecological theorists.

Yet most contemporary green thinkers have little to say about those who called on nature before them. They are too busy noting how far today's liberal social order has strayed from their ideal of an acceptable ecological ethic. In such a mission we would expect that classic liberal philosophers such as Locke or Wollstonecraft would rarely appear.[31] The work of younger environmentalist scholars such as Joe Bowersox and John Meyer does, however, give some hope for the future. Such young scholars appreciate that present and past cannot be so easily severed, and they understand that it would be foolish not to learn from the past.[32]

Several dimensions of modern-day liberalism draw the most intense dissent from environmentalist intellectuals, who especially reject what they believe is liberalism's devotion to the human being and the individual above all else. They reject the idea that the human is at the center of the universe or of nature; instead, they endorse ecocentrism, which holds that all parts of nature are equal and interconnected with all other parts in a marvelous web. No part of nature, including the human being, has special rights or privileges, although each part has its own integrity and all must be honored as part of the whole. Thus, as John Rodman has argued, ecocentrism promises liberation from human-centeredness and the pernicious idea that the rest of nature exists for humans to exploit as they see fit.[33]

Objections to the liberal emphasis on the individual are also essential and common. No one has made a more thorough or passionate green attack on this side of liberalism than William Ophuls in his contemporary *Requiem for Modern Politics: The Tragedy of the Enlightenment and the Challenge of the New Millennium*.[34] For Ophuls, the urgent radical critique of liberalism must include a full-scale demystification of the liberal Enlightenment and its ideals of individualism in civilization. For him, what Western civilization has been about is "theft"—stealing from nature and from each other, often in the name of the false ideals of selfish individualism and unconstrained individual liberty.[35]

For all its high-minded talk, the Enlightenment and its child liberalism, according to Ophuls, are best understood as the sanctioning of appalling "predatory development" for selfish economic gain. Moreover, he charges, the liberal Enlightenment outlook pursues the folly of trying to solve all problems by increasing production and overcoming scarcity. The result is as clear as it is tragic to Ophuls. Our present Hobbesian condition, in which selfish power and domination reign under the gods of Science, Reason, and Greed, has led to the rape of nature, impending scarcity, a breakdown of community, and the rise of a kind of friendly fascism—a democracy that is metamorphosing into a Hobbesian totalitarian state.[36]

Green dissent regarding liberalism in the West today often singles out capitalism as a principal, often the principal, evil. Routinely connected to liberalism, capitalism's image is as an engine propelled by individual greed, relentlessly controlling and destroying nature—often in alliance with its dubious twin, technology. Wherever both are prominent, a shockingly desecrated natural world follows, one that cannot easily be rejuvenated.[37]

While critical public intellectuals frequently identify liberalism, or selected "liberal" institutions, as central causes of our ecological travail, few make them the sole causes of environmental crisis. They could not be, after all, since Western liberalism is a relatively recent phenomenon, hardly a presence before the seventeenth century. This is why many green intellectuals also blame Christianity, a religion whose doctrines and practices they consistently single out for its alleged negative effects on nature.[38]

The now nearly orthodox critique complains that Christian theology based in the Bible has been human-centered—declaring the human person special and the most important part of Creation, being made in God's image. As a result, critics insist, Christianity has viewed the rest of nature as inferior and all too available for exploitation by humans at their discretion. The most frequently cited Bible passage, which is taken as deeply damning, is from the Book of Genesis: "Fill the earth and subdue it. Have dominion over the fish of the sea, the birds of the air, and all the living things that are on the earth" (Gen. 1:28).[39]

Many Christian thinkers share this mood of dissatisfaction, especially with the record of Christian practice, which they tend to identify as the culprit rather than Christianity as a religion. But some complain also about theological misdirections (or perceived misdirections) toward nature by such influential Christian theologians as Saint Augustine or Saint Thomas Aquinas. They often proceed to offer what they consider to be a better Christian theology, one that is invariably respectful of all nature as God's precious creation and that God calls human beings to love. Their prized exemplar of this Christian theology displayed in a life of witness is the story of Saint Francis of Assisi (1182–1226). Saint Francis's famous love of the birds and all living things in nature is their Christianity in action.[40]

Alternate Ethical Foundations for
an Environmental Redirection

There is little doubt that many in the community movement take community's good as a given, especially in contrast to liberalism (or the side of liberalism they dislike). This reflexive attitude is equally present in modern environmentalist thought regarding its main assumptions. Yet the good news is that green intellectuals are increasingly engaging in serious reflection about alternative ethical outlooks and justifications for them. These reflections sometimes provide environmentalism with an unexpected philosophical side that is both welcome and stimulating.

There are, as Robyn Eckersley says, many ways to grapple with contemporary ecological thought and its tendencies, issues, divisions, and history. Eckersley concentrates on how the different branches of green thought address the environment, working with the particular history of each. This proves fruitful, but to get the clearest sense of various environmentalist ethics and justifications, my focus is more strictly analytical. The goal is to present some sense of the major alternatives and the distinctions among them. Without this awareness, it is not possible to understand contemporary green thought.[41]

Recourse to natural rights claims is one standard approach. In fact, contemporary green thought is suffused with rights talk and rights arguments—and with disputes over rights arguments. Intellectual proponents of a natural rights perspective make a wide range of claims, from suggesting a few domestic animals or large mammals have natural rights to maintaining that all of nature has rights. The case is made, for instance, that animals have a right to life or a right to equal consideration with humans and, in some arguments, a host of other rights as well.

This effort to extend rights to (or acknowledge the rights of) part or all of nature is a recognizably liberal project, predictable from some American intellectuals. But it is not self-evident, which is why there is plenty of argument about whether it makes sense to say there is such a thing as animal rights (or, for that matter, natural rights for anyone or anything). The debate is predictable in part because such rights talk flies in the face of postmodernism and postmodern intellectuals, who are hardly few in number in the United States. From a postmodern perspective, nature cannot provide a true foundation for ethics, and there are no true "rights" in nature. There are no such certain foundations or truths, and to believe there are is to delude oneself. Yet in this era of supposed postmodern skepticism, rights talk has never been more prevalent in environmental thought— and elsewhere. It is equally interesting to observe green thinkers lambasting liberal values or liberal culture while invoking the name of rights, a concept that has long been integral to both.

A crucial issue in the natural rights discourse is who has natural rights. Does a dog? Does a flea? Does an amoeba? And how should this be decided? For example, must an organism be beneficial to nature as a whole, including human nature, in order to have rights? That is, does a cancer cell have rights? Also in dispute is whether, and to what extent, an organism must be aware to have rights. Some argue that definite self-consciousness in an organism is required. Others contend that some feeling is sufficient. Yet others propose that just a glimmer of consciousness will do. Adequate answers are far from clear.

Another recent effort to get humans to go "beyond prejudice" and accept the natural rights of other organisms maintains that what is required is the presence of "causation," defined as the presence in an animal of purposefulness. As a standard, purposefulness is meant to be broad, and as a result it is not obvious what living thing lacks it. By this view, moreover, all purposes are equal, and so all living things have equal rights.[42]

There is also the matter of what rights an animal or other organism might possess besides the right to life. Often the answer is the right to some kind of liberty, but how liberty should be conceived and then defended in such a context is controversial and difficult to determine. And there is the significant question of how the limitless multitude of rights-bearing living things that would or do constitute nature can be held together in satisfactory equilibrium. Rights are often proclaimed in isolation, but nothing lives in isolation from other humans or the rest of nature. How would the putative right to life of the human fit with the same right for the wolf or the cancer cell?

Intellectual historian Roderick Nash is perhaps the most well-known exponent of a rights approach to environmental ethics. His primary work on the subject, *Rights of Nature,* is a fascinating history of environmental ethics but also an essay on behalf of a rights approach. Nash believes that all nature, not just the animal kingdom, has rights, but his defense of rights also proceeds from a pragmatic calculation that a rights argument for environmentalism is effective in the American context. At heart he is a pragmatist who likes a rights approach because he concludes it fits with our liberal, rights-oriented political tradition, enshrined in the Declaration of Independence. For Nash, an extension of rights to nonhuman nature is just another logical step in the history of America's affinity with rights. While this move might seem radical to some, Nash says it would be no more radical than other chapters in the story of the expansion of rights in American history. As he sees it, he is calling on people to acknowledge all nature's rights to be free of human enslavement, just as almost 150 years ago Americans finally acknowledged African Americans' rights and ended their enslavement.

A second important ethical framework among environmentalist intellectuals is the intrinsic value approach. This outlook attracts some of the more philosophical thinkers within environmentalism, who argue that nature's ethical value is intrinsic to nature and therefore derived from itself. They understand nature to be good in and of itself. Its value is not grounded in claims that it is God's creation or in some humans' assertions that it has rights.

Pioneering scientist and thinker Aldo Leopold (1887–1948) has become something of a hero to many who are attracted to this persuasion. Leopold's most influential work is *A Sand County Almanac*, which is now second only to Thoreau's *Walden* in the honored corpus of American nature literature. Although Leopold was a fairly prolific writer, he was not a philosopher and did not fashion an elaborate intrinsic environmental ethic. Leopold maintained that nature contained within itself its own natural and therefore proper values, especially integrity, stability, and beauty. Since these were intrinsic to nature, Leopold insisted they were appropriate for an ethic for all living things. He favored policies and institutions that served these values and opposed those that did not.[43]

The intrinsic outlook can be a close cousin of the rights of nature perspective. Indeed, one might argue that those who talk of the rights of or in nature share a kind of intrinsic analysis. Both discern normative value in nature. The difference is often that rights thinkers discern rights in parts of nature that carry special normative weight. Intrinsic thinkers tend to valorize all nature.[44]

The intrinsic approach is also sometimes confused with ecocentrism, which is now a standard perspective among green intellectuals and activists. Ecocentrism, in fact, is more a claim about what nature is like and what it includes than it is a justification for environmentalism or even an ethic of ecological concern.[45] It understands nature as a complex, interwoven whole in which nothing and no one, including human beings, has special status. It also often defines nature broadly to encompass more than living things, including rocks, rivers, or entire ecosystems.[46]

Since Leopold, many environmental theorists have argued within a self-conscious intrinsic framework.[47] One who profoundly admires Leopold but continually refines and improves his own version of the intrinsic approach to nature is J. Baird Callicott, a professional philosopher. Skeptical of natural rights claims and resistant to romantic conceptions of nature, Callicott believes that people do not really question nature's intrinsic moral imperatives and that we should not do so. He is well aware that many analytic philosophers protest that the fact or "is" of nature must be separated from "ought" (that is, from the claim that nature somehow has intrinsic worth and thus ethical force). Callicott rejects this conventional philosophical distinction, in effect holding that it has no logic outside the arbitrary disciplinary rules of analytic philosophy. At other moments he leaves philosophical disputes over nature far behind and relates to nature in a decidedly mystical fashion—as he did when he discovered that the Mississippi River was intrinsically part of himself.[48] In such images, the intrinsic approach reminds one of the intuitive ways of Thoreau. Thoreau was certainly a memorable mystic and something of an intrinsic ethicist, if not enough of a philosopher or political theorist for some public intellectuals in the environmentalist mode.[49]

Callicott's important environmental thought has evolved and includes several significant dimensions, but his affirmation of nature, its intrinsic worth, its beauty, and the interdependence of its parts has always included much respect for Native Americans, who, he argues, often related to nature in an ideal way. Callicott's respect, however, is not uncritical. He understands that few Native Americans were self-conscious ecologists and that few tribes had flawless environmentalist records in practice.[50]

Spiritually based environmental ethics and justifications are another common approach today. One sign is that even Tom Hayden, famous as a former New Left activist but not previously noted for his spiritual concerns, has joined in. Hayden's manifesto, *The Lost Gospel of the Earth*, published by the Sierra Club, proclaims his desire for people to rediscover nature religions such as Native American faiths, as well as the sides of historical Christianity that celebrated nature as a possible framework for an ecological ethics.[51]

One spiritually grounded ethics emphasizes "caring for creation: responsible stewardship of God's handiwork," as the title of a contemporary book defines the position.[52] Many Jewish and Christian scholars defend the stewardship stance by drawing on relevant passages in the Book of Genesis that they read to hold that God commands humans to care for Creation, for example, "The Lord God then took the man and settled him in the Garden of Eden, to cultivate and care for it" (Gen. 2:15).

While Christian scholars sometimes find a few verses in the New Testament to add to the picture, ones that suggest God will liberate all nature in the Second Coming, the main New Testament emphasis falls on its core event, the Incarnation.[53] The usual claim is that the Incarnation of God as Jesus Christ is the most important imaginable indication of the Creator's overwhelming connection with and love of the natural world.[54]

What stewardship of Creation by humans means, individual thinkers interpret differently. Some argue that stewardship requires active human direction and protection of nature. Others spurn this understanding and view stewardship as something all nature must somehow participate in. For them, nature is holistic, human beings are just one part of it, and each part has its own dignity and role. Romans 8:21 is often cited: "The world itself will be freed from its slavery to corruption and share in the glorious freedom of the children of God."[55]

Despite such differences, there is agreement that the Bible, whether inspired by God or God's literal word, justifies an environmental ethic of stewardship, however much it may have been ignored in Western and Christian history.[56] In this spirit there is great confidence that the "Bible is not an enemy of the environmental cause, but its greatest asset."[57]

Creation theology is a second example of a spiritually based ethic enlisted for ecological redirection. Some exponents align themselves with Christianity or Judaism, while many others do not, yet they share a vision of a universe in which the core is a divine, glorious, and continuing evolution, a universe in which nature is wonderfully creative. These intellectuals, often theologians, concentrate on ongoing creation in nature, including human beings. They are less interested in any original Creation. This is why they radiate confidence about the future of the divinely biocentric and evolving universe. Matthew Fox, a former Roman Catholic priest, and Thomas Berry, a well-known ecotheologian, among the leading voices of creation theology, suggest that the ethical implications of their perspective are radical. Profoundly communitarian, they see a holistic and evolving nature, which sharply clashes with the selfish and divided world men and women inhabit today.[58]

Creation theology has had substantial intellectual impact and has generated predictable controversy within Christianity over whether it can even be considered a legitimate form of Christianity. Isn't it really a distinct spirituality in which the special divinity of Jesus Christ disappears and the central, dynamic, first Creation of God is rendered unimportant? Some within Christianity charge that it is, and others outside of Christianity happily agree.[59]

Yet creation theology is not nearly as controversial as another spiritually based standard for environmental ethics. This is ecofeminism, a perspective that has entered mainstream religious intellectual consciousness and has generated a lot of sparks.[60] While not all ecofeminists are self-consciously spiritual, many are. Some, like the well-known Starhawk, are involved in the wiccan and other witch movements.[61] There are as well a wide variety of goddess worshipers,[62] adherents to nature religions, variously defined,[63] and those within established religious traditions who are sympathetic to much (though rarely all) of the ecofeminist outlook; Roman Catholic Rosemary Radford Ruether is the most prominent of this last group.[64]

The heart of the ecofeminist argument is that nature is the ground of proper authority either in itself or by the inevitable fact that we are beings of nature. As it is understood in ecofeminism, moreover, women are especially identified with nature because of their unique role in childbearing. There are the usual variations, but the common message affirms women and nature together and insists that both have been denied respect and often treated terribly throughout much of human history. There is also considerable agreement on the necessity of the liberation of both women and nature and on the value of a variety of means to enhance both objectives.[65]

Most environmental ethics based in religion have much in common with secular environmental ethics. For example, most seek a radical ecological redirection of American ethics and life, basing this goal on a kind of foundationalism that derives from their shared perceptions of nature as a place of the greatest worth. Thus it is ironic that secular environmentalists (sometimes joined with religious compatriots) regularly criticize religion as a major impediment to environmentalism. The truth is, however, that many intellectual voices in the major U.S. religions are eagerly joining the cause, although some of their secular critics are blissfully unaware of the fact.

The pragmatic approach is another example of the many ethical perspectives in green thought today. There has long been a pragmatic tradition in American environmental thought, just as there has been in other areas of political and social theory. Historically, the preservationist Gifford Pinchot represented this orientation. He shared pragmatism's desire to proceed in a practical, rational manner, taking account of what works in practice, and always avoiding absolutist claims.[66] Like Pinchot, some environmentalist pragmatists today are human-centered; others are ecocentrists. Either way, their ethical outlook combines great respect for nature with a pragmatic conviction that assisting nature requires an ethic rooted in practice and experience, not abstract absolutes or statements of faith or romantic effusions.[67]

These ethical perspectives and others are concerned with how to defend the struggle toward an ecological redirection. As we have seen, they are alike in much of their attitude toward nature and in many of their ethical attitudes, yet they often differ a good deal on the justifications they posit for their respective environmental ethics. If one steps back, though, it is their range of agreement that is more significant and justifies some self-confidence about the possibility of a transforming ecological ethic. There is little existential skepticism or postmodern uncertainty to be found in these ranks. The result reflects the growing energy making for environmental change, energy that manifests itself more and more in American intellectual life today, energy that could transform the beleaguered earth.

Images of the Good Society

American intellectuals concerned with a green redirection today go beyond matters of alternative ethics or value justification. The nation's intellectual life abounds in ecological visions of a good society, of social orders that respect, honor, and seek to embody nature. In fact, images of the good community have now become integral to environmental theorizing, and they increasingly take a significant place in contemporary American social and political thought.

One image, which is best described as an antiutopia, a dreaded possibility rather than a dearly sought ideal, is the authoritarian model. It is fiercely controversial and often denounced, but its consideration cannot be avoided.[68] This view insists that environmental crises and the slow and halfhearted responses they generate cast doubt on whether democracy has the capacity to make necessary changes fast and effectively enough. Its frankest proponents go further, doubting that Western democracy, including the United States, will be able to meet the task and wondering if some sort of Hobbesian authoritarian government may be necessary.

To avoid such an alternative, this view argues that what will be needed is not just a whirlwind of action to address ecological crises, but also a direct challenge to aspects of liberal democratic society. There will have to be a confrontation with Americans' infatuation with individualism, their romance with property rights, their stubborn resistance to serious state action to confront ecological problems, and their continued willingness to cater to each other's selfish, short-run interests.

For example, Robert Heilbroner in his widely read book, *An Inquiry into the Human Prospect* has questioned whether the First World is able to discipline itself sufficiently to save the environment.[69] If it cannot, he predicts authoritarian resolutions will be inevitable—and perhaps appropriate. Heilbroner is anxious to avoid this possibility, and he wrote his book in part so that it might be escaped. He is a self-declared, left-leaning social democrat whose commitment to this ideal is very real. Yet his argument is that inequities between the West and the Third World and contemporary environmental problems together threaten the globe. Western democracy must address these problems on an international scale or face the fact that necessity will create authoritarian regimes that can.

In the back of the mind of more than a few green intellectuals there exists a fear that such worries may be justified. Those who cautiously approach the conclusion that if we are not careful we may have to turn to authoritarian resolutions are different, however, from others in the green movement for whom the only legitimate society must be one where "true" authority governs. Adherents to these views of course reject the sort of democracy practiced in Western governments. Such views are no strangers in American or European green thinking. In their most robust expressions, such as among some eco-Marxists, capitalism remains the core problem, and Marxist historical analysis constitutes the true authority, one that urges a powerful role for the state in meeting environmental demands. In less firmly Marxist versions of ecosocialism, more common in the U.S. green movement, there is greater emphasis on civil liberties and a greater hostility toward state authority. Yet there is at the same time an assumption that protecting the environment will necessitate a great deal of state planning and control of the economy.[70]

A second and decidedly more alluring ecological image of the good life is eco-anarchism. For eco-anarchists, the best social order is one in which everything in nature, nonhuman as well as human, does as its nature dictates. In this sense it seeks a fully "natural" social order that would involve a free nature, living in community with itself and its parts. For some time Murray Bookchin has been the best-known voice for this ideal, which he calls the "ecology of freedom."

This view assumes that for nature to realize liberation it will have to escape the intense pressures that human populations now put on it. In turn, eco-anarchists will have to "liberate" society from capitalism and from freedom conceptualized as the liberty to acquire private property, make private economic investments, or exercise wide consumer choice. Capitalism terribly damages nature through its encouragement of the values of wasteful production, competition, and pollution at the expense of nature. For eco-anarchists, moreover, liberal capitalist freedoms do not constitute real freedom at all. They involve the false freedom that is always entailed in manipulated consumer choices in a market or semimarket society.[71]

There is rarely much attention to politics in eco-anarchist analyses. But that is not unusual in green thinking, where one eye typically is cast on present crises and the other on future ideals. Eco-anarchist Murray Bookchin, however, is an impressive exception to this too-frequent situation. He criticizes this tendency among some eco-anarchists as well as other green thinkers. For him, there will have to be a great deal of politics on "the pathways to a green future," and it cannot be escaped by choosing national community or the market as the social ideal.[72]

Eco-anarchists are interested in both quasi-Marxist analyses and classic nineteenth-century communitarian anarchist thought. Both approaches may be "dead" elsewhere in contemporary intellectual life, but they are far from dead among eco-anarchist intellectuals. This is why, while sometimes eco-anarchist perspectives are labeled "postliberal," their spirit is actually closer to that of the late nineteenth century. The effort devoted to attacking capitalism and the market in the name of nature cannot help but remind some readers of Peter Kropotkin a century ago.

In this view, human domination of nature is not at all inevitable. Its origins lie in the hegemony of some humans over others, especially in economic relations. Indeed, eco-anarchists argue that transforming socioeconomic relationships is the gateway to transforming the relations of people with nature as well as with each other. For them, the resulting "social ecology" can be an ideal, egalitarian community, living in accord with nature. Left behind will be the corrupt hierarchies among people and between people and the rest of nature.[73]

This perspective on society, of course, has no confidence in government. Eco-anarchists are convinced that governments are all about the regular denial of precious natural liberty. They are equally certain that the proper ecological society will require only a modest bureaucracy. Since eco-anarchists expect to have the most participatory and communal society possible, one where all take part in common tasks, to them it makes no sense to depend on an unnecessary activist government. Community members will regulate themselves and have scant need to employ more than Marx's "administration of things."

Skeptics, of course, doubt whether such a vision is realistic. In particular they question whether a small, administrative government in an anticapitalist society will nourish the environment. Critics note that problems of management, coordination, and control necessarily will loom large in the enterprise of achieving a green society, as in any other social order, and they wonder how an eco-anarchist society can meet them. Even if that were possible, skeptics doubt the result would yield increased human freedom. They ask, How could a tight community built on shared values result in expanded freedom?

These are troubling questions, and eco-anarchists know it. They understand the doubts and rarely promise easy solutions. They especially recognize that the issue of liberation or freedom and what one means by it is important. Yet they insist that if one defines freedom as allowing people—and the rest of nature—the chance to control their life, their proposals are about liberation and liberty, and are the best means to expand them. They have few doubts that freedom from the rule of capitalism, consumerism, and the alienating big state/representative "democracy" that afflicts too many humans —and the rest of nature—would be liberation indeed.

There are variations among eco-anarchists, as with any group. Robyn Eckersley is especially impressed with the differences within their environmentalist agendas. Thus, she notes, some eco-anarchists favor controlling the human population, while others want to move toward its gradual reduction, meanwhile putting more and more of the planet into wilderness areas out of the reach of humans for the entire ecosystem's benefit.[74] There are also plenty of variations among eco-anarchists when it comes to the proper means of change. Most characteristic is a spirit that is willing to break with conventional or even legal modes of behavior to stop alleged outrages against nature. Among eco-anarchists it is not unusual to encounter celebrations of classic monkey-wrenching as a means to help the ecological cause.[75]

Another image of the good society, the participatory green society, is perhaps the most popular one among American green intellectuals arguing for an environmental redirection. This perspective is also a significant part of many green activists' outlook. Indeed, this expression of the participatory ideal of democratic action originally articulated in the 1960s now permeates the green movement. The environmental slogan "Think Globally, Act Locally" reflects this disposition when it means that local action, taken by real people in highly participatory democratic settings, is a moral imperative that must be honored in practice. While eco-anarchism is also sympathetic to a localist and participatory order, proponents of the participatory ideal differ crucially in their attitude toward government and its positive possibilities for the green cause.

This approach, which is often summarized or lauded as a commitment by environmentalists to "true democracy," has long been significant in European green thought.[76] It has been slower to catch on in the United States, although it has had enthusiasts for decades. Now, however, it is gaining an important place here.[77]

While the case for participatory activism assumes the results will positively affect the global environment, some accounts are far from transparent about why they will.[78] To critics, this belief is naive and does not address the deep-seated structural problems that lie beneath particular environmental crises. Moreover, while in some cases, as with such an able theorist as Adolf Gundersen, there is a mature awareness of the conceivable conflicts between participatory democracy and the urgent ecological agenda, in others there is not. Where the awareness exists, the usual argument is that this problem is greater in theory than it will be in practice.

This is mostly because adherents to this approach have high trust in human beings, which is hardly a universal sentiment among environmentalist theorists. Participatory environmentalists express considerable assurance that people, *when they are in a participatory and deliberative setting,* will decide rightly. As a result, there is often no real tension among participatory environmentalists regarding their twin goals. For them, participatory democracy and a truly ecological society can go together. They can be a splendid exemplification of their ideal: humans and the rest of nature united as one community.[79]

In this connection Gundersen and others have been intrigued by the Native American experience. To be sure, Gundersen carefully distances himself from the uncritical environmentalist celebrants of everything and anything Native American. He knows it is pointless to pursue romantic, reactionary efforts to resuscitate the lost worlds of past Indian civilizations. Nor, he advises, should we think we can carve out a favorite part of those lost worlds and pretend it can be carried forward to today, no matter how different the present world may be. What Gundersen does consider worthwhile is exploring Native American experience as it took place in tribes' "embedded membranes," in Native Americans' actual lives, in their particular practices, their villages, and their culture. There we can perceive how Native Americans participated with nature and each other and, perhaps, learn from them.[80]

Another image of the good society in green thought today is what I would call the "creation society." This image visualizes the good ecological society as one faithful to God's holy and beneficent will. What this invariably means is a society dwelling in accord with God's created natural universe, defined in the familiar ways: cherishing nature, creating an ecologically sustainable society, and fostering community within the human and all other species. Perhaps the most assertive steps toward achieving this image are taking place today in evangelical (not fundamentalist) Protestant Christian circles. Led by Calvin DeWitt and other committed Protestant evangelical greens, the progress toward this conception of the good society depends in part on the growing evangelical support that it is receiving. DeWitt characterizes this current effort as more than a movement. It is best understood "more as a revival. . . . People are finding new life in their faith as they encounter God in all his fullness."[81]

Predictably, such efforts encounter roadblocks, divisions, and disputes. For example, the many parallels with the secular environmental movement lead some Christian critics to ask whether green Christian efforts distinguish themselves enough "from a secular environmental movement laden with humanistic and pantheistic views."[82] Others argue that the Bible of green Christians treats nature far too respectfully. It ignores the fact that the Bible holds that all nature, not just human beings, is corrupted, which is a claim most religious environmentalists firmly deny.[83]

Another, final image (of many possible alternatives) of the good ecological society posits a holistic order as its ideal. As with some other images, public intellectuals and theorists drawn to this outlook hardly reject all the alternatives; indeed, they frequently incorporate part of them, just as other intellectuals make use of the holistic ideal in their conceptions of the good society. What distinguishes the holistic ideal is its stress on the theme of community among people and with nature. It is a communitarian vision, above all, one that concentrates on a holistic natural community as the special objective.

Two expressions that illustrate this outlook may be noted here. One is the considerable intellectual interest among greens in Native American culture as a splendid expression of a lived holistic ideal. This view is familiar enough in pop culture today, but the holistic image is also invoked often in the expanding arena of religious environmentalism. For example, process theologians lift up what they see as a sacred, holistic cosmos. In such a universe God is integral to the whole and not a remote transcendent figure.[84]

Moreover, process theologies particularly accent development and evolution as part of holistic nature. To them, static perceptions of nature are misunderstandings of the dynamic and divine holism that nature so grandly embodies.[85] Equally attracted to the holistic view are many ecofeminists. Pioneer Charlene Spretnak, along with a host of others, experiences the natural universe as a unity and resists visualizing it in what she views as an analytical, discrete, "male" fashion.[86]

While already widespread in environmentalist writings, the holistic metaphor is spreading. Thus there is interest today in ecology conceived as a moral concept. Proponents of this idea stress the complex and interdependent dimensions of a moral environment, note how society is affected by various moral relations, and observe that these relations are often more far-reaching than a less integrated and holistic analysis might predict. One example of this kind of environment-influenced analysis holds that there is a moral-environmental system in every social order and that in the United States today it is so damaged by media violence, family decline, and the like that it may be on the verge of collapse.[87]

Conclusion

There is little doubt that there is a growing momentum toward an ecological focus in contemporary American political and social theory. It has not yet attained the legitimacy among the most elite public intellectuals in the United States that considerations on liberalism and its failures, civil society, or community have, but it is making progress. Even this gap, moreover, may be more apparent than real. Intellectuals engaged with environmentalism, after all, certainly consider liberalism and its failures. They are also as much engaged with the idea of community as is contemporary political thinking in general. Indeed, one way to understand green political and social thought may be to interpret it as mostly a kind of community-oriented thinking. And it is fair to conclude that there is, in fact, more commitment to "community" in green thought than among many sometimes ambivalent communitarians in other discourses.

Of course, there are often differences between green intellectuals and those addressing more conventional understandings of community. The communities most attractive to environmental theorists are holistic biotic communities. They rarely are the same communities that attract many other community-oriented thinkers, which tend to be political communities ranging from national communities to participatory democratic ones. Nor is there much interest in local, decentralized communities in the ecological literature.

Support for community in green thought is inevitably, as well, part of the affirmation of all nature so prominent in this literature. Nature is the beloved ideal, and community is honored because it is intrinsic to nature. Community is not an independent good for a proper political or social theory or practice. It is not the end, except as envisioned by some theorists of global civil society or ecoreligion.[88]

Ecological thought, however, has not formed a bridge to a third important, current direction in American political thought, toward a civil society analysis. Environmental theorists on the whole show little interest in—and, frequently, little respect for—intermediate institutions of any sort, from the family to cultural groups or to ethnic, racial, or religious organizations. The civil society often disappears before nature among green intellectuals, for whom ordinary days and ordinary institutions seem to hold little interest.

Despite the attacks on liberalism in green thought, a liberal vocabulary of politics retains a tenacious hold in these uncongenial waters. Those who want to argue that liberalism remains the dominant mode of American political intellectuals can find material to work with in contemporary environmental thought. There are a fair number of liberal moments: frequent rights language, celebrations of the goal of "liberation" in nature, insistence that each aspect of nature has its own individual integrity and, in its way, independence. Indeed, given the history of liberal thought and its frequent recourse to "nature" as a self-evident justification for values, it is no surprise that much of the basic conceptual languages of ecological thought and liberalism do not clash.

This picture may or may not fade as environmental thought develops and the green movement surges forward. It definitely runs counter to the desire of many intellectuals in the more radical and self-consciously theoretical environmental cause. But once again there is no choice but to conclude that while liberalism hardly rules all American intellectual thought, it is hardly gone either.

Still, contemporary green political and social theory proposes an important redirection. Its intellectual enthusiasts badly want a sharp break with liberal thought and practice in the United States, where a holistic and egalitarian community fully integrated with the rest of nature is not exactly foremost on the liberal agenda. Such green thought, however, has a long way to go in terms of intellectual acceptance and popular approval. It is hardly poised to become the basis for the emergence of a new consensus in American political and social thought.

The ecological strain of American thought today, taking into account its several dimensions, continues to serve as evidence that there is no consensus among intellectuals on American political thought. Liberalism may have become more and more the practice in American culture, and it certainly can be found in green thought as well. But the rise of environmentalist thought is fundamentally no affirmation of liberalism. Nor is it evidence for consensus among public intellectuals on the future direction for the United States.

Chapter Eight

To Revive Civil Society

American intellectuals' recent rediscovery of the importance of civil society was far from predictable. After all, many of today's intellectuals grew to adulthood in the 1960s or early 1970s, when agitation against society and its institutions was considerably more common than concern with, much less affection for, civil society. Not a few others, moreover, although born later, look back to that era with obvious affection, perhaps wishing they also had come to maturity then. From such backgrounds, one would not predict the current engagement with civil society—and even less the conviction of many public intellectuals that restoring civil society to health is the essential redirection required for the American polity in the new millennium.

Yet perhaps the contemporary interest in civil society should occasion no surprise. After all, in part it is just a straightforward response to the times. In a society plagued with a nasty politics and too little civil discourse, rampant disrespect for teachers and police, road rage, and frequent "loss of common decency," alarm about the condition of basic civility and civil society may be a matter of simple logic.[1]

In any case, such concerns unite a good many observers, including Stephen Carter, who bewails the situation in his sometimes tart analysis in *Civility: Manners, Morals, and the Etiquette of Democracy*.[2] For Carter, as for a number of other public intellectuals, the stakes involve more than the burdens incivility put on daily living—although he appreciates that these can matter painfully. The issue of civility is also ultimately and intimately connected with what kind of society, including what kind of political system, we want to have. Nothing could be more important, and this is exactly why the question of civil society is of such broad and intense concern to many American intellectuals.

Civility is not the sole concern here. It is tightly connected with the issue of civil society as a whole—the institutions of family, religion, and local organized life and the world they form. The overall mood is that civil society faces a dangerous crisis in our age. The atmosphere is alive with anxiety about family collapse, deterioration of the school systems, violent youth crime, and the like, all evident since the 1960s. Some public intellectuals fear that the voluntary organizations in particular that have been so important to civil society in the United States are weakening. They believe political, neighborhood, and charitable groups attract less and less interest, and thus citizens experience fewer and fewer chances to build a civil society together. Exceptions such as Habitat for Humanity just prove the rule.[3]

Given this context, a rebirth of attention to civil society was entirely predictable in the long run. After all, family, friendships, religion, and other dimensions of civil society are always at the center of most people's existence, including that of public intellectuals. They can rarely be avoided. They are more immediate and more tangible to almost everyone than the status of "community" or the health of planet Earth, not to speak of the latest intellectual fashion.

Of course, American public intellectuals are not alone in considering civil society, just as they are not alone in addressing environmentalism or community. The condition of civil society is increasingly of global interest, of serious concern to intellectuals in many places. Three particular characteristics distinguish many American public intellectuals' encounter with civil society, however, as this chapter and the next argue. One is a sense that the nation's civil society problems are unusually grave, that the condition of the family, institutional religion, and relations among the races are in dangerously poor shape. Intellectual discussion of civil society radiates a crisis aura, especially regarding the family, the basic unit of civil society.

A second characteristic is the public intellectual concentration on family and religion as the eventual bridges to fostering responsible and effective citizens. Many American intellectuals' focus on civil society, in other words, is more instrumental and political than anything else. The health of civil society and the political order are rarely separated; each is key to the other. Thus civil society is often valued more as a ground for the fading ideal of an active citizenry and a lively political democracy than as a good in itself.

There is nothing obvious in this way of thinking. After all, how many people conceive of religion or family in terms of a putative connection with citizenship or a role in building a good nation? One suspects that few view civil society and its institutions in such an instrumental fashion. For believers, religion is about worshiping and following God, not encouraging the development of good citizens. For family members, family is about love, support, care for children, and much else, but not promoting good citizenship or a healthy polity.

Yet intellectual discourse about civil society proceeds differently, and its concerns often are directed to linkages between civil society and politics. Its sense of crisis, moreover, legitimizes the common instrumental approach to civil society and its institutions. Some prominent public intellectuals, such as Jean Elshtain, who view religion and the family instrumentally also acknowledge, honor, or defend their more ordinary and intrinsic purposes.

Third, much of the contemporary public intellectual discourse on civil society is now empirically based and depends enormously on social science evidence and counterevidence. Social science intellectuals and their modes of discourse are now at the heart of contemporary civil society debates. Their empirical focus—like their taste for instrumentalism—is familiarly American. What is not clear, however, is how far this approach has gone toward discovering how to construct a better civil society. To this point, its practitioners have been most successful at the grim business of documenting current pathologies damaging civil society.[4]

Alexis de Tocqueville was the great pioneer in the analysis of American civil society.[5] His argument in the 1830s famously leaned on the view that the United States' rich and vibrant group life was essential to the success of society. It was the medium through which a free people participated in society, formed bonds with others, and learned the moral restraints needed for life. For Tocqueville, the family, religion, and religious groups were especially crucial components of civil society, and they could not be taken for granted—a sentiment now heard once again from many public intellectuals.

In our era, in which the topic of civil society attracts innumerable analysts—and a legion of intellectual proponents—there is no shortage of guides to approaching a conceptual understanding of civil society.[6] Few, however, can match anthropologist Ernest Gellner's insights, which greatly influence what follows.[7] Gellner tries to define civil society in a commonsense fashion, carefully avoiding a definition that is either too inclusive or too narrow. For him, a civil society is a social arrangement characterized by substantial pluralism of diverse social groups, forces, and organizations. All of these have some share of power, and thus can and do block the power of others, including that of government.

Gellner believes that such an arrangement—sometimes in better or worse health—accurately describes most contemporary Western societies, including the United States, but it does not describe most societies in the past or today. In his view, civil society is always weak where a controlling and largely unchecked government rules, whether it was the Soviet regime in 1960, autocratic monarchies of the past, or military regimes today. Such a government snuffs out other social groupings or renders them impotent.

In Gellner's analysis, civil society also is likely to be underdeveloped in nations with relatively weak governments. In such societies it is common to find little pluralism and the population tightly encased in existent social arrangements. Such arrangements have often existed in the past and they do still, Gellner argues, in agrarian societies where class, caste, ethnicity, or family and kin prevent the personal liberty that strong civil societies foster. Oppression is just as real in these circumstances, he insists, as in societies dominated by the authoritarianism of an oppressive government.[8]

In this understanding of civil society, one Tocqueville could easily endorse, the United States has long had a genuine civil society. The issues today, however, are two: What is the current condition of civil society in the United States, and how important is strengthening it for the United States as a nation? For many of those looking for a renewed civil society, their answer to the first query is pessimistic and to the second is a strong affirmative.

On Reviving Civil Society in General

The widespread contemporary argument that it is time to strengthen civil society implies (or declares) that liberal values (or a certain liberalism) are ever more triumphant in the United States and have eroded civil society and institutions, networks, and values. Sometimes the engagement with liberalism is more direct, but it is always there. At its best the discussion is intriguing and sensitive to the paradoxes and dilemmas that lie in the troubled way of liberalism and civil society in America.

Some public intellectuals who seek the renewal of civil society speak less of "civil society" and more of the need to revive institutions, promote shared values, or build local communities. More common now, however, is an approach that calls directly for a revival of civil society. Consider social scientist Alan Wolfe. No one has made a more thoughtful case for helping civil society than this social observer in his book *Whose Keeper? Social Science and Moral Obligation.*[9]

Wolfe insists that the failure of American society to serve many of its citizens in acquiring meaningful values and developing a satisfactory place in society is obvious in the problems besetting our country: crime, suicide, drug abuse, and the rest of the depressingly familiar litany. Part of the difficulty, he also insists, is that the word *duty* has faded from the American vocabulary. While never a core word in the liberal vocabulary, it had remained important in the private spheres of liberal societies until recently. Now it has slipped away everywhere, leaving little in its wake besides alienating institutions and selfish wills. Given the twin and synergistic realities of giant but weak institutions and lost but selfish individuals, Wolfe argues that fortifying the primary and intermediate institutions of society has become an urgent necessity.

For Wolfe, as for others, the growth of the mammoth state is another part of the civil society problem. In his analysis, the liberal state has greatly expanded in good part because it has become a substitute for the shared meaning and local institutions that civil society provided in the past. The irony for Wolfe is that while the state has grown markedly, it has not proved particularly effective as a substitute provider of social integration. It has not and it cannot. The state can do mechanical tasks more or less well, such as delivering welfare checks or putting up stop signs, but it is less successful in creating intangible values or nurturing social institutions. To get people to stop at red lights, to cease robbing 7–Elevens, or to stop having babies out of wedlock is difficult at best for any government.

The idea that the modern liberal state is muscle-bound and has not delivered despite its size is far from a unique perception by Wolfe, who is no conservative. It leads him on to deconstruct the

Scandinavian experience, which once was the darling of many American public intellectuals. In Wolfe's reading, Scandinavia, especially Sweden, provides a sad case study of what happens when the state replaces civil society. The number of out-of-wedlock children has soared, the abortion rate is high, and the marriage rate is falling, as is commitment to work and other collective enterprises. The state rules over an increasingly empty shell.[10]

Similar concerns have animated Jean Bethke Elshtain of the University of Chicago Divinity School, who in the 1980s and 1990s shifted from her earlier concentration on feminist issues and became preoccupied with making the case for reviving civil society. Among her many forums have been numerous books, public appearances, and journal essays, including a regular column in the *New Republic.* At this point, no one plays a more important role in the civil society project in the United States.

Elshtain underlines the kinds of grim social policy outcomes that she believes our weakened civil society now yields, evils others, such as Wolfe, also record and lament. But her gaze falls particularly on what she perceives to be the costs in terms of precious democratic citizenship. The steep decline of active democratic citizenship, Elshtain argues in her recent *Democracy on Trial,* is closely connected with the degeneration of civil society. As politics has become increasingly distorted by individual and group resentments and conflicts, and poisoned by those who push to the fore issues that arise from their private lives—often from their individual psyches—as if they were major public issues, democratic citizenship retreats and democracy becomes more and more fragile.[11]

Elshtain is convinced that a healthy civil society, where the communities of family, friendship, neighborhood, and local associations flourish, is what most people dearly seek, although they are increasingly bewildered about how to achieve it in our present age. They may not want to draw sharp lines between their individual lives and civil society, nor between civil society and the larger political order. Yet they want a society that supports each, defined flexibly and taking into account the ever-changing world. People also want a society in which there is a basic agreement among people based on good will and respect, and an escape from quarrelsome conflict.

These goals, she contends, are equally valuable for both a healthy civil society and a functioning democracy. For Elshtain, both must respect diverse communities and accept the legitimacy of many roles, including people as private persons, members of civil society, and citizens. Both will recognize that people are simultaneously rational and emotive, independent and communal, and interested in liberty and community.[12]

Elshtain argues in *Democracy on Trial* that among the steps needed to achieve a flourishing civil society and an authentic democracy is a "new social covenant." This covenant would commit government to assist civil society and its institutions. Put another way, a rebirth of a kind of a national community where government action helps energize the community's parts is vital for Elshtain. Civil society needs that assistance and should expect it from government in a democratic order, just as government in turn depends on civil society to aid the polity. After all, it is in civil society, Elshtain affirms, that we can learn about citizenship and service while also learning to reject selfishness as our supreme goal in life. Implicit here is a prime difference between Elshtain and some other intellectuals focused on civil society. She does not hate government or consider it all but useless. It has a central role to play, although it must never be allowed to try to replace civil society.[13]

Elshtain believes, however, that civil society cannot proceed with our current conception of rights as something individuals possess quite apart from any duties toward civil society, not to speak of the national community or others in our lives. Such raw selfishness is just too hard on civil society relationships. Elshtain does not have much use for worshipers of the market either or for those who desire to obliterate all private existence and civil society itself in the name of authoritarian agendas. All these tendencies not only undermine civil society but also hurt the large democratic polity. Again and again Elshtain returns to her agreement with Tocqueville's claim that a democratic government characterized by restraint and intelligent civic discourse can exist only when there is an equally successful civil society that teaches the wisdom of these norms.[14]

For Elshtain, ordinary civility both within civil society and in democratic government is, as she emphasizes in *Democracy on Trial*, desperately required in our time. She contends that our increasing lack of such civility bodes ill for our civil society and our form of government, as both struggle to come to terms with unprecedented diversity. To accept incivility is to accept abusive and divisive behavior in an already fragmented social fabric.

This is why Elshtain is so involved in the Council on Civil Society, which she chairs, and which in 1998 issued "A Call to Civil Society," a document that reflects her outlook. It insists people must treat each other as persons of great value, worth listening to and worth including in their lives. Shouting at each other and splitting into self-segregating groups must be rejected, and the ever more abundant signs of these pernicious practices are tragic.

The "Call to Civil Society" presents forty-one ideas for changing the beleaguered situation of American civil society, a list that is long on entries but short on new or definitive "solutions." But for Elshtain, mundane work to aid families, religious groups, local organizations, and the like is the only plausible approach to reviving civility and civil society in the United States. We must recognize that there is no magic wand that can produce a quick and easy solution. Thus she makes no apologies for what her group offers, knowing that the road to be traveled is going to be long and hard.[15]

Elshtain has an acute sense of just the right balance of factors that would benefit society. Civil society is important, but so is a democratic polity. Pluralism in society and the freedom to enjoy diverse lifestyles are valuable, but so is the unity that she judges is so lacking in the United States. Putting all these elements together is exquisitely difficult, she understands, but she is no pessimist. For her this aspiration is not a chimera but an age-old ideal worth steadily pursuing. This religious public intellectual characteristically expresses her ideal as the notion that "the body is one but has many members," a model whose original author wrote First Corinthians and knew a great deal about dedicated struggles toward difficult goals.[16]

As with any theorist, Elshtain's balanced and textured analyses and goals sometimes sound better than messy reality might prove them to be. In fact, one can be more reassured about the directions one should take when reading the eloquent Elshtain than one probably should be. Yet in her essays for the *New Republic* that address specific issues, she often demonstrates a welcome feel for the complexities, paradoxes, and ironies of politics and civil society. She also has a delightful sense of existential realities. It is typical of her cast of mind that she wisely offers few neat answers, instead inviting her readers to enter into a reflective conversation designed to make a difference. In the process she honors her commitment to both civility and civil society.

Civil society enthusiasts such as Elshtain, however, worry some other public intellectuals, whose reservations are part of what is sometimes a very public argument over civil society. Some critics challenge the enthusiasm for civil society by asking who will really benefit besides established local elites and the hierarchies they impose. Others are equally skeptical of celebrations of individual duty and service working at the local level. They are reminded of George Bush's "thousand points of light" and doubt that promoting local acts of charity and helpfulness will deliver much change.

Some civil society proponents do have Bush's idea in mind, however they may reformulate it, although they are rarely eager to put it quite this way. They want people to act locally to help others and to fashion the social connections that they trust will build the communal lives essential, as Tocqueville argued, for public liberalism to exist. And they do not agree that such activities will produce little change. For them, this kind of change is the deepest. It is change that transforms lives.

Other critics insist that "reinventing government" would be a better project for reformers. But this goal receives little support from those interested in civil society, who contend that it appears to assume that somehow government is the answer, or much of the answer, to what ails society. It continues the pleasant faith of many modern liberals that government can be done right this time—to the great benefit of society.

While proponents of a civil society revival seek the most effective government possible, they often view the "reinvention of government" project as romantic at best. To them, it can look like a dead end that those still in love with government—as well as considerable numbers of government employees and clients—cling to. They prefer to emphasize their continuing theme that government is no substitute for civil society, and they judge that that should be obvious to all by now.

Still other critics fear that concentrating on civil society may weaken the state, only to have it replaced by capitalism and capitalists. Wolfe and Elshtain, among other defenders of civil society, are aware of this danger. They, too, are cautious about American capitalism and its giant mergers, multinational corporate alliances, and significant income inequalities. They hope that socially shared values, as well as an enhanced civil society, will block any institution that gets too powerful, but they also understand that the government must be available to check the corporation and vice versa.

Despite such observations, I am struck by how little energy participants in the civil society debates spend on the subject of capitalism. Does liberal capitalism damage American civil society, for example, by its ethic of the free mobility of persons and goods in the market? Many European intellectuals have long complained about capitalism's putative costs to civil society, but in the American civil society debates attacks on capitalism are modest. They exist, but mostly they are muted and ignored. Part of the reason, surely, is the eclipse of Communism and the success of the market in many places in the world. Part is the temper of the age, where wholesale assault on institutions is not exactly standard practice. Part is the specific attitude of most civil society revivalists, which prefers to help American institutions rather than tear any down.

Yet this is not the entire story. The careful reader cannot miss the lack of enthusiasm for the market among the ideas of many civil society advocates. If there is rarely an unrestrained critique in this post-Marxian age, nevertheless uneasiness about capitalism hovers in the background. This is certainly true of Jean Elshtain. It is also the case with Michael Walzer, who may be the most important theorist of civil society in the contemporary United States.

Walzer, of Princeton's Advanced Institute, has given serious thought to civil society, as is reflected in his prodigious intellectual output of the past thirty years.[17] He is keenly aware of the virtues of a flourishing civil society, but he also has reservations about the present-day enthusiasm for civil society. He particularly wants "to warn against the antipolitical tendencies that commonly accompany the celebration of civil society."[18] His fear derives from his commitment to democracy and his suspicion that in some hands civil society is to become a substitute for democracy.

In Walzer's analysis, egalitarian democracy must have as its companion authentic pluralism, respecting each individual and providing wide human freedom, an argument he first made in his masterwork, *Spheres of Justice,* and has developed since. The setting for a real pluralism, Walzer thinks, is civil society, and this is why he considers it important too, *and* why he counts himself among those who want to fortify civil society in the contemporary age. Thus while Walzer indicates he is "uneasy" about too great a stress on civil society, at the same time he is determined to help it.[19] He concludes that "we have neglected the networks through which civility is produced and reproduced," and he wants that inattention to be reversed.[20] In this spirit Walzer calls for "a new sensitivity for what is local, specific, contingent" and a dedication to remembering, as he elegantly puts it, "that the good life is in the details."[21]

For Walzer, there are several perspectives that may harm "the necessary pluralism of any civil society."[22] One is the threat of capitalism. Another is the unchecked market. The crucial issue is the power of capitalism and the market to rip civil society apart—and overwhelm a democratic polity. It is typical of Walzer, however, that he is not interested in those on the Left who seek some collective economic ideal that supposedly will lead to the state's withering away. This is a fantasy, he insists. By now we should have learned that when such schemes are tried there is, in fact, a tremendous growth in the state at the cost of human liberty, a democratic polity, and a living civil society.

Walzer rejects militant nationalism on the same grounds, but his criticism of currently fashionable "republicanism" is more surprising. For him, the problem with republicanism is that it does not take civil society seriously. It focuses too much on public community and therefore is out of touch with most people whose lives are centered in civil society and who want them to be.[23]

Put another way, Walzer's argument is that all these challenges to a civil society focus fail because of "their singularity."[24] They do not understand or respect the complexity of people's existence and the fascinating phenomenon that is society. They are all *an* or *the* "answer," and thus fall short before the complex and wonderful reality of life and the pluralistic good that it produces.[25]

The sum of Walzer's view is, as always, a careful balance. Concentration on civil society can become a retreat from commitment to a democratic, egalitarian political order. Yet failure to appreciate and support civil society can deny people their valued, diverse lives and society its pluralistic reality. Walzer would pursue both democracy and civil society at once, and he summons his readers to do the same.

All this fits nicely with how Walzer conceives civil discourse, which he contends is essential to a healthy democratic politics as well as to civil society. He criticizes public discussions and debate in the United States today because they are so often "thin" or superficial and frequently degenerate into meaningless or downright fatuous rhetoric. The kind of moral discourse that Walzer admires—and embodies in his own writings[26]—is of an entirely different order. His civil discourse would be "thick," aware of the complex many-sidedness, really of the depth, of people, society, and the moral and policy issues that swirl around them. In this, civil discourse would model real people and serve society: "Thick, divided selves . . . re-quire a thick, differentiated, and pluralist society."[27]

Walzer's argument has recently taken yet another turn in his explicit attention to the defense of toleration.[28] Walzer cannot conceive of a decent civil society that does not have generous space not just for pluralism in discourse but also in terms of ways of living. For him, tolerance is close to the heart of a proper civil society, although he is predictably much less clear—or, he might prefer to say, his discussion on tolerance is much "thicker"—when it comes to drawing the boundaries of tolerance. After all, he knows how the dynamics of diversity can destroy society—especially the contentious pluralism of combative groups and individuals, a phenomenon that is hardly fading in contemporary American culture. But Walzer is guardedly optimistic, hoping that the very diversity will work for a viable democratic civil and political society.

Implicit in his discussion of tolerance, thick discourse, and civil society more broadly is Walzer's ethical affinity for moral conventionalism. That is, Walzer praises diversity within and among societies because he has great sympathy for particular civil societies and their respective ways of (ethical) life. He is a genuine, if not limitless, ethical pluralist who respects the particular, the historical, the individual in almost all civil societies—and wants us to do the same.[29] Indeed, he is quite suspicious of any alternative approach to ethics, civil society, or anything else, especially one that proclaims narrow absolutes or indulges in grand, global theory. Such approaches are inevitably dismissive of the particular texture of people and societies as Walzer understands them. He wants us to remember the sometimes murderous historical record of some true believers proclaiming universal truths.[30]

This does not mean Walzer opposes a certain, if very vague, ethical universalism, what he terms "moral minimalism."[31] He maintains there is such a thing among the world cultures, although he also insists that it is "not foundational," appears only at crisis times, and is "recognized" only from the "thick" specifics of particular people, traditions, and cultures.[32] The putative content of Walzer's "ethical minimum" is decidedly uncertain, perhaps deliberately. But that does not bother him as much as would some system of binding natural or religious law or as would any effort "to impose a complete set of moral principles across the range of cultural difference."[33]

Ironically, perhaps, critics of Walzer often fault him for being too abstract, despite the fact that he fills all his books with specific illustrations, bringing his arguments down to earth. Walzer's writing is not so much abstract, in fact, as it is "thick."[34] For him, we may conclude, civil society and what goes with it—tolerance and civil discourse—translate in complicated ways in particular places and times in individual civil societies. Most of them are special, he argues, just because they vary so much. In their diversity and "details," which parallel those of life itself, lies a human grandeur that exceeds any great theory.[35]

Conservative public intellectuals have also played a major role in the civil society debates. Indeed, to some critics the effort to revive civil society—especially the two-parent family—is largely a project of open or disguised conservatives. This is hardly true, but conservatives of several varieties have, in fact, been zealous in the civil society movement in the contemporary United States, including those associated with the Christian Coalition and other Christian, Jewish, and Muslim conservative groups.

Yet revival of civil society is far from automatically a part of the conventional conservative program, despite protestations about the big state and the importance of moral values that permeate the political talk of contemporary conservatism. After all, so much of American conservatism is intensely committed to a kind of hyperliberalism reflected in its sometimes romantic affection for market capitalism and private property above almost all else. In such libertarian contexts civil society tends to disappear amid the celebration of the market.[36]

Former education secretary and drug czar William Bennett well represents the civil society concern within conservatism. Bennett's famous best-seller, *The Book of Virtues*, and other books indicate his strong dedication to strengthening civil society. While Bennett ostensibly wrote *The Book of Virtues* for children, it definitely constitutes an argument for adults also.[37]

At first glance *The Book of Virtues* may not appear to be about civil society. Composed of stories and poems and organized into sections devoted to the values Bennett admires—honesty, compassion, self-discipline, faith, and loyalty, among others—it devotes little explicit attention to society as a whole or to particular social institutions. Yet as the reader goes along it becomes clear that the virtues Bennett lauds are valuable mostly for their social benefits. His objective is the fashioning of character for a responsible, useful participant in society. Bennett's virtues turn out to be mostly indispensable building blocks for what he judges to be a humane and functioning civil society.[38]

Elsewhere in his writings, in *The De-valuing of America*, for example, Bennett makes explicit institutional analyses and a determined defense of civil society. He lambastes cultural and intellectual elites who deconstruct American civil society and thereby consistently attempt to undermine it. Like Elshtain, Bennett thinks ideas and their purveyors have a real impact and that too many intellectual elites have succeeded in their negative mission, assisting in the unraveling of American civil society. No wonder he denounces these cultural elites and insists they no longer merit deference.[39]

Yet Bennett's characteristic mood is optimistic, and he is not lured by siren calls of cynicism or despair.[40] His approach is to work steadily to reinforce civil society's main components—the family, the neighborhood, and, not surprisingly for a former secretary of the Department of Education, local schools. A revitalized civil society is the answer, and achieving this goal through institutions is the practical road to follow. Bennett's organized expression of this commitment in recent years has fittingly been entitled Empower America (not the government or the intellectual elites!).

Notably, the considerable intellectual engagement with civil society renewal is mirrored in (or mirrors) the disposition of the general public. While the concept of civil society is no part of Americans' ordinary discourse, alarm over the decline of the family, confidence in the value of religion and church membership, and support for marriage, children, and the web of small groups that composes American civil society is broad. We know, for example, that public support for the family easily survived the libertarian 1960s and early 1970s and the changes that took place then regarding such social issues as premarital sexual relations and abortion. In the contemporary era, when politicians of virtually every stripe praise "the family" and civil society institutions such as organized religion, decline of public commitment to civil society is not in view.[41]

Moreover, concern with civil society crosses all conventional political lines. Indeed, to many of its proponents the issue teaches the uselessness of traditional divisions between the Right and the Left. Bennett illustrates conservative involvement, and Wolfe and Elshtain show how theorists on the moderate Left address this concern. Perhaps Hillary Rodham Clinton is the most well known proponent of a civil society revival in popular culture. Her use of the proverbial claim that "it takes a village to raise a child" is an affirmation of the value of community in civil society.

The Revival of Family

Intellectual proponents of the revival of civil society regularly criticize the disintegrative liberal individualism they see at work in many social sectors, but nowhere more so than in the family. Moreover, the "pro-family" cause is gaining supporters from a number of sources. Indeed, it has metamorphosed into a family revival movement, promoted by a burgeoning literature from family practitioners and specialists who insist on the importance of family. The best-selling work of Mary Pipher is an example. In *The Shelter of Each Other*, Pipher vigorously defends the family and identifies some of the many cultural barriers—the telephone, TV, and consumerism, for example—that she judges make life so perilous for the ordinary family today. Her strategy for family revival involves a typically American determination to act and a distaste for mere praise for action. Much of her program depends on families themselves, such as committing to time for family interaction and turning off such competitors as the telephone and the TV.[42]

The so-called family revival movement has important advocates in Washington. William Galston, a social and political theorist who was a close aide to President Clinton, has been an example in his outspoken defense of family as a necessary institution for the health of civil society. He has publicly bewailed the family's decline and thinks its vitality should be integral to the domestic agenda of the Democratic Party. In fact, Galston left the Clinton administration when his son, Ezra, complained that his father was seldom available to watch him play sports.[43]

Despite the family revival movement, however, there is still plenty of controversy over "the family" and civil society. Among political intellectuals and family policy "experts" there are distinct points of view, pursued with intensity and passion. Serious matters are at stake, and the resulting controversies justify the term "war over the family."[44]

What counts as a family and what merits approval as a good family are sensitive issues that open up major sore points from the start. Beyond these matters, however, there are a fair number of public intellectuals who are not sympathetic to family revival in any terms. Some object that families are inevitably patriarchal and thus unjust. Some object that families are regularly parochial and stultifying. Some argue for radical alternatives to "family," sometimes communal arrangements, sometimes free-form methods of child rearing.[45]

What perhaps gets less attention are the debates rooted in serious historical or philosophical considerations on the family, especially in terms of the family in the liberal tradition over time. There are exceptions, but there is a considerable belief that the liberal tradition has too little positive to offer for thinking about the family and family policy today.[46] Political theorist Andrew Spalding maintains, however, that liberals need not accept that there is an inherent conflict between the family and liberal values, and they should not conceive of either family or liberalism in such a manner that will promote or legitimize such a conflict. After all, he argues, key portions of the liberal tradition, especially the work of John Stuart Mill and Alexis de Tocqueville, acknowledge how important the family is for teaching liberal values *and* responsibilities. In this conception of the liberal tradition, then, the family is not an enemy to liberalism but an essential ally.[47]

Views critical of conventional families today also confront a fierce counterattack from those who defend its practical importance for society and for the individual. For family advocates, this means at least two things. It means appreciating the individual and the social benefits they believe come from stable family lives (in comparison with the increasingly demonstrable social pathologies now resulting from damaged family life). First, defending the family means recognizing the family's importance in terms of individual happiness. Some defenders of the family among public intellectuals argue that the inability to form happy, intimate relationships, which is a widespread curse of the contemporary era, originates in childhood family problems such as divorce, alcoholism, and child abuse. Thus one's family experience has an enormous effect on one's life chances for happiness. Second, it means respecting the family's social and moral benefits. Harvard professor Mary Ann Glendon's defense of the family is one illustration among many. For her, families are vital to the "communities of memory and mutual aid" that are the "seedbeds of virtue" in an attractive civil society. They can nurture virtue, in fact, as no other institution can begin to do. They can also promote good citizens as well as decent human beings, and in the process the entire society benefits.[48]

Consider the argument of social scientist James Q. Wilson. He contends that comparative study of world cultures shows what people know intuitively: that everywhere family is basic to the human story and is the crucible for the teaching of morality to children. After all, he observes, children must learn a "moral sense" and such moral norms as fairness, duty, sympathy, and concern for the group. We are not born with them. For Wilson, the family is the usual place—and generally the best place—for such learning. Moreover, Wilson argues that morality will not be acquired through highly rational discourse, despite the claims of some fancy intellectual outlooks; nor is it true that "the highest moral stage is one in which people talk like college professors."[49] To develop morality, children need a functioning family, not classes in philosophy.

This is why Wilson is skeptical of many proposals to turn to schools to promote the moral sense that is so plainly missing among many young people who are victims of divorce, poverty, and neglect. He maintains that morality rarely develops in schools or in any other formal setting. Family and friends teach people morality as they live their lives, a process that cannot be replicated in the classroom.

No wonder Wilson praises the ordinary family as a vital part of a successful civil society and worries when it is not working. It provides the morality that matters enormously to the achievement of an enduring and satisfied nation. The family and other groups in civil society as a whole, therefore, must be a major project of Americans. The answer does not lie in well-intentioned government legislation but in encouraging something that is much harder than passing laws. It resides in individuals and society providing a supportive environment for the family and other elements of civil society. They are the means to decent, ethical people.[50]

Marriage and Divorce

Another part of the family movement is the burgeoning literature devoted to the defense and renewal of marriage. Sometimes grounded in serious research, but at least as often the expression of pop psychology, these works and their arguments are addressed to mixed audiences. They range from Judith Wallerstein's sober, research-based book *The Good Marriage* to Ed Wheat's popular and practical *Love Life for Every Married Couple*, with much in between.[51] Such a range is entirely predictable because it mirrors the meteoric rise of discussion on marriage and the family in all sectors of society. This revival of interest and support is a good indicator of perceptions of the health of marriage and the family. Only rarely is the mood of this literature optimistic. Studies such as that by Rosalind Barnett and Caryl Rivers, which notes how strong some families are today, are rare.[52]

The entire movement focused on marriage and divorce and determined to change the current situation has been appropriately dubbed the "antidivorce revolution." There is little doubt that there is great interest in bringing down the million-plus divorces per year in the United States. All sorts of intensive premarital counseling by religious and other groups, as well as marital counseling for couples in trouble, now exist. More are proposed, and some are proposed to be mandated. There are also increasing efforts to challenge no-fault divorce laws, which opponents see as "easy" divorce.[53]

Why all this effort is under way, an effort joined by a number of public intellectuals, is an interesting question. Much of the time nothing so grand as the vitality of civil society receives explicit mention. Even the general strength of marriage or family is not always emphasized. The most frequently discussed issue is children and their lives. Around them turns the attack on family collapse and divorce, although the issue of the civil society necessarily hovers in the background, for the condition of the family is a crucial aspect of every civil society, and family failure means civil society failure.

Thus while a wide variety of issues arise in the contemporary intellectual disputes over family and civil society, the largest concerns focus on divorce, single mothers, and, above all, children. Indeed, most of the fight over the family today is about children, which is to say about our future as a society.

Family Breakdown and Children

Public intellectuals critical of the consequences of family breakdown increasingly demand that, for children's sake, an integral and functioning family must be supported. Perhaps the most public expression of this view came in Barbara Whitehead's famous 1993 article in the *Atlantic Monthly*, entitled "Dan Quayle Was Right." There she declares it is just plain wrong to glamorize single parenthood as former Vice President Quayle felt the *Murphy Brown* TV show did.[54] Whitehead is hardly a conservative Republican, but her straightforward argument, which she later expanded, is that children of divorce experience a far greater range of problems, both personal and social, than those whose parents are not divorced. In her work Whitehead combines detailed research with empathetic discussion to bring home to the reader the pain and problems of children trapped in families of divorce.[55]

Helping children must mean helping parents, argue Sylvia Hewlett and Cornel West in their *War Against Parents*,[56] an example of the growing literature by intellectuals that defends parenthood and at the same time tries somewhat desperately to help parents. The book's subtitle gets at their practical agenda: *What We Can Do for America's Beleaguered Moms and Dads*. Not inclined to much theory, but affronted by the present situation, Hewlett and West offer a scattershot set of ideas, some more plausible than others, but all with the goal of trying to ease the pressures that are so intense for many families: financial pressures and other difficulties brought on by very complicated and busy lives. They appreciate very well that unless contemporary pressures diminish, marriages, families, children, parents, and the larger society will suffer even more pain and dislocation than they do now.

Perhaps the two most influential public intellectual advocates for two-parent families for the sake of children and, through them, civil society, have been David Popenoe and David Blankenhorn. Popenoe wants people to acknowledge the reality of what he describes as "family decline." He means both divorce statistics and their consequences for children who grow up outside a "conventional" family structure. He is convinced that the selfish individualism and general social disarray prevalent in American culture are the primary causes for the deterioration of the two-parent family. And he believes that family decline, in turn, has speeded the general deterioration of civil society.[57]

Blankenhorn is the head of the Institute for American Values, a New York think tank. His controversial thesis is that the absence of men in more and more families in the United States is a disaster for the family and for civil society. While Blankenhorn recognizes that divorce is not going away, he contends that children of divorce need their fathers at least as much as do children in a two-parent family— and not just for their father's child support money. Children need a father's love, care, and participation in their lives, just as they need these things from their mother. Since fathers' absence has enormous costs that we all live with every day, in the form of social problems and in personal unhappiness, Blankenhorn argues that our society's most pressing challenge is to get men to remain an active part of every family.[58]

The most intense intellectual and social science disputes today address the effects of divorce on children and on civil society as a whole. The issues are complex and difficult, but the battle lines can be rigid. In the manner of social science intellectuals, the matter frequently takes the form of arguments over whether there are scientifically demonstrable effects of divorce on children and, if so, whether these are good for children and for civil society.

The literature has moved slowly but surely in recent years to conclude that children of divorce are disadvantaged in society. Among the many difficulties they face, they have lower odds for economic and educational success and for escaping crime and the criminal justice system. As social scientists Gary Sandefur and Sara McLanahan (who are hardly conservative shills) sum up the data, children in single-parent families are likely to have a much harder time succeeding in school and later by standard measures of achievement than are the offspring in two-parent families. This pattern, moreover, is likely to be manifest repeatedly throughout such children's lives. Sandefur and McLanahan agree that we must develop a much greater commitment to marriage and step away from an ethic of individual satisfaction that imposes heavy costs on others. But as practical social scientists and social policy advocates, they are more interested in making the one-parent family work better than in pontificating on the virtues of the two-parent family.[59]

Of course, these arguments grant that the effects of divorce vary according to specific situations and particular children. Of course, they recognize that divorce is not always worse for every child than its alternative. Of course, they point out that some children of divorce do beautifully in life, and many do fine by conventional measures. Yet the overall record for children of divorce is less and less open to debate. No matter how fiercely arguments rage over whether it is divorce itself or the aftermath of divorce—poor economic conditions, lack of a male presence, and the like—the standard (if sometimes reluctant) intellectual argument now is that social costs are real for children of divorce and for children whose mothers never married. The larger conclusion, moreover, is that the consequences also place terrific burdens on civil society and its institutions.[60]

Critics Revisited

The intellectual critics of the family revival movement, however, do not go away. Judith Stacey, perhaps the most well known dissenter,[61] has no sympathy for the "family" revivalists who yearn to rebuild family and expresses no regrets over its decline. After all, she argues, marriage itself in any form is suspect, since the foundation of marriage is always coercion of women. Thus "family" is also very much about coercion and merits no approval. The only vision of family that Stacey welcomes enthusiastically is the gay family. She agrees that having two parents might be a good thing, but she contends that having three or four (or whatever) number of parents would be "even better."[62] There is nothing unfortunate about having just one parent either. She reassures us that most kids turn out fine, no matter what their family structure. Quality time from a parent or parents is what counts.

Stacey is not much interested in or impressed with social science data, and she has no trouble arguing that children can often benefit, in fact, from their parents' divorce. For example, she points out, divorce is often better for children than living with two battling parents. Family revivalists would be better advised to spend their time attacking "corporate greed" and low pay for women if they really want to help children. She insists their moral hand-wringing about "family" is irrelevant to anything important and hides the truth about the "pro-family" movement: it is homophobic and anti-black, and it cares only for the middle class.[63]

Stacey's position is not one she occupies alone, although others who agree with her often are more cautious. Thus some argue that the family is important, but they urge observers to develop some perspective when they think of the family, which has changed a great deal throughout human history and taken many forms in human culture. That it is changing in our time does not mean that somehow it is collapsing, and all civil society with it. Perhaps we are merely in a time of "transition," not necessarily an indication of decline.[64]

While Stacey-like proclamations—"Good riddance to the family"—may not be the norm among critics, attacks on "the new crusade for the old family" are plentiful. Again and again the argument is that the pro-family movement is locked into the model of the 1950s family—or some other period of the recent past. It is a "fantasy" for today, although one with little appeal in any circumstance for critics. They contend, moreover, that the best explanation for family problems today is poverty and other economic difficulties, not social values or defects in family structure, such as divorce.[65]

Some intellectuals who spurn the pro-family movement are self-conscious family liberationists. They favor a loosely bound family, one in which each member is radically free and radically equal. For them the eclipse of most expressions of "family" in our time is good news, representing a growing triumph of human "self-development, freedom, and androgyny." Family revivalists, in turn, lambaste such views—"utopia against the family"—as a dangerous and destructive outlook with great human cost in terms of personal happiness and social stability.[66] They also note that single motherhood, in the light of single mothers' increasing numbers and frequently difficult life conditions, garners little enthusiasm.[67]

Conclusion

Controversies over marriage and divorce and the "proper" family structure are hardly the only contested areas in civil society debates. There also are those who are suspicious of the entire civil society revival program, with its implicit or explicit warm and fuzzy overtones of community. There are those who raise the issue of whether many of the ideas of the civil society revival are not really projections toward reactionary utopias. They suggest these ideas are mostly attempts to create a utopian decentralized world that has no relevance today in a world order with a global economy, corporate domination of the national marketplaces, two-wage-earner families, day care, computers, and TV that is here to stay.[68]

Among the many skeptical voices, the late Christopher Lasch was one of the most interesting. Lasch long understood and respected the place of civil society and the home in most people's lives.[69] At the same time, like Walzer and Elshtain and others, he was concerned to achieve a social order with other goods as well. For Lasch, the effects of capitalism on civil society and individual Americans were largely negative, reinforcing materialism, greed, and the shallowest kind of selfishness. Indeed, Lasch's work is especially engaging because he grappled with the question of our capitalist political economy and what he considered its price for civil society. We have an unfortunate consumer culture, Lasch argued, which is daily gaining a greater and greater destructive grip on Americans and American culture.[70]

Like Tocqueville, Lasch turned to the family and civil society in general as the best means to impart norms that he judged integral to a good life, including love and trust, a sense of community, respect for every person, basic equality, and democracy. As he did so, he expressed a certain ambivalence about the feminist movement. Of course, Lasch rallied to full equality for women as an immensely worthy goal, but he worried that the feminist movement did not honor stay-at-home moms enough and did not care enough about women prepared to serve as volunteers in local organizations, women who are important to family and other institutions of civil society.

Lasch recognized that more than the family is in trouble in American civil society. Everywhere he looked, he identified declining institutions and practices that once served to weave bonds among Americans, to build the community an individualistic, capitalist culture badly needs. While he blamed capitalist elites for the situation, he also singled out intellectual elites. For him, both groups played too great a role in promoting the disaggregation of U.S. society that has come with the celebration of selfish materialism and the worship of individual self-realization.[71]

Lasch insisted, however, that there can be no going back to earlier eras. This was not merely a commonsense assessment of the march of American history; it was his personal preference. He reluctantly seemed to accept liberal capitalism, as he did liberal feminism—even as he noted their putative civil society costs. His dilemma was not unusual for civil society advocates—only his frankness.

Lasch and others who seek a rebirth of civil society in the United States agree that decay of civil society is all around them. Much less often do they agree on the specifics of what to do about it. Often they do not pretend to know what to do in any dramatic or sweeping sense. The usual fare they offer is slogging through particular policy changes and taking individual actions. This widespread awareness of the difficulty of achieving a successful civil society rebirth is a tribute of sorts to civil society thinkers such as Lasch and Walzer. They perceive the complexity of civil society problems and know that working on them means traveling a long and not especially well-marked road. Thus those who turn to the revival of civil society as the best approach to America's woes and expect today's public intellectuals to have that answer face major disappointment. Sharp and shared outlines to accomplish a civil society redirection do not exist.

Yet at this juncture, consideration of the intellectual concerns over civil society can hardly stop. Far from it. Thus there is much discussion of the African-American family, its challenges, and the implications for African Americans and the entire civil society. There is also increasing attention to the role of religion and religious institutions in civil society. Chapter 9 turns to these aspects of contemporary civil society discourse, which are very much a part of the search through civil society for new directions in American life.

Chapter Nine

To Revive Civil Society II

While intellectual discourse over civil society is in full flower, it is unclear whether the result has illuminated civil society or provided much substantive guidance about how to promote its improvement. The subject is a large one, as are its challenges. They include questions about how much any civil society can be constructed or reconstructed by intellectuals or governments. They also include the question of whether the overwhelmingly instrumental approach of many intellectual revivalists of civil society will work. Yet the public intellectual engagement with civil society is almost endless, and more needs to be said to explicate contemporary considerations on the revival of civil society as a redirection for American thought and life.

The African-American Family

No aspect of civil society discourse attracts more attention than the condition of the family in the African-American community and its implications for society as a whole. No area is more sensitive, and in none is there more widespread recognition by intellectuals of all colors of the existence of a crisis regarding the family that is deleterious for civil society.

Daniel Patrick Moynihan first brought the health of the African-American family to broad intellectual consciousness in the 1960s, and he has continued to grapple with a situation that he realizes has deteriorated.[1] The statistics are now well established and widely known. The most important is that the two-parent family is in serious straits and that about three-quarters of black children are born to single mothers and will grow up in homes without fathers. Terrible problems of youth delinquency and crime, drug abuse, failure to complete high school, and still more children produced out of wedlock are also part of a picture that causes great concern virtually everywhere.

Contemporary works describe the situation many African-American children face when they are mired in a fatherless world of poverty, welfare, and crime. Alex Kotlowitz's *There Are No Children Here* is one heartrending account of the life of poor African-American children in Chicago projects.[2] Lealan Jones and Lloyd Newman's *Our America* is another, a compilation of two black teenagers' depressing firsthand reports for National Public Radio of their experiences as residents of Chicago's South Side.[3] In less evocative terms, the situation has long been recognized—and for as long deplored.[4]

To be sure, not quite everyone agrees on how real the crisis is. There are complaints that "the crisis" is mostly an artifact of a white conception of the family and does not exist at all in terms of African-American culture. Understandably, there are also those, like Robert B. Hill, who want the good news about African-American families to be told much more often. After all, as Hill remarks, there are plenty of success stories among African-American families, and there are also decided communal virtues in many black family arrangements that help ease the current situation. He asks, When and where do they get much attention?[5]

One reason such a perspective is not the usual fare in the intellectual conversation today is that the problems of troubled families in the African-American community (as well as elsewhere in the U.S. population) are just too overwhelming to be avoided. Another is that historians of the black family, such as Kenneth Clark and Herbert Gutman, insist that the current situation is no fixed cultural norm in the history of African Americans. Far from it. They argue that it departs from the historic story of the black family in slavery and in freedom. They note that until the 1960s a two-parent family was the rule in the black community and that most African-American children were born to married couples. Only in the 1960s did this pattern undergo sharp—and controversial—declension toward the present situation.[6]

Most discussion regarding the African-American family today, then, starts from the reality of its vulnerable condition, a judgment shared within and without the black community. Focus falls on the question of what has caused the present situation, which begs for an answer if there is to be any hope of practically addressing the problems.

Despite some assumptions to the contrary, there is considerable diversity among African-American intellectuals today.[7] Discussions about the origins of the difficulties in the African-American family reflect this fact, and thus it is no surprise that there are a variety of explanations among African-American as well as other analysts.

Structural and Other Economic Problems

Some identify (and blame) the lack of employment opportunities for many African Americans, especially black men, as the crucial cause for the difficulties in black family life. William Julius Wilson is the best-known exponent of this view, although it has also attracted other articulate expositors.[8] Wilson's classic argument in his book *The Truly Disadvantaged* has created an enormous interest in his thesis. Wilson is now a highly respected and placed (at Harvard) social scientist advocate for African Americans, known for his reflective considerations on the challenges faced by the black poor, including the black family in urban poverty.[9]

Wilson grounds his argument in ample data from impoverished sections of African-American Chicago. In his most recent work his conclusions continue to be that black men—and through them the African-American family—have suffered in recent decades largely because of the loss of serious jobs, especially solid manufacturing jobs, in the central cities of the United States. For Wilson, the superstructure of other African-American troubles rests on this underlying economic tragedy. Like others of similar persuasion, Wilson concludes that other explanations for the situation of the African-American family, including racism, may have a role but fall short of the explanatory power of the structural economic variable.[10]

Government Failure

A second view identifies government failure as an important element in exploring difficulties in the African-American family structure. Many travel this road, but there is plenty of disagreement along the way about what constitutes government failure. One side of this outlook complains that government's failure is that it has not done enough—often has not begun to do enough—to help many needy African Americans (or the poor in general) to become economically independent. Proponents, who have included Donna Shalala and others in the Clinton administration, believe that meeting this goal requires activist policies to strengthen the family in the black community. They insist, for example, that as traditional welfare ends, government will have to offer much more health care, day care, and other services—at least for a few years and maybe long after that.

Another side of the government failure view diagnoses the cause of the failure as too much government. Its proponents maintain that government has created the very problems it was supposedly relieving. They reject the idea that they consider paradoxical—that the answer to government failure should be more government expenditures and programs. Instead, they insist that as government has embraced a welfare model, it has encouraged women—whether intentionally or not—to be dependent clients of government and to turn away from their family communities. They also note that government has abandoned many efforts to support or enforce a family-oriented ethic. They conclude that these consequences badly damaged the once well-established, two-parent, African-American family. Routine in conservative intellectual circles, this argument has long since ceased to be heard only there.[11]

Stephan and Abigail Thernstrom offer another take on the role of government, the black family, and the overall African-American situation in the United States in their widely discussed and controversial book *America in Black and White*.[12] In this lengthy study the Thernstroms shower their readers with data, much of which suggest that many public intellectuals' view of the general situation of African Americans has been far too negative. They insist that African Americans have made dramatic advances in the twentieth century in terms of their economic condition, civil and political rights, and education. For the Thernstroms, however, the explanation for this good news, while complicated, is not primarily the events and the government laws of the civil rights era and its struggles. These factors mattered, but World War II and subsequent economic growth mattered more, as has the erosion of white prejudice that they contend has steadily occurred.

The Thernstroms understand very well that all is not good in parts of the African-American community, and that includes serious erosion of the two-parent family, with terrible consequences for many black children. Yet they are convinced that government action has only worsened the situation. Modern government at the behest of liberals—especially affirmative action—has poisoned race relations, they suggest, and impeded efforts by African Americans to address black problems such as family stability.

Cultural Problems

A third perspective holds that the principal cause of African-American family deterioration is the widespread, if hardly universal, growth of cultural attitudes in the black community that undermine marriage and family bonds. In this sensitive area two matters attract the most discussion. One focuses on attitudes regarding personal discipline, including evidence of diminished acceptance of marriage and fatherhood and a willingness to pursue short-run over long-run pleasures. A second concentrates specifically on selected attitudes that some young black males and females have toward each other—and toward children. These include the outlook of males who take (sexual) pride in producing children but feel no responsibility for them, and that of young women who want to have children to mark their maturity.

By some calculations, the strength of these attitudes is not declining. While prior to the 1960s single mothers sometimes received sympathetic support because they were in difficult straits, they did not do so because single motherhood somehow merited approval. Now analysts explore whether some sectors of the black community admire it.[13] Black and white cultural analysts agree that it will be no simple task to alter such attitudes. While they know government programs can try, they suspect that only the African-American community itself can lead the way to real change.

Racism

Yet another outlook concentrates on race as the main explanatory factor for the condition of the African-American family, an explanation that often accompanies other analyses. Those who consider race the key maintain that blacks suffer so much discrimination from the majority culture that the resulting pressures make family life painfully difficult.

This often-angry literature details the myriad consequences some African Americans perceive as originating in pervasive racism in the United States, including scant government help for black families. Its proponents often concentrate on what they consider the pernicious and prominent role of the liberal media in sustaining the stereotypes and misconceptions of African Americans that allow racism to continue. These include allowing people to blame the life conditions of poor blacks on poor blacks rather than exploring broader causes—including racism.

Social scientists Paul Sniderman and Thomas Piazza discuss the racial thesis gingerly but thoroughly in their landmark exploration of the evidence regarding "the scar of race" in the United States.[14] They know that racial bigotry still exists in the United States, but they report that it is not a significant factor among the majority of Americans. Sniderman and Piazza find that many whites have negative stereotypes of blacks, but they distinguish such attitudes from racial prejudice. They contend that it is these stereotypes rather than blatant racism that best explain white attitudes.

Sniderman and Piazza also report that white opposition to policies intended to assist African Americans often stems from whites' personal values and politics rather than their racial feelings or their stereotypes about African Americans. What white people think about African Americans and how they evaluate particular policies turn out to be by no means the same thing. Nor are white reactions to policies regarding African Americans uniform. Thus, for Sniderman and Piazza, the situation is far too complex to be reduced to the single explanation of white racism. They conclude that this fact offers hope for positive change in the future, since stereotypes and policy differences may be far easier to overcome than racism.

On the other hand, Lawrence Bobo, a prominent African-American social scientist, has brought together a number of other social scientists whose findings suggest that racism remains a powerful and destructive force in American life.[15] While there is no disagreement that much of the overt racism of the past has eroded, Bobo notes that white stereotyping of blacks—and vice versa—is common, as is much "symbolic" white racism. The definition he offers of "symbolic" racism may be viewed as surreptitious racism, which hides in such claims as that blacks are lazy, show little initiative, and live off the government. These findings and a good many others do not make these social scientists very optimistic about the future of race relations in the United States.[16]

Unfortunately, the social science dispute over the evidence for racism in the United States does not help much in resolving the competing claims about the extent of racism. So much turns around interpretation and labeling of results. In fact, Sniderman and Piazza and the Bobo group do not present dramatically different data. The real differences arise in their interpretations. One voice accents black and white differences based in policy disputes; another says racism is the issue. Both agree that there is plenty of racial stereotyping.

It is in this context that David Shipler's *Company of Strangers: Blacks and Whites in America* has appeared.[17] This book pursues quite another methodology, one that Shipler maintains leads to a heightened sense of the dynamics involved and thus to a more plausible understanding of American racial reality. Shipler's approach is to talk with people and to report their racial stories. This method yields lively reading, since he offers no systematic survey data, but rather quite fascinating black and white stories about racial experiences. Whether it is particularly accurate is another matter.

Shipler contends that if one actually gets out and talks with Americans about race, one discovers that there is still plenty of racism around, although nowadays it is often unselfconscious. Moreover, relations are terribly complicated quite apart from racism because blacks and whites repeatedly understand even the most ordinary gestures and comments in strikingly different ways. Racism does not cause these misunderstandings, but they matter because they, too, make relations between whites and blacks difficult.

Some critics of Shipler within the African-American community charge that his stories come from no random sample of blacks and reflect the views of African Americans who accent racism and claims of victimhood.[18] In any case, his unsystematic selection of interviewees proves fascinating and insightful even as its social scientific claims of accuracy are questionable.

On balance, Shipler is not really a pessimist regarding the racial future of the United States, but he considers it absurd to ignore racism as a continuing problem for African Americans. Airy reassurances that racism is all but irrelevant for the condition of blacks and the black family get nowhere with him, and he wonders how they could with any aware American.

Discussions about racism in the United States now often circle around the contention that it has brought disaster for the black male in particular, leaving many African-American males undereducated, underemployed, and with little useful role in society or in the family. Indeed, today there is rising attention to the fate of black males in the United States among intellectuals and social scientists. Many applaud this development as good news for the black family and society in general. The problem is that there is as yet no agreement on what to do to help.[19]

Makes Me Wanna Holler is journalist Nathan McCall's best-selling autobiography about his troubled youth. Filled with tales of sexual machismo and criminal activity, it is a striking testimony to the problems, including racism, African-American males may face, even those who come from better than average backgrounds.[20] Now a successful writer, McCall gives his readers little happy news. He argues that his escape is no guide to the fate typical for many others he knew as a young man. McCall survived his youth—and a prison sentence—but many of his African-American friends did not. McCall is no potential ally, however, of those like William Julius Wilson. For McCall, racism, not the economic situation, is the most important single problem facing most black men, and until it is confronted they have a bleak future in the United States.

Others in the African-American community agree, especially on the need for attention to the plight of the black male. While the now famous Million Man March and the activities associated with it that followed in some localities are an effort to call more African-American men to responsible adulthood and especially fatherhood, they also involve concern with and respect for black males as men. Some male African-American commentators now address this topic, often complaining that the larger culture—as well as many black women—have negative attitudes toward African-American males. The result, some contend, is a disturbing and costly "assassination of the black male image."[21]

Some African Americans and others fault the welfare system for a good portion of what Bill Stephney considers male marginalization by a welfare system that defines "family" as "any woman with children and a check from AFDC for support." The welfare system has thus "devalued and replaced" men.[22] This outlook maintains that it is hardly surprising that as a result some black men display deep contempt for African-American women. Altogether there is a poison here that critics suggest will last until welfare is no longer integral to a segment of African-American life. What changes the new welfare system of the late 1990s will bring to this situation remains to be seen.

For some black men involved with helping African-American boys "reaching up for manhood," the situation is depressing. Especially in the inner city, natural adolescent risk-taking can go unchecked, "ruthless marketing" fans the flames of materialism and crime, and sex, but not fatherhood, is celebrated.[23] Many argue that black men themselves have the answer and that they alone can reverse the situation by working with young African-American males, serving as role models of a socially integrative life in manhood. This may be possible because African-American boys badly "need to be connected to men so that they see examples of what they can become."[24]

For still others the crisis of the black male is an example of the age-old problem of how to cope with young males, whatever their race or culture.[25] It is the task of dealing with the plentiful biological aggressiveness in young men's genes. This challenge is compounded in the United States because the culture is poorly equipped to deal with young males, including young inner-city African-American males. American culture often fails to integrate some young males of all races into civil society due to its damaged family structures and the absence of adequate male role models; excessive respect for personal "honor"; too many guns; the power of gangs; male resistance to marriage; and a favorable gender ratio that frees men from the need to marry to obtain sex. The result, according to David Courtwright, is that "young American men . . . are . . . among the most dangerous people on earth."[26]

Both black Muslim and Christian leaders agree that the answer for many African-American males must involve religion. As Tony Evans, an African-American leader in Promise Keepers puts it, there is no other way that a black male can be "the man God made you to be."[27] The goal here is the male who is above all responsible to the women and children in his life—to his family. The argument is that quarreling over who or what is to blame for the situation of many black males should not be the main focus. African-American men have to grapple with things as they are, not the excuses people may have, however legitimate, for their circumstances. The Million Man March attracted men of all faiths (and those of no faith) to this ideal of the proper role for black men, as has the integrated Christian Promise Keepers movement.

All these perspectives are controversial, but George Gilder's view is even more so. Gilder insists that welfare "culture" is crucial to comprehending the situation of some African-American males today. For him, welfare has created a situation in which there is almost no legitimate social role for many poor black males, and thus they have fallen on bad times. Gilder's view is that society requires a robust economy (here he and Wilson echo each other) in order to provide black males the opportunity for a decent economic life, which in turn will provide them with a legitimate role in society. Whenever and wherever this economic situation exists, Gilder contends, African-American males become providers and then husbands. Moreover, he declares, this is the way for young males from any race to live disciplined and purposeful lives in any society.

Gilder does not care that his argument clashes with some feminist assumptions about proper role sharing by men and women. He is convinced there is no other effective means to help young African-American men and women, who are often trapped in a system where the two-parent family is gone—with tremendous costs to African Americans and to civil society.[28]

Few concerned public intellectuals subscribe to any one of these theories as the complete explanation of the situation facing the African-American family. Treatments such as William Kelso's *Poverty and the Underclass* are especially valuable because they compare the alternative explanations.[29] While Kelso has his own theory, he appreciates the essential point: that family problems in the black community (as elsewhere) cannot be quickly explained or corrected. What he and so many other public intellectuals also recognize is the importance of this issue for the black community—and for the entire civil society.

This is exactly the analysis of African-American Harvard sociologist Orlando Patterson. He sees many factors at work, some general and some specific. Of course, he says, racial pressures place stress on many black families. Of course, economic conditions take a huge toll too. Who could possibly think otherwise, he asks? Patterson maintains, however, that the influence of cultural factors in the African-American community needs to be acknowledged as well. He believes that some lower-class black males have an ethic that is disastrous for the black family. The ethic puts too much emphasis on being cool, celebrating sexual conquests, using drugs and alcohol, and accepting violence, including violence against women and children.

In the black middle class, Patterson suggests, African-American women are liberated, often have careers, and yet face a shortage of eligible men, in part because too many of the middle-class men they meet are sexists, dinosaurs from another era unable to deal with modern women. The situation is complex, Patterson agrees, but he recoils at the thought that nothing can be done. The first step is acknowledgment of the problems of African-American gender relations and family formation, followed by an aggressive effort to address the problems.[30]

Perhaps the most hopeful sign about the family—of whatever race, description, or problems—is that it is now recognized to be central to civil society. Its health is acknowledged by public intellectuals of many persuasions and concerns to be integral to the lives of children and to their future, which means to the future of civil society. But this can also amount to mere Panglossian pap if nothing substantive results from addressing its challenges.

Religion and Religious Institutions and Civil Society

The contemporary discourse on civil society does not focus only on the family. In particular, there is growing attention to religion and religious institutions in American civil society. Part of the explanation for this expanding interest involves the discovery by a number of public intellectuals of the practical value of this dimension. As in so many other instances, American practicality once again comes to the fore.

One path to this point starts from a simple recognition of the role that religion and its social networks play in U.S. civil society now, as in the past. They provide innumerable people with spiritual, moral, and communal places, exactly what many lack today. In this light more than a few public intellectuals cast hopeful glances at religion as a potential agent for the revival of civil society. This is more and more common despite the fact that many public intellectuals in America do not like religion, especially organized religion. Welcoming religion for the sake of civil society is thus not always a natural or congenial task—and rarely is it a noncontroversial one. Thus some public intellectuals who identify the potential of religion for civil society do so even though they personally lack religious belief. Some push ahead anyway, convinced that "America needs religion" to provide a moral basis for society and thus sustain civil society itself.[31]

Another impediment for many political intellectuals who are inclined to look to religion to help revive civil society is the nation's traditional separation of church and state. This is not really a matter of what the practice is regarding such separation. There is, in fact, more separation of church and state in theory than in practice in the United States. After all, most major religions in the United States receive tangible benefits from government, including the immensely valuable property tax forgiveness, although no religion or church is formally established by the state.

Yet there is widespread support for the abstract principle of nonestablishment among the general public, public intellectuals, and religious leaders. The most common reason is fear that a religion too closely allied with government will diminish or end religious toleration—or toleration in general. How real a concern this should be is debatable in the light of the tremendous diversity—and often contentious division—within American religion. Religion in the United States is no single behemoth, nor does it seem likely to become one, but fear of its potential power is real.[32]

Despite these reservations, more than a few intellectuals today defend religion's—and organized religion's—value for civil society. In the process, they make one or more of the following three points.

Religion and Social Virtue

One argument holds that religion promotes moral values in civil society and thus aids social integration and social stability. This is an old belief in American thought, one, as we have seen, subtly articulated by Alexis de Tocqueville.[33] Those impressed with the classic Tocquevillian claim echo it in contemporary terms. Yale law professor Stephen Carter does so in his best-seller, *The Culture of Disbelief.*[34] Carter expresses his sympathy for religion in part because he is sure that it benefits America through the moral order it can encourage. This is why he does not want the wall of separation of church and state in the United States to be too high and why he has little use for militant separatists of church and state and religion and society. They simply have no appreciation of religion's contribution to a social life.

Whether religion actually has any empirically demonstrable positive effects on civil society is a fascinating question. Many people in the United States believe that it does, including on their own behavior. About half the population claims that the ethical teachings of Christianity or Judaism are "very important" in their life decisions in beneficial ways. Only about one-quarter rate them as "not very important." These perceptions have been a constant in American public opinion for decades. At the same time, however, most Americans believe that religion's moral influence over others' ethical values and behavior has steeply declined since the 1960s.[35]

Apart from perceptions of influence, there is also a quarrelsome empirical social science literature that looks for specific demonstrable social effects of religion. It is often mired in methodological disputes, but the efforts of social scientists to provide insight on this subject are nonetheless interesting. In particular, social scientists have paid serious attention to possible connections between religious belief and juvenile delinquency, sexual behavior, and marital commitment.

There has been extensive social science work on the subject of delinquency and religious background. One analysis of the data suggests that children with a religious background are more likely to avoid becoming involved in crime than are other children, a finding that reinforces the longtime "hellfire hypothesis" that a religious upbringing discourages criminal behavior. Yet the data are mixed, no correlations are strong, and nuanced explanations of the connection, if any, between religious background and noncriminal behavior in youth are hardly clear.

Moreover, how to measure religious background is a vexing methodological issue. So is whether religious background is as relevant a measure as one's current religious affiliation, or involvement, or beliefs—none of which are easy to gauge either. Some studies start with decidedly modest amounts of data regarding youths' religious background and proceed from there, often with little or no information about youths' current religious affiliation, involvement, or convictions.[36]

Other contemporary work contends that measures of religious involvement or noninvolvement for youth provide scant insight into their religious orientation or its behavioral effects. It also argues that there is no solid evidence that standard measures of religious commitment correlate with youths who commit serious crime. For less serious "status offenses"—for example, arrests for underage drinking—there may be an inverse correlation with measures of religious involvement. Yet even here family situations and youths' moral beliefs correlate more closely than does religious involvement. Participation by youths in religious evangelism, however, is positively related to youth nonparticipation in serious crime. In other words, serious and committed religious involvement may indeed work against delinquency.[37]

A recent review of the data and the literature by sociologists Rodney Stark and William Sims Bainbridge leads them to conclude that there is little, if any, independent effect of religion or church involvement on youth drinking. This is not the case with marijuana use, however. Church involvement is negatively correlated with marijuana use, especially among evangelical and fundamentalist youth.[38] But Stark and Bainbridge do not find any particular connection between youth delinquency and religious beliefs. They do note, however, that rates of delinquency vary depending on the geographic location, which they suggest shows the effect of different moral climates in which the varying strengths of organized religion play a major role.[39] This fits well with another of their conclusions: that crime rates and church membership rates in differing regions correlate inversely. Thus the highest crime area in the United States, which is the West Coast, has by far the lowest church membership.[40]

Similar efforts have been made to explore the relationship between religion and sexual behavior, out-of-wedlock pregnancies, marital commitment, and religious belief and practice. Some studies indicate a connection between religious variables and conservative views on sexual issues (not necessarily to be conflated with sexual behavior).

Yet how religion works in individual lives remains something of a mystery, despite sometimes-heated social scientific disagreements. What is clear is that few in the debate over the connections between civil society, individual behavior, and religion can claim certain social science ground on which to stand. Public intellectuals who assert religion has scant—or substantial—effects on the incidence of divorce, pregnancy, or juvenile delinquency are alike in being unable to make a definitive social scientific case. The jury is still out.[41]

Religion and the Polity

A second view stresses the benefits of religion for the political system and, through it, for civil society. Here theoretical arguments have mattered more than social science ones. Richard John Neuhaus has been the most prominent intellectual voice addressing the political dimension. In *The Naked Public Square* he insists that religion—he means the Christian and Jewish religions—has a long history of helping the American political community. It has encouraged a political order based on democratic values, especially by teaching respect for every person as a moral equal of every other, each equally worthy as a child of God.[42]

Neuhaus fears that to diminish the role of religion, particularly to drive it from the public realm, will necessarily undermine democratic values in American life in the long run and replace them with the norms of materialism, status seeking, or even violence. This is why he asks those seeking a revival of religion for civil society to be on guard against any strict separation of religion and government and politics. This policy's legacy of such bad values will hurt both civil society and American democracy, neither of which is in good shape as it is. This is why Neuhaus supports government assistance for religious schools, believing it will help sustain civil society, benefit American democracy, and push away such norms as materialism and selfish individualism.

Neuhaus, like Stephen Carter and William Bennett, is a committed Christian, and his faith in God comes first. He does not approach religion only from this utilitarian perspective concerned to sustain a democracy and a civil society drifting toward serious difficulties. But this practical argument is important to him, and he agrees with Carter that for both practical and spiritual reasons God or religion cannot be a hobby. For Neuhaus and Carter, religion is not something reserved for the private moment or a private realm—and then left there. Religion must and does engage all parts of life, and it can and should aid civil society and democratic polity—help that is required now.

Some recent social science evidence for the claim that religion plays a significant role in the health of the American order follows a somewhat different path. In their massive study of American civic consciousness, social scientist Sidney Verba and associates discovered that people who undertake active roles in church life acquire major skills that often lead them toward becoming active citizens in public life. Their study, *Voice and Equality: Civic Voluntarism in American Politics*, recognizes that participation in public life varies by income, ethnicity, education, and age. They were surprised by their discovery that organizational experience in civil society, especially in religious institutions, also matters. While they found that involvement in any religious institution made a difference, those serving in Protestant churches with a tradition of lay leadership were most likely to obtain valuable experience for public life.[43]

The general population rarely thinks of the relation of religion to civil society or political society in any formal sense. The language of work, home, and the streets is not the language of the academy. Yet a majority of Americans believe that religion and the well-being of society are connected, and they have thought so for decades. Even more believe religion is relevant to or can solve today's problems. Studies repeatedly show, moreover, that many Americans associate their sense of the decline of the United States with their conviction that religion is experiencing a similar decline and with their feeling that American elites are hostile to religion.[44]

At another level, many in the general population also think that a revival of religion, or of certain religious practices, will reinforce the social fabric of the United States. The most obvious illustration of this sentiment is the overwhelming support for prayer in the public schools. About 75 percent of the population favors prayer in the schools and has done so since the Supreme Court outlawed organized school prayer in 1962. This support derives largely from the public's assumption that religion has beneficial social effects on youth (and all of us).[45]

The Value of Particular Traditions

Advocates of a third outlook maintain that one or another particular religious tradition is especially valuable for America's civil society. This perspective touches some very sensitive issues, but there is nothing unusual about public intellectuals who proceed down this road. For example, a number of Roman Catholic intellectuals contend that Catholicism in particular has much to contribute to a vibrant civil society. For example, Ken Grasso, Gerald Bradley, and Robert Hunt, among other Catholic intellectuals, visualize Roman Catholicism's ancient principle of subsidiarity as an especially valuable norm for civil society. This principle affirms the dignity of human beings in God's created universe and holds that to best realize this dignity humans should live in decentralized social settings, where local governments and the world of civil society matter.[46]

Put another way, these Catholic thinkers contend that Catholicism, through its subsidiarity principle, incorporates civil society as a vital feature of the divine order, one that should be nourished at all times. Other Roman Catholics also celebrate civil society as especially coincident with Roman Catholic theology. Jean Elshtain urges subsidiarity as well as one basis for revival of civil society.[47] Christopher Wolfe lauds subsidiarity as a norm by which Roman Catholics can work to improve civil society and at the same time hold off the menacing state.[48]

Conclusion

Critics wonder if all the discussion about civil society by intellectuals and social scientists is much ado about nothing. Some return to Harvard social scientist Robert Putnam's alarming conclusion that Americans are increasingly "bowling alone," less and less involved in social groups that must necessarily make up any robust civil society. They wonder if civil society is likely to be very relevant to the American future. Putnam's claims certainly fit well with popular and intellectual perceptions about civil society decline. Yet they also serve as ready fuel for the many voices today calling for a renewal of civil society as the essential new direction for the American polity.[49]

Other skeptics grant that some groups have lost membership, but they reject the claim that this is true of all civil society involvement by American citizens. While union groups may have lost members, sports organizations of all sorts have soared in membership—and, in fact, few people are bowling alone. They also note that recent decades have seen a great expansion of the informal groups that are increasingly important in people's lives. To them, this is evidence that civil society matters very much and that it may be the proper path to follow for American renewal.[50]

The growth of support for a refurbished civil society in the United States does not necessarily clash with the considerable interest in environmentalism and community as possible pathways to a better future. All three directions want to strengthen the communal side of an increasingly pluralistic and sometimes fissured American society. The civil society option is explicitly communal, with its primary concern people's lives outside the public realm. Thus one can certainly accommodate community conceived in terms of the components of a flourishing civil society. Of course, there are other definitions of community, as we know, that are not interested in community in terms of civil society so much as in community as national unity or as a participatory democracy or a public philosophy of the common good.

At least as congruent with intellectual interest in community is the thought of the environmental movement. Indeed, what is interesting about the green movement in this context is how much of it concerns community. To be sure, the community is nature and includes far more than the human being, much less the United States. Yet the environmental movement, like the civil society and community movements, is in good part a revolt against contemporary liberal individualism. This is an important theme in American political thought today: the urgent search from many different starting points toward a more community-oriented life, toward bringing the "second language" of community to the fore.

Proponents who develop this theme with special emphasis on the civil society are convinced that without a robust civil society there will be no society at all—including a stable functioning political order—and certainly no community. Their suspicions cannot be blithely ignored by those who do not like institutions or, indeed, society in any guise except for a kind of egalitarian anarchism on the Left or an idealized free market on the Right.

Nor can they be brushed aside by those such as Gertrude Himmelfarb, for whom the entire concentration on civil society renewal, announced "to near-universal acclaim," makes scant sense.[51] "It sounds too good to be true. And it is too good to be true," Himmelfarb insists. Granted, "the intentions of the proponents of civil society are admirable, and today more than ever the idea of a mediating structure between an unrestrained individualism and an overweening state is commendable. The difficulty is that civil society . . . cannot bear the burden of the charge" given to it.[52] It cannot somehow save us because "much of civil society has been infected" itself by "disease."[53]

Moving toward a more robust civil society is a valuable redirection, perhaps an absolutely necessary one in the present age. What form that civil society should take is much less certain—as is the shape of any institutions within it. Parallel to the danger of downgrading this project is the danger of confusing its present (perhaps desiccated) forms with eternal forms. This confusion can lead one to miss the possibility that the changes before us may reflect a valuable evolution and not simply decline. This is, perhaps, merely a sentiment of hope, and it may prove false, but there is nothing wrong with hope in this world.

Chapter Ten

Conclusion

A conclusion to my voyage into the treacherous waters of interpretation of American political thinking may do two things. One is to focus on the big picture; a second is to reflect personally on what I believe I have seen. The second I do with some skepticism about what someone such as myself—part Enlightenment liberal, part Burkean conservative, part Emersonian anarchist, and part religious existentialist—can offer that might be of interest.

I started this journey wondering if those who have insisted, sometimes since the 1960s, that there is no consensus on political values in the United States are correct. My research confirms that while they are right, it is often for the wrong reason. There is little doubt that if there was such a consensus in the glory years of consensus analysis in the 1950s, it has long since disappeared. Opening Louis Hartz's brilliant *Liberal Tradition in America* is still very much worth doing, but it is hardly the best route to understanding American political perspectives at the beginning of the new millennium.

Yet there must be an argument about what it means to say there is no such consensus, a demonstration that this conclusion is accurate, and some effort toward explaining its origins. This book has sought to address these goals.

One familiar explanation for the absence of a consensus on political values today, of course, is the observation that America has become a land of cultural diversity. But there are troubles with this explanation, which has been almost automatic in our time. After all, cultural diversity is hardly new in the United States. Moreover, there is no reason to assume that cultural diversity necessarily means diversity in political values. The cultural diversity explanation, in short, explains nothing in itself.

There is even less validity to the argument that the bulk of the American population is segmented into political divisions that reflect long-existent ideological conflicts. The difficulty with this common view is that there is scant evidence of such warring ideologies within the public.

Indeed, as I have argued, evidence exists that the American public overwhelmingly shares basic liberal political norms. To be sure, there are important variations that one cannot and should not ignore. Of course, there are different shadings of meanings of key concepts and somewhat different rankings of shared values. Of course, there are sometimes fierce disputes in the expression of these variations, especially when it comes to their translation into policy decisions in a world of finite resources. Yet in assessing public attitudes today, there is more substantive evidence of consensus in the contemporary American public than ever, and certainly more than there was in the consensus heyday of the 1950s.

The reason for this unprecedented situation, I have insisted, is that liberal values—above all the celebration of the individual and individual rights, choice, and self-expression—have swept into the so-called private realms of life. This is true, as I have undertaken to show, in the family and in people's religious communities in particular to an extent unimagined in the 1950s or earlier. In these realms, untouched by Hartz and judged nonliberal by Tocqueville, what may be fairly characterized as a liberal revolution has occurred.

While it is a dubious enterprise to try to dismiss the consistent social scientific findings of broad public agreement on fundamental liberal values, questioning their significance is more than legitimate. An ineluctable query arises: Does such broad agreement matter much in real-world terms, or does it merely constitute a formalistic or "weak" consensus? Are there consequences in terms of concrete lives or actual government policies if we have a popular consensus on liberal values in the United States?

My argument in this book has been that it does matter in practice. I have offered examples, although again, this does not mean that disputes over policy and value priorities do not abound within the American public. Sometimes they do. But it would be rare indeed to encounter such conflict taking place outside the current liberal framework, which sets the terms of popular debate in ever more firmly liberal categories.

The sharpest setting for such disagreements today, as I have noted, lies in the racial divides that so mar American life, especially those between black and white. Yet however much or little racism remains in Americans of whatever color, and however deep the splits over policies independent of racial feelings, there is scant evidence that these debates proceed outside a mutually shared contemporary liberal perspective.

Given the racial tension in the United States, I discussed race at some length to explore the limits of the broad value agreement in the United States. The reality of the considerable consensus and the limits it imposes remain, however. The fact is that there is widespread agreement on basic liberal values in the American polity among every race.

Some may not wish to label my general conclusion regarding public norms as the discovery of a consensus, and they need not do so to acknowledge the situation. Consensus may imply too broad, or too tight, or too nonconflictual a reality for contemporary America. I am more bold or more foolish. I do call it a consensus—not unanimity, but a general consensus. I do so because that is what we have among most of the public in the United States, as I read the meaning of the studies of American attitudes and practice. Why not name it what it is?

In this light, the recent, much-discussed study from the indefatigable Alan Wolfe hardly comes as a surprise.[1] Wolfe's contention that Americans are "one nation after all" has proved to be controversial to some reviewers who, unlike Wolfe, continue to confuse policy disputes with fundamental value differences or intellectual disputations with value conflict within the broader public.[2]

Wolfe's considerations have their acknowledged class limitations.[3] His main empirical procedure of conducting serious interviews with several hundred people in selected localities across the nation, moreover, offends some social scientists (while it pleases others who doubt the depth and thus the accuracy of standard public opinion surveys). Yet Wolfe's conclusions are sound. They accord with standard public opinion studies, as we know, and repeat this book's argument that most Americans have a recognizably liberal faith in individual freedom, broad tolerance, the norms of liberal capitalism, and, Wolfe adds, a mild patriotism.

To be sure, Wolfe's report that there is considerable uneasiness and division about homosexuality has attracted attention. In some cases it has even led to puzzling misdiagnoses of the American situation—and of Wolfe's analysis as focused on conflict just because homosexuality divides Americans. This kind of occasional reaction is predictable, given the gap between much of intellectual opinion and Wolfe's middle-class Americans regarding gays. But it is in error. The essential fact is that Wolfe could find only one area where the values of liberal individualism and tolerance had not (yet) captured the popular mind, demonstrating just how entrenched the liberal consensus is in the culture. It also shows just how transforming liberal values have become. Arguing over gay rights was inconceivable forty years ago, when even publicly mentioning the subject was taboo.

Wolfe is at least as interested in investigating the notions of religious conservatives—Christian conservatives particularly. He is curious whether Christian conservatives do reject the liberal constellation of norms, as some charge and others hope.

Certainly Wolfe encountered in these Americans and many others the powerful presence of religious and spiritual concerns. We know to expect this discovery and also that such a religious orientation rarely poses much challenge to Americans' liberal ethic. Wolfe found the same with Christian conservatives. He could discern no separate religious Right defined in terms of basic political perspectives. He encountered plenty of resentments and felt conflicts with others in the United States, as others in the American public have. But they proved to be mostly a matter of contrasting judgments about who currently benefits from the American system and who should. Their origins do not lie in alternative political value structures. To be sure, there are religious differences in the United States—more every day—but they are much more sweeping than are the popular differences over root political values.

Wolfe, like most other important contemporary cultural analysts, carefully steers away from much explicit liberal consensus talk. That makes sense, perhaps, given the swirl of controversy and sometimes hardened stances on this subject in recent decades. But there is little about Wolfe's work that would surprise Louis Hartz. Times have changed in the past half century, but they have also stayed the same.

Wolfe explicitly recognizes that his conclusions clash with a good slice of dominant intellectual opinion, which insists that the cultural pluralism it perceives and celebrates in American life is paralleled by a similar diversity in the public's thinking about fundamental political norms. Wolfe concludes that his interviews do not support this claim—any more than do many major studies of political attitudes.

I argue, however, that such diversity does genuinely exist among public intellectuals in the present-day United States. It includes many public intellectuals who are in revolt either against liberalism or at least against liberal America. Many of them simply cannot be twisted or squeezed into a liberal framework even by the most energetic Hartzian mind—and they don't want to be. Thus in the end I agree with those who deny and decry consensus claims regarding the United States today. There is no such consensus, but the main reason has more to do with intellectual pluralism than with an imagined widely divided public.

In this book I discuss the evidence of intellectual ideological diversity at some length. There is no need to retrace that ground here, but it may be worthwhile to reflect on this phenomenon. At the start, I acknowledge that there is reason for some skepticism about the reality of intellectual pluralism itself, as there is for the view that the public largely shares a general liberalism. Indeed, I share the suspicion that much intellectual criticism of liberal institutions or even liberal ideology—often in language that quite explicitly repudiates liberalism—amounts to much less than it appears.

Such perspectives repeatedly turn out to mean that their authors have not repudiated liberalism—even, one must say, when they insist sincerely that they have. Much of the confusion is interpretive, deriving from differing conceptions of what liberalism and liberal values mean, are made to mean, and come to mean. The most important example may be those American intellectuals who declare themselves conservatives (or neoconservatives) and proceed to attack liberalism. But, of course, most of them are philosophical liberals. Positions along the spectrum of American politics should not be

conflated with philosophical perspectives. Most of American conservatism is, as I have argued, just a garden variety of philosophical liberalism.

Many of the public intellectuals who proudly align themselves
with the political Left are by no means aliens to liberalism either.
Richard Rorty is an obvious case in point, as he himself acknowledges. In Rorty's brief but widely discussed contemporary manifesto, *Achieving Our Country: Leftist Thought in Twentieth-Century
America,* he emerges a dedicated liberal. His frequent objections to
American liberalism come down to complaints that it does not act
on his policy agenda, which is hardly in conflict with philosophical
liberalism. That agenda is mostly a 1930s or 1960s set of programs
promoted to encourage greater economic equality and designed, in
turn, to advance Rorty's version of substantive individual freedom
and democratic government. In its mustiness it recalls the outlook
of Rorty's hero, John Dewey, who strove to "save" the liberal tradition he, too, loved. No wonder Rorty offers no alternative ideology,
no brief for Marxism or anarchism or any other vision of the good.
His is a familiar American liberal voice of a certain tenor: earnest,
blustery, liberal in its values, left-leaning in its politics.[4]

The same point can be made in exploring the arguments of other
self-declared critics of liberalism. Yet there are many public intellectuals today whose views really are not in the liberal tradition. For
example, consider Ronald Beiner, who asks, as so many public
intellectual critics do today, "What's the matter with liberalism?"[5]

Beiner dissociates himself from the cult of individual rights and
individual self-indulgence. He is intensely concerned with the concept of the public good and upset that the liberalism he knows does
not seem to be. His goal is a kind of republicanism that acknowledges the necessity of selective civic virtues as the basis for what
matters: a community committed, above all else, to the public good.
Should we somehow interpret a thinker such as Beiner as a spokesman for liberalism? I would say no. The diversity he embodies is real.

I grant that the push toward "community" that is a core theme
of contemporary intellectual political and social thought in the
United States sometimes hides more than it reveals. It can hide the
fact that much of the intellectual and popular enthusiasm for community is actually thin and represents little serious challenge to
liberal values. Sometimes it is little more than parlor chitchat, prom-

ising and entailing no costs. At worst it is a con, as John Freie contends in his hard-hitting *Counterfeit Community: The Exploitation of Our Longings for Connectedness.*[6]

When public intellectuals begin to assert that "community" deserves celebration as an alternative to liberalism, caution is appropriate. "Community" is not necessarily such an alternative. Of course, some conceptions of community may be, but many who invoke its name have something decidedly more modest in mind, as this book has argued.

A good deal of the political thought of contemporary public intellectuals, nonetheless, is a repudiation of liberalism, especially as radical individualism, individual rights, and market capitalism. Because that repudiation is far from rare, I argue that the thought of public intellectuals in the United States today yields unpromising material for consensus seekers.

Chapter 2 demonstrates the widespread intellectual pluralism as it is expressed by American Marxists, some environmentalists, many communitarians, radical feminists, a host of radical postmoderns, and Christian conservatives.[7]

At the same time, as we have seen, liberalism today comes in many forms among public intellectuals. One tendency is the search for a liberalism that is more communal and concerned for the public good while carefully affirming the almost sacred worth of the individual. No doubt much of the best current political thought in the United States proceeds on this edge between liberalism and community as it undertakes to strengthen the community side of liberalism. Jean Bethke Elshtain and Michael Walzer are two obvious examples. Their projects are highly sympathetic to community both in civil society and in the public realm. They are equally resistant to community, however, conceived as the opponent of liberalism, not its companion. They celebrate the individual, the particular, the details of life and have no interest in their disappearing into "community."

Market liberalism is another important strand in contemporary liberalism, although it earns the enmity of many public intellectuals. There can be no doubt that such intellectuals and social scientists as Milton Friedman and Charles Murray have had an enormous impact on liberal thought in our day. Indeed, like it or not, there is solid reason to propose that in retrospect the celebrants of this view may turn out to be the most influential voices of liberalism in our time.

Perhaps identity liberalism, often devoted to multiculturalism, also belongs on any short list. So does that liberalism whose foundational skepticism is its central constituting definition. It comes in many forms: in the militancy of Richard Rorty, the dourness of Judith Shklar, or the cheerful pragmatism of Charles Anderson. Any list of variations within the liberal constellation today would be lengthy, in fact, and the discourse among them is a large part of intellectual political argument.

This is only to be expected, for reasons quite beyond the (very liberal) inclination toward intellectual diversity of our era. It is inherent in liberalism itself. James Young, in his reflective book *Reconsidering American Liberalism: The Troubled Odyssey of the Liberal Idea*, details many of the "tensions and confusions of American liberal political theory" throughout our history and reminds us that the present situation is not really new.[8] Liberalism is a complex outlook, after all, with somewhat porous and highly contested definitional boundaries and many internal tensions. As Young argues, perceiving these multiple dimensions is essential to understanding liberalism and allows us to have a more accurate view of liberalism than that presented by the classic consensus liberalism literature. Thus a serious problem with Hartz was not only that he did not see beyond liberalism but what he did not observe within the liberal consensus itself.[9]

A rich sense of liberalism also makes the study of public intellectuals' political and social thought all the more fascinating. For such a study must be about diversity within as well as without liberalism, and it leads one into a dynamic, contentious, and sometimes enlightening world. It certainly does not lead one, however, into any realm of consensus.

Does It Matter?

I suppose I reveal my Enlightenment side when I contend it does matter for us to reach toward some grasp of the contours of political thinking in the United States. My goal is to increase understanding in part because we inevitably confront social and political problems now just as we will face them in the new millennium.

To address such problems, whatever they may prove to be, we have to understand the public's widely shared liberal values that lie below the sometime raucous policy disputes. They will likely matter. Perhaps they will facilitate problem solving, or perhaps they will constrain how we meet our problems in the twenty-first century and force us to challenge them if we are to tackle our future successfully.

We also have to keep in mind that there is no consensus, nor anything like it, among contemporary public intellectuals in America about what values we most require or what redirections we should follow. From another angle, the creativity in American political intellectual life springs from its disagreements. It represents freedom in action, and in its many points of direction it provides alternatives, a situation that some may judge, as I do, both exciting and inspiring. It would be unwise, however, to predict that somehow American problems will fade away as a result. Caution rather than Millian optimism seems appropriate here. But Mill is surely right that the potential for new ideas and conceptions to aid us in a new millennium is very much part of the promise of our intellectual diversity. The long-lost consensus of the 1950s is gone (if it ever existed), and there is no tragedy in that. What it may represent is promise and, in any case, what it does represent is an unavoidable reality.

A Distinctly Unscientific Postscript

At the same time, I feel no apologia is necessary for a certain detachment that Epicurus would recognize from the earnest arguments over whether understanding American political thinking makes a crucial practical difference. It may or it may not, but there are other roles for committed intellectuals and scholars besides being in (inevitably dubious) battle. There is room for those who are sometimes just trying to understand.

Yet I agree with Burke, among many others, that as humans we have a responsibility to do what we can to help others and ourselves together, working within our time and place. To that end we must know our environment—and we need ideas about current directions and possible redirections. In this study I have tried to present both as they appear in American political thinking today.

That I am committed in particular to an ideal of community among men and women—rooted in spiritual values—is certainly true. And thus I welcome (and not merely imagine, I think) the unmistakable, if slow and incredibly diverse, drift of American civilization toward a reawakening regarding "community." There is no reason to assume that a more community-oriented society must involve abandonment of liberalism. Yet there is every reason to argue that liberalism must move more firmly to explore whether it can exist politically, in terms of civil society and as part of the growing global environment, without embracing a keener sense of community.

The risks are great. I am skeptical of naive communitarians (of whom there are too many) as well as of those who would create authoritarianism in the name of community. There always is danger, too, from those for whom community has become The Great End, which must (but never will) be realized once and for all. By its very nature, community is only an existential project, always in creation and never fully created.

Amid all the fascinating sides of contemporary American political thinking and the not entirely comforting signs that America's centrifugal tendencies flourish, I come back to hope. The Founders had a dream that their nation might become "a company of Enginemen," a free people who seek community, coming together for the good of the whole—as does a successful volunteer fire company. Movement in that direction will not be easy, but I am an optimist. I plan to enter the next millennium with such a hope.

Notes

1. Classic Interpretations

1. Some recent studies well worth exploring are Joshua Mitchell, *The Fragility of Freedom: Tocqueville on Religion, Democracy, and the American Future* (Chicago: University of Chicago Press, 1995); Peter Lawler, *The Restless Mind: Alexis de Tocqueville on the Origin and Perpetuation of Human Liberty* (Lanham, Md.: Rowman and Littlefield, 1992); Alan S. Kahn, *Aristocratic Liberalism: The Social and Political Thought of Jacob Burkhardt, John Stuart Mill, and Alexis de Tocqueville* (New York: Oxford University Press, 1992); Roger Boesche, *The Strange Liberalism of Alexis de Tocqueville* (Ithaca, N.Y.: Cornell University Press, 1987); Bruce Frohnen, *Virtue and the Promise of Communitarianism: The Legacy of Burke and Tocqueville* (Lawrence: University Press of Kansas, 1993).

2. Comments by Cornel West, in "The Democratic Soul," a symposium covered in *Religion and Values in Public Life* 6 (Fall 1997): 6.

3. Comments by Michael Sandel, in "The Democratic Soul," a symposium covered in *Religion and Values in Public Life* 6 (Fall 1997): 6–7.

4. Alexis de Tocqueville, *Democracy in America,* edited by Phillips Bradley, vol. 2 (New York: Vintage, 1957), 21.

5. Ibid., 2: 23.

6. Alexis de Tocqueville, *Democracy in America,* edited by Phillips Bradley, vol. 1 (New York: Vintage, 1954), 45.

7. Tocqueville, *Democracy in America,* 2: 225.

8. Ibid., 209, 202–14, 222–25.

9. Ibid., 105–6.

10. See note 8.

11. Tocqueville, *Democracy in America,* 2: 42–49, 99–103.

12. Frederick Jackson Turner, *The Significance of the Frontier in American History* (New York: Unger, 1982).

13. For a judicious and far more sympathetic treatment, see Ray A. Billington, *Frederick Jackson Turner: Historian, Scholar, Teacher* (New York: Oxford University Press, 1973).

14. On this matter, as on so many others, see Allan G. Bogue, *Frederick Jackson Turner: Strange Roads Going Down* (Norman: University of Oklahoma Press, 1998), 166.

15. Two treatments that I especially like are Gene Wise, *American Historical Explanations* (Homewood, Ill.: Dorsey, 1973), chap. 7; and Richard Hofstadter, *The Progressive Historians: Turner, Beard, Parrington* (New York: Vintage, 1970; reprint, Chicago: University of Chicago Press, 1979), chaps. 2–4.

16. Bogue, *Turner*, 184.

17. Ibid., 435.

18. Turner, *Significance of the Frontier*, 27.

19. Bogue, *Turner*, 245.

20. Ibid., 435.

21. Ibid., 343.

22. Clyde A. Milner II, Carol A. O'Connor, and Martha A. Sandweiss, *The Oxford History of the American West* (New York: Oxford University Press, 1994).

23. Bogue, *Turner*, 451–64.

24. Ibid., 46.

25. John Higham, *Writing American History* (Bloomington: Indiana University Press, 1970), 123.

26. For two quite recent discussions of Turner, see Wilfred M. McClay, *The Masterless: Self and Society in Modern America* (Chapel Hill: University of North Carolina Press, 1994), chap. 4; and Patricia Nelson Limerick, *The Legacy of Conquest: The Unbroken Past of the American West* (New York: Norton, 1986), 20–32.

27. Higham, *Writing American History*, 59.

28. See the recent H. Lark Hall, *V. L. Parrington: Through the Avenue of Art* (Kent, Ohio: Kent State University Press, 1994); and Daniel Aaron, "The Mid-American Scholar," *New Republic*, September 5, 1994, 47, 49.

29. Higham, *Writing American History*, 57; Hofstadter, *Progressive Historians*, chap. 10.

30. Higham, *Writing American History*, 56–57.

31. V. L. Parrington, *Main Currents in American Thought: An Interpretation of American Literature from the Beginnings to 1920*, 3 vols. (New York: Harcourt, Brace and World, 1930), for example, 1: i, v, 151, 267–91, 342–56; 3: 17, 23, 132; Hofstadter, *Progressive Historians*, chaps. 10–11; Higham, *Writing American History*, 62.

32. Parrington, *Main Currents*, 1: 159–60; 2: 413, 386–409.

33. Ibid., 3: 240, 170–71; Hofstadter, *Progressive Historians*, 390–91.

34. Hofstadter, *Progressive Historians*, 355, 401.

35. Ibid.

36. Hall, *Parrington*; Aaron, "The Mid-American Scholar," 47–49.

37. Hall, *Parrington*, is replete with textual arguments, well worth exploring; for Parrington on Adams and Calhoun, see *Main Currents*, 1: 292–307, 2: 82.

38. See the treatments of Beard in Ellen Nore, *Charles A. Beard: An Intellectual Biography* (Carbondale: Southern Illinois University Press, 1983); and Hofstadter, *Progressive Historians*.

39. Charles A. Beard, *An Economic Interpretation of the Constitution of the United States* (New York: Free Press, 1941), 324.

40. Ibid., 325.

41. Ibid., chap. 7.

42. The best-detailed critique is Robert E. Brown, *Charles Beard and the Constitution* (New York: Norton, 1956).

43. There are, of course, innumerable conflicting accounts. A good one is Forrest McDonald, *Novus Ordo Seclorum: The Intellectual Origins of the Constitution* (Lawrence: University Press of Kansas, 1985).

44. Charles A. Beard and Mary Beard, *The Rise of American Civilization* (New York: Macmillan, 1930); Higham, *Writing American History*, 60.

45. Higham, *Writing American History*, chap. 7.

46. See chapter 3.

47. Henry James, *The American Scene* (New York: Penguin, 1994). See Leon Edel, *Henry James: A Life* (Philadelphia: Lippincott, 1953); and Bryan R. Washington, *The Politics of Exile: Ideology, in Henry James, F. Scott Fitzgerald, and James Baldwin* (Boston: Northeastern University Press, 1995).

48. James, *The American Scene*, 12–13, 43.

49. Ibid., chap. 3.

50. Ibid., 175–76.

51. Ibid., 53.

52. Ibid., 37, 239–40.

53. Ibid., 91.

54. Ibid., 12.

55. Ibid., chap. 3.

56. Ibid., 249–53.

57. Ibid., 280–81, 270–71.

58. Bernard Sternsher, *Consensus, Conflict, and American Historians* (Bloomington: Indiana University Press, 1975).

59. Richard Hofstadter, *The American Political Tradition* (New York: Knopf, 1948); for a view of Hofstadter's early years politically and as a historian, see Susan Stout Baker, *Radical Beginnings: Richard Hofstadter and the 1930s* (Westport, Conn.: Greenwood, 1985).

60. Hofstadter, *Progressive Historians*, 451.

61. Ibid., 442.

62. Ibid., 462; and Hofstadter, *The Progressive Historians* (Chicago: University of Chicago Press, 1979), 240.

63. Ibid., 458–59.

64. A very nice collection of the writings of Reinhold Niebuhr is Harry R. Davis and Robert C. Good, eds., *Reinhold Niebuhr on Politics* (New York: Scribner's, 1960); see also Richard Wightman Fox, *Reinhold Niebuhr: A Biography* (New York: Pantheon, 1985).

65. Reinhold Niebuhr, *Moral Man and Immoral Society* (New York: Scribner's, 1932).

66. Reinhold Niebuhr, *The Children of Light and the Children of Darkness* (New York: Scribner's, 1945).

67. Reinhold Niebuhr, *The Irony of American History* (New York: Scribner's, 1952).

68. Louis Hartz, *The Liberal Tradition in America* (New York: Harcourt, Brace and World, 1955); Louis Hartz, *The Founding of New Societies* (New York: Harcourt, Brace and World, 1964).

69. Hartz, *Liberal Tradition*.

70. Hartz, *New Societies*.

71. Hartz, *Liberal Tradition*, chap. 1.

72. For a reflection on Hartz's use of Locke, see Sternsher, *Consensus*, 350.

73. For example, see Donald J. Devine, *The Political Culture of the United States* (Boston: Little, Brown, 1972).

74. See the argument of Marvin Meyers, "Louis Hartz, *The Liberal Tradition in America*: An Appraisal," *Comparative Studies in Society and History* 5 (1963): 261–68.

75. Hartz, *Liberal Tradition*, chap. 9, part 3.

76. Hofstadter, *Progressive Historians*, 449.

77. John P. Diggins, "Knowledge and Sorrow: Louis Hartz's Quarrel with American History," *Political Theory* 16 (August 1988): 355–76.

78. Hofstadter, *Progressive Historians*, chap. 11.

79. Hartz, *Liberal Tradition*, chap. 2.

80. Sternsher, *Consensus*, 353.

81. Hartz, *Liberal Tradition*, chap. 10.

82. Hofstadter, *Progressive Historians*, 448–49.

83. Sternsher, *Consensus*, chap. 6.

84. Hofstadter, *Progressive Historians*, 448.

85. For an interesting essay on Boorstin, see John P. Diggins, "Consciousness and Ideology in American History: The Burden of Daniel J. Boorstin," *American Historical Review* 76 (February 1971): 100–117.

86. Daniel Boorstin, *The Genius of American Politics* (Chicago: University of Chicago Press, 1953).

87. Daniel Boorstin, *The Americans: The National Experience* (New York: Vintage, 1965); Daniel Boorstin, *The Americans: The Democratic Experience* (New York: Vintage, 1974).

88. Daniel Boorstin, *The Creators* (New York: Random House, 1992).

89. Boorstin, *Genius,* chap. 1 and pp. 22, 30.

90. Michael E. Meagher, "The Multiple Personalities of Daniel J. Boorstin: A Third Image Analysis," *American Review of Politics* 15 (Winter 1995): 462–80.

91. Boorstin, *Genius,* 63.

92. Ibid., 94.

93. Ibid., 84.

94. Ibid., 68–98.

95. Ibid., chap. 4.

96. Boorstin, *National Experience,* 430.

97. Boorstin, *Democratic Experience,* ix.

98. Ibid., 1.

99. Ibid., 600.

100. Boorstin, *Genius,* 1.

101. Ibid., 180.

102. Ibid., 188.

103. Boorstin, *Democratic Experience,* 327.

104. Ibid., 306.

105. Ibid., 408.

106. Ibid., 287.

2. The Fall of Consensus

1. Daniel Bell, *The End of Ideology* (New York: Colliers, 1962).

2. For example, see "Ideology: A Debate," *Commentary* 38 (October 1964): 69–76.

3. Robert Booth Fowler, *Believing Skeptics: American Political Intellectuals, 1945–1964* (Westport, Conn.: Greenwood, 1978).

4. Garry Wills, *Nixon Agonistes: The Crisis of the Self-Made Man* (New York: Signet, 1970).

5. Ibid., 229–30.

6. Barton J. Bernstein, ed., *Towards a New Past* (New York: Vintage, 1969); and Staughton Lynd, *The Intellectual Origins of American Radicalism* (London: Faber, 1969).

7. Including this author.

8. C. Wright Mills, *The Power Elite* (New York: Oxford University Press, 1956).

9. For example, ibid., 87, 77.

10. C. Wright Mills, *White Collar* (New York: Oxford University Press, 1951).

11. C. Wright Mills, *The Sociological Imagination* (New York: Oxford University Press, 1959).

12. Herbert Marcuse, *One-Dimensional Man* (Boston: Beacon, 1964).

13. Herbert Marcuse, *An Essay on Liberation* (Boston: Beacon, 1969); and Herbert Marcuse et al., *Critique of Pure Tolerance* (Boston: Beacon, 1965).

14. John Higham, *Writing American History* (Bloomington: Indiana University Press, 1970), 146.

15. Ibid.

16. Ibid., 159, 146.

17. Iwan W. Morgan, *Beyond the Liberal Consensus: A Political History of the United States Since 1965* (New York: St. Martin's, 1994).

18. Charles Kadushin, *The American Political Elite* (Boston: Little, Brown, 1974).

19. Peter Clecak, *America's Quest for the Ideal Self: Dissent and Fulfillment in the 60s and 70s* (New York: Oxford University Press, 1983).

20. David McConnell, "The 1970s and Failure" (unpublished lecture, University of Wisconsin–Madison, 1978).

21. Daniel Bell, *The Cultural Contradictions of Capitalism* (New York: Basic Books, 1978).

22. Alan Wolfe, *Marginalized in the Middle* (Chicago: University of Chicago Press, 1996).

23. See the analysis of Gil Green, *The New Radicalism: Anarchist or Marxist?* (New York: International Publishers, 1971).

24. Lynd, *Intellectual Origins;* Jerome Weinstein, *The Corporate Ideal in the Liberal State: 1900–1918* (Boston: Beacon, 1968).

25. Robert Paul Wolff, *The Poverty of Liberalism* (Boston: Beacon, 1968).

26. Carole Pateman, *Participation and Democratic Theory* (Cambridge: Cambridge University Press, 1970).

27. Joshua Cohen and Joel Rogers, *On Democracy: Toward a Transformation of American Society* (New York: Penguin, 1983).

28. For example, Arthur Stein, *Seeds of the Seventies* (Hanover, N.H.: University Press of New England, 1985); and Harry C. Boyte and Frank Riessman, eds., *The New Populism* (Philadelphia: Temple University Press, 1986).

29. See, for example, Noam Chomsky, *Deterring Democracy* (New York: Verso, 1991); Noam Chomsky, *The Culture of Terrorism* (New York: South End Press, 1988); Noam Chomsky, *Class Warfare: Interviews with David Barsamian* (Monroe, Maine: Common Courage Press, 1996).

30. Todd Gitlin, *The Twilight of Common Dreams: Why America Is Wracked by Culture Wars* (New York: Holt, 1995), 37.

31. Ibid., chap. 1.

32. Ibid., 124, 150.

33. Ibid., 157.

34. Ibid., 151–69.

35. See Hester Eisenstein, *Contemporary Feminist Thought* (Boston: G. K. Hall, 1983).

36. A good treatment of feminism and feminist thought is found in Myra Ferree and Beth B. Hess, *Controversy and Coalition: The New Feminist Movement* (Boston: Twayne, 1985); an example of a feminist analysis that talks in terms of liberal feminism, Marxist feminism, and so forth, is Eisenstein, *Contemporary Feminist Thought*.

37. Eisenstein's *Contemporary Feminist Thought* is an excellent example of this approach, and I have gratefully drawn on her work; I thank Marion Smiley for directing me to it.

38. Kate Millett, *Sexual Politics* (New York: Avon, 1971); and Shulamith Firestone, *The Dialectic of Sex: The Case for Feminist Revolution* (New York: Bantam, 1971).

39. An illustration: Mary C. Segers, "Feminism, Liberalism, and Catholicism," in *Catholicism and Liberalism: Contributions to American Public Philosophy*, edited by R. Bruce Douglass and David Hollenbach (New York: Cambridge University Press, 1994).

40. Susan Griffin, *Woman and Nature: The Roaring Inside Her* (New York: Harper and Row, 1978).

41. Carol Gilligan, *In a Different Voice: Psychological Theory and Women's Development* (Cambridge, Mass.: Harvard University Press, 1982).

42. Joan C. Tronto, *Moral Boundaries: A Political Argument for an Ethic of Care* (New York: Routledge, 1993).

43. Ibid., chap. 6.

44. Mary Daly, *Pure Lust: Elemental Feminist Philosophy* (Boston: Beacon, 1984); Susan Brownmiller, *Against Our Will: Men, Women, and Rape* (New York: Simon and Schuster, 1975).

45. For example, Daly, *Pure Lust;* Catharine A. MacKinnon, *Feminism Unmodified* (Cambridge, Mass.: Harvard University Press, 1987); and see Eisenstein's treatment in *Contemporary Feminist Thought*.

46. Jill Johnston, *Lesbian Nation: The Feminist Solution* (New York: Simon and Schuster, 1973); Adrienne Rich, *Compulsory Heterosexuality and Lesbian Experience* (London: Only Women Press, 1981); Adrienne Rich, *On Lies, Secrets and Silence* (New York: Norton, 1979).

47. See, for example, Shane Phelan, *Getting Specific: Postmodern Lesbian Politics* (Minneapolis: University of Minnesota Press, 1994); Dana R. Shugar, *Separatism and Women's Community* (Lincoln: University of Nebraska Press, 1995); and Sarah Lucia Hoagland and Julia Penelope, eds., *For Lesbians Only: A Separatist Anthology* (London: Only Women Press, 1988).

48. Nancy J. Hirschmann and Christine DiStefano, eds., *Revisioning the Political: Feminist Reconstructions of Traditional Concepts in Western Political Theory* (Boulder, Colo.: Westview, 1996).

49. Betty Friedan, *The Second Stage* (New York: Summit, 1981).

50. bell hooks, *Ain't I a Woman: Black Women and Feminism* (Boston: South End Press, 1981); and bell hooks, *Feminist Theory from Margin to Center* (Boston: South End Press, 1984).

51. Nancy Hartsock, *The Feminist Standpoint Revisited and Other Essays* (Boulder, Colo.: Westview, 1996).

52. Eisenstein, *Contemporary Feminist Thought*, chaps. 2–3; and Marion Smiley, "Feminist Theory and the Question of Identity," *Women and Politics* 13 (1993): 91–122.

53. Charlene Haddock Seigfried, *Pragmatism and Feminism: Reweaving the Social Fabric* (Chicago: University of Chicago Press, 1996).

54. Jean Bethke Elshtain, *Public Man, Private Woman: Women in Social and Political Thought* (Princeton, N.J.: Princeton University Press, 1981).

55. Susan Faludi, *Backlash: The Undeclared War Against American Women* (New York: Anchor, 1992).

56. Two studies, quite different but both valuable, are George H. Nash, *The Conservative Intellectual Movement in America Since 1945* (New York: Basic Books, 1979); and David Frum, *Dead Right* (New York: Basic Books, 1994).

57. See, for example, Russell Kirk, "The Cultural Conservatives," *The Heritage Lectures* 151 (Washington, D.C.: Heritage Foundation, 1989); Russell Kirk, "The Neoconservatives," *The Heritage Lectures* 178 (Washington, D.C.: Heritage Foundation, 1988); and Russell Kirk, "A Dispassionate Assessment of Libertarians," *The Heritage Lectures* (Washington, D.C.: Heritage Foundation, 1988). Russell Kirk, *The Conservative Mind* (Chicago: Regnery, 1953), is Kirk's masterwork.

58. Milton Friedman, *Capitalism and Freedom* (Chicago: University of Chicago Press, 1963); and Milton Friedman and Rose Friedman, *Free to Choose: A Personal Statement* (New York: Harcourt Brace, 1990).

59. Charles Murray, *What It Means to Be a Libertarian* (New York: Broadway, 1997).

60. For example, see Frank Meyer, "Recrudescent Conservatism," in *Left, Right, and Center*, edited by Robert Goldwin (Chicago: Rand McNally, 1965), chap. 4; and Dick Armey, "Freedom's Choir," *Policy Review* 67 (Winter 1994): 27–34.

61. Pat Robertson, *The Turning Tide* (Dallas: Word, 1993); Ralph Reed, *Politically Incorrect: The Emerging Faith Factor in American Politics* (Dallas: Word, 1994).

62. Irving Kristol, *Two Cheers for Capitalism* (New York: Meridian, 1977); for the foreign policy side of neoconservatism, see John Ehrman, *The Rise of the Neoconservatives* (New Haven, Conn.: Yale University Press, 1995).

63. Jeane Kirkpatrick, *Dictatorships and Double Standards* (New York: Simon and Schuster, 1982); and Norman Podhoretz, *The Present Danger* (New York: Simon and Schuster, 1980).

64. Kristol, *Two Cheers*, chaps. 10, 1.

65. Gene Edward Veith Jr., *Postmodern Times: A Christian Guide to Contemporary Thought and Culture* (Wheaton, Ill.: Crossway, 1994).

66. James W. Ceaser, *Reconstructing America: The Symbol of America in Modern Thought* (New Haven, Conn.: Yale University Press, 1997).

67. Richard Rorty, *Contingency, Irony, and Solidarity* (New York: Cambridge University Press, 1989).

68. Michael J. Shapiro, *Reading the Postmodern Polity: Political Theory as Textual Practice* (Minneapolis: University of Minnesota Press, 1992).

69. William E. Connolly, *The Augustinian Imperative: A Reflection on the Politics of Morality* (Newbury Park, Calif.: Sage, 1993).

70. William E. Connolly, *The Ethos of Pluralization* (Minneapolis: University of Minnesota Press, 1995), 36, xii.

71. Ibid., 183, 192, 178.

72. Ibid., 179.

73. Stanley Fish, *There's No Such Thing as Free Speech . . . and It's a Good Thing Too* (New York: Oxford University Press, 1994).

74. Kenneth R. Craycroft Jr., "Free Speech or True Speech?" *Chronicles,* August 1994, 30–32.

75. See the discussion by Linda Nicholson, *Feminism and Postmodernism* (New York: Routledge, 1990).

76. Iris Marion Young, *Justice and the Politics of Difference* (Princeton, N.J.: Princeton University Press, 1990).

77. Patricia Williams, *The Alchemy of Race and Rights: Diary of a Law Professor* (Cambridge, Mass.: Harvard University Press, 1991).

78. Ibid., 130.

79. The acclaimed master here is Quentin Skinner, *Foundations of Modern Political Thought* (New York: Cambridge University Press, 1978).

80. For example, Walter Truett Anderson, *Reality Isn't What It Used To Be* (San Francisco: Harper and Row, 1990).

81. Marion Smiley is an able example of a theorist who discusses and supports pragmatic constructivism; see her "Feminist Theory and the Question of Identity," 91–122.

82. Sheldon Wolin, "Democracy in the Discourse of Postmodernism," *Social Research* 57 (Spring 1990): 5–30.

83. Bernard Yack, *The Fetishism of Modernities: Epochal Self-Consciousness in Contemporary Social and Political Thought* (Notre Dame, Ind.: University of Notre Dame Press, 1997), 6.

84. Ibid., chap. 3.

85. Robert Booth Fowler, *The Dance with Community: The Contemporary Debate in American Political Thought* (Lawrence: University Press of Kansas, 1991).

86. Robert Bellah, Richard Madsen, William Sullivan, Ann Swidler, and Steven M. Tipton, *Habits of the Heart: Individualism and Commitment in American Life* (Berkeley: University of California Press, 1985); Michael Sandel, *Liberalism and Its Critics* (New York: New York University Press, 1984).

87. Fowler, *The Dance with Community,* chap. 5, has an account of this focus.

88. Amitai Etzioni, ed., *New Communitarian Thinking: Persons, Virtues, Institutions, and Communities* (Charlottesville: University Press of Virginia, 1995).

89. John Rawls, *A Theory of Justice* (Cambridge, Mass.: Harvard University Press, 1971).

90. John Rawls, *Political Liberalism* (New York: Columbia University Press, 1993).

91. Michael Walzer, *Spheres of Justice: A Defense of Pluralism and Equality* (New York: Basic Books, 1983); Michael Walzer, *On Toleration* (New Haven, Conn.: Yale University Press, 1997); Michael Walzer, *Thick and Thin: Moral Argument at Home and Abroad* (Notre Dame, Ind.: University of Notre Dame Press, 1994).

92. Kenneth Grasso, "Man, Society, and the State: A Catholic Perspective," in *Caesar's Coin Revisited,* edited by Michael Cromartie (Grand Rapids, Mich.: Eerdmans, 1996), 139.

93. Stephen Holmes, *The Anatomy of Antiliberalism* (Cambridge, Mass.: Harvard University Press, 1993).

94. Ibid., 134.

95. Bernard Yack, "Liberalism Without Illusions," in *Essays on Liberal Theory and the Political Vision of Judith N. Shklar*, edited by Bernard Yack (Chicago: University of Chicago Press, 1996).

96. Judith Shklar, *Ordinary Vices* (Cambridge, Mass.: Harvard University Press, 1984).

97. Judith Shklar, *Faces of Injustice* (New Haven, Conn.: Yale University Press, 1990).

98. Ibid., p. 9 and chap. 2.

99. Ibid., 3, 6, 13, 40, 81, 83, 90.

100. Ibid., pp. 32, 49 and chap. 1.

101. Amy Gutmann and Dennis Thompson, *Democracy and Disagreement* (Cambridge, Mass.: Harvard University Press, 1996).

102. Thomas Spragens, *The Irony of Liberal Reason* (Chicago: University of Chicago Press, 1981).

103. Charles W. Anderson, *Pragmatic Liberalism* (Chicago: University of Chicago Press, 1990), chap. 2.

104. Ibid., chaps. 10–12.

105. R. Bruce Douglass, "Liberalism After the Good Times," in *Catholicism and Liberalism: Contributions to American Public Philosophy*, edited by R. Bruce Douglass and David Hollenbach (New York: Cambridge University Press, 1994), 111–12.

106. Seymour Martin Lipset, *American Exceptionalism: A Double-Edged Sword* (New York: Norton, 1996).

107. Ibid., introduction.

108. Ibid., chap. 4.

109. Ibid., chap. 8.

110. Ben Page and Robert Shapiro, *The Rational Public: Fifty Years of Trends in Americans' Policy Preferences* (Chicago: University of Chicago Press, 1992).

111. See, for example, John R. Zaller, *The Nature and Origins of Mass Opinion* (New York: Cambridge University Press, 1992).

112. Jerome Kluegel and Eliot R. Smith, *Beliefs About Inequality: Americans' Views of What Is and What Ought To Be* (New York: Aldine, 1986).

113. "The US in Cross-National Perspective: On Equality," *Public Perspective*, April–May 1995, 20.

114. Kluegel and Smith, *Beliefs About Inequality*.

115. Jervis Anderson, "Black and Blue," *New Yorker*, April 29, 1996, 62–64.

116. William G. Mayer, *The Changing American Mind: How and Why American Public Opinion Changed Between 1960 and 1988* (Ann Arbor: University of Michigan Press, 1992).

117. Herbert McClosky and John Zaller, *The American Ethos: Public Attitudes Toward Capitalism and Democracy* (Cambridge, Mass.: Harvard University Press, 1984), chap. 1.

118. Ibid., 186.

119. Jack Dennis, "Do We Believe Aristotle: A Study of American Beliefs About Democracy" (paper presented at Midwest Political Science Association, 1993), 17–19.

120. Stephen C. Craig, *The Malevolent Leaders: Popular Discontent in America* (Boulder, Colo.: Westview, 1993).

121. Dennis, "Do We Believe Aristotle," 18–37.

122. I want to thank those at the Carl Albert Institute of the University of Oklahoma, where I gave a talk in the spring of 1995, for their vigorous criti-

cism of my argument. Nowhere did I face tougher critics. Nowhere did I learn more that I hope improved this manuscript.

123. Alan Wolfe, *One Nation, After All: What Middle-Class Americans Think About God, Country, Family, Poverty, Racism, Welfare, Homosexuality, Immigration, the Left, the Right, and Each Other* (New York: Viking, 1998).

3. The Broader Critique and Alternative Perspectives

1. Several of the most comprehensive works reflecting on consensus analysis are Richard Hofstadter, *The Progressive Historians: Turner, Beard, Parrington* (New York: Vintage, 1970; reprint, Chicago: University of Chicago Press, 1979); Richard J. Ellis, *American Political Cultures* (New York: Oxford University Press, 1993); and Bernard Sternsher, *Consensus, Conflict, and American Historians* (Bloomington: Indiana University Press, 1975).

2. Karen Orren, *Belated Feudalism: Labor, Law, and Liberal Development in the United States* (New York: Cambridge University Press, 1991).

3. Sternsher, *Consensus,* 212–13 and passim.

4. Aileen Kraditor, "American Radical Historians on Their Heritage," *Past and Present* 56 (1972): 136–53.

5. Most recently, Seymour Martin Lipset, *American Exceptionalism: A Double-Edged Sword* (New York: Norton, 1996).

6. Gabriel Kolko, *The Triumph of Conservatism: A Reinterpretation of American History, 1900–1916* (Glencoe, Ill.: Free Press, 1963).

7. For example, John Higham, "The Cult of the 'American Consensus': Homogenizing Our History," *Commentary* 27 (February 1959): 93–100; Ronald Takaki, *A Different Mirror: A History of Multicultural America* (Boston: Little, Brown, 1993); Rudolph J. Vecoli, "Ethnicity: A Neglected Dimension of American History," in *The State of American History,* edited by Herbert J. Bags (Chicago: University of Chicago Press, 1970), 70–88; I. A. Newby, "Historians and Negroes," *Journal of Negro History* 54 (January 1969): 32–47; Joyce Appleby, Lynn Hunt, and Margaret Jacob, *Telling the Truth About History* (New York: Norton, 1994).

8. See, for example, J. R. Pole, "Daniel J. Boorstin," in *Pastmasters: Some Essays on American Historians,* edited by Marcus Cunliffe and Robin W. Winks (New York: Harper and Row, 1969), 210–38; Sternsher, *Consensus,* p. 123 and chap. 7.

9. Gary B. Nash, "American History Reconsidered: Asking New Questions About the Past," in *Learning from the Past,* edited by Diane Ravitch and Maria A. Vinovskis (Baltimore, Md.: Johns Hopkins University Press, 1995), 135–63.

10. See, for example, Michael Wallace, "The Uses of Violence in American History," *American Scholar* 40 (Winter 1970–1971): 81–100; Richard Hofstadter, "Reflections on Violence in the United States," in *American Violence,* edited by Richard Hofstadter and Michael Wallace (New York: Vintage, 1971), 3–43; Sternsher, *Consensus.*

11. An interesting discussion of the international perspective is Ian Tyrrell, "American Exceptionalism in an Age of International History," *American Historical Review* 96 (October 1991): 1031–55.

12. John Higham, *Writing American History* (Bloomington: Indiana University Press, 1970), 73.

13. Sternsher, *Consensus;* David Greenstone, *The Lincoln Persuasion: Remaking American Liberalism* (Princeton, N.J.: Princeton University Press, 1993).

14. See Seymour Martin Lipset, *The First New Nation: The United States in Historical and Comparative Perspective* (New York: Norton, 1979).

15. Greenstone, *Lincoln Persuasion.*

16. Alan Dawley, *Struggles for Justice: Social Responsibility and the Liberal State* (Cambridge, Mass.: Harvard University Press, 1991).

17. See Richard K. Matthews, "Liberalism, Civic Humanism, and the American Political Tradition: Understanding Genesis," *Journal of Politics* 49 (November 1987): 1127–53; Daniel T. Rodgers, "Republicanism: The Career of a Concept," *Journal of American History* 79 (June 1992): 11–38.

18. Robert M. Crunden, *A Brief History of American Culture* (New York: Paragon, 1994).

19. Robert H. Wiebe, *Self-Rule: A Cultural History of American Democracy* (Chicago: University of Chicago Press, 1995).

20. Paul Leinberger and Bruce Tucker, *The New Individualists: The Generation After the Organization Man* (New York: HarperCollins, 1991).

21. Michael Kammen, *People of Paradox: An Inquiry Concerning the Origins of American Civilization* (New York: Knopf, 1972).

22. Michael Kammen, *Historical Perspectives on American Culture* (New York: Oxford University Press, 1997).

23. Ibid., p. xi and chap. 7.

24. Ibid., chap. 2.

25. Ibid., chap. 5.

26. Theda Skocpol, *Protecting Soldiers and Mothers* (Cambridge, Mass.: Harvard University Press, 1992), 17.

27. Ibid., 21.

28. Wilson Carey McWilliams, *The Idea of Fraternity in America* (Berkeley: University of California Press, 1973).

29. Robert Bellah, Richard Madsen, William Sullivan, Ann Swidler, and Steven M. Tipton, *Habits of the Heart: Individualism and Commitment in American Life* (Berkeley: University of California Press, 1985).

30. Michael Sandel, *Democracy's Discontent: America in Search of a Public Philosophy* (Cambridge, Mass.: Harvard University Press, 1996).

31. Hofstadter, *Progressive Historians,* 240.

32. Philip Abbott, *Political Thought in America: Conversations and Debates* (Itasca, Ill.: Peacock, 1991).

33. Linda Kerber, "Can a Woman Be an Individual? The Discourse of Self-Reliance," in *American Chameleon,* edited by Richard O. Curry and Lawrence B. Goodheart (Kent, Ohio: Kent State University Press, 1991), 151–66.

34. For example, see Wilfred M. McClay, *The Masterless: Self and Society in Modern America* (Chapel Hill: University of North Carolina Press, 1994), 283.

35. As became very clear among many of the historians and other intellectuals promoting the multiple-strands approach in the national history standards controversy of 1994–96.

36. Rogers Smith, *Civic Ideals: Conflicting Visions of Citizenship in U.S. History* (New Haven, Conn.: Yale University Press, 1997), 17, 24.

37. Rogers Smith, "Beyond Tocqueville, Myrdal, and Hartz: The Multiple Traditions in America," *American Political Science Review* 87 (1993): 549–66;

Rogers Smith, "Response," *American Political Science Review* 89 (December 1995): 990–95.

38. Smith, *Civic Ideals*, 198, 128.

39. Ibid., 5.

40. Smith, "Response," 991.

41. Smith, "Beyond Tocqueville."

42. Ibid.

43. Smith, *Civic Ideals*, chaps. 2, 3, 8.

44. Ibid., 489.

45. Rogers Smith, "The Unfinished Tasks of Liberalism," in *Liberalism Without Illusions: Essays on Liberal Theory and the Political Vision of Judith Shklar*, edited by Bernard Yack (Chicago: University of Chicago Press, 1996), 241–62.

46. Smith, *Civic Ideals*, 496, 503, 473.

47. Ibid., 478.

48. Jacqueline Stevens, "Comment: Beyond Tocqueville, Please!" *American Political Science Review* 89 (December 1995): 987–90.

49. Ibid., 989.

50. Ellis, *American Political Cultures*.

51. Ibid., chap. 4.

52. Ibid., chap. 5.

53. Ibid., chap. 1.

54. Ibid., chap. 6.

55. Ibid., chap. 8.

56. Ibid., chap. 7.

57. As one reviewer of my manuscript suggested.

58. Theodore Lowi, *The End of the Republican Era* (Norman: University of Oklahoma Press, 1995).

59. Ibid., 221, 226.

60. Ibid., 259.

61. For a good introductory treatment of postmodern views, see Joseph Natoli and Linda Hutcheon, eds., *A Postmodern Reader* (Albany: State University of New York Press, 1993); the distinctions here are ones that my colleague Marion Smiley urged me to clarify.

62. Appleby, Hunt, and Jacob, *Telling the Truth*.

63. See, for example, Thomas Dumm, *Democracy and Punishment: Disciplinary Origins of the United States* (Madison: University of Wisconsin Press, 1987).

64. Anne Norton, *The Republic of Signs: Liberal Theory and American Popular Culture* (Chicago: University of Chicago Press, 1993).

65. See Barry Alan Shain's scathing critique of *The Republic of Signs* in *Review of Politics* 57 (Fall 1995): 755–58.

66. Gordon Wood, *The Creation of the American Republic, 1776–1787* (New York: Norton, 1972); Gordon Wood, *The Radicalism of the American Revolution* (New York: Knopf, 1992).

67. J. G. A. Pocock, *The Machiavellian Moment: Florentine Political Thought and the Atlantic Republican Tradition* (Princeton, N.J.: Princeton University Press, 1975).

68. Bernard Bailyn, *Ideological Origins of the American Revolution* (Cambridge, Mass.: Harvard University Press, 1967).

69. On republicanism and capitalism Ed Countryman is especially useful: "Of Republicanism, Capitalism, and the American Mind," *William and Mary Quarterly* 44 (July 1987): 556–62.

70. Bailyn, *Ideological Origins.*

71. Christopher Duncan, *The Anti-Federalists and Early American Political Thought* (De Kalb: Northern Illinois University Press, 1995).

72. Ellis, *American Political Cultures.*

73. Wood, *The Creation;* also Lance Banning, "Republican Identity and the Triumph of the Constitution, 1789 to 1793," *William and Mary Quarterly* 31 (April 1974): 167–88.

74. Rodgers, "Republicanism," brought out this theme for me, and Sean Wilentz, *Chants Democratic: New York City and the Rise of the American Working Class, 1788–1850* (New York: Oxford University Press, 1984), illustrates it.

75. Russell L. Hanson, *The Democratic Imagination in America: Conversations with Our Past* (Princeton, N.J.: Princeton University Press, 1985).

76. George C. Rable, *The Confederate Republic: A Revolution Against Politics* (Chapel Hill: University of North Carolina Press, 1994); Philip J. Ethington, *The Public City: The Political Contruction of Urban Life in San Francisco, 1850–1900* (New York: Cambridge University Press, 1994).

77. Paul A. Rahe, *Republics Ancient and Modern: Classical Republicanism and the American Revolution* (Chapel Hill: University of North Carolina Press, 1992), 570–72.

78. Thomas L. Pangle, *The Spirit of Modern Republicanism: The Moral Vision of the American Founders and the Philosophy of Locke* (Chicago: University of Chicago Press, 1988).

79. A splendid example of this is Richard Vetterli and Gary Bryner, *In Search of the Republic: Public Virtue and the Roots of American Government* (Lanham, Md.: Rowman and Littlefield, 1987).

80. Melvin Yazawa, *From Colonies to Commonwealth: Familial Ideology and the Beginnings of the American Republic* (Baltimore, Md.: Johns Hopkins University Press, 1985).

81. See especially Rodgers, "Republicanism"; for an engagement with contemporary "republicans," see Don Herzog, "Some Questions for Republicans," *Political Theory* 14 (August 1986): 473–93.

82. See Robert Booth Fowler, *The Dance with Community: The Contemporary Debate in American Political Thought* (Lawrence: University Press of Kansas, 1991), chap. 5.

83. Gary B. Nash, *The Urban Crucible: Social Change, Political Consciousness, and the Origins of American Revolution* (Cambridge, Mass.: Harvard University Press, 1979).

84. Marc Egnal and Joseph A. Ernst, "An Economic Interpretation of the American Revolution," *William and Mary Quarterly* 29 (January 1972): 3–32.

85. Joyce Appleby, *Capitalism and a New Social Order: The Republican Vision of the 1790s* (New York: New York University Press, 1984).

86. Ruth Bloch, "Religion, Literary Sentimentalism, and Popular Revolutionary Ideology," in *Religion in a Revolutionary Age,* edited by Ronald Hoffman and Peter J. Albert (Charlottesville: University Press of Virginia, 1994), 308–30.

87. John P. Diggins, *The Lost Soul of American Politics: Virtue, Self-Interest, and the Foundations of Liberalism* (Chicago: University of Chicago Press, 1984).

88. Ellis Sandoz, *A Government of Laws: Political Theory, Religion and the American Mind* (Baton Rouge: Louisiana State University Press, 1990), chap. 6.

89. Jon Butler, "Coercion, Miracle, Reason: Rethinking the American Religious Experience in the Revolutionary Age," in Hoffman and Albert, *Religion in a Revolutionary Age,* 1–30.

90. Patricia U. Bonomi, "Religious Dissent and the Case for American Exceptionalism," in Hoffman and Albert, *Religion in a Revolutionary Age*, 31–51.

91. William McLoughlin, "'Enthusiasm for Liberty': The Great Awakening as the Key to the Revolution," in *Preachers and Politicians: Two Essays on the Origins of the American Revolution*, edited by Jack P. Greene and William McLoughlin, 47–73 (Worcester, Mass.: American Antiquarian Society, 1977).

92. For example, see Charles Royster, *A Revolutionary People at War: The Continental Army and American Character, 1775–1783* (Chapel Hill: University of North Carolina Press, 1979).

93. Barry Alan Shain, *The Myth of American Individualism: The Protestant Origins of American Political Thought* (Princeton, N.J.: Princeton University Press, 1994).

94. Steven M. Dworetz, *The Unvarnished Doctrine: Locke, Liberalism, and the American Revolution* (Durham, N.C.: Duke University Press, 1990).

95. Robert H. Webking, *The American Revolution and the Politics of Liberty* (Baton Rouge: Louisiana State University Press, 1988).

96. Jack N. Rakove, *Original Meanings: Politics and Ideas in the Making of the Constitution* (New York: Knopf, 1996).

97. Pauline Maier, "A Pearl in a Gnarled Shell: Gordon S. Wood's *The Creation of the American Republic* Reconsidered," *William and Mary Quarterly* 44 (July 1987): 583–90.

98. James T. Kloppenberg, "The Virtues of Liberalism: Christianity, Republicanism, and Ethics in Early American Political Discourses," *Journal of American History* 74 (June 1987): 9–33.

99. Donald S. Lutz, *A Preface to American Political Theory* (Lawrence: University Press of Kansas, 1992).

100. Forrest McDonald, *Novus Ordo Seclorum: The Intellectual Origins of the Constitution* (Lawrence: University Press of Kansas, 1985).

101. Michael Lienesch, *New Order of the Ages: Time, the Constitution, and the Making of Modern American Political Thought* (Princeton, N.J.: Princeton University Press, 1988); Michael Allen Gillespie and Michael Lienesch, "Introduction," in *Ratifying the Constitution*, edited by Michael Allen Gillespie and Michael Lienesch (Lawrence: University Press of Kansas, 1989), 1–26.

102. Appleby, *Capitalism*.

103. Jerome Huyler, *Locke in America: The Moral Philosophy of the Founding Era* (Lawrence: University Press of Kansas, 1995).

104. Some works worth noting in this context are Mary Beth Norton, *Liberty's Daughters: The Revolutionary Experience of American Women, 1750–1800* (Boston: Little, Brown, 1980); Jan Lewis, "The Republican Wife: Virtue and Seduction in the Early Republic," *William and Mary Quarterly* 44 (October 1987): 689–721; and Linda Kerber, *Women of the Republic: Intellect and Ideology in Revolutionary America* (Chapel Hill: University of North Carolina Press, 1980).

105. Kerber, *Women of the Republic*.

106. Linda Kerber, *Toward an Intellectual History of Women* (Chapel Hill: University of North Carolina Press, 1997).

107. Norton, *Liberty's Daughters*.

108. As Marion Smiley put it to me.

109. See Pauline Schloesser, "Mercy Otis Warren's Critique of the U.S. Constitution" (paper, Midwest Political Science Association, April 1995).

110. For example, see Mark Kann, "A Republic of Men: Manhood, Citizenship, and Leadership during the American Founding" (unpublished manuscript, chaps. 1–2).

111. Mark Kann, *On the Man Question: Gender and Civic Virtue in America* (Philadelphia: Temple University Press, 1991).

112. Samuel P. Huntington Jr., *American Politics: The Promise of Disharmony* (Cambridge, Mass.: Harvard University Press, 1981).

4. Liberalism in the Public Sphere

1. For example, Seymour Martin Lipset, "American Exceptionalism," in *Is America Different?* edited by Byron E. Shafer (New York: Oxford University Press, 1991), chap. 1.

2. Some useful sources among a multitude: Stephen C. Craig, *The Malevolent Leaders: Popular Discontent in America* (Boulder, Colo.: Westview, 1993); Paul Abramson, *Political Attitudes in America* (San Francisco: W. H. Freeman, 1983); Herbert McClosky and John Zaller, *The American Ethos: Public Attitudes Toward Capitalism and Democracy* (Cambridge, Mass.: Harvard University Press, 1984); Jack Dennis, "Do We Believe Aristotle: A Study of American Beliefs About Democracy" (paper, Midwest Political Science Association, 1985); Thomas B. Edsall, "The GOP Gains as Trust in Government Erodes," *Washington Post National Weekly Edition*, February 12–18, 1996, 11–12.

3. Especially valuable here is John R. Hibbing and Elizabeth Theiss-Morse, *Congress as Public Enemy* (New York: Cambridge University Press, 1995).

4. McClosky and Zaller, *American Ethos*.

5. Joseph Nye Jr., Philip D. Zelikow, and David C. King, eds., *Why People Don't Trust Government* (Cambridge, Mass.: Harvard University Press, 1997).

6. Seymour Martin Lipset and Earl Raab, *Jews and the New American Scene* (Cambridge, Mass.: Harvard University Press, 1995).

7. Ben Page and Robert Shapiro, *The Rational Public: Fifty Years of Trends in Americans' Policy Preferences* (Chicago: University of Chicago Press, 1992).

8. William G. Mayer, *The Changing American Mind: How and Why American Public Opinion Changed Between 1960 and 1988* (Ann Arbor: University of Michigan Press, 1992).

9. Sidney Verba, Kay Lehman Schlozman, and Henry E. Brady, eds., *Voice and Equality: Civic Voluntarism in American Politics* (Cambridge, Mass.: Harvard University Press, 1995).

10. Jerome Kluegel and Eliot R. Smith, *Beliefs About Inequality: Americans' Views of What Is and What Ought to Be* (New York: Aldine, 1986).

11. Ronald Inglehart, *Culture Shift in Advanced Industrial Society* (Princeton, N.J.: Princeton University Press, 1990); Daniel Yankelovich, "How Changes in the Economy Are Reshaping American Values," in *Values and Public Policy*, edited by Henry J. Aaron, Thomas E. Mann, and Timothy Taylor (Washington, D.C.: Brookings, 1994), 16–53.

12. In the discussion that follows, besides the empirical literature on tolerance that I cite, I draw on the excellent analysis in Andrew R. Murphy, "Tolerance and Toleration: Political Psychology and Liberal Theory" (paper, International Society of Political Psychology, July 1996).

13. Some interesting studies: Herbert McClosky and Alida Brill, *Dimensions of Tolerance: What Americans Believe About Civil Liberties* (New York: Russell Sage,

1983); James L. Gibson and Richard D. Bingham, "On the Conceptualization and Measurement of Political Tolerance," *American Political Science Review* 76 (1982): 603–20; James H. Kuklinski, Ellen Riggle, Victor Ottati, Norbert Schwarz, and Robert S. Wyer Jr., "The Cognitive and Affective Bases of Political Tolerance Judgments," *American Journal of Political Science* 35 (February 1991): 1–27.

14. Herbert McClosky, "Consensus and Ideology in American Politics," *American Political Science Review* 58 (1964): 361–82; James W. Prothro and Charles M. Grigg, "Fundamental Principles of Democracy: Bases of Agreement and Disagreement," *Journal of Politics* 22 (1963): 276–94.

15. See John L. Sullivan, James Piereson, and George E. Marcus, *Political Tolerance and American Democracy* (Chicago: University of Chicago Press, 1982).

16. George E. Marcus, John L. Sullivan, Elizabeth Theiss-Morse, and Sandra L. Wood, *With Malice Toward Some: How People Make Civil Liberties Judgments* (New York: Cambridge University Press, 1995).

17. For a more pessimistic reading, see James L. Gibson, "The Structure of Attitudinal Tolerance in the United States," *British Journal of Political Science* 19 (1989): 562–72; James L. Gibson, "The Political Consequences of Intolerance," *American Political Science Review* 86 (1992): 338–56.

18. Jennifer L. Hochschild, *Facing Up to the American Dream: Race, Class, and the Soul of the Nation* (Princeton, N.J.: Princeton University Press, 1995).

19. Kluegel and Smith, *Beliefs About Inequality*.

20. Nathan Glazer, "Polls Apart," *New Republic*, October 23, 1995, 43–45.

21. Compare Dinesh D'Souza, *The End of Racism* (New York: Free Press, 1995), with Glenn C. Loury, "Not so Black and White: The Two Americas Are Actually Converging," *Washington Post*, October 15, 1995, CO3.

22. Myra Ferree and Beth B. Hess, *Controversy and Coalition: The New Feminist Movement* (Boston: Twayne, 1985); Hester Eisenstein, *Contemporary Feminist Thought* (Boston: G. K. Hall, 1983); Mary Daly, *Gyn/Ecology: The Metaethics of Radical Feminism* (Boston: Beacon, 1978), is an interesting effort to combine the feminist and gay agendas; Peter Clecak, *America's Quest for the Ideal Self: Dissent and Fulfillment in the 60s and 70s* (New York: Oxford University Press, 1983).

23. Several good examples worth looking at here are Lani Guinier, *The Tyranny of the Majority: Fundamental Fairness in Representative Democracy* (New York: Free Press, 1995); and Iris Marion Young, *Justice and the Politics of Difference* (Princeton, N.J.: Princeton University Press, 1990).

24. William M. Banks, *Black Intellectuals: Race and Responsibility in American Life* (New York: Norton, 1996).

25. Charles W. Anderson, *Pragmatic Liberalism* (Chicago: University of Chicago Press, 1990).

26. Elizabeth Fox-Genovese, *Feminism Without Illusions: A Critique of Individualism* (Chapel Hill: University of North Carolina Press, 1991).

27. Although Bellah has not taken the path of conversion to Roman Catholicism as has Fox-Genovese.

28. Fox-Genovese, *Feminism Without Illusions*.

29. Robert Bellah, Richard Madsen, William Sullivan, Ann Swidler, and Steven M. Tipton, *Habits of the Heart: Individualism and Commitment in American Life* (Berkeley: University of California Press, 1985), chap. 6.

30. Robert Booth Fowler, *The Dance with Community: The Contemporary Debate in American Political Thought* (Lawrence: University Press of Kansas, 1991), chap. 2.

31. Amitai Etzioni, *The Spirit of Community: Rights, Responsibilities and the Communitarian Agenda* (New York: Crown, 1993).

32. Bruce Frohnen, *The New Communitarians and the Crisis of Modern Liberalism* (Lawrence: University Press of Kansas, 1996).

33. Ibid.

34. Fowler, *The Dance with Community*, chap. 2.

35. See, for example, Abramson, *Political Attitudes in America;* Dennis, "Do We Believe Aristotle"; Pat Dunham, *Electoral Behavior in the United States* (Englewood Cliffs, N.J.: Prentice Hall, 1991); and Herbert B. Asher, *Presidential Elections and American Politics* (Pacific Grove, Calif.: Brooks/Cole, 1992). For a dissenting view, see Bruce E. Keith, *The Myth of the Independent Voter* (Berkeley: University of California Press, 1992).

36. Jack Dennis and Diana Owen, "Anti-Partyism and Support for Perot, 1992–93" (paper, Workshop on Anti-Party Sentiment, European Consortium for Political Research, 1994).

37. Ibid.; Jack Dennis, "Political Independence in America, Part II: Towards a Theory," *British Journal of Political Science* 18 (1988): 197–219.

38. See Paul S. Herrnson and John C. Green, *Multiparty Politics in America* (Lanham, Md.: Rowman and Littlefield, 1997); and Gordon S. Black and Benjamin D. Black, *The Politics of American Discontent* (New York: Wiley, 1994).

39. Arthur G. Powell, Eleanor Farrar, and David C. Cohen, *The Shopping Mall High School: Winners and Losers in the Educational Marketplace* (Boston: Houghton Mifflin, 1985).

40. For a balanced discussion (if such a thing is possible on this topic), see the following: Nathan Glazer, *We Are All Multiculturalists Now* (Cambridge, Mass.: Harvard University Press, 1997); Diane Ravitch and Maris A. Vinovskis, eds., *Learning from the Past: What History Teaches Us About School Reform* (Baltimore, Md.: Johns Hopkins University Press, 1995); Will Kymlicka, *Multicultural Citizenship: A Liberal Theory of Minority Rights* (New York: Oxford University Press, 1995); Lawrence Levine, *The Opening of the American Mind* (Boston: Beacon, 1996); and David A. Hollinger, *PostEthnic America: Beyond Multiculturalism* (New York: Basic Books, 1995).

41. Two views on school choice: Jeffrey R. Henig, *Rethinking School Choice: Limits of the Market Metaphor* (Princeton, N.J.: Princeton University Press, 1994); and John Chubb and Terry Moe, *Politics, Markets, and America's Schools* (Washington, D.C.: Brookings, 1990).

42. See Chubb and Moe, *Politics, Markets, and America's Schools;* Paul E. Peterson, "The New Politics of Choice," in *Learning from the Past: What History Teaches Us About School Reform,* edited by Diane Ravitch and Maris A. Vinovskis (Baltimore, Md.: Johns Hopkins University Press, 1995), 217–40; and John Witte and Mark Rigdon, "Education Choice Reforms: Will They Change America's Schools?" *Publius* 23 (Summer 1993): 95–114.

43. John Witte, Troy D. Sterr, and Christopher A. Thorn, *Fifth Year Report: Milwaukee Parental Choice Program* (Madison: University of Wisconsin, 1995); Paul E. Peterson, Jay P. Greene, and Chad Noyes, "School Choice in Milwaukee," *Public Interest* 125 (Fall 1996): 38–56.

44. Witte, Sterr, and Thorn, *Fifth-Year Report.*

45. See Anthony S. Bryk, Valerie E. Lee, and Peter B. Holland, *Catholic Schools and the Common Good* (Cambridge, Mass.: Harvard University Press, 1993).

46. For an argument on the limited evidence, which is from Milwaukee, see John Witte, who collected the data, *Fifth Year Report;* and Peterson, Greene, and Noyes, "School Choice in Milwaukee."

47. George H. Nash, *The Conservative Intellectual Movement in America Since 1945* (New York: Basic Books, 1979); David Frum, *Dead Right* (New York: Basic Books, 1994); Bruce Frohnen, *Virtue and the Promise of Communitarianism: The Legacy of Burke and Tocqueville* (Lawrence: University Press of Kansas, 1993).

48. I would especially recommend, for a historical treatment, Nash, *The Conservative Intellectual Movement*, and, for a controversial but clear-eyed current analysis Frum, *Dead Right.*

49. Milton Friedman, *Capitalism and Freedom* (Chicago: University of Chicago Press, 1963), chaps. 1, 2.

50. Charles Murray, *What It Means to Be a Libertarian* (New York: Broadway, 1997).

51. Russell Kirk's classic: *The Conservative Mind* (Chicago: Regnery, 1953).

52. See Eric Voegelin, *The New Science of Politics* (Chicago: University of Chicago Press, 1952); and Leo Strauss, *Natural Right and History* (Chicago: University of Chicago Press, 1965).

53. We are fortunate, now at last, to have a sophisticated treatment and comparison of these two thinkers in one book: Ted V. McAllister, *Revolt Against Modernity: Leo Strauss, Eric Voegelin, and the Search for a Postliberal Order* (Lawrence: University Press of Kansas, 1996).

54. Allan Bloom, *The Closing of the American Mind* (New York: Simon and Schuster, 1987).

55. Ralph Reed, *Politically Incorrect: The Emerging Faith Factor in American Politics* (Dallas: Word, 1994); and Pat Robertson, *The Turning Tide* (Dallas: Word, 1993).

56. Kenneth L. Grasso, Gerald V. Bradley, and Robert P. Hunt, eds., *Catholicism, Liberalism, and Communitarianism* (Lanham, Md.: Rowman and Littlefield, 1995).

57. See J. Budziszewski, "The Problem with Conservatism," *First Things* 62 (April 1996): 38–44.

58. James Q. Wilson, *The Moral Sense* (New York: Free Press, 1993).

59. William A. Kelso, *Poverty and the Underclass* (New York: New York University Press, 1994).

60. William J. Bennett, *The De-valuing of America: The Fight for Our Culture and Our Children* (New York: Simon and Schuster, 1992).

61. Frank Meyer, "Recrudescent Conservatism," in *Left, Right, and Center,* edited by Robert Goldwin (Chicago: Rand McNally, 1965), chap. 4.

62. Dick Armey, "Freedom's Choir," *Policy Review* 67 (Winter 1994): 27–34.

63. See Mark Gerson, *The Essential Neoconservative Reader* (Reading, Mass.: Addison-Wesley, 1996).

64. For example, see Irving Kristol, *Two Cheers for Capitalism* (New York: Meridian, 1977); Jeane Kirkpatrick, *Dictatorships and Double Standards* (New York: Simon and Schuster, 1982).

65. See Jeane Kirkpatrick, *Human Rights and American Foreign Policy* (Gambier, Ohio: Kenyon College Public Affairs Conference Center, 1982); Kirkpatrick, *Dictatorships.*

66. See Norman Podhoretz, *Why We Were in Vietnam* (New York: Simon and Schuster, 1983); and Norman Podhoretz, *Breaking Ranks* (New York: Harper and Row, 1979).

67. Kristol, *Two Cheers.*

68. Irving Kristol, *Reflections of a Neoconservative* (New York: Basic Books, 1983); and Irving Kristol, *Neoconservatism: The Autobiography of an Ideal* (New York: Free Press, 1995).

69. The best book on neoconservatism is Mark Gerson, *The Neoconservative Vision* (Lanham, Md.: Madison Books, 1996); also see the valuable discussion in James Nuechterlein, "The End of Neoconservatism," *First Things* 63 (May 1996): 14–15.

70. Theodore Lowi, *The End of the Republican Era* (Norman: University of Oklahoma Press, 1995).

71. Ibid., chap. 4.

72. Ibid., 23–32.

73. Ibid., chap. 5.

74. Ibid., 215.

75. Ibid.

76. Arthur A. Ekirch Jr., *The Decline of American Liberalism* (New York: Longman's, 1955).

5. Liberalism in the Private Realm

1. Robert Bellah, Richard Madsen, William Sullivan, Ann Swidler, and Steven M. Tipton, *Habits of the Heart: Individualism and Commitment in American Life* (Berkeley: University of California Press, 1985), vii–viii.

2. Louis Hartz, *The Liberal Tradition in America* (New York: Harcourt, Brace and World, 1955).

3. See the discussion of Tocqueville in chapter 1.

4. *Statistical Abstract of the United States, 1993* (Washington, D.C.: Bureau of the Census, 1994), 396, 399.

5. See, for example, "Individualism vs. Community," *American Enterprise* 4 (March–April 1993): 108.

6. Sam Roberts, *Who We Are: A Portrait of America Based on the Latest U.S. Census* (New York: New York Times Books, 1993), 4, 47; also see *Statistical Abstract 1993.*

7. Barbara Ehrenreich, *The Hearts of Men: American Dreams and the Flight from Responsibility* (Garden City, N.Y.: Anchor, 1983).

8. William G. Mayer, *The Changing American Mind: How and Why American Public Opinion Changed Between 1960 and 1988* (Ann Arbor: University of Michigan Press, 1992); Herbert McClosky and John Zaller, *The American Ethos: Public Attitudes Toward Capitalism and Democracy* (Cambridge, Mass.: Harvard University Press, 1984).

9. For another account that confirms and approves, see Ben Page and Robert Shapiro, *The Rational Public: Fifty Years of Trends in Americans' Policy Preferences* (Chicago: University of Chicago Press, 1992).

10. Mayer, *Changing American Mind,* chaps. 3, 6–9; McClosky and Zaller, *American Ethos;* Page and Shapiro, *The Rational Public.*

11. George Gilder, *Men and Marriage* (Gretna, La.: Pelican, 1986); and Ehrenreich, *Hearts of Men.*

12. bell hooks, *Ain't I a Woman: Black Women and Feminism* (Boston: South End Press, 1981).

13. Shane Phelan, *Lesbian Feminism and the Limits of Community* (Philadelphia: Temple University Press, 1995).

14. Susan Okin, *Justice, Gender, and the Family* (New York: Basic Books, 1989).

15. Bellah et al., *Habits of the Heart.*

16. Mary Daly, *Gyn/Ecology: The Metaethics of Radical Feminism* (Boston: Beacon, 1978); see the excellent discussion by Virginia Sapiro, "Gender Politics, Gendered Politics: The State of the Field" (paper, Midwest Political Science Conference, April 1989).

17. See, for example, the discussions in Hester Eisenstein, *Contemporary Feminist Thought* (Boston: G. K. Hall, 1983); Myra Ferree and Beth B. Hess, *Controversy and Coalition: The New Feminist Movement* (Boston: Twayne, 1985); Jean Grimshaw, *Philosophy and Feminist Thinking* (Minneapolis: University of Minnesota Press, 1986); and Rosemarie Tong, *Feminist Thought: A Comprehensive Introduction* (Boulder, Colo.: Westview, 1989).

18. Carol Gilligan, *In a Different Voice: Psychological Theory and Women's Development* (Cambridge, Mass.: Harvard University Press, 1982); Joan C. Tronto, *Moral Boundaries: A Political Argument for an Ethic of Care* (New York: Routledge, 1993). See Sneja Gunew and Anna Yeatman, *Feminism and the Politics of Difference* (Boulder, Colo.: Westview, 1994), for a good collection.

19. Alan Wolfe, *Marginalized in the Middle* (Chicago: University of Chicago Press, 1996), provides some interesting and controversial reflections on these topics.

20. See identity discussion in chapter 7.

21. Naomi Wolf, *Fire with Fire: The New Female Power and How to Use It* (New York: Random House, 1993).

22. Christine Hoff Sommers, *Who Stole Feminism? How Women Have Betrayed Women* (New York: Simon and Schuster, 1994).

23. Katha Pollitt, "Are Women Morally Superior to Men?" *Nation*, December 28, 1992, 799–802.

24. Elizabeth Fox-Genovese, *Feminism Without Illusions: A Critique of Individualism* (Chapel Hill: University of North Carolina Press, 1991); Elizabeth Fox-Genovese, *"Feminism Is Not the Story of My Life": How Today's Feminist Elite Has Lost Touch with the Real Concerns of Women* (New York: Doubleday, 1996).

25. Fox-Genovese, *Feminism Without Illusions*, 7.

26. Ibid., 10.

27. Ibid., 53, 40.

28. Ibid., 9.

29. Ibid., 40.

30. Roberts, *Who We Are?*, 47, 12, 30, 34, 53, 4.

31. Michael Sandel, *Democracy's Discontent: America in Search of a Public Philosophy* (Cambridge, Mass.: Harvard University Press, 1996), chaps. 3–4.

32. For a discussion, see Dana R. Shugar, *Separatism and Women's Community* (Lincoln: University of Nebraska Press, 1995); and Sally Munt, ed., *New Lesbian Criticism: Literary and Cultural Readings* (New York: Columbia University Press, 1992).

33. Ehrenreich, *Hearts of Men.*

34. Linda Gordon, ed., *Women, the State, and Welfare* (Madison: University of Wisconsin Press, 1990).

35. For example, see Okin, *Justice, Gender, and the Family.*

36. See Sommers, *Who Stole Feminism?*

37. Betty Friedan, *The Second Stage* (New York: Summit, 1981).

38. Sylvia Hewlett, *A Lesser Life: The Myth of Women's Liberation in America* (New York: Morrow, 1986).

39. Jean Bethke Elshtain, "Feminists Against the Family," *Nation*, November 17, 1979, front cover and 497–500; Jean Bethke Elshtain, *Public Man, Private Woman: Women in Social and Political Thought* (Princeton, N.J.: Princeton University Press, 1981).

40. Ibid.; Jean Bethke Elshtain, *The Family in Political Thought* (Amherst: University of Massachusetts Press, 1982).

41. Sommers, *Who Stole Feminism?*

42. See Alexis de Tocqueville, *Democracy in America*, edited by Richard D. Heffner (New York: Mentor, 1956); and Robert Booth Fowler, *Unconventional Partners: Religion and Liberal Culture in the United States* (Grand Rapids, Mich.: Eerdmans, 1989).

43. I make a much fuller argument on this point in Fowler, *Unconventional Partners*.

44. See Phillip Hammond, *Religion and Personal Autonomy: The Third Disestablishment in America* (Columbia: University of South Carolina Press, 1992).

45. Wade Clark Roof, *A Generation of Seekers: The Spiritual Journey of the Baby Boom Generation* (San Francisco: HarperCollins 1993).

46. Ibid., 194.

47. Jack Wertheimer, *A People Divided: Judaism in Contemporary America* (New York: Basic Books, 1993); Charles Silberman, *A Certain People: American Jews and Their Lives Today* (New York: Summit, 1985); Steven M. Cohen, *Survey of American Jews* (New York: American Jewish Committee, 1991); and Seymour Martin Lipset and Earl Raab, *Jews and the New American Scene* (Cambridge, Mass.: Harvard University Press, 1995).

48. For a general discussion of Roman Catholic beliefs and practice, see George Gallup Jr. and Jim Castelli, *The American Catholic People* (Garden City, N.Y.: Doubleday, 1987); and for up-to-date and more focused discussion regarding the pope and conscience issues, see *The New York Times/CBS News Poll*, September 18–22, 1995.

49. Robert Wuthnow, *Sharing the Journey: Support Groups and America's New Quest for Community* (New York: Free Press, 1994); my own experiences in a Bible-study group have proved to be fully in line with the findings in Wuthnow's systematic work.

50. William V. D'Antonio, James Davidson, and Ruth Wallace, *Laity American and Catholic: Transforming the Church* (Kansas City, Mo.: Sheed and Ward, 1996).

51. Ibid.

52. See Robert Booth Fowler and Allen Hertzke, *Religion and Politics in America: Faith, Culture, and Strategic Choices* (Boulder, Colo.: Westview, 1995).

53. For a splendid discussion of the more mixed findings of technical social science studies on tolerance in general, see Andrew R. Murphy, "Tolerance and Toleration: Political Psychology and Liberal Theory" (paper, International Society of Political Psychology, 1996).

54. For the best "market" analysis of religion in U.S. history, see Roger Finke and Rodney Stark, *The Churching of America, 1776–1990* (New Brunswick, N.J.: Rutgers University Press, 1992).

55. Ibid., chap. 6.

56. Two good analyses are Richard Neuhaus, *The Naked Public Square: Religion and Democracy in America* (Grand Rapids, Mich.: Eerdmans, 1984); and David F. Wells, *No Place for Truth, or Whatever Happened to Evangelical Theology?* (Grand Rapids, Mich.: Eerdmans, 1993).

57. For an able discussion of the secularization debate, see David Yamane, "Secularization on Trial: A Defense of a Neosecularization Paradigm," *Journal for the Scientific Study of Religion* 36 (1997): 109–22.

58. Francis Fukuyama, *Trust: The Social Virtues of the Creation of Prosperity* (New York: Free Press, 1995), makes an interesting argument on this topic.

59. Hewlett, *A Lesser Life*; Susan Faludi, *Backlash: The Undeclared War Against American Women* (New York: Anchor, 1992).

60. Susan Brownmiller, *Against Our Will* (New York: Simon and Schuster, 1975); Andrea Dworkin, *Pornography: Men Possessing Women* (New York: Perigee, 1981).

61. For example, Steven Goldberg, *The Inevitability of Patriarchy* (New York: Morrow, 1973).

62. For example, Michael Levin, *Feminism and Freedom* (New Brunswick, N.J.: Transaction Books, 1977).

6. Community as a Point of Redirection

1. Some valuable discussions that reflect on the definition of community are David B. Clark, "The Concept of Community: A Re-examination," *Sociological Review* 21 (August 1973): 397–416; Glenn Tinder, *Community: Reflections on a Tragic Ideal* (Baton Rouge: Louisiana State University Press, 1980); Robert Nisbet, *The Quest for Community* (New York: Oxford University Press, 1953); Philip Selznick, *The Moral Commonwealth: Social Theory and the Promise of Community* (Berkeley: University of California Press, 1992); C. F. Delaney, ed., *The Liberalism and Communitarianism Debate* (London: Rowman and Littlefield, 1994); Robert Booth Fowler, *The Dance with Community: The Contemporary Debate in American Political Thought* (Lawrence: University Press of Kansas, 1991); Amitai Etzioni, ed., *The Spirit of Community: Rights, Responsibilities and the Communitarian Agenda* (New York: Crown, 1993).

2. Fowler, *The Dance with Community*, chap. 1.

3. Michael Sandel, *Democracy's Discontent: America in Search of a Public Philosophy* (Cambridge, Mass.: Harvard University Press, 1996).

4. Ibid.

5. Ibid.; see also Mary Ann Glendon, "Civil Service," *New Republic*, April 1, 1996, 39–40.

6. Sandel, *Democracy's Discontent*; Alasdair MacIntyre, *After Virtue: A Study in Moral Theory* (Notre Dame, Ind.: University of Notre Dame Press, 1981).

7. Selznick, *The Moral Commonwealth*.

8. Amy Gutmann, "The Disharmony of Democracy," in *Democratic Community*, edited by John W. Chapman and Ian Shapiro (New York: New York University Press, 1993), 126–60.

9. Three examples from a large literature: Daniel Bell, *Communitarianism and Its Critics* (New York: Oxford University Press, 1993); Delaney, *The Liberalism and Communitarianism Debate*; and Clarke E. Cochran, "The Thin Theory of Community: The Communitarians and Their Critics," *Political Studies* 37 (1989): 422–35.

10. Terence Ball, *Reappraising Political Theory* (New York: Oxford University Press, 1995), 295.

11. Ann Swidler in Robert Bellah, Richard Madsen, William Sullivan, Ann Swidler, and Steven M. Tipton, *Habits of the Heart: Individualism and Commitment in American Life* (Berkeley: University of California Press, 1985), chap. 4.

12. Ibid., 82.

13. Benjamin Barber, *Strong Democracy* (Berkeley: University of California Press, 1984).

14. Ibid.

15. Bellah et al., *Habits of the Heart*.

16. Robert Bellah, Richard Madsen, William Sullivan, Ann Swidler, and Steven M. Tipton, *The Good Society* (New York: Knopf, 1991).

17. Daniel Kemmis, *Community and the Politics of Place* (Norman: University of Oklahoma Press, 1990).

18. David F. Wells, *No Place for Truth, or Whatever Happened to Evangelical Theology?* (Grand Rapids, Mich.: Eerdmans, 1993).

19. William Damon, *Greater Expectations* (New York: Free Press, 1995), chaps. 1–4.

20. J. Budziszewski, "The Problem of Communitarianism," *First Things* 51 (March 1995): 22–26.

21. For example, see Joshua Cohen and Joel Rogers, *On Democracy: Toward a Transformation of American Society* (New York: Penguin, 1983).

22. Robert Bellah, Richard Madsen, William Sullivan, Ann Swidler, and Steven M. Tipton, "Individualism and the Crisis of Civic Membership," *Christian Century*, May 8, 1996, 510–15.

23. Amitai Etzioni, *The New Golden Rule: Community and Morality in a Democratic Society* (New York: Basic Books, 1997); Amitai Etzioni, ed., *Rights and the Common Good: The Communitarian Perspective* (New York: St. Martin's, 1995); Amitai Etzioni, ed., *Communitarian Thinking: New Essays* (Charlottesville: University Press of Virginia, 1995); Etzioni, *Spirit of Community*.

24. Amitai Etzioni, "On Restoring the Moral Voice," in *Rights and the Common Good: The Communitarian Perspective*, edited by Amitai Etzioni (New York: St. Martin's, 1995), 271–76.

25. Etzioni, *Spirit of Community*.

26. Joan C. Tronto, *Moral Boundaries: A Political Argument for an Ethic of Care* (New York: Routledge, 1993).

27. Wilson Carey McWilliams, *The Idea of Fraternity in America* (Berkeley: University of California Press, 1973), 34.

28. Ibid., 109.

29. Ibid., 5.

30. Ibid., chaps. 5, 9.

31. Ibid., chap. 9.

32. Michael Lind, *The Next American Nation: The New Nationalism and the Fourth American Revolution* (New York: Free Press, 1995).

33. Michael Lind, *Up from Conservatism: Why the Right Is Wrong for America* (New York: Free Press, 1996).

34. Michael Lind, *Hamilton's Republic: Readings in the American Democratic Nationalist Tradition* (New York: Free Press, 1997).

35. Barbara Ehrenreich, "Another Communitarianism," *New Republic*, May 9, 1988, 21.

36. Corinne McLaughlin and Gordon Davidson, *Builders of the Dawn: Community Lifestyles in a Changing World* (Shutesbury, Mass.: Sirius, 1986).

37. R. Jeffrey Lustig, *Corporate Liberalism: Origins of Modern American Political Theory, 1890–1920* (Berkeley: University of California Press, 1982).

38. For example, see Robert Dahl, *A Preface to Economic Democracy* (Berkeley: University of California Press, 1985); Cohen and Rogers, *On Democracy*.

39. Edward J. Blakely and Mary Gail Snyder, *Fortress America: Gated Communities in the United States* (Washington, D.C.: Brookings, 1987).

40. Stephen Holmes, "The Polis State," *New Republic,* June 6, 1988, 32–39.

41. Derek Phillips, *Looking Backward: A Critical Appraisal of Communitarian Thought* (Princeton, N.J.: Princeton University Press, 1993).

42. Alan Ehrenhalt, *The Lost City: Discovering the Forgotten Virtue of Community in the Chicago of the 1950s* (New York: Basic Books, 1995).

43. Ibid., 40.

44. Jane Mansbridge, *Beyond Adversary Democracy* (Chicago: University of Chicago Press, 1983).

45. The classic case here continues to be Carole Pateman's enthusiastic celebration of Yugoslavia as the ideal of modern participatory democracy in her *Participation and Democratic Theory* (Cambridge: Cambridge University Press, 1970).

46. Sheldon Wolin, *Politics and Vision* (Boston: Little, Brown, 1960); Sheldon Wolin and John H. Schaar, *The Berkeley Rebellion and Beyond* (New York: Vintage, 1970).

47. Sheldon Wolin, "Democracy in the Discourse of Postmodernism," *Social Research* 57 (Spring 1990): 5–30.

48. John S. Dryzek, *Discursive Democracy: Politics, Policy and Political Science* (Cambridge: Cambridge University Press, 1990), 22.

49. Dryzek is not an American citizen, but his work on democracy was done while he was teaching in the United States.

50. Robert Wuthnow, *Sharing the Journey: Support Groups and America's New Quest for Community* (New York: Free Press, 1994).

51. Ibid.; Robert Wuthnow, "How Small Groups Are Transforming Our Lives," *Christianity Today,* February 7, 1994, 19–24.

52. Milbrey W. McLaughlin, Merita A. Irby, and Juliet Longman, *Urban Sanctuaries: Neighborhood Organizations in the Lives and Future of Inner-City Youth* (San Francisco: Jossey-Bass, 1994).

53. Ann Swidler, "In Groups We Trust," *New York Times Book Review,* March 20, 1994, 13.

54. Wuthnow, *Sharing the Journey.*

55. For example, see the excellent book by Irene Diamond and Gloria Feman Orenstein, eds., *Reweaving the World: The Emergence of Ecofeminism* (San Francisco: Sierra Club, 1990).

56. Wuthnow, *Sharing the Journey;* and Wuthnow, "How Small Groups Are Transforming Our Lives."

57. Neuhaus, *Naked Public Square.*

58. A recent discussion is found in Kenneth L. Grasso, Gerald V. Bradley, and Robert P. Hunt, eds., *Catholicism, Liberalism, and Communitarianism* (Lanham, Md.: Rowman and Littlefield, 1995).

59. Robert P. Hunt, "Moral Orthodoxy and the Procedural Republic," in *John Courtney Murray and the American Civil Conversation,* edited by Robert P. Hunt and Kenneth L. Grasso (Grand Rapids, Mich.: Eerdmans, 1992), 249–70.

60. Kenneth L. Grasso, "'We Hold These Truths': The Transformation of American Pluralism and the Future of American Democracy," in Hunt and Grasso, *John Courtney Murray and the American Civil Conversation*, 109.

61. Mary Ann Hinsdale, Helen M. Lervis, and S. Maxine Waller, *It Comes from the People: Community Development and Local Theology* (Philadelphia: Temple University Press, 1995).

62. Kathleen Norris, *Dakota: A Spiritual Geography* (New York: Ticknor and Fields, 1993); Kathleen Norris, *The Cloister Walk* (New York: Riverhead Books, 1996).

63. Tinder, *Community*.

64. Russell Kirk, *The Conservative Mind* (Chicago: Regnery, 1953).

65. Richard Moe and Carter Wilkie, *Changing Places: Rebuilding Community in the Age of Sprawl* (New York: Holt, 1987).

66. Nisbet, *Quest for Community*.

67. Stephen Macedo, *Liberal Virtues: Citizenship, Virtue, and Community in Liberal Constitutionalism* (New York: Oxford University Press, 1990).

68. Peter Berger, *Pyramids of Sacrifice* (Garden City, N.Y.: Doubleday, 1976).

69. Amitai Etzioni, "Too Many Rights, Too Many Responsibilities," in *Toward a Global Civil Society*, edited by Michael Walzer (Providence, R.I.: Berghahn, 1995), 99–111.

70. Wilfred M. McClay, *The Masterless: Self and Society in Modern America* (Chapel Hill: University of North Carolina Press, 1994), 282.

71. Ibid.

72. Iris Marion Young, *Justice and the Politics of Difference* (Princeton, N.J.: Princeton University Press, 1990).

73. Although how this might be achieved Nicholson does not discuss; Linda Nicholson talk, University of Wisconsin–Madison, March 5, 1996.

74. Lani Guinier, *The Tyranny of the Majority: Fundamental Fairness in Representative Democracy* (New York: Free Press, 1995).

75. Marilyn Friedman, "Feminism and Modern Friendship: Dislocating the Community," in *Social and Political Philosophy: Classical Texts in Feminist and Multi-cultural Perspective*, edited by James P. Sterba (Belmont, Calif.: Wadsworth, 1995), 501–12; Susan Okin, *Justice, Gender, and the Family* (New York: Basic Books, 1989).

76. Shelby Steele, *The Content of Our Character* (New York: HarperCollins, 1991), 47, 55, 68, 72, 132.

77. Ibid., 141, 148.

78. Ibid., 70–72.

79. J. Donald Moon, *Constructing Community: Moral Pluralism and Tragic Conflicts* (Princeton, N.J.: Princeton University Press, 1993).

80. As one reviewer of this manuscript suggested.

81. For example, see Damon, *Greater Expectations*.

82. See chapters 5 and 6 for discussion and data.

7. Environmentalism as a Point of Redirection

1. For an interesting argument on this theme, see Ian Tyrrell, "American Exceptionalism in an Age of International History," *American Historical Review* 96 (October 1991): 1031–55.

2. See the account, for example, by Kirkpatrick Sale, *The Green Revolution: The American Environmental Movement, 1962–1992* (New York: Hill and Wang, 1993).

3. See the bibliographic direction and the data analyses in Riley E. Dunlap, "Trends in Public Opinion Toward Environmental Issues: 1965–1990," in *American Environmentalism: The U.S. Environmental Movement, 1970–1990*, edited by Riley E. Dunlap and Angela G. Mertig (Philadelphia: Taylor and Francis, 1990), 89–116; Riley E. Dunlap, George Gallup Jr., and Alec M. Gallup, *Health of the Planet: Results of a 1992 International Environmental Opinion Survey of Citizens in Twenty-four Nations* (Princeton, N.J.: George H. Gallup International Institute, 1993); John C. Green, Lyman A. Kellstedt, and Corwin E. Smidt, "Faith and the Environment: Religious Beliefs and Attitudes on Environmental Policy" (paper, Southern Political Science Association, 1993); Robyn Eckersley, "Green Politics and the New Class: Selfishness or Virtue?" *Political Studies* 37 (June 1989): 205–43; Robert Rohrschneider, "Citizens' Attitudes Toward Environmental Issues: Selfish or Selfless?" *Comparative Political Studies* 21 (October 1988): 347–67; Adolf Gundersen, *The Environmental Promise of Democratic Deliberation* (Madison: University of Wisconsin Press, 1995); Robert Booth Fowler, *The Greening of Protestant Thought: 1970–1990* (Chapel Hill: University of North Carolina Press, 1995), chap. 1. For earlier information, see Lester Milbrath, *Environmentalists: Vanguard for a New Society* (Albany: State University of New York Press, 1984); Nicholas Watts and Geoffrey Wandesforde-Smith, "Moral Outrage and the Progress of Environmental Policy," in *Environmental Policy in the 1990s*, edited by Norman J. Vig and Michael E. Kraft (Washington, D.C.: Congressional Quarterly Press, 1990), 325–47; in fact, the sources are endless, although the results are rarely in conflict.

4. For relevant data and bibliographies, see Mary Anne E. Steger and Stephanie L. Witt, "Gender Differences in Environmental Orientations," *Western Political Quarterly* 42 (December 1989): 627–49; Doceta E. Taylor, "Blacks and the Environment: Toward an Explanation of the Concern and Action Gap Between Blacks and Whites," *Environmental Behavior* 21 (March 1989): 175–205; Douglas Lee Eckberg and T. Jean Blocker, "Christianity, Environmentalism, and the Theoretical Problem of Fundamentalism," *Journal for the Scientific Study of Religion* 35 (December 1996): 343–55.

5. Richard J. Ellis and Fred Thompson, "The Culture War by Other Means: Environmental Attitudes and Cultural Bias in the Northwest" (paper, Western Political Science Association, 1996).

6. Rachel Carson, *Silent Spring* (Greenwich, Conn.: Fawcett, 1962).

7. Barry Commoner, *The Closing Circle: Nature, Man, and Technology* (New York: Bantam Books, 1974); Jonathan Schell, *The Fate of the Earth* (New York: Knopf, 1982); Paul Ehrlich, *The Population Bomb* (New York: Ballantine, 1968); Paul Ehrlich and Anne H. Ehrlich, *The Population Explosion* (New York: Simon and Schuster, 1990).

8. For example, see Michael Renner, *Fighting for Survival* (New York: Norton, 1996).

9. Arthur Herman, *The Idea of Decline in Western History* (New York: Free Press, 1997).

10. Ibid.

11. Garrett Hardin, "The Tragedy of the Commons," *Science* 162 (December 1968): 243–48.

12. Herman E. Daly and John B. Cobb Jr., *For the Common Good: Redirecting the Economy Toward Community, the Environment, and a Sustainable Future* (Boston: Beacon, 1989).

13. Roderick Nash, *The Rights of Nature: A History of Environmental Ethics* (Madison: University of Wisconsin Press, 1989); J. Baird Callicott, *In Defense of the Land Ethic* (Albany: State University of New York Press, 1989).

14. Bill Devall and George Sessions, *Deep Ecology* (Salt Lake City, Utah: Peregrine Smith Books, 1985); Murray Bookchin, *The Ecology of Freedom: The Emergence and Dissolution of Hierarchy* (Palo Alto, Calif.: Cheshire Books, 1982); Murray Bookchin, *The Philosophy of Social Ecology* (Montreal: Black Rose Books, 1990).

15. Julian L. Simon and Herman Kahn, *The Resourceful Earth* (New York: Basil Blackwell, 1984).

16. Wilfred Beckerman, *Through Green-Colored Glasses: Environmentalism Reconsidered* (Washington, D.C.: Cato Institute, 1996).

17. Paul Ehrlich and Anne H. Ehrlich, *Betrayal of Science and Reason* (Washington, D.C.: Island Press, 1996).

18. Greg Easterbrook, *A Moment on the Earth: The Coming Age of Environmental Optimism* (New York: Viking, 1995).

19. Todd Gitlin, *The Twilight of Common Dreams: Why America Is Wracked with Cultural Wars* (New York: Holt, 1995), 235.

20. Bob Pepperman Taylor, *Our Limits Transgressed: Environmental Political Thought in America* (Lawrence: University Press of Kansas, 1992).

21. Bob Pepperman Taylor, *America's Bachelor Uncle: Thoreau and the American Polity* (Lawrence: University Press of Kansas, 1996).

22. Carolyn Merchant, *The Death of Nature: Women, Ecology, and the Scientific Revolution* (San Francisco: Harper, 1980).

23. Joni Seager, *Earth Follies: Coming to Feminist Terms with the Global Environmental Crisis* (New York: Routledge, 1993).

24. See Fowler, *The Greening*.

25. Lynn White, "The Historic Roots of Our Ecologic Crisis," *Science*, March 10, 1967, 1203–7.

26. White recognized alternative Christian traditions himself.

27. See H. Paul Santmire, *The Travail of Nature: The Ambiguous Ecological Promise of Christian Theology* (Philadelphia: Fortress, 1985); Calvin DeWitt, ed., *The Environment and the Christian: What Does the New Testament Say About the Environment?* (Grand Rapids, Mich.: Baker, 1991).

28. See, for example, Sale, *The Green Revolution*.

29. "Evangelical Environmentalism Comes of Age," *Christianity Today*, November 11, 1996, 84.

30. Michael Barkun, "Divided Apocalypse: Talking About the End in Contemporary America," *Soundings* 66 (Fall 1983): 257–80.

31. William Ophuls, *Ecology and the Politics of Scarcity* (San Francisco: W. H. Freeman, 1977); Katrina Schwartz, "Possibilities and Limits of an Ecological Social Contract: Survival, Ecocentrism, and Lockean Liberalism" (unpublished paper, University of Wisconsin–Madison, 1993).

32. Joe Bowersox, "The Moral and Spiritual Potential of Environmentalism" (Ph.D. dissertation, University of Wisconsin–Madison, 1995); John Meyer, "The Politics of Nature: Political Theory, Environmentalism, and the Evasion of Political Judgment" (Ph.D. dissertation, University of Wisconsin–Madison, 1997).

33. John Rodman, "Paradigm Change in Political Science: An Ecological Perspective," *American Behavioral Scientist* 24 (1980): 49–78.

34. William Ophuls, *Requiem for Modern Politics: The Tragedy of the Enlightenment and the Challenge of the New Millennium* (Boulder, Colo.: Westview, 1997).

35. Ibid., 96.

36. Ibid.

37. For example, Daly and Cobb, *For the Common Good*; Lewis W. Moncrief, "The Cultural Basis for Our Environmental Crisis," *Science*, October 30, 1970, 506–11; and Eugene Hargrove, *Religion and the Environmental Crisis* (Athens: University of Georgia Press, 1986). It is important to note also the considerable ecosocialist literature; a good place to start is with James O'Connor and his journal, *Capitalism, Nature, Socialism*.

38. See Fowler, *The Greening*.

39. White, "Historic Roots."

40. Francis Schaeffer, *Pollution and the Death of Man* (Wheaton, Ill.: Tyndale House, 1970); Loren Wilkinson, "What Can We Learn from the New Testament?" in *The Environment and the Christian: What Does the New Testament Say About the Environment?* edited by Calvin DeWitt (Grand Rapids, Mich.: Baker, 1991), chap. 1; Santmire, *Travail of Nature*, chaps. 2, 4–5.

41. Robyn Eckersley, *Environmentalism and Political Theory: Toward an Ecocentric Approach* (Albany: State University of New York Press, 1992), chap. 2.

42. Evelyn Pluhar, *Beyond Prejudice: The Moral Significance of Human and Nonhuman Animals* (Durham, N.C.: Duke University Press, 1995).

43. On Leopold, see his "Conservation as a Moral Issue," in *Ethics and the Environment*, edited by Donald Scherer and Thomas Attig, 9–12 (Englewood Cliffs, N.J.: Prentice-Hall, 1983); "The Land Ethic," in *Ethics and the Environment*, 6–9; and *A Sand County Almanac* (New York: Oxford University Press, 1949).

44. A distinction made to me by John Meyer.

45. Eckersley, *Environmentalism and Political Theory*, chap. 3.

46. As my colleague John Meyer has pointed out to me.

47. Paul Taylor, *Respect for Nature* (Princeton, N.J.: Princeton University Press, 1986).

48. Callicott, *In Defense*.

49. But see Taylor's *America's Bachelor Uncle*, arguing that Thoreau was very much a public intellectual and political theorist.

50. J. Baird Callicott, "Traditional American Indian and Traditional Western European Attitudes Towards Nature: An Overview," in *Environmental Philosophy: A Collection of Readings*, edited by Robert Elliot and Arran Gare (University Park: Pennsylvania State University Press, 1983), 231–59.

51. Tom Hayden, *The Lost Gospel of the Earth* (San Francisco: Sierra Club Books, 1996).

52. Calvin B. DeWitt, *Caring for Creation: Responsible Stewardship of God's Handiwork* (Grand Rapids, Mich.: Baker, 1998).

53. See Romans 8:21.

54. DeWitt, *The Environment and the Christian*.

55. Santmire, *Travail of Nature*.

56. Tim Stafford, "Animal Liberation," *Christianity Today*, June 16, 1990, 19–23.

57. "It's Not Easy Being Green," *Christianity Today*, May 18, 1992, 14.

58. Matthew Fox, *Original Blessing: A Primer in Creation Spirituality* (Santa Fe, N.M.: Bear and Co., 1983); Thomas Berry, *The Dream of the Earth* (San Francisco: Sierra Books, 1988).

59. Wayne Boulton, "The Thoroughly Modern Mysticism of Matthew Fox," *Christian Century*, April 25, 1990, 428–32.

60. An excellent introduction to ecofeminism is Irene Diamond and Gloria Feman Orenstein, eds., *Reweaving the World: The Political Emergence of Ecofeminism* (San Francisco: Sierra Club, 1990); see also Charlene Spretnak, *The Politics of Women's Spirituality* (Garden City, N.Y.: Anchor, 1982).

61. Starhawk, *Truth or Dare: Encounters with Power, Authority and Mystery* (San Francisco: Harper, 1990).

62. Compare Carol Christ, *Laughter of Aphrodite: Reflections on a Journey to the Goddess* (San Francisco: Harper and Row, 1987), with Susanne Heine, *Matriarchs, Goddesses, Images of God: A Critique of a Feminist Theology* (Minneapolis: Augsburg, 1988).

63. Charlene Spretnak, *The Spiritual Dimension of Green Politics* (San Francisco: Bear and Co., 1986); Spretnak, *Women's Spirituality*.

64. Rosemary Ruether, *Gaia and God* (New York: HarperCollins, 1992).

65. Merchant, *Death of Nature*.

66. Taylor, *Our Limits Transgressed*.

67. On green pragmatism, see Bryan Norton, *Toward Unity Among Environmentalists* (New York: Oxford University Press, 1991); an impressive argument for pragmatism in the context of contemporary practice is found in Charles W. Anderson, *Pragmatic Liberalism* (Chicago: University of Chicago Press, 1990).

68. This view was first made famous by Ophuls in *Ecology and the Politics of Scarcity* (San Francisco: W. H. Freeman, 1977); William Ophuls, *Ecology and the Politics of Scarcity Revisited* (San Francisco: W. H. Freeman, 1992).

69. Robert Heilbroner, *An Inquiry into the Human Prospect* (New York: Norton, 1974).

70. For a discussion of these approaches that accurately concentrates on their strength in the European green movement, see Eckersley, *Environmentalism*, chaps. 4, 6.

71. Bookchin, *Ecology of Freedom*; Bookchin, *Social Ecology*; Rodman, "Paradigm Change"; Eckersley, *Environmentalism*.

72. Murray Bookchin, *Remaking Society: Pathways to a Green Future* (Boston: South End Press, 1990).

73. Bookchin, *Ecology of Freedom*; Eckersley, *Environmentalism*, chap. 7.

74. Eckersley, *Environmentalism*, chaps. 1, 2.

75. Mark Mowry and Tim Redmond, *Not in Our Backyard: The People and Events That Shaped America's Modern Environmental Movement* (New York: Morrow, 1993).

76. For example, see Brian Roherty and Marius de Geus, *Democracy and Green Political Thought: Sustainability, Rights and Citizenship* (New York: Routledge, 1996).

77. Bookchin, *Remaking Society* and *Ecology of Freedom*.

78. For example, see Bruce Stokes, *Helping Ourselves: Local Solutions to Global Problems* (New York: Norton, 1981).

79. Gundersen, *Environmental Promise*; John S. Dryzek, *Discursive Democracy: Politics, Policy and Political Science* (Cambridge: Cambridge University

Press, 1990). Dryzek is an Australian, but he did his work on democracy while living in the United States.

80. Adolf Gundersen, "Native American Political Theory: The Lesson for Contemporary Ecological Governance" (paper, Fourth Annual Symposium on Society and Resource Management, May 1992).

81. Quoted by Randy Frame in "Greening of the Gospel?" *Christianity Today*, November 11, 1996, 82–86.

82. Ibid., 83.

83. Ibid.

84. Fox, *Original Blessing*.

85. John B. Cobb Jr., "Process Theology and an Ecological Model," in *Cry of the Environment*, edited by Philip N. Joranson and Ken Butigan (Santa Fe, N.M.: Bear and Co., 1984), 329–36.

86. Spretnak, *Green Politics;* Fowler, *The Greening*, chap. 8.

87. Allen Hertzke and Chris McRorie, "The Concept of Moral Ecology" (paper, Conference on Communitarianism and Civil Society, 1996).

88. On global dimensions, see Paul Wapner, *Environmental Activism and World Civic Politics* (Albany: State University of New York Press, 1996); and Ronnie D. Lipschutz, *Global Civil Society and Global Environmental Governance* (Albany: State University of New York Press, 1996); on the religious side, see Fowler, *The Greening*.

8. To Revive Civil Society

1. James B. Twitchell, *For Shame: The Loss of Common Decency in American Culture* (New York: St. Martin's, 1997).

2. Stephen Carter, *Civility: Manners, Morals, and the Etiquette of Democracy* (New York: Basic Books, 1998).

3. Robert Putnam, "Bowling Alone: America's Declining Social Capital," *Current*, no. 373 (June 1995): 3–9.

4. In these opening reflections, the contribution by Charlie Anderson is large.

5. Alexis de Tocqueville, *Democracy in America*, edited by Richard D. Heffner (New York: Mentor, 1956).

6. Thus, for an interesting contemporary discussion of civil society, see Michael Walzer, "The Concept of Civil Society," in *Toward a Global Civil Society* (Providence, R.I.: Berghahn, 1995), part 1, pp. 7–67.

7. Gellner is used here because of his insight, not with the suggestion that he is an American.

8. Ernest Gellner, *Conditions of Liberty: Civil Society and Its Rivals* (London: Hamish, Hamilton, 1994).

9. Alan Wolfe, *Whose Keeper? Social Science and Moral Obligation* (Berkeley: University of California Press, 1989).

10. Ibid.

11. Jean Bethke Elshtain, *Democracy on Trial* (New York: Basic Books, 1995).

12. Jean Bethke Elshtain, *Public Man, Private Woman: Women in Social and Political Thought* (Princeton, N.J.: Princeton University Press, 1981).

13. Ibid.

14. Ibid.; indeed, this is what much of *Democracy on Trial* is about.

15. See the discussion in Martin E. Marty, "Sightings: Issues from the Public Religion Project," June 4, 1998.

16. Jean Bethke Elshtain, "In Common Together: Unity, Diversity, and Civic Virtue," in *Toward a Global Civil Society*, edited by Michael Walzer (Providence, R.I.: Berghahn, 1995), 77–97.

17. Among key Walzer works are *Spheres of Justice: A Defense of Pluralism and Equality* (New York: Basic Books, 1983); *The Company of Critics: Social Criticism and Political Commitment in the Twentieth Century* (New York: Basic Books, 1988); *On Toleration* (New Haven, Conn.: Yale University Press, 1997); *Thick and Thin: Moral Argument at Home and Abroad* (Notre Dame, Ind.: University of Notre Dame Press, 1994); and "Concept of Civil Society."

18. Walzer, "Concept of Civil Society," 22.

19. Ibid., 26.

20. Ibid., 8.

21. Ibid., 27.

22. Ibid., 8.

23. Ibid., 9–15.

24. Ibid., 16.

25. Ibid.

26. Although his column in the *New Republic* tends to lack much substance.

27. Walzer, *Thick and Thin*, p. 101.

28. See Walzer, *On Toleration*.

29. Although not those devoted to the rejection of pluralism and worse, for example, the societies of Hitler, Stalin, and Mao.

30. See Walzer, *Company of Critics*.

31. As presented in *Thick and Thin*.

32. Ibid., chap. 1.

33. Ibid., 49.

34. See J. Peter Euben's excellent review of *The Company of Critics*: "Fanfare for the Common Complaints," *New York Times Book Review*, January 8, 1989, 18.

35. The argument in *Company of Critics*.

36. Milton Friedman, *Capitalism and Freedom* (Chicago: University of Chicago Press, 1963).

37. William J. Bennett, *The Book of Virtues: A Treasury of Great Moral Stories* (New York: Simon and Schuster, 1993); and William J. Bennett, *The De-valuing of America: The Fight for Our Culture and Our Children* (New York: Simon and Schuster, 1992).

38. Bennett, *Book of Virtues*.

39. Bennett, *De-valuing*, 13, 38, 256.

40. Ibid., 252.

41. See, for example, William G. Mayer, *The Changing American Mind: How and Why American Public Opinion Changed Between 1960 and 1988* (Ann Arbor: University of Michigan Press, 1992).

42. Mary B. Pipher, *The Shelter of Each Other: Rebuilding Our Families* (New York: Putnam, 1996).

43. William Galston, "A Liberal-Democratic Case for the Two-Parent Family," in *The Spirit of Community*, edited by Amitai Etzioni (New York: Crown, 1993); 139–49; Murray Dubin, "Advisor Leaves White House to Spend More Time at Home," *Wisconsin State Journal*, May 27, 1995, 1C.

44. Brigitte Berger and Peter L. Berger, *The War over the Family: Capturing the Middle Ground* (Garden City, N.Y.: Anchor, 1983).

45. James Q. Wilson, "Justice vs. Humanity in the Family," in *The Neoconservative Imagination*, chap. 14.

46. Susan Okin, *Justice, Gender, and the Family* (New York: Basic Books, 1989).

47. Andrew Kurvers Spalding, "Finding the Liberal Family: Moral Education and the Family in Liberal Political Thought" (unpublished paper, 1997).

48. Mary Ann Glendon and David Blankenhorn, eds., *Seedbeds of Virtue: Sources of Competence, Character, and Citizenship in American Society* (Lanham, Md.: Madison Books, 1995).

49. Wilson, "Justice vs. Humanity," 182.

50. James Q. Wilson, *The Moral Sense* (New York: Free Press, 1993).

51. Judith Wallerstein, *The Good Marriage: How and Why Love Lasts* (Boston: Houghton Mifflin, 1995); John Gottman, *Why Marriages Succeed or Fail: And How You Can Make Yours Last* (New York: Simon and Schuster, 1995); Willard F. Harley Jr., *His Needs/Her Needs: Building an Affair-Proof Marriage* (Ada, Mich.: Revell, 1990); Ed Wheat, *Love Life for Every Married Couple* (Grand Rapids, Mich.: Zondervan, 1987).

52. Rosalind C. Barnett and Caryl Rivers, *She Works/He Works: How Two-Income Families Are Happier, Healthier, and Better Off* (San Francisco: Harper, 1996).

53. Pia Nordlinger, "The Anti-divorce Revolution," *Weekly Standard*, March 2, 1998, 25–29.

54. Barbara Whitehead, "Dan Quayle Was Right," *Atlantic Monthly*, April 1993, 47–50.

55. Barbara Whitehead, *The Divorce Culture* (New York: Knopf, 1996).

56. Sylvia Hewlett and Cornel West, *The War Against Parents: What We Can Do for America's Beleaguered Moms and Dads* (Boston: Houghton Mifflin, 1998).

57. David Popenoe, *Disturbing the Nest: Family Change and Decline in Modern Societies* (New York: Aldine, 1988).

58. David Blankenhorn, *Fatherless America: Confronting America's Most Urgent Social Problem* (New York: Basic Books, 1995).

59. Gary Sandefur and Sara McLanahan, *Growing Up with a Single Parent: What Hurts, What Helps* (Cambridge, Mass.: Harvard University Press, 1994), 121–24.

60. Sara McLanahan, "The Consequences of Single Motherhood," *American Prospect* 18 (Summer 1994): 48–58; Susan E. Krantz. "The Impact of Divorce on Children," in *Family in Transition*, edited by Arlene Skolnick and Jerome Skolnick (New York: HarperCollins, 1992), 242–65; Richard Weissbourd, "Divided Families, Whole Children," *American Prospect* 18 (Summer 1994): 66–72.

61. Judith Stacey, *In the Name of the Family: Rethinking Family Values in the Postmodern Age* (Boston: Beacon, 1996).

62. Judith Stacey, "The New Family Values Crusade," *Nation* 259 (1992): 119–22.

63. Ibid.

64. Skolnick and Skolnick, *Family in Transition*; Kathleen Gough, "The Origin of the Family," in Skolnick and Skolnick, *Family in Transition*, 23–39; Tamara K. Hareven, "American Families in Transition: Historical Perspectives on Change," in Skolnick and Skolnick, *Family in Transition*, 40–57; Jean Seligmann, "Variations on a Theme," in Skolnick and Skolneck, *Family in Transition*, 518–23.

65. Jerome Skolnick and Stacey Rosencrantz, "The New Crusade for the Old Family," *American Prospect* 18 (Summer 1994): 59–65.

66. Bryce J. Christensen, *Utopia Against the Family: The Problems and Politics of the American Family* (San Francisco: Ignatius Press, 1990).

67. For example, Martha Mednick, "Single Mothers: A Review and Critique of Current Research," in Skolnick and Skolnick, *Family In Transition*, 363–78; Laura Benkov, *Reinventing the Family: The Emerging Story of Lesbian and Gay Parents* (New York: Crown, 1994).

68. As suggested by my usually not so suspicious friend Charlie Anderson.

69. Christopher Lasch, *Haven in a Heartless World: The Family Besieged* (New York: Basic Books, 1977).

70. Christopher Lasch, *Women and the Common Life: Love, Marriage, and Feminism*, edited by Elisabeth Lasch-Quinn (New York: Norton, 1996).

71. Christopher Lasch, *The Revolt of the Elites and the Betrayal of Democracy* (New York: Norton, 1994).

9. To Revive Civil Society II

1. For example, Daniel Patrick Moynihan, *Family and Nation* (New York: Harcourt Brace Jovanovich, 1986).

2. Alex Kotlowitz, *There Are No Children Here* (New York: Doubleday, 1991).

3. LeAlan Jones and Lloyd Newman, *Our America: Life and Death in the South Side of Chicago* (New York: Scribner's, 1997).

4. Glenn C. Loury, "The Family as Context for Delinquency Prevention," in *Families, Schools, and Delinquency Prevention*, edited by James Q. Wilson and Glenn C. Loury (New York: Springer, 1987), 3–26; Harold E. Cheatham and James B. Stewart, eds., *Black Families* (New Brunswick, N.J.: Transaction Books, 1990).

5. Robert B. Hill, *The Strength of Black Families* (New York: Norton, 1989).

6. Kenneth B. Clark, *Dark Ghetto* (New York: Harper and Row, 1965); Herbert Gutman, *The Black Family in Slavery and Freedom: 1750–1925* (New York: Pantheon, 1976); Myron Magnet, *The Dream and the Nightmare: The Sixties Legacy to the Underclass* (New York: Morrow, 1993); Charles Murray, *Losing Ground: American Social Policy, 1950–1981* (New York: Basic Books, 1984).

7. See William M. Banks, *Black Intellectuals: Race and Responsibility in American Life* (New York: Norton, 1996).

8. Wilson's first influential book: *The Truly Disadvantaged* (Chicago: University of Chicago Press, 1990); Maxine Baca Zinn, "Family, Race, and Poverty in the Eighties" in *Family in Transition*, edited by Arlene Skolnick and Jerome Skolnick (New York: HarperCollins, 1992), 399–413.

9. See, for example, Joe Klein, "The True Disadvantage," *New Republic*, October 28, 1996, 32.

10. William Julius Wilson, *When Work Disappears: The World of the New Urban Poor* (New York: Knopf, 1996).

11. For example, Murray, *Losing Ground;* Moynihan, *Family and Nation;* Magnet, *The Dream and the Nightmare.*

12. Stephan Thernstrom and Abigail Thernstrom, *America in Black and White* (New York: Simon and Schuster, 1997).

13. Glenn C. Loury, "Not So Black and White: The Two Americas Are Actually Converging," *Washington Post*, October 15, 1995, C03. Lawrence Mead,

The New Politics of Poverty: The Nonworking Poor in America (New York: Basic Books, 1991); Eugene Genovese, "The Southern Tradition and the Black Experience," *Chronicles* 18 (August 1994): 20–22; Clark, *Dark Ghetto*, on past attitudes.

14. Paul M. Sniderman and Thomas Piazza, *The Scar of Race* (Cambridge, Mass.: Harvard University Press, 1993).

15. Lawrence Bobo, ed., "Special Issue on Race," *Public Opinion Quarterly* 61 (Spring 1997).

16. Lawrence Bobo, "Introduction: Special Issue on Race," *Public Opinion Quarterly* 61 (Spring 1997): 1–15.

17. David Shipler, *A Country of Strangers: Blacks and Whites in America* (New York: Knopf, 1997).

18. Robert L. Woodson, "Strangers in a Divided House: Race in America," *Washington Times*, November 2, 1997, B8.

19. Joe R. Feagin and Melvin P. Sikes, *Living with Racism: The Black Middle-Class Experience* (Boston: Beacon, 1994); Mitchell Duneier, *Slim's Table: Race, Respectability, and Masculinity* (Chicago: University of Chicago Press, 1992); John Edgar Wideman, *Fatheralong: A Meditation on Fathers and Sons, Race and Society* (New York: Pantheon, 1994).

20. Nathan McCall, *Makes Me Wanna Holler: A Young Black Man in America* (New York: Random House, 1995).

21. Earl Ofai Hutchinson, *The Assassination of the Black Male Image* (New York: Simon and Schuster, 1996).

22. Bill Stephney, "The Welfare Rap: Why Black Men Hate It," *New Republic*, September 16/23, 1996, 11.

23. Geoffrey Canada, *Reaching Up for Manhood: Transforming the Lives of Boys in America* (Boston: Beacon, 1998).

24. Ibid., 154.

25. David T. Courtwright, *Violent Land: Single Men and Social Disorder from the Frontier to the Inner City* (Cambridge, Mass.: Harvard University Press, 1996).

26. Ibid., 9.

27. For example, see Anthony T. Evans, *No More Excuses* (Wheaton, Ill.: Crossway Books, 1996).

28. George Gilder, "End Welfare Reform as We Know It," *American Spectator* 28 (June 1995): 24–27.

29. William A. Kelso, *Poverty and the Underclass* (New York: New York University Press, 1994).

30. Orlando Patterson, "The Crisis of Gender Relations Among African Americans," in *Race, Gender, and Power in America: The Legacy of the Hill-Thomas Hearings*, edited by Anita Faye Hill and Emma Coleman Jordan (New York: Oxford University Press, 1995), 56–104.

31. Guenter Lewy, *Why America Needs Religion: Secular Modernity and Its Discontents* (Grand Rapids, Mich.: Eerdmans, 1997).

32. Ted Jelen and Clyde Wilcox, *Public Attitudes Toward Church and State* (Armonk, N.Y.: M. E. Sharpe, 1995).

33. Alexis de Tocqueville, *Democracy in America*, edited by Richard D. Heffner (New York: Mentor, 1956).

34. Stephen Carter, *The Culture of Disbelief* (New York: Basic Books, 1993).

35. See, for example, the standard findings from the Roper Center's publication *The Public Perspective* (for example, May/June 1990, 109).

36. For example, see Steven R. Burkett and Mervin White, "Hellfire and

Delinquency: Another Look," *Journal for the Scientific Study of Religion* 13 (1974): 455–62; Gary F. Jensen and Maynard L. Erickson, "The Religious Factor and Delinquency: Another Look at the Hellfire Hypothesis," in *The Religious Dimension*, edited by Robert Wuthnow (New York: Academic Press, 1979), 157–78; Paul C. Higgins and Gary L. Albrecht, "Hellfire and Delinquency Revisited," *Social Forces* 55 (1977): 952–58; Douglas M. Sloane and Raymond H. Potvin, "Religion and Delinquency: Cutting Through the Maze," *Social Forces* 65 (1986): 87–105; Scott H. Beck, Bettie S. Cole, and Judith A. Hammond, "Religious Heritage and Premarital Sex," *Journal for the Scientific Study of Religion* 30 (1991): 177–80; Lee Ellis, "Religiosity and Criminality: Evidence and Explorations of Complex Relationships," *Sociological Perspectives* 28 (1985): 501–20; Rodney Stark et al., "Rediscovering Moral Communities: Church Membership and Crime," in *Understanding Crime: Current Theory and Research*, edited by Travis Hirschi and Michael Gottfredwson (Beverly Hills, Calif.: Sage, 1980), 43–52; William Sims Bainbridge, "The Religious Ecology of Deviance," *American Sociological Review* 54 (1989): 288–95; Joseph P. Fitzpatrick, "The Role of Religion in Programming for the Prevention and Correction of Crime and Delinquency," in *Task Force Report: Juvenile Delinquency and Youth Crimes* (Washington, D.C.: Government Printing Office, 1967); and Travis Hirschi and Rodney Stark, "Hellfire and Delinquency," *Social Problems* 17 (1969): 202–13.

37. See Brent B. Benda and Robert Flynn Corwyn, "Religion and Delinquency," *Journal for the Scientific Study of Religion* 36 (March 1997): 81–92.

38. Rodney Stark and William Sims Bainbridge, *Religion, Deviance, and Social Control* (New York: Routledge, 1997), chap. 6.

39. Ibid., chap. 5.

40. Ibid., chap. 4.

41. E. R. Mahoney, "Religiosity and Sexual Behavior Among Heterosexual College Students," *Journal of Sex Research* 16 (1980): 97–113; Jensen, "The Religious Factor"; Beck, Cole, and Hammond, "Religious Heritage"; William V. D'Antonio and Joan Aldous, eds., *Families and Religion* (Beverly Hills, Calif.: Sage, 1983); Lee Kunz, "Religiosity and Criminality," *Sociological Perspectives* 28 (1985): 501–20.

42. Richard Neuhaus, *The Naked Public Square: Religion and Democracy in America* (Grand Rapids, Mich.: Eerdmans, 1984).

43. Sidney Verba, Kay Lehman Schlozman, and Henry E. Brody, eds., *Voice and Equality: Civic Voluntarism in American Politics* (Cambridge, Mass.: Harvard University Press, 1995), pp. 333, 390, chaps. 7, 8, 15.

44. Especially good for a longitudinal look: Robert Bezilla, *Religion in America* (Princeton, N.J.: Princeton Religion Research Center, 1993).

45. An excellent source of data on these matters may be found in *Religion in America*. These regular reports from the Princeton Religion Research Center in cooperation with George Gallup Jr., though, are but an excellent version of a common message from multiple surveys that include questions on prayer in the public schools with highly consistent results.

46. Kenneth L. Grasso, Gerald V. Bradley, and Robert P. Hunt, eds., *Catholicism, Liberalism, and Communitarianism* (Lanham, Md.: Rowman and Littlefield, 1995).

47. Jean Bethke Elshtain, "Catholic Social Thought, the City, and Liberal America," in *Catholicism, Liberalism, and Communitarianism*, edited by Kenneth L. Grasso, Gerald V. Bradley, and Robert P. Hunt (Lanham, Md.: Rowman and Littlefield, 1995), 97–114.

48. Christopher Wolfe, "Subsidiarity: The 'Other' Ground of Limited Government," in *Catholicism, Liberalism, and Communitarianism*, edited by Kenneth L. Grasso, Gerald V. Bradley, and Robert P. Hunt (Lanham, Md.: Rowman and Littlefield, 1995), 81–96.

49. Robert Putnam, "Bowling Alone: America's Declining Social Capital," *Current*, no. 373 (June 1995): 3–9.

50. Ibid.; Robert J. Samuelson, "Join the Club," *Washington Post National Weekly Edition*, April 15–21, 1996, 5.

51. Gertrude Himmelfarb, "Democratic Remedies for Democratic Disorders," *Public Interest* 131 (Spring 1998): 3–35.

52. Ibid., 6–7.

53. Ibid., 7; for her the worst form of disease is relativism.

10. Conclusion

1. Alan Wolfe, *One Nation, After All: What Middle-Class Americans Really Think About God, Country, Family, Poverty, Racism, Welfare, Homosexuality, Immigration, the Left, the Right, and Each Other* (New York: Viking, 1998).

2. James T. Patterson, "Big Country, Small World," *Washington Post National Weekly Edition*, March 2, 1998, 33.

3. His focus is the middle class, although he includes most Americans in his conception of middle class.

4. Richard Rorty, *Achieving Our Country: Leftist Thought in Twentieth-Century America* (Cambridge, Mass.: Harvard University Press, 1998).

5. Ronald Beiner, *What's the Matter with Liberalism?* (Berkeley: University of California Press, 1992).

6. John F. Freie, *Counterfeit Community: The Exploitation of Our Longings for Connectedness* (Lanham, Md.: Rowman and Littlefield, 1998).

7. See Richard J. Ellis, *The Dark Side of the Left: Illiberal Egalitarianism in America* (Lawrence: University Press of Kansas, 1998).

8. James P. Young, *Reconsidering American Liberalism: The Troubled Odyssey of the Liberal Idea* (Boulder, Colo.: Westview, 1996), 39.

9. Ibid., 91.

Bibliography

Aaron, Daniel. "The Mid-American Scholar." *New Republic,* September 5, 1994, 47–49.

Aaron, Henry J., Thomas E. Mann, and Timothy Taylor, eds. *Values and Public Policy.* Washington, D.C.: Brookings, 1994.

Abbott, Philip. *Political Thought in America: Conversations and Debates.* Itasca, Ill.: Peacock, 1991.

Abramson, Paul. *Political Attitudes in America.* San Francisco: W. H. Freeman, 1983.

Anderson, Charles W. *Pragmatic Liberalism.* Chicago: University of Chicago Press, 1990.

Anderson, Jervis. "Black and Blue." *New Yorker,* April 29, 1996, 62–64.

Anderson, Walter Truett. *Reality Isn't What It Used To Be.* San Francisco: Harper and Row, 1990.

Appleby, Joyce. *Capitalism and a New Social Order: The Republican Vision of the 1790s.* New York: New York University Press, 1984.

Appleby, Joyce, Lynn Hunt, and Margaret Jacob. *Telling the Truth About History.* New York: Norton, 1994.

Arendell, Terry. "Divorce: A Women's Issue." In *Perspectives on the Family,* edited by Christopher Carlson, 497–95. Belmont, Calif.: Wadsworth, 1990.

Armey, Dick. "Freedom's Choir." *Policy Review* 67 (Winter 1994): 27–34.

Asher, Herbert B. *Presidential Elections and American Politics.* Pacific Grove, Calif.: Brooks/Cole, 1972.

Bailyn, Bernard. *Ideological Origins of the American Revolution.* Cambridge, Mass.: Harvard University Press, 1967.

Bainbridge, William Sims. "The Religious Ecology of Deviance." *American Sociological Review* 54 (1989): 288–95.

Baker, Susan Stout. *Radical Beginnings: Richard Hofstadter and the 1930s.* Westport, Conn.: Greenwood, 1985.

Ball, Terence. *Reappraising Political Theory.* New York: Oxford University Press, 1995.

Banks, William M. *Black Intellectuals: Race and Responsibility in American Life.* New York: Norton, 1996.

Banning, Lance. "Republican Identity and the Triumph of the Constitution, 1789 to 1793." *William and Mary Quarterly* 31 (April 1974): 167–88.

Barber, Benjamin. "A Mandate for Liberty: Requiring Education-Based Community Service." In *Rights and the Common Good: The Communitarian Perspective,* edited by Amitai Etzioni, 193–201. New York: St. Martin's, 1995.
———. *Strong Democracy.* Berkeley: University of California Press, 1984.
Barkun, Michael. "Divided Apocalypse: Talking About the End in Contemporary America." *Soundings* 66 (Fall 1983): 257–80.
Barnett, Rosalind C., and Caryl Rivers. *She Works/He Works: How Two-Income Families Are Happier, Healthier, and Better Off.* San Francisco: Harper, 1996.
Beard, Charles A. *An Economic Interpretation of the Constitution of the United States.* New York: Free Press, 1941.
Beard, Charles A., and Mary Beard. *The Rise of American Civilization.* New York: Macmillan, 1930.
Beck, Scott, Bettie S. Cole, and Judith A. Hammond. "Religious Heritage and Premarital Sex." *Journal for the Scientific Study of Religion* 30 (1991): 177–89.
Beckerman, Wilfred. *Through Green-Colored Glasses: Environmentalism Reconsidered.* Washington, D.C.: Cato Institute, 1996.
Beeman, Richard, Stephen Botein, and Edward C. Carter II. *Beyond Confederation: Origins of the Constitution and American National Identity.* Chapel Hill: University of North Carolina Press, 1987.
Beiner, Ronald. *What's the Matter with Liberalism?* Berkeley: University of California Press, 1992.
Beisner, E. Calvin. *Where Garden Meets Wilderness: Evangelical Entry into the Environmental Debate.* Grand Rapids, Mich.: Eerdmans, 1998.
Bell, Daniel. *Communitarianism and Its Critics.* New York: Oxford University Press, 1993.
———. *The Cultural Contradictions of Capitalism.* New York: Basic Books, 1978.
———. *The End of Ideology.* New York: Colliers, 1962.
———. "The 'Hegelian Secret': Civil Society and American Exceptionalism." In *Is America Different?* edited by Byron E. Schafer. New York: Oxford University Press, 1991.
Bellah, Robert, Richard Madsen, William Sullivan, Ann Swidler, and Steven M. Tipton. *The Good Society.* New York: Knopf, 1991.
———. *Habits of the Heart: Individualism and Commitment in American Life.* Berkeley: University of California Press, 1985.
———. "Individualism and the Crisis of Civic Membership." *Christian Century,* May 8, 1996, 510–15.
Benda, Brent B., and Robert Flynn Corwyn. "Religion and Delinquency." *Journal for the Scientific Study of Religion* 36 (March 1997): 81–92.
Benkov, Laura. *Reinventing the Family: The Emerging Story of Lesbian and Gay Parents.* New York: Crown, 1994.
Bennett, William J. *The Book of Virtues: A Treasury of Great Moral Stories.* New York: Simon and Schuster, 1993.
———. *The De-valuing of America: The Fight for Our Culture and Our Children.* New York: Simon and Schuster, 1992.
———. *The Index of Leading Cultural Indicators.* Washington, D.C.: Empower America, March 1993.
Berger, Brigitte, and Peter L. Berger. *The War over the Family: Capturing the Middle Ground.* Garden City, N.Y.: Anchor, 1983.
Berger, Peter. *Pyramids of Sacrifice.* Garden City, N.Y.: Doubleday, 1976.
Bernstein, Barton J., ed. *Towards a New Past.* New York: Vintage, 1969.
Berry, Thomas. *The Dream of the Earth.* San Francisco: Sierra Books, 1988.

Bezilla, Robert. *Religion in America.* Princeton, N.J.: Princeton Religion Research Center, 1993.

Billington, Ray A. *Frederick Jackson Turner: Historian, Scholar, Teacher.* New York: Oxford University Press, 1973.

Bird, Warren. "The Great Small-Group Takeover." *Christianity Today,* February 7, 1994, 25–29.

Black, Gordon S., and Benjamin D. Black. *The Politics of American Discontent.* New York: Wiley, 1994.

Blakely, Edward J., and Mary Gail Snyder. *Fortress America: Gated Communities in the United States.* Washington, D.C.: Brookings, 1987.

Blankenhorn, David. *Fatherless America: Confronting America's Most Urgent Social Problem.* New York: Basic Books, 1995.

———. *Rebuilding the Nest: A New Commitment to the American Family.* Milwaukee, Wis.: Family Service America, 1990.

Bloch, Ruth. "The Constitution and Culture." In "The Creation of the American Republic, 1776–1789: A Symposium of Views and Reviews." *William and Mary Quarterly* 44 (July 1987): 550–55.

———. "Religion, Literary Sentimentalism, and Popular Revolutionary Ideology." In *Religion in a Revolutionary Age,* edited by Ronald Hoffman and Peter J. Albert, 308–30. Charlottesville: University Press of Virginia, 1994.

Bloom, Allan. *The Closing of the American Mind.* New York: Simon and Schuster, 1987.

Bobo, Lawrence. "Introduction: Special Issue on Race." *Public Opinion Quarterly* 61 (Spring 1997): 1–15.

———, ed. "Special Issue on Race." *Public Opinion Quarterly* 61 (Spring 1997).

Boesche, Roger. *The Strange Liberalism of Alexis de Tocqueville.* Ithaca, N.Y.: Cornell University Press, 1987.

Bogue, Allan G. *Frederick Jackson Turner: Strange Roads Going Down.* Norman: University of Oklahoma Press, 1998.

Bonomi, Patricia U. "Religious Dissent and the Case for American Exceptionalism." In *Religion in a Revolutionary Age,* edited by Ronald Hoffman and Peter J. Albert, 31–51. Charlottesville: University Press of Virginia, 1994.

Bookchin, Murray. *The Ecology of Freedom: The Emergence and Dissolution of Hierarchy.* Palo Alto, Calif.: Cheshire Books, 1982.

———. *The Philosophy of Social Ecology.* Montreal: Black Rose Books, 1990.

———. *Remaking Society: Pathways to a Green Future.* Boston: South End Press, 1990.

Boorstin, Daniel. *The Americans: The Democratic Experience.* New York: Vintage, 1974.

———. *The Americans: The National Experience.* New York: Vintage, 1965.

———. *The Creators.* New York: Random House, 1992.

———. *The Genius of American Politics.* Chicago: University of Chicago Press, 1953.

Boulton, Wayne. "The Thoroughly Modern Mysticism of Matthew Fox." *Christian Century,* April 25, 1990, 428–32.

Bowersox, Joe. "The Moral and Spiritual Potential of Environmentalism." Ph.D. Dissertation, University of Wisconsin–Madison, 1995.

Boyer, Paul. *When Time Shall Be No More: Prophecy Belief in Modern American Culture.* Cambridge, Mass.: Harvard University Press, 1992.

Boyte, Harry C., and Frank Riessman, eds. *The New Populism.* Philadelphia: Temple University Press, 1986.

Brint, Michael. "Review of Richard J. Ellis's *American Political Cultures.*" *American Political Science Review* 88 (1994): 759–60.

Brown, Robert E. *Charles Beard and the Constitution.* New York: Norton, 1956.

Brownmiller, Susan. *Against Our Will: Men, Women, and Rape.* New York: Simon and Schuster, 1975.

Bryk, Anthony S., Valerie E. Lee, and Peter B. Holland, *Catholic Schools and the Common Good.* Cambridge, Mass.: Harvard University Press, 1993.

Budziszewski, J. "The Problem of Communitarianism." *First Things* 51 (March 1995): 22–26.

———. "The Problem with Conservatism." *First Things* 62 (April 1996): 38–44.

Burkett, Steven R., and Mervin White. "Hellfire and Delinquency: Another Look." *Journal for the Scientific Study of Religion* 13 (1974): 455–62.

Butler, Jon. "Coercion, Miracle, Reason: Rethinking the American Religious Experience in the Revolutionary Age." In *Religion in a Revolutionary Age,* edited by Ronald Hoffman and Peter J. Albert, 1–30. Charlottesville: University Press of Virginia, 1994.

Callicott, J. Baird. *In Defense of the Land Ethic.* Albany: State University of New York Press, 1989.

———. "Traditional American Indian and Traditional Western European Attitudes Towards Nature: An Overview." In *Environmental Philosophy: A Collection of Readings,* edited by Robert Elliot and Arran Gare, 231–59. University Park: Pennsylvania State University Press, 1983.

Canada, Geoffrey. *Reaching Up for Manhood: Transforming the Lives of Boys in America.* Boston: Beacon, 1998.

Cancian, Francesca M. "Gender Politics." In *Family in Transition,* edited by Arlene Skolnick and Jerome Skolnick, 193–204. New York: HarperCollins, 1992.

Carlson, Christopher, ed. *Perspectives on the Family.* Belmont, Calif.: Wadsworth, 1990.

Carson, Rachel. *Silent Spring.* Greenwich, Conn.: Fawcett, 1962.

Carter, Stephen. *Civility: Manners, Morals, and the Etiquette of Democracy.* New York: Basic Books, 1998.

———. *The Culture of Disbelief.* New York: Basic Books, 1993.

Ceaser, James W. *Reconstructing America: The Symbol of America in Modern Thought.* New Haven, Conn.: Yale University Press, 1997.

Chapman, John W., and Ian Shapiro, eds. *Democratic Community.* New York: New York University Press, 1993.

Cheatham, Harold E., and James B. Stewart, eds. *Black Families.* New Brunswick, N.J.: Transaction Books, 1990.

Cherlin, Andrew J. *Marriage, Divorce, and Remarriage.* Cambridge, Mass.: Harvard University Press, 1992.

Chodorow, Nancy. *The Reproduction of Motherhood: Psychoanalysis and the Sociology of Gender.* Berkeley: University of California Press, 1978.

Chomsky, Noam. *Class Warfare: Interviews with David Barsamian.* Monroe, Maine: Common Courage Press, 1996.

———. *The Culture of Terrorism.* New York: South End Press, 1988.

———. *Deterring Democracy.* New York: Verso, 1991.

Christ, Carol. *Laughter of Aphrodite: Reflections on a Journey to the Goddess.* San Francisco: Harper and Row, 1987.

Christensen, Bryce J. *Utopia Against the Family: The Problems and Politics of the American Family.* San Francisco: Ignatius Press, 1990.

Chubb, John, and Terry Moe. *Politics, Markets, and America's Schools.* Washington, D.C.: Brookings, 1990.

Clark, David B. "The Concept of Community: A Re-examination." *Sociological Review* 21 (August 1973): 397–416.

Clark, Kenneth B. *Dark Ghetto.* New York: Harper and Row, 1965.

Clecak, Peter. *America's Quest for the Ideal Self: Dissent and Fulfillment in the 60s and 70s.* New York: Oxford University Press, 1983.

Cobb, John B., Jr. "Process Theology and an Ecological Model." In *Cry of the Environment,* edited by Philip N. Joranson and Ken Butigan, 329–36. Santa Fe, N.M.: Bear and Co., 1984.

Cochran, Clarke E. "The Thin Theory of Community: The Communitarians and Their Critics." *Political Studies* 37 (1989): 422–35.

Cohen, Joshua, and Joel Rogers. *On Democracy: Toward a Transformation of American Society.* New York: Penguin, 1983.

Cohen, Steven M. *Survey of American Jews.* New York: American Jewish Committee, 1991.

Commoner, Barry. *The Closing Circle: Nature, Man, and Technology.* New York: Bantam, 1974.

Connolly, William E. *The Augustinian Imperative: A Reflection on the Politics of Morality.* Newbury Park, Calif.: Sage, 1993.

———. *The Ethos of Pluralization.* Minneapolis: University of Minnesota Press, 1995.

———. *The Terms of Political Discourse.* Lexington, Mass.: D. C. Heath, 1974.

Countryman, Ed. "Of Republicanism, Capitalism, and the American Mind." *William and Mary Quarterly* 44 (July 1987): 556–62.

Courtwright, David T. *Violent Land: Single Men and Social Disorder from the Frontier to the Inner City.* Cambridge, Mass.: Harvard University Press, 1996.

Cowan, Philip A., and Mavis Hetherington, eds. *Family Transitions.* Hillsdale, N.J.: Lawrence Erlbaum, 1991.

Cowan, Ruth Schwartz. "Twentieth-Century Changes in Household Technology." In *Family in Transition,* edited by Arlene Skolnick and Jerome Skolnick, 82–92. New York: HarperCollins, 1992.

Craig, Stephen C. *The Malevolent Leaders: Popular Discontent in America.* Boulder, Colo.: Westview, 1993.

Craycroft, Kenneth R., Jr. "Free Speech or True Speech?" *Chronicles,* August 1994, 30–32.

Cromartie, Michael, ed. *Caesar's Coin Revisited.* Grand Rapids, Mich.: Eerdmans, 1996.

Crunden, Robert M. *A Brief History of American Culture.* New York: Paragon, 1994.

Dahl, Robert. *A Preface to Economic Democracy.* Berkeley: University of California Press, 1985.

Daly, Mary. *Gyn/Ecology: The Metaethics of Radical Feminism.* Boston: Beacon, 1978.

———. *Pure Lust: Elemental Feminist Philosophy.* Boston: Beacon, 1984.

Daly, Herman E., and John B. Cobb Jr. *For the Common Good: Redirecting the Economy Toward Community, the Environment, and a Sustainable Future.* Boston: Beacon, 1989.

Damon, William. *Greater Expectations.* New York: Free Press, 1995.

D'Antonio, William V. "Family Life, Religion and Societal Values and Structures." In *Families and Religion,* edited by William V. D'Antonio and Joan Aldous. Beverly Hills, Calif.: Sage, 1983.

D'Antonio, William V., and Joan Aldous, eds. *Families and Religion.* Beverly Hills, Calif.: Sage, 1983.

D'Antonio, William V., James Davidson, and Ruth Wallace. *Laity American and Catholic: Transforming the Church.* Kansas City, Mo.: Sheed and Ward, 1996.

Davidson, Nicholas. *The Failure of Feminism.* Buffalo, N.Y.: Prometheus Press, 1988.

Davis, Harry R., and Robert C. Good, eds. *Reinhold Niebuhr on Politics.* New York: Scribner's, 1960.

Dawley, Alan. *Struggles for Justice: Social Responsibility and the Liberal State.* Cambridge, Mass.: Harvard University Press, 1991.

Delaney, C. F., ed. *The Liberalism and Communitarianism Debate.* London: Rowman and Littlefield, 1994.

Delbanco, Andrew. "Consuming Passions.*" New York Times Book Review,* January 19, 1997, 19.

DeLue, Steven M. *Political Thinking, Political Theory, and Civil Society.* Boston: Allyn and Bacon, 1997.

DeMuth, Christopher, and William Kristol, eds. *The Neoconservative Imagination: Essays in Honor of Irving Kristol.* Washington, D.C.: American Enterprise Institute, 1995.

Dennis, Jack. "Do We Believe Aristotle: A Study of American Beliefs About Democracy." Paper, Midwest Political Science Association, 1993.

———. "Political Independence in America, Part II: Towards a Theory." *British Journal of Political Science* 18 (1988): 197–219.

Dennis, Jack, and Diana Owen. "Anti-partyism and Support for Perot, 1992–93." Paper, Workshop on Anti-party Sentiment, European Consortium for Political Research, 1994.

Devall, Bill, and George Sessions. *Deep Ecology.* Salt Lake City, Utah: Peregrine Smith Books, 1985.

Devine, Donald J. *The Political Culture of the United States.* Boston: Little, Brown, 1972.

DeWitt, Calvin. *Caring for Creation: Responsible Stewardship of God's Handiwork.* Grand Rapids, Mich.: Baker, 1998.

———, ed. *The Environmental and the Christian: What Does the New Testament Say About the Environment?* Grand Rapids, Mich.: Baker, 1991.

Diamond, Irene, and Gloria Feman Orenstein, eds. *Reweaving the World: The Emergence of Ecofeminism.* San Francisco: Sierra Club, 1990.

Diggins, John P. "Consciousness and Ideology in American History: The Burden of Daniel J. Boorstin." *American Historical Review* 76 (February 1971): 100–117.

———. "Knowledge and Sorrow: Louis Hartz's Quarrel with American History." *Political Theory* 16 (August 1988): 355–76.

———. *The Lost Soul of American Politics: Virtue, Self-Interest, and the Foundations of Liberalism.* Chicago: University of Chicago Press, 1984.

Di Stefano, Christine. "Dilemmas of Difference: Feminism, Modernity, and Postmodernism." In *Feminism/postmodernism,* edited by Linda J. Nicholson, 63–82. New York: Routledge, 1990.

Doherty, Brian, and Marius de Geus, eds. *Democracy and Green Political Thought.* New York: Routledge, 1996.

Douglass, R. Bruce, and David Hollenbach, eds. *Catholicism and Liberalism: Contributions to American Public Philosophy.* New York: Cambridge University Press, 1994.

Dryzek, John S. *Discursive Democracy: Politics, Policy and Political Science.* Cambridge: Cambridge University Press, 1990.

D'Souza, Dinesh. *The End of Racism.* New York: Free Press, 1995.

Dubin, Murray. "Advisor Leaves White House to Spend More Time at Home." *Wisconsin State Journal,* May 27, 1995, 1C.

Dumm, Thomas. *Democracy and Punishment: Disciplinary Origins of the United States.* Madison: University of Wisconsin Press, 1987.

―――. *United States.* Ithaca, N.Y.: Cornell University Press, 1994.

Duncan, Christopher. *The Anti-Federalists and Early American Political Thought.* De Kalb: Northern Illinois University Press, 1995.

Duneier, Mitchell. *Slim's Table: Race, Respectability, and Masculinity.* Chicago: University of Chicago Press, 1992.

Dunham, Pat. *Electoral Behavior in the United States.* Englewood Cliffs, N.J.: Prentice Hall, 1991.

Dunlap, Riley E. "Trends in Public Opinion Toward Environmental Issues: 1965–1990." In *American Environmentalism: The U.S. Environmental Movement, 1970–1990,* edited by Riley E. Dunlap and Angela G. Mertig, 89–116. Philadelphia: Taylor and Francis, 1990.

Dunlap, Riley E., George Gallup Jr., and Alec M. Gallup. *Health of the Planet: Results of a 1992 International Environmental Survey of Citizens in Twenty-four Nations.* Princeton, N.J.: George H. Gallup International Institute, 1993.

Dworetz, Steven M. *The Unvarnished Doctrine: Locke, Liberalism, and the American Revolution.* Durham, N.C.: Duke University Press, 1990.

Dworkin, Andrea. *Intercourse.* New York: Free Press, 1987.

―――. *Pornography: Men Possessing Women.* New York: Perigee, 1981.

Dyer, Charles H., and Angela E. Hunt. *The Rise of Babylon.* Wheaton, Ill.: Tyndale, 1991.

Easterbrook, Greg. *A Moment on the Earth: The Coming Age of Environmental Optimism.* New York: Viking, 1995.

Eckberg, Douglas Lee, and T. Jean Blocker. "Christianity, Environmentalism, and the Theoretical Problem of Fundamentalism." *Journal for the Scientific Study of Religion* 35 (December 1996): 343–55.

―――. "Varieties of Religious Involvement and Environmental Concern." *Journal for the Scientific Study of Religion* 28 (1989): 509–17.

Eckersley, Robyn. *Environmentalism and Political Theory: Toward an Ecocentric Approach.* Albany: State University of New York Press, 1992.

―――. "Green Politics and the New Class: Selfishness or Virtue?" *Political Studies* 37 (June 1989): 205–43.

Edel, Leon. *Henry James: A Life.* Philadelphia: Lippincott, 1953.

Edsall, Thomas B. "The GOP Gains as Trust in Government Erodes." *Washington Post National Weekly Edition,* February 12–18, 1996, 11–12.

Egnal, Marc, and Joseph A. Ernst. "An Economic Interpretation of the American Revolution." *William and Mary Quarterly* 29 (January 1972): 3–32.

Ehrenhalt, Alan. *The Lost City: Discovering the Forgotten Virtue of Community in the Chicago of the 1950s.* New York: Basic Books, 1995.

Ehrenreich, Barbara. "Another Communitarianism." *New Republic,* May 9, 1988, 21.

―――. *The Hearts of Men: American Dreams and the Flight from Responsibility.* Garden City, N.Y.: Anchor, 1983.

―――. "Oh, Those Family Values." *Time,* July 18, 1994, 62.

Ehrlich, Paul. *The Population Bomb.* New York: Ballantine, 1968.

Ehrlich, Paul, and Anne H. Ehrlich. *Betrayal of Science and Reason.* Washington, D.C.: Island Press, 1996.

―――. *The Population Explosion.* New York: Simon and Schuster, 1990.

Ehrman, John. *The Rise of the Neoconservatives.* New Haven, Conn.: Yale University Press, 1995.

Eisenstein, Hester. *Contemporary Feminist Thought.* Boston: G. K. Hall, 1983.

Eisenstein, Zillah R. *The Radical Future of Liberal Feminism.* New York: Longman's, 1981.

Ekirch, Arthur A., Jr. *The Decline of American Liberalism.* New York: Longman's, 1955.

Elifson, Kirk, David W. Petersen, and C. Kirk Hadaway. "Religiosity and Delinquency." *Criminology* 21 (1983): 505–27.

Eller, Cynthia. *The Feminist Spirituality Movement in America.* New York: Crossroad, 1993.

Elliott, Michael. "The Ties That Bind." *New York Times Book Review,* February 23, 1997, 18.

Ellis, Lee. "Religiosity and Criminality: Evidence and Explanations of Complex Relationships." *Sociological Perspectives* 28 (1985): 501–20.

Ellis, Richard J. *American Political Cultures.* New York: Oxford University Press, 1993.

———. *The Dark Side of the Left: Illiberal Egalitarianism in America.* Lawrence: University Press of Kansas, 1998.

Ellis, Richard J., and Fred Thompson. "The Cultural Wars by Other Means: Environmental Attitudes and Cultural Bias in the Northwest." Paper, Western Political Science Association, 1996.

Elshtain, Jean Bethke. "Catholic Social Thought, the City, and Liberal America." In *Catholicism, Liberalism, and Communitarianism,* edited by Kenneth L. Grasso, Gerald V. Bradley, and Robert P. Hunt, 97–114. Lanham, Md.: Rowman and Littlefield, 1995.

———. *Democracy on Trial.* New York: Basic Books, 1995.

———. *The Family in Political Thought.* Amherst: University of Massachusetts Press, 1982.

———. "Feminists Against the Family." *Nation,* November 17, 1979, front cover and 497–500.

———. "In Common Together: Unity, Diversity, and Civic Virtue." In *Toward a Global Civil Society,* edited by Michael Walzer, 77–97. Providence, R.I.: Berghahn, 1995.

———. *Public Man, Private Woman: Women in Social and Political Thought.* Princeton, N.J.: Princeton University Press, 1981.

Ethington, Philip J. *The Public City: The Political Construction of Urban Life in San Francisco, 1850–1900.* New York: Cambridge University Press, 1994.

Etzioni, Amitai. *The New Golden Rule: Community and Morality in a Democratic Society.* New York: Basic Books, 1997.

———. "On Restoring the Moral Voice." In *Rights and the Common Good: The Communitarian Perspective,* edited by Amitai Etzioni, 271–76. New York: St. Martin's, 1995.

———. "Too Many Rights, Too Few Responsibilities." In *Toward a Global Civil Society,* edited by Michael Walzer, 99–111. Providence, R.I.: Berghahn, 1995.

———, ed. *New Communitarian Thinking: Persons, Virtues, Institutions, Communities.* Charlottesville: University Press of Virginia, 1995.

———. *The Spirit of Community: Rights, Responsibilities and the Communitarian Agenda.* New York: Crown, 1993.

Euben, J. Peter. "Fanfare for the Common Complaints." *New York Times Book Review,* January 8, 1989, 18.

"Evangelical Environmentalism Comes of Age." *Christianity Today,* November 11, 1996, 84.

Evans, Anthony T. *No More Excuses.* Wheaton, Ill.: Crossway Books, 1996.

Faludi, Susan. *Backlash: The Undeclared War Against American Women.* New York: Anchor, 1992.

Feagin, Joe R., and Melvin P. Sikes. *Living with Racism: The Black Middle-Class Experience*. Boston: Beacon, 1994.

Ferree, Myra, and Beth B. Hess. *Controversy and Coalition: The New Feminist Movement*. Boston: Twayne, 1985.

Finke, Roger, and Rodney Stark. *The Churching of America, 1776–1990*. New Brunswick, N.J.: Rutgers University Press, 1992.

Firestone, Shulamith. *The Dialectic of Sex: The Case for Feminist Revolution*. New York: Bantam, 1971.

Fish, Stanley. *There's No Such Thing as Free Speech . . . and It's a Good Thing Too*. New York: Oxford University Press, 1994.

Fitzpatrick, Joseph P. "The Role of Religion in Programming for the Prevention and Correction of Crime and Delinquency." In *Task Force Report: Juvenile Delinquency and Youth Crimes*, 317–30. Washington, D.C.: Government Printing Office, 1967.

Foreman, Dave. *Confessions of an Eco-Warrior*. New York: Harmony, 1991.

Fowler, Robert Booth. *Believing Skeptics: American Political Intellectuals, 1945–1964*. Westport: Conn.: Greenwood, 1978.

———. *The Dance with Community: The Contemporary Debate in American Political Thought*. Lawrence: University Press of Kansas, 1991.

———. *The Greening of Protestant Thought: 1970–1990*. Chapel Hill: University of North Carolina Press, 1995.

———. *Unconventional Partners: Religion and Liberal Culture in the United States*. Grand Rapids, Mich.: Eerdmans, 1989.

Fowler, Robert Booth, and Allen Hertzke. *Religion and Politics in America: Faith, Culture, and Strategic Choices*. Boulder, Colo.: Westview, 1995.

Fox, Matthew. *Original Blessing: A Primer in Creation Spirituality*. Santa Fe, N.M.: Bear and Co., 1983.

Fox, Richard Wightman, *Reinhold Niebuhr: A Biography*. New York: Pantheon, 1985.

Fox-Genovese, Elizabeth. *"Feminism Is Not the Story of My Life": How Today's Feminist Elite Has Lost Touch with the Real Concerns of Women*. New York: Doubleday, 1996.

———. *Feminism Without Illusions: A Critique of Individualism*. Chapel Hill: University of North Carolina Press, 1991.

Frame, Randy. "Greening of the Gospel?" *Christianity Today,* November 11, 1996, 82–86.

Freie, John F. *Counterfeit Community: The Exploitation of Our Longings for Connectedness*. Lanham, Md.: Rowman and Littlefield, 1998.

Friedan, Betty. *The Second Stage*. New York: Summit, 1981.

Friedman, Marilyn. "Feminism and Modern Friendship: Dislocating the Community." In *Social and Political Philosophy: Classical Texts in Feminist and Multi-cultural Perspective,* edited by James P. Sterba, 501–12. Belmont, Calif.: Wadsworth, 1995.

Friedman, Milton. *Capitalism and Freedom*. Chicago: University of Chicago Press, 1963.

Friedman, Milton, and Rose Friedman. *Free to Choose: A Personal Statement*. New York: Harcourt Brace, 1990.

Frohnen, Bruce. *The New Communitarians and the Crisis of Modern Liberalism*. Lawrence: University Press of Kansas, 1996.

———. *Virtue and the Promise of Communitarianism: The Legacy of Burke and Tocqueville*. Lawrence: University Press of Kansas, 1993.

Frum, David. *Dead Right*. New York: Basic Books, 1994.

Fukuyama, Francis. *The End of History and the Last Man*. New York: Macmillan, 1992.

————. *Trust: The Social Virtues of the Creation of Prosperity.* New York: Free Press, 1995.

Furstenberg, Frank F., Jr., and Christine Winquist Nord. "Patterns of Childrearing After Marital Disruption." In *Perspectives on the Family,* edited by Christopher Carlson, 496–514. Belmont, Calif.: Wadsworth, 1990.

Gallup, George, Jr., and Jim Castelli. *The American Catholic People.* Garden City, N.Y.: Doubleday, 1987.

Galston, William. "A Liberal-Democratic Case for the Two-Parent Family." In *The Spirit of Community,* edited by Amitai Etzioni, 139–49. New York: Crown, 1993.

————. "Public Morality and Religion in the Liberal State." *PS* 19 (Fall 1986): 807–24.

Gellner, Ernest. *Conditions of Liberty: Civil Society and Its Rivals.* London: Hamish, Hamilton, 1994.

Genovese, Eugene. "The Southern Tradition and the Black Experience." 18 *Chronicles,* August 1994, 20–22.

Gerson, Mark. *The Essential Neoconservative Reader.* Reading, Mass.: Addison-Wesley, 1996.

————. *The Neoconservative Vision.* Lanham, Md.: Madison Books, 1996.

Gestel, Naomi. "Divorce and Stigma." In *Perspectives on the Family,* edited by Christopher Carlson, 460–78. Belmont, Calif.:Wadsworth, 1990.

Gibson, James L. "The Political Consequences of Intolerance." *American Political Science Review* 86 (1992): 338–56.

————. "The Structure of Attitudinal Tolerance in the United States." *British Journal of Political Science* 19 (1989): 562–72.

Gibson, James L., and Richard D. Bingham. "On the Conceptualization and Measurement of Political Tolerance." *American Political Science Review* 76 (1982): 603–20.

Gilder, George. "End Welfare Reform as We Know It." *American Spectator* 28 (June 1995): 24–27.

————. *Men and Marriage.* Gretna, La.: Pelican, 1986.

Gillespie, Michael Allen, and Michael Lienesch, "Introduction." In *Ratifying the Constitution,* edited by Michael Allen Gillespie and Michael Lienesch, 1–26. Lawrence: University Press of Kansas, 1989.

Gilligan, Carol. *In a Different Voice: Psychological Theory and Women's Development.* Cambridge, Mass.: Harvard University Press, 1982.

Gitlin, Todd. *The Twilight of Common Dreams: Why America Is Wracked by Cultural Wars.* New York: Holt, 1995.

Glazer, Nathan. "Polls Apart." *New Republic,* October 23, 1995, 43–45.

————. *We Are All Multiculturalists Now.* Cambridge, Mass.: Harvard University Press, 1997.

Glendon, Mary Ann. "Civil Service." *New Republic,* April 1, 1996, 39–40.

Glendon, Mary Ann, and David Blankenhorn, eds. *Seedbeds of Virtue: Sources of Competence, Character, and Citizenship in American Society.* Lanham, Md.: Madison Books, 1995.

Goldberg, Steven. *The Inevitability of Patriarchy.* New York: Morrow, 1973.

Goldenberg, Naomi. *Changing of the Gods: Feminism and the End of Traditional Religions.* Boston: Beacon, 1979.

Goodman, Paul. *Growing Up Absurd.* New York: Vintage, 1960.

Gordon, Linda, ed. *Women, the State, and Welfare.* Madison: University of Wisconsin Press, 1990.

Gottman, John. *Why Marriages Succeed or Fail: And How You Can Make Yours Last.* New York: Simon and Schuster, 1995.

Gough, Kathleen. "The Origin of the Family." In *Family in Transition,* edited by Arlene Skolnick and Jerome Skolnick, 23–39. New York: HarperCollins, 1992.

Grasso, Kenneth L. "Man, Society, and the State: A Catholic Perspective." In *Caesar's Coin Revisited,* edited by Michael Cromartie. Grand Rapids, Mich.: Eerdmans, 1996.

———. "'We Hold These Truths': The Transformation of American Pluralism and the Future of American Democracy." In *John Courtney Murray and the American Civil Conversation,* edited by Robert P. Hunt and Kenneth L. Grasso, 89–115. Grand Rapids, Mich.: Eerdmans, 1992.

Grasso, Kenneth L., Gerald V. Bradley, and Robert P. Hunt, eds. *Catholicism, Liberalism, and Communitarianism.* Lanham, Md.: Rowman and Littlefield, 1995.

Greeley, Andrew. "Religion and Attitudes Toward the Environment." *Journal for the Scientific Study of Religion* 32 (1993): 19–28.

Green, Gil. *The New Radicalism: Anarchist or Marxist?* New York: International Publishers, 1971.

Green, John C., Lyman A. Kellstedt, and Corwin E. Smidt. "Faith and the Environment: Religious Beliefs and Attitudes on Environment of Policy." Paper, Southern Political Science Association, 1993.

Greenstone, David. *The Lincoln Persuasion: Remaking American Liberalism.* Princeton, N.J.: Princeton University Press, 1993.

———. "Political Culture and American Political Development," 2 (1987): 1–49.

Griffin, Susan. *Woman and Nature: The Roaring Inside Her.* New York: Harper and Row, 1978.

Grimshaw, Jean. *Philosophy and Feminist Thinking.* Minneapolis: University of Minnesota Press, 1986.

Guinier, Lani. *The Tyranny of the Majority: Fundamental Fairness in Representative Democracy.* New York: Free Press, 1995.

Gundersen, Adolf. *The Environmental Promise of Democratic Deliberation.* Madison: University of Wisconsin Press, 1995.

———. "Finding the Kosmos in the Agora." Ph.D. dissertation, University of Wisconsin–Madison, 1990.

———. "Native American Political Theory: The Lesson for Contemporary Ecological Governance." Paper, Fourth Annual Symposium on Society and Resource Management, May 1992.

Gunew, Sneja, and Anna Yeatman. *Feminism and the Politics of Difference.* Boulder, Colo.: Westview, 1994.

Guth, James L., John C. Green, Lyman A. Kellstedt, and Corwin E. Smidt. "Faith and the Environment: Religious Beliefs and Attitudes on Environmental Policy." Paper, Southern Political Science Association, 1993.

Gutman, Herbert. *The Black Family in Slavery and Freedom: 1750–1925.* New York: Pantheon, 1976.

Gutmann, Amy. *Democratic Education.* Princeton, N.J.: Princeton University Press, 1987.

———. "The Disharmony of Democracy." In *Democratic Community,* edited by John W. Chapman and Ian Shapiro, 126–60. New York: New York University Press, 1993.

Gutmann, Amy, and Dennis Thompson. *Democracy and Disagreement.* Cambridge, Mass.: Harvard University Press, 1996.

Hadjor, Kofi Buenor. *Another America: The Politics of Race and Blame.* Boston: South End Press, 1995.

Hall, H. Lark. *V. L. Parrington: Through the Avenue of Art.* Kent, Ohio: Kent State University Press, 1994.

Hammond, Phillip. *Religion and Personal Autonomy: The Third Disestablishment in America.* Columbia: University of South Carolina Press, 1992.

Hand, Carl, and Kent Van Liere. "Religion, Mastery-over-Nature, and Environmental Concern." *Social Forces* 63 (1984): 555–70.

Hanson, Russell L. *The Democratic Imagination in America: Conversations with Our Past.* Princeton, N.J.: Princeton University Press, 1985.

Hardin, Garrett. "The Tragedy of the Commons." *Science* 162 (December 1968): 243–48.

Hareven, Tamara K. "American Families in Transition: Historical Perspectives on Change." In *Family in Transition,* edited by Arlene Skolnick and Jerome Skolnick, 40–57. New York: HarperCollins, 1992.

Hargrove, Eugene. *Religion and the Environmental Crisis.* Athens: University of Georgia Press, 1986.

Harley, Willard F., Jr. *His Needs/Her Needs: Building an Affair-Proof Marriage.* Ada, Mich.: Revell, 1990.

Hartsock, Nancy. *The Feminist Standpoint Revisited and Other Essays.* Boulder, Colo.: Westview, 1996.

Hartz, Louis. *The Founding of New Societies.* New York: Harcourt, Brace and World, 1964.

———. *The Liberal Tradition in America.* New York: Harcourt, Brace and World, 1955.

———. *The Necessity of Choice: Nineteenth-Century Political Thought.* Edited by Paul Roazen. New Brunswick, N.J.: Transaction, 1990.

Hatch, Nathan. *The Democratization of Christianity.* New Haven, Conn.: Yale University Press, 1989.

Hayden, Tom. *The Lost Gospel of the Earth.* San Francisco: Sierra Club Books, 1996.

Heilbroner, Robert. *An Inquiry into the Human Prospect.* New York: Norton, 1974.

Heine, Susanne. *Matriarchs, Goddesses, Images of God: A Critique of a Feminist Theology.* Minneapolis, Minn.: Augsburg, 1988.

Henig, Jeffrey R. *Rethinking School Choice: Limits of the Market Metaphor.* Princeton, N.J.: Princeton University Press, 1994.

Herman, Arthur. *The Idea of Decline in Western History.* New York: Free Press, 1997.

Herrnson, Paul S., and John C. Green. *Multiparty Politics in America.* Lanham, Md.: Rowman and Littlefield, 1997.

Hertzke, Allen, and Chris McRorie. "The Concept of Moral Ecology." Paper, Conference on Communitarianism and Civil Society, 1996.

Herzog, Don. "Some Questions for Republicans." *Political Theory* 14 (August 1986): 473–93.

Hetherington, E. Mavis. "The Role of Individual Differences and Family Relationships in Children's Coping with Divorce and Remarriage." In *Family Transitions,* edited by Philip A. Cowan and Mavis Hetherington, 165–94. Hillsdale, N.J.: Erlbaum, 1991.

Hewlett, Sylvia. *A Lesser Life: The Myth of Women's Liberation in America.* New York: Morrow, 1986.

Hewlett, Sylvia, and Cornel West. *The War Against Parents: What We Can Do for America's Beleaguered Moms and Dads.* Boston: Houghton Mifflin, 1998.

Hibbing, John R., and Elizabeth Theiss-Morse. *Congress as Public Enemy.* New York: Cambridge University Press, 1995.

Higgins, Paul C., and Gary L. Albrecht. "Hellfire and Delinquency Revisited." *Social Forces* 55 (1977): 952–58.

Higham, John. "The Cult of the 'American Consensus': Homogenizing Our History." *Commentary* 27 (February 1959): 93–100.

———. *Writing American History.* Bloomington: Indiana University Press, 1970.

Hill, Robert B. *The Strength of Black Families.* New York: Norton, 1989.

Himmelfarb, Gertrude. "Democratic Remedies for Democratic Disorders." *Public Interest* 131 (Spring 1998): 3–35.

————. *The De-moralization of Society: From Victorian Virtues to Modern Values.* New York: Knopf, 1995.

Hinsdale, Mary Ann, Helen M. Lervis, and S. Maxine Waller. *It Comes from the People: Community Development and Local Theology.* Philadelphia: Temple University Press, 1995.

Hirschi, Travis, and Rodney Stark. "Hellfire and Delinquency." *Social Problems* 17 (1969): 202–13.

Hirschmann, Nancy J. *Rethinking Obligation: A Feminist Method for Political Theory.* Ithaca, N.Y.: Cornell University Press, 1992.

Hirschmann, Nancy J., and Christine DiStefano, eds. *Revisioning the Political: Feminist Reconstructions of Traditional Concepts in Western Political Theory.* Boulder, Colo.: Westview, 1996.

Hoagland, Sarah Lucia, and Julia Penelope, eds. *For Lesbians Only: A Separatist Anthology.* London: Only Women Press, 1988.

Hochschild, Arlie, with Anne Machung. *The Second Shift.* New York: Viking, 1989.

————. "The Second Shift: Working Parents and the Revolution at Home." In *Family in Transition,* edited by Arlene Skolnick and Jerome Skolnick, 431–38. New York: HarperCollins, 1992.

Hochschild, Jennifer L. *Facing Up to the American Dream: Race, Class, and the Soul of the Nation.* Princeton, N.J.: Princeton University Press, 1995.

Hoffman, Ronald, and Peter J. Albert, eds. *Religion in a Revolutionary Age.* Charlottesville: University Press of Virginia, 1994.

————. *The Transforming Hand of Revolution: Reconsidering the American Revolution as a Social Movement.* Charlottesville: University Press of Virginia, 1995.

Hofstadter, Richard. *The American Political Tradition.* New York: Knopf, 1948.

————. *The Progressive Historians: Turner, Beard, Parrington.* New York: Vintage, 1970. Reprint, Chicago: University of Chicago Press, 1979.

————. "Reflections on Violence in the United States." In *American Violence,* edited by Richard Hofstadter and Michael Wallace, 3–43. New York: Vintage, 1971.

Holmes, Stephen. *The Anatomy of Antiliberalism.* Cambridge, Mass.: Harvard University Press, 1993.

————. "The Polis State." *New Republic,* June 6, 1988, 32–39.

hooks, bell. *Ain't I a Woman: Black Women and Feminism.* Boston: South End Press, 1981.

————. *Feminist Theory from Margin to Center.* Boston: South End Press, 1984.

————. *Killing Rage: Ending Racism.* New York: Holt, 1995.

Howe, John. "Gordon S. Wood and the Analysis of Political Culture in the American Revolutionary Era." *William and Mary Quarterly* 44 (July 1987): 569–82.

Hunt, Robert P. "Moral Orthodoxy and the Procedural Republic." In *John Courtney Murray and the American Civil Conversation,* edited by Robert P. Hunt and Kenneth L. Grasso, 249–70. Grand Rapids, Mich.: Eerdmans, 1992.

Hunt, Robert P., and Kenneth L. Grasso, eds. *John Courtney Murray and the American Civil Conversation.* Grand Rapids, Mich.: Eerdmans, 1992.

Huntington, Samuel P., Jr. *American Politics: The Promise of Disharmony.* Cambridge, Mass.: Harvard University Press, 1981.

Hutchinson, Earl Ofai. *The Assassination of the Black Male Image.* New York: Simon and Schuster, 1996.

Huyler, Jerome. *Locke in America: The Moral Philosophy of the Founding Era.* Lawrence: University Press of Kansas, 1995.

Inglehart, Ronald, *Culture Shift in Advanced Industrial Society.* Princeton, N.J.: Princeton University Press, 1990.

"It's Not Easy Being Green." *Christianity Today,* May 18, 1992, 14.

James, Henry. *The American Scene.* New York: Penguin, 1994.

Jeffrey, Grant R. *Armageddon: Appointment with Destiny.* New York: Bantam, 1990.

Jelen, Ted, and Clyde Wilcox. *Public Attitudes Toward Church and State.* Armonk, N.Y.: M. E. Sharpe, 1995.

Jensen, Gary F., and Maynard L. Erickson. "The Religious Factor and Delinquency: Another Look at the Hellfire Hypothesis." In *The Religious Dimension,* edited by Robert Wuthnow, 157–78. New York: Academic Press, 1979.

Jensen, Larry, Rea J. Newell, and Tom Holman. "Sexual Behavior, Church Attendance, and Permissive Beliefs Among Unmarried Young Men and Women." *Journal for the Scientific Study of Religion* 29 (1990): 113–17.

Jones, Lealan, and Lloyd Newman. *Our America: Life and Death on the South Side of Chicago.* New York: Scribner's, 1997.

Kadushin, Charles. *The American Political Elite.* Boston: Little, Brown, 1974.

Kahn, Alan S. *Aristocratic Liberalism: The Social and Political Thought of Jacob Burkhardt, John Stuart Mill, and Alexis de Tocqueville.* New York: Oxford University Press, 1992.

Kammen, Michael. *Historical Perspectives on American Culture.* New York: Oxford University Press, 1972.

———. *People of Paradox: An Inquiry Concerning the Origins of American Civilization.* New York: Knopf, 1970.

Kanagy, Conrad, and Fern Willits. "A 'Greening' of Religion? Some Evidence from a Pennsylvania Sample." *Social Science Quarterly* 74 (1993): 674–83.

Kann, Mark. *On the Man Question: Gender and Civic Virtue in America.* Philadelphia: Temple University Press, 1991.

———. Letter to the author, March 12, 1997.

———. *A Republic of Men.* New York: New York University Press, 1998.

Keith, Bruce E. *The Myth of the Independent Voter.* Berkeley: University of California Press, 1992.

Kelso, William A. *Poverty and the Underclass.* New York: New York University Press, 1994.

Kemmis, Daniel. *Community and the Politics of Place.* Norman: University of Oklahoma Press, 1990.

Kerber, Linda. "Can a Woman Be an Individual? The Discourse of Self-Reliance." In *American Chameleon,* edited by Richard O. Curry and Lawrence B. Goodhart, 151–66. Kent, Ohio: Kent State University Press, 1991.

———. *Toward an Intellectual History of Women.* Chapel Hill: University of North Carolina Press, 1997.

———. *Women of the Republic: Intellect and Ideology in Revolutionary America.* Chapel Hill: University of North Carolina Press, 1980.

Kirk, Russell. *The Conservative Mind.* Chicago: Regnery, 1953.

———. "The Cultural Conservatives." *The Heritage Lectures.* Washington, D.C.: Heritage Foundation, 1989.

———. "A Dispassionate Assessment of Libertarians." *The Heritage Lectures.* Washington, D.C.: Heritage Foundation, 1988.

———. "The Neoconservatives." *The Heritage Lectures.* Washington, D.C.: Heritage Foundation, 1988.

———. *A Program for Conservatives.* Chicago: Regnery, 1962.

Kirkpatrick, Jeane. *Dictatorships and Double Standards.* New York: Simon and Schuster, 1982.

————. *Human Rights and American Foreign Policy.* Gambier, Ohio: Kenyon College Public Affairs Conference Center, 1982.

Klein, Joe. "The True Disadvantage." *New Republic,* October 28, 1996, 32.

Kloppenberg, James T. "The Virtues of Liberalism: Christianity, Republicanism, and Ethics in the Early American Political Discourses." *Journal of American History* 74 (June 1987): 9–33.

Kluegel, Jerome, and Eliot R. Smith. *Beliefs About Inequality: Americans' Views of What Is and What Ought To Be.* New York: Aldine, 1986.

Kolko, Gabriel. *The Triumph of Conservatism: A Reinterpretation of American History, 1900–1916.* Glencoe, Ill.: Free Press, 1963.

Kotlowitz, Alex. *There Are No Children Here.* New York: Doubleday, 1991.

Kraditor, Aileen. "American Radical Historians on Their Heritage." *Past and Present* 56 (1972): 136–53.

Krantz, Susan E. "The Impact of Divorce on Children." In *Family in Transition,* edited by Arlene Skolnick and Jerome Skolnick, 242–65. New York: HarperCollins, 1992.

Kristol, Irving. *Neoconservatism: The Autobiography of an Ideal.* New York: Free Press, 1995.

————. *Reflections of a Neoconservative.* New York: Basic Books, 1983.

————. *Two Cheers for Capitalism.* New York: Meridian, 1977.

Kuklinski, James H., Ellen Riggle, Victor Ottati, Norbert Schwartz, and Robert S. Wyer Jr. "The Cognitive and Affective Bases of Political Tolerance Judgments." *American Journal of Political Science* 35 (February 1991): 1–27.

————. "Thinking About Political Tolerance, More or Less, with More or Less Information." In *Reconsidering the Democratic Public,* edited by George E. Marcus and Russell L. Hanson. University Park: Pennsylvania State University Press, 1993.

Kunz, Lee. "Religiosity and Criminality." *Sociological Perspectives* 28 (1985): 501–20.

Kunz, Philip R., and Stan L. Albrecht. "Religion, Marital Happiness and Divorce." *International Journal of Sociology of the Family* 7 (January–June 1977): 227–32.

Kymlicka, Will. *Multicultural Citizenship: A Liberal Theory of Minority Rights.* New York: Oxford University Press, 1995.

Lane, Roger. "Philadelphia, Then and Now." *Public Interest* 108 (Summer 1992): 35–52.

Lasch, Christopher. *Haven in a Heartless World: The Family Besieged.* New York: Basic Books, 1977.

————. *The Revolt of the Elites and the Betrayal of Democracy.* New York: Norton, 1994.

————. *Women and the Common Life: Love, Marriage, and Feminism.* Edited by Elisabeth Lasch-Quinn. New York: Norton, 1996.

Lauber, Volkmar. "Ecology, Politics and Liberal Democracy." *Government and Opposition* 13 (Spring 1978): 199–217.

Lawler, Peter. *The Restless Mind: Alexis de Tocqueville on the Origin and Perpetuation of Human Liberty.* Lanham, Md.: Rowman and Littlefield, 1992.

Lears, T. J. Jackson. *No Place of Grace: Antimodernism and the Transformation of American Culture, 1880–1920.* New York: Pantheon, 1981.

Leinberger, Paul, and Bruce Tucker. *The New Individualists: The Generation After the Organization Man.* New York: HarperCollins, 1991.

Lens, Sidney. *Radicalism in America.* New York: Crowell, 1969.

Leopold, Aldo. "Conservation as a Moral Issue." In *Ethics and the Environment,* edited by Donald Scherer and Thomas Attig, 9–12. Englewood Cliffs, N.J.: Prentice-Hall, 1983.

————. "The Land Ethic." In *Ethics and the Environment,* edited by Donald Scherer and Thomas Attig, 6–9. Englewood Cliffs, N.J.: Prentice-Hall, 1983.

————. *A Sand County Almanac.* New York: Oxford University Press, 1949.

Lerner, Robert, Althea K. Nagai, and Stanley Rothman. "Elites vs. Mass Opinion: Another Look at a Classic Relationship." *International Journal of Public Opinion Research* 3 (1991): 1–31.

Levin, Michael. *Feminism and Freedom.* New Brunswick, N.J.: Transaction, 1977.

Levine, Lawrence. *The Opening of the American Mind.* Boston: Beacon, 1996.

Lewis, Jan. "The Republican Wife: Virtue and Seduction in the Early Republic." *William and Mary Quarterly* 44 (October 1987): 689–721.

Lewy, Guenter. *Why America Needs Religion: Secular Modernity and Its Discontents.* Grand Rapids, Mich.: Eerdmans, 1997.

Lienesch, Michael. *New Order of the Ages: Time, the Constitution, and the Making of Modern American Political Thought.* Princeton, N.J.: Princeton University Press, 1988.

Limerick, Patricia Nelson. *The Legacy of Conquest: The Unbroken Past of the American West.* New York: Norton, 1986.

Limerick, Patricia Nelson, Clyde A. Milner II, and Charles E. Rankin. *Trails: Toward a New Western History.* Lawrence: University Press of Kansas, 1991.

Lind, Michael. *Hamilton's Republic: Readings in the American Democratic Nationalist Tradition.* New York: Free Press, 1997.

————. *The Next American Nation: The New Nationalism and the Fourth American Revolution.* New York: Free Press, 1995.

————. *Up from Conservatism: Why the Right Is Wrong for America.* New York: Free Press, 1996.

Lindsey, Hal. *The Late Great Planet Earth.* New York: Bantam, 1981.

Lipschutz, Ronnie D. *Global Civil Society and Global Environmental Governance.* Albany: State University of New York Press, 1996.

Lipset, Seymour Martin. "American Exceptionalism." In *Is America Different?* edited by Byron E. Schafer, chap. 1. New York: Oxford University Press, 1991.

————. *American Exceptionalism: A Double-Edged Sword.* New York: Norton, 1996.

————. *The First New Nation: The United States in Historical and Comparative Perspective.* New York: Norton, 1979.

Lipset, Seymour Martin, and Earl Raab. *Jews and the New American Scene.* Cambridge, Mass.: Harvard University Press, 1995.

Loury, Glenn C. "The Family as Context for Delinquency Prevention." In *Families, Schools, and Delinquency Prevention,* edited by James Q. Wilson and Glenn C. Loury, 3–26. New York: Springer, 1987.

————. "Not so Black and White: The Two Americas Are Actually Converging." *Washington Post,* October 15, 1995, CO3.

Lowi, Theodore. *The End of the Republican Era.* Norman: University of Oklahoma Press, 1995.

Lustig, R. Jeffrey. *Corporate Liberalism: Origins of Modern American Political Theory, 1890–1920.* Berkeley: University of California Press, 1982.

Lutz, Donald S. *A Preface to American Political Theory.* Lawrence: University Press of Kansas, 1992.

Lynd, Staughton. *The Intellectual Origins of American Radicalism.* London: Faber, 1969.

Macedo, Stephen. *Liberal Virtues: Citizenship, Virtue, and Community in Liberal Constitutionalism.* New York: Oxford University Press, 1990.

MacIntyre, Alasdair. *After Virtue: A Study in Moral Theory.* Notre Dame, Ind.: University of Notre Dame Press, 1981.

MacKinnon, Catharine A. *Feminism Unmodified.* Cambridge, Mass.: Harvard University Press, 1987.

———. *Only Words.* Cambridge, Mass.: Harvard University Press, 1993.

Magnet, Myron. *The Dream and the Nightmare: The Sixties Legacy to the Underclass.* New York: Morrow, 1993.

Mahoney, E. R. "Religiosity and Sexual Behavior Among Heterosexual College Students." *Journal of Sex Research* 16 (1980): 97–113.

Maier, Pauline. "A Pearl in a Gnarled Shell: Gordon S. Wood's *The Creation of the American Republic* Reconsidered." *William and Mary Quarterly* 44 (July 1987): 583–90.

Mansbridge, Jane. *Beyond Adversary Democracy.* Chicago: University of Chicago Press, 1983.

———. "Feminism and Democratic Community." In *Democratic Community,* edited by John W. Chapman and Ian Shapiro, 339–95. New York: New York University Press, 1993.

Marcus, George E., John L. Sullivan, Elizabeth Theiss-Morse, and Sandra L. Wood. *With Malice Toward Some: How People Make Civil Liberties Judgments.* New York: Cambridge University Press, 1995.

Marcuse, Herbert. *An Essay on Liberation.* Boston: Beacon, 1969.

———. *One-Dimensional Man.* Boston: Beacon, 1964.

Marcuse, Herbert, et al. *Critique of Pure Tolerance.* Boston: Beacon, 1965.

Marty, Martin E. "Sightings: Issues from the Public Religion Project." June 4, 1998.

Matthews, Richard K. "Liberalism, Civic Humanism, and the American Political Tradition: Understanding Genesis." *Journal of Politics* 49 (November 1987): 1127–53.

Mayer, William G. *The Changing American Mind: How and Why American Public Opinion Changed Between 1960 and 1988.* Ann Arbor: University of Michigan Press, 1992.

McAllister, Ted V. *Revolt Against Modernity: Leo Strauss, Eric Voegelin, and the Search for a Postliberal Order.* Lawrence: University Press of Kansas, 1996.

McCall, Nathan. *Makes Me Wanna Holler: A Young Black Man in America.* New York: Random House, 1995.

McClay, Wilfred M. *The Masterless: Self and Society in Modern America.* Chapel Hill: University of North Carolina Press, 1994.

McClosky, Herbert. "Consensus and Ideology in American Politics." *American Political Science Review* 58 (1964): 361–82.

McClosky, Herbert, and Alida Brill. *Dimensions of Tolerance: What Americans Believe About Civil Liberties.* New York: Russell Sage, 1983.

McClosky, Herbert, and John Zaller. *The American Ethos: Public Attitudes Toward Capitalism and Democracy.* Cambridge, Mass.: Harvard University Press, 1984.

McConnell, David. "The 1970s and Failure." Unpublished lecture, University of Wisconsin–Madison, 1978.

McDonald, Forrest. *Novus Ordo Seclorum: The Intellectual Origins of the Constitution.* Lawrence: University Press of Kansas, 1985.

McLanahan, Sara. "The Consequences of Single Motherhood." *American Prospect* 18 (Summer 1994): 48–58.

McLaughlin, Corrine, and Gordon Davidson. *Builders of the Dawn: Community Lifestyles in a Changing World.* Shutesbury, Mass.: Sirius, 1986.

McLaughlin, Milbrey W., Merita A. Irby, and Juliet Longman. *Urban Sanctuaries: Neighborhood Organizations in the Lives and Future of Inner-City Youth.* San Francisco: Jossey-Bass, 1994.

McLoughlin, William. "'Enthusiasm for Liberty': The Great Awakening as the Key to the Revolution." In *Preachers and Politicians: Two Essays on the Origins of the American Revolution,* edited by Jack P. Greene and William McLoughlin, 47–73. Worcester, Mass.: American Antiquarian Society, 1977.

McWilliams, Wilson Carey. *The Idea of Fraternity in America.* Berkeley: University of California Press, 1973.

Mead, Lawrence. *Beyond Entitlement: The Social Obligations of Citizenship.* New York: Free Press, 1986.

———. *The New Politics of Poverty: The Nonworking Poor in America.* New York: Basic Books, 1991.

Meagher, Michael E. "Daniel Boorstin and Russell Kirk: Religion and American Political Development." *Journal of Interdisciplinary Studies* 7 (1995): 135–48.

———. "The Multiple Personalities of Daniel J. Boorstin: A Third Image Analysis." *American Review of Politics* 15 (Winter 1995): 462–80.

Mednick, Martha. "Single Mothers: A Review and Critique of Current Research." In *Family in Transition,* edited by Arlene Skolnick and Jerome Skolnick, 363–78. New York: HarperCollins, 1992.

Merchant, Carolyn. *The Death of Nature: Women, Ecology, and the Scientific Revolution.* San Francisco: Harper, 1980.

Merelman, Richard. "Inequality and Political Legitimacy in the United States." Paper, American Political Science Convention, 1996.

———. *Making Something of Ourselves: On Culture and Politics in the U.S.* Berkeley: University of California Press, 1984.

———. *Representing Black Culture: Racial Conflict and Cultural Politics in the United States.* New York: Routledge, 1995.

Meyer, Frank. "Recrudescent Conservatism." In *Left, Right, and Center,* edited by Robert Goldwin, chap. 4. Chicago: Rand McNally, 1965.

Meyer, John. "The Politics of Nature: Political Theory, Environmentalism, and the Evasion of Political Judgment." Ph.D. dissertation, University of Wisconsin–Madison, 1997.

Meyers, Marvin. "Louis Hartz, *The Liberal Tradition in America:* An Appraisal." *Comparative Studies in Society and History* 5 (1963): 261–68.

Milbrath, Lester. *Environmentalists: Vanguard for a New Society.* Albany: State University of New York Press, 1984.

Miller, Jean Baker. *Toward a New Psychology of Women.* Boston: Beacon, 1986.

Millett, Kate. *Sexual Politics.* New York: Avon, 1971.

Mills, C. Wright. *The Power Elite.* New York: Oxford University Press, 1956.

———. *The Sociological Imagination.* New York: Oxford University Press, 1959.

———. *White Collar.* New York: Oxford University Press, 1951.

Milner, Clyde A., II, Carol A. O'Connor, and Martha A. Sandweiss. *The Oxford History of the American West.* New York: Oxford University Press, 1994.

Mitchell, Joshua. *The Fragility of Freedom: Tocqueville on Religion, Democracy, and the American Future.* Chicago: University of Chicago Press, 1995.

Moe, Richard, and Carter Wilkie. *Changing Places: Rebuilding Community in the Age of Sprawl.* New York: Holt, 1987.

Moncrief, Lewis W. "The Cultural Basis for Our Environmental Crisis." *Science,* October 30, 1970, 506–11.

Moon, J. Donald. *Constructing Community: Moral Pluralism and Tragic Conflicts.* Princeton, N.J.: Princeton University Press, 1993.

Morgan, Iwan W. *Beyond the Liberal Consensus: A Political History of the United States Since 1965.* New York: St. Martin's, 1994.

Mowrey, Mark, and Tim Redmond. *Not in Our Backyard: The People and Events that Shaped America's Modern Environmental Movement.* New York: Morrow, 1993.

Moynihan, Daniel Patrick. *Family and Nation.* New York: Harcourt Brace Jovanovich, 1986.

Munt, Sally, ed. *New Lesbian Criticism: Literacy and Cultural Readings.* New York: Columbia University Press, 1992.

Murphy, Andrew R. "Tolerance and Toleration: Political Psychology and Liberal Theory." Paper, International Society of Political Psychology, 1996.

Murray, Charles. "The Legacy of the Sixties." *Commentary,* July 1992, 23–24.

———. *Losing Ground: American Social Policy, 1950–1981.* New York: Basic Books, 1984.

———. *What It Means to Be a Libertarian.* New York: Broadway, 1997.

Murrin, John W. "Gordon S. Wood and the Search for Liberal America." *William and Mary Quarterly* 44 (July 1987): 597–601.

Nash, Gary B. "American History Reconsidered: Asking New Questions About the Past." In *Learning from the Past,* edited by Diane Ravitch and Maria A. Vinovskis, 135–63. Baltimore, Md.: Johns Hopkins University Press, 1995.

———. *The Urban Crucible: Social Change, Political Consciousness, and the Origins of American Revolution.* Cambridge, Mass.: Harvard University Press, 1979.

Nash, George H. *The Conservative Intellectual Movement in America Since 1945.* New York: Basic Books, 1979.

Nash, Roderick. *The Rights of Nature: A History of Environmental Ethics.* Madison: University of Wisconsin Press, 1989.

Natoli, Joseph, and Linda Hutcheon, eds. *A Postmodern Reader.* Albany: State University of New York Press, 1993.

Naylor, Thomas H., and William H. Willimon. *Downsizing the U.S.A.* Grand Rapids, Mich.: Eerdmans, 1997.

Neuhaus, Richard. *The Naked Public Square: Religion and Democracy in America.* Grand Rapids, Mich.: Eerdmans, 1984.

Newby, I. A. "Historians and Negroes." *Journal of Negro History* 54 (January 1969): 32–47.

Nicholson, Linda. *Feminism and Postmodernism.* New York: Routledge, 1990.

Niebuhr, Reinhold. *The Children of Light and the Children of Darkness.* New York: Scribner's, 1945.

———. *The Irony of American History.* New York: Scribner's, 1952.

———. *Moral Man and Immoral Soc*iety. New York: Scribner's, 1932.

Nisbet, Robert. *The Quest for Community.* New York: Oxford University Press, 1953.

Nordlinger, Pia. "The Anti-divorce Revolution." *Weekly Standard,* March 2, 1998, 25–29.

Nore, Ellen. *Charles A. Beard: An Intellectual Biography.* Carbondale: Southern Illinois University Press, 1983.

Norris, Kathleen. *The Cloister Walk.* New York: Riverhead Books, 1996.

———. *Dakota: A Spiritual Geography.* New York: Ticknor and Fields, 1993.

Norton, Anne. *The Republic of Signs: Liberal Theory and American Popular Culture.* Chicago: University of Chicago Press, 1993.

Norton, Bryan. *Toward Unity Among Environmentalists.* New York: Oxford University Press, 1991.

Norton, Mary Beth. *Liberty's Daughters: The Revolutionary Experience of American Women, 1750–1800.* Boston: Little, Brown, 1980.

Novak, Michael, ed. *To Empower People: From State to Civil Society.* Washington, D.C.: American Enterprise Institute, 1995.

Nuechterlein, James. "The End of Neoconservatism." *First Things* 63 (May 1996): 14–15.

Nye, Joseph, Jr., Philip D. Zelikov, and David C. King, eds. *Why People Don't Trust Government.* Cambridge, Mass.: Harvard University Press, 1997.

Okin, Susan. *Justice, Gender, and the Family.* New York: Basic Books, 1989.

Ophuls, William. *Ecology and the Politics of Scarcity.* San Francisco: W. H. Freeman, 1977.

———. *Ecology and the Politics of Scarcity Revisited.* San Francisco: W. H. Freeman, 1992.

———. *Requiem for Modern Politics: The Tragedy of the Enlightenment and the Challenge of the New Millennium.* Boulder, Colo.: Westview, 1997.

Orren, Karen. *Belated Feudalism: Labor, Law, and Liberal Development in the United States.* New York: Cambridge University Press, 1991.

Ortner, Sherry. "Is Female to Male as Nature Is to Culture?" In *Women, Culture and Society,* edited by Michelle Zimbalist Rosaldo and Louise Lamphere, 67–87. Palo Alto, Calif.: Stanford University Press, 1974.

Page, Ben, and Robert Shapiro. *The Rational Public: Fifty Years of Trends in Americans' Policy Preferences.* Chicago: University of Chicago Press, 1992.

Palmer, Parker. *The Company of Strangers.* New York: Crossroad, 1981.

———. *To Know as We Are Known: A Spirituality of Education.* San Francisco: HarperCollins, 1983.

Pangle, Thomas L. *The Spirit of Modern Republicanism: The Moral Vision of the American Founders and the Philosophy of Locke.* Chicago: University of Chicago Press, 1988.

Parrington, V. L. *Main Currents in American Thought: An Interpretation of American Literature from the Beginnings to 1920.* 3 vols. New York: Harcourt, Brace and World, 1930.

Passmore, John. *Man's Responsibility for Nature: Ecological Problems and Western Traditions.* New York: Scribner's, 1974.

Patai, Daphne, and Nooretta Koertge. *Professing Feminism: Cautionary Tales from the Strange New World of Women's Studies.* New York: Basic Books, 1994.

Pateman, Carole. *Participation and Democratic Theory.* Cambridge: Cambridge University Press, 1970.

Patterson, Orlando. "The Crisis of Gender Relations Among African Americans." In *Race, Gender, and Power in America: The Legacy of the Hill-Thomas Hearings,* edited by Anita Faye Hill and Emma Coleman Jordan, 56–104. New York: Oxford University Press, 1995.

Peek, Charles W., Evans W. Curry, and H. Paul Chalfant. "Religiosity and Delinquency over Time." *Social Science Quarterly* 66 (1985): 120–31.

Perkins, John. *Beyond Charity: The Call to Christian Community Development.* Grand Rapids, Mich.: Baker, 1993.

Peterson, Paul E. "The New Politics of Choice." In *Learning from the Past: What History Teaches Us About School Reform,* edited by Diane Ravitch and Maris A. Vinovskis, 217–40. Baltimore, Md.: Johns Hopkins University Press, 1995.

Peterson, Paul E., Jay P. Greene, and Chad Noyes. "School Choice in Milwaukee." *Public Interest* 125 (Fall 1996): 38–56.

Phelan, Shane. *Getting Specific: Postmodern Lesbian Politics.* Minneapolis: University of Minnesota Press, 1994.

———. *Lesbian Feminism and the Limits of Community.* Philadelphia: Temple University Press, 1995.

Phillips, Derek. *Looking Backward: A Critical Appraisal of Communitarian Thought.* Princeton, N.J.: Princeton University Press, 1993.

Pierce, Gregory. *Activism that Makes Sense.* Chicago: ACTA Publications, 1991.

Pipher, Mary B. *The Shelter of Each Other: Rebuilding Our Families.* New York: Putnam, 1996.

Plant, Judith. *Ecofeminism.* Philadelphia: New Societies, 1989.

Pluhar, Evelyn. *Beyond Prejudice: The Moral Significance of Human and Nonhuman Animals.* Durham, N.C.: Duke University Press, 1995.

Pocock, J. G. A. *The Machiavellian Moment: Florentine Political Thought and the Atlantic Republican Tradition.* Princeton, N.J.: Princeton University Press, 1975.

Podhoretz, Norman. *Breaking Ranks.* New York: Harper and Row, 1979.

———. *Making It.* New York: Random House, 1967.

———. *The Present Danger.* New York: Simon and Schuster, 1980.

———. *Why We Were in Vietnam.* New York: Simon and Schuster, 1983.

Pole, J. R. "Daniel J. Boorstin." In *Pastmasters: Some Essays on American Historians,* edited by Marcus Cunliffe and Robin W. Winks, 210–38. New York: Harper and Row, 1969.

Pollitt, Katha. "Are Women Morally Superior to Men?" *Nation,* December 28, 1992, 799–802.

Popenoe, David. *Disturbing the Nest: Family Change and Decline in Modern Societies.* New York: Aldine, 1988.

Powell, Arthur G., Eleanor Farrar, and David C. Cohen. *The Shopping Mall High School: Winners and Losers in the Educational Marketplace.* Boston: Houghton Mifflin, 1985.

Prothro, James W., and Charles M. Grigg. "Fundamental Principles of Democracy: Bases of Agreement and Disagreement." *Journal of Politics* 22 (1963): 276–94.

Putnam, Robert. "Bowling Alone: America's Declining Social Capital." *Current,* no. 373 (June 1995): 3–9.

Rabinow, Paul, ed. *The Foucault Reader.* New York: Pantheon, 1984.

Rable, George C. *The Confederate Republic: A Revolution Against Politics.* Chapel Hill: University of North Carolina Press, 1994.

Rahe, Paul A. *Republics Ancient and Modern: Classical Republicanism and the American Revolution.* Chapel Hill: University of North Carolina Press, 1992.

Rakove, Jack N. *Original Meanings: Politics and Ideas in the Making of the Constitution.* New York: Knopf, 1996.

Ravitch, Diane. "Pluralism Within Unity: A Communitarian Version of Multiculturalism." In *Rights and the Common Good: The Communitarian Perspective,* edited by Amitai Etzioni, 179–85. New York: St. Martin's, 1995.

Ravitch, Diane, and Maris A. Vinovskis, eds. *Learning from the Past: What History Teaches Us About School Reform.* Baltimore, Md.: Johns Hopkins University Press, 1995.

Rawls, John. *Political Liberalism.* New York: Columbia University Press, 1993.

———. *A Theory of Justice.* Cambridge, Mass.: Harvard University Press, 1971.

Reed, Ralph. *Politically Incorrect: The Emerging Faith Factor in American Politics.* Dallas: Word, 1994.

Regan, Tom. *The Case for Animal Liberation.* Berkeley: University of California Press, 1983.

Regenstein, Lewis G. *Replenish the Earth: A History of Organized Religion's Treatment of Animals and Nature.* New York: Crossroad, 1991.

Reinitz, Richard. *Irony and Consciousness: American Historiography and Reinhold Niebuhr's Vision.* Lewisburg, Penn.: Bucknell University Press, 1980.

"Religious Institutions as Partners in Community-Based Development." *Progressions* 5 (February 1995): 1–21.

Renner, Michael. *Fighting for Survival.* New York: Norton, 1996.

Rich, Adrienne. *Compulsory Heterosexuality and Lesbian Experience.* London: Only Women Press, 1981.

———. *On Lies, Secrets and Silence.* New York: Norton, 1979.

Riessman, Catherine Kohler. "Starting a New Life: The Positive Consequences of Divorce." In *Family in Transition,* edited by Arlene Skolnick and Jerome Skolnick. New York: HarperCollins, 1992.

Roberts, Sam. "More Americans Are Loners, and a Scholar Wants to Know Why." *Wisconsin State Journal,* December 26, 1995, 6A.

———. *Who We Are: A Portrait of Americans Based on the Latest U.S. Census.* New York: New York Times Books, 1993.

Robertson, James Oliver. *American Myth, American Reality.* New York: Hill and Wang, 1980.

Robertson, Pat. *The Turning Tide.* Dallas: Word, 1993.

Rodgers, Daniel T. "Republicanism: The Career of a Concept." *Journal of American History* 79 (June 1992): 11–38.

Rodman, John. "The Liberation of Nature?" *Inquiry* (1977): 83–131.

———. "Paradigm Change in Political Science: An Ecological Perspective." *American Behavioral Scientist* 24 (1980): 49–78.

Roherty, Brian, and Marius de Geus. *Democracy and Green Political Thought: Sustainability, Rights, and Citizenship.* New York: Routledge, 1996.

Rohrschneider, Robert. "Citizens' Attitudes Toward Environmental Issues: Selfish or Selfless?" *Comparative Political Studies* 21 (October 1988): 347–67.

Roof, Wade Clark. *A Generation of Seekers: The Spiritual Journey of the Baby Boom Generation.* San Francisco: HarperCollins, 1993.

Rorty, Richard. *Achieving Our Country: Leftist Thought in Twentieth-Century America.* Cambridge, Mass.: Harvard University Press, 1998.

———. *Contingency, Irony, and Solidarity.* New York: Cambridge University Press, 1989.

Rose, Richard. "Is American Public Policy Exceptional?" In *Is America Different?* edited by Byron E. Schafer, chap. 7. New York: Oxford University Press, 1991.

Rosenblum, Nancy. *Another Liberalism: Romanticism and the Reconstruction of Liberal Thought.* Cambridge, Mass.: Harvard University Press, 1987.

Royster, Charles. *A Revolutionary People at War: The Continental Army and American Character, 1775–1783.* Chapel Hill: University of North Carolina Press, 1979.

Rubin, Lillian B. *Worlds of Pain: Life in the Working-Class Family.* New York: Basic Books, 1992.

Ruether, Rosemary Radford. *Gaia and God.* New York: HarperCollins, 1992.

Sagoff, Mark. *The Economy of the Earth.* Cambridge: Cambridge University Press, 1988.

Sale, Kirkpatrick. *The Green Revolution: The American Environmental Movement, 1962–1992.* New York: Hill and Wang, 1993.

———. *Human Scale.* New York: Coward, McCann, Geoghegan, 1980.

Samuelson, Robert J. "Join the Club." *Washington Post National Weekly Edition,* April 15–21, 1996, 5.

Sandefur, Gary, and Sara McLanahan. *Growing Up with a Single Parent: What Hurts, What Helps.* Cambridge, Mass.: Harvard University Press, 1994.

Sandel, Michael. *Democracy's Discontent: America in Search of a Public Philosophy.* Cambridge, Mass.: Harvard University Press, 1996.

———. "The Democratic Soul." *Religion and Values in Public Life* 6 (Fall 1997): 6–7.

———. "Democrats and Community." *New Republic,* February 22, 1988, 20–23.

————. *Liberalism and Its Critics.* New York: New York University Press, 1984.
————. *Liberalism and the Limits of Justice.* Cambridge: Cambridge University Press, 1982.
Sandoz, Ellis. *A Government of Laws: Political Theory, Religion and the American Mind.* Baton Rouge: Louisiana State University Press, 1990.
Santmire, H. Paul. *The Travail of Nature: The Ambiguous Ecological Promise of Christian Theology.* Philadelphia: Fortress, 1985.
Sapiro, Virginia. "Gender Politics, Gendered Politics: The State of the Field." Paper, Midwest Political Science Conference, April 1989.
Scar, Sandra, Deborah Phillips, and Kathleen McCartney. "Working Mothers and Their Families." In *Family in Transition,* edited by Arlene Skolnick and Jerome Skolnick, 414–30. New York: HarperCollins, 1992.
Schaeffer, Francis. *Pollution and the Death of Man.* Wheaton, Ill.: Tyndale House, 1970.
Schell, Jonathan. *The Fate of the Earth.* New York: Knopf, 1982.
Schlafly, Phyllis. *The Power of the Christian Woman.* Cincinnati, Ohio: Standard, 1981.
Schlesinger, Arthur M., Jr. "Richard Hofstadter." In *Pastmasters: Some Essays on American Historians,* edited by Marcus Cunliffe and Robin W. Winks, 278–315. New York: Harper and Row, 1969.
Schloesser, Pauline. 'Mercy Otis Warren's Critique of the U.S. Constitution." Paper, Midwest Political Science Association, 1995.
Schwartz, Barry. "George Washington and the Whig Conception of Heroic Leadership." In *American Models of Revolutionary Leadership,* edited by Daniel J. Elazar and Ellis Katz, 59–92. Lanham, Md.: University Press of America, 1992.
Schwartz, Katrina. "Possibilities and Limits of an Ecological Social Contract: Survival, Ecocentrism, and Lockean Liberalism." Unpublished paper, University of Wisconsin–Madison, 1993.
Seager, Joni. *Earth Follies: Coming to Feminist Terms with the Global Environmental Crisis.* New York: Routledge, 1993.
Segers, Mary C. "Feminism, Liberalism, and Catholicism." In *Catholicism and Liberalism: Contributions to American Public Philosophy,* edited by R. Bruce Douglass and David Hollenbach, chap. 10. New York: Cambridge University Press, 1994.
Seigfried, Charlene Haddock. *Pragmatism and Feminism: Reweaving the Social Fabric.* Chicago: University of Chicago Press, 1996.
Seligman, Adam. *The Idea of Civil Society.* New York: Free Press, 1992.
Seligmann, Jean. "Variations on a Theme." In *Family in Transition,* edited by Arlene Skolnick and Jerome Skolnick, 518–23. New York: HarperCollins, 1992.
Selznick, Philip. *The Moral Commonwealth: Social Theory and the Promise of Community.* Berkeley: University of California Press, 1992.
Shafer, Byron E. *Is America Different? A New Look at American Exceptionalism.* New York: Oxford University Press, 1991.
————. "What Is the American Way? Four Themes in Search of Their Next Incarnation." In *Is America Different?* edited by Byron E. Shafer, chap. 8. New York: Oxford University Press, 1991.
Shaiko, Ronald. "Religion, Politics and Environmental Concern." *Social Science Quarterly* 68 (1987): 244–62.
Shain, Barry Alan. *The Myth of American Individualism: The Protestant Origins of American Political Thought.* Princeton, N.J.: Princeton University Press, 1994.
————. "Wine and Cheese at the Roller Derby." *Review of Politics* 57 (Fall 1995): 755–58.
Shapiro, Michael J. *Reading the Postmodern Polity: Political Theory as Textual Practice.* Minneapolis: University of Minnesota Press, 1992.

Sheie, David M., et al. *Better Together? Religious Institutions as Partners in Commu-nity-Based Development.* Minneapolis: Rainbow Research, 1994.

Shipler, David. *A Country of Strangers: Blacks and Whites in America.* New York: Knopf, 1997.

Shklar, Judith. *The Faces of Injustice.* New Haven, Conn.: Yale University Press, 1990.

———. *Ordinary Vices.* Cambridge, Mass.: Harvard University Press, 1984.

Shugar, Dana R. *Separatism and Women's Community.* Lincoln: University of Nebraska Press, 1995.

Siemers, David. "Revolutionary Origins, Neglected Resolutions." Unpublished paper, 1994.

Silberman, Charles. *A Certain People: American Jews and Their Lives Today.* New York: Summit, 1985.

Simon, Julian L., and Herman Kahn. *The Resourceful Earth.* New York: Basil Blackwell, 1984.

Singer, Peter. *Animal Liberation.* New York: Random House, 1975.

Skinner, Quentin. *Foundations of Modern Political Thought.* New York: Cambridge University Press, 1978.

Skocpol, Theda. *Protecting Soldiers and Mothers.* Cambridge, Mass.: Harvard University Press, 1992.

Skolnick, Arlene, and Stacey Rosencrantz. "The New Crusade for the Old Family." *American Prospect* 18 (Summer 1994): 59–65.

Skolnick, Arlene, and Jerome Skolnick, eds. *Family in Transition: Rethinking Marriage, Sexuality, Child Rearing, and Family Organization.* 7th ed. New York: HarperCollins, 1992.

Skotheim, Robert Allen. *American Intellectual Histories and Historians.* Princeton, N.J.: Princeton University Press, 1966.

Sloane, Douglas M., and Raymond H. Potvin. "Religion and Delinquency: Cutting Through the Maze." *Social Forces* 65 (1986): 87–105.

Smiley, Marion. "Feminist Theory and the Question of Identity." *Women and Politics* 13 (1993): 91–122.

Smith, Rogers. "Beyond Tocqueville, Myrdal, and Hartz: The Multiple Traditions in America." *American Political Science Review* 87 (1993): 549–66.

———. *Civic Ideals: Conflicting Visions of Citizenship in U.S. History.* New Haven, Conn.: Yale University Press, 1997.

———. "Response." *American Political Science Review* 89 (December 1995): 990–95.

———. "The Unfinished Tasks of Liberalism." In *Liberalism Without Illusions: Essays on Liberal Theory and the Political Vision of Judith Shklar,* edited by Bernard Yack, 241–62. Chicago: University of Chicago Press, 1996.

Sniderman, Paul M., and Thomas Piazza. *The Scar of Race.* Cambridge, Mass.: Harvard University Press, 1993.

Sommers, Christine Hoff. *Who Stole Feminism? How Women Have Betrayed Women.* New York: Simon and Schuster, 1994.

Spalding, Andrew Kurvers. "Finding the Liberal Family: Moral Education and the Family in Liberal Political Thought." Unpublished paper, 1997.

Spelman, Elizabeth. *Inessential Woman.* Boston: Beacon, 1988.

Spragens, Thomas. *The Irony of Liberal Reason.* Chicago: University of Chicago Press, 1981.

Spretnak, Charlene. *The Politics of Women's Spirituality.* Garden City, N.Y.: Anchor, 1982.

———. *The Spiritual Dimension of Green Politics.* San Francisco: Bear and Co., 1986.

Stacey, Judith. *In the Name of the Family: Rethinking Family Values in the Postmodern Age.* Boston: Beacon Press, 1996.

———. "The New Family Values Crusade." *Nation* 259 (1992): 119–22.

Stafford, Tim. "Animal Liberation." *Christianity Today,* June 16, 1990, 19–23.

Starhawk. *Truth or Dare: Encounters with Power, Authority and Mystery.* San Francisco: Harper, 1990.

Stark, Rodney, and William Sims Bainbridge. *The Future of Religion: Secularization, Revival, and Culture Formation.* Berkeley: University of California Press, 1985.

———. *Religion, Deviance, and Social Control.* New York: Routledge, 1997.

Stark, Rodney, et al. "Rediscovering Moral Communities: Church Membership and Crime." In *Understanding Crime: Current Theory and Research,* edited by Travis Hirschi and Michael Gottfredwson, 43–52. Beverly Hills, Calif.: Sage, 1980.

Steele, Shelby. *The Content of Our Character.* New York: HarperCollins, 1991.

Steger, Mary Anne E., and Stephanie L. Witt. "Gender Differences in Environmental Orientations." *Western Political Quarterly* 42 (December 1989): 627–49.

Stein, Arthur. *Seeds of the Seventies.* Hanover, N.H.: University Press of New England, 1985.

Stephney, Bill. "The Welfare Rap: Why Black Men Hate It." *New Republic,* September 16/23, 1996, 11.

Sternsher, Bernard. *Consensus, Conflict, and American Historians.* Bloomington: Indiana University Press, 1975.

Stevens, Jacqueline. "Comment: Beyond Tocqueville, Please!" *American Political Science Review* 89 (December 1995): 987–89.

Stokes, Bruce. *Helping Ourselves: Local Solutions to Global Problems.* New York: Norton, 1981.

Storing, Herbert J. *What the Anti-Federalist Were For.* Chicago: University of Chicago Press, 1981.

Strauss, Leo. *Natural Right and History.* Chicago: University of Chicago Press, 1965.

Streichen, Donna. *Ungodly Rage: The Hidden Face of Catholic Feminism.* San Francisco: Ignatius Press, 1991.

Sullivan, Andrew. "Washington Diarist." *New Republic,* October 18, 1993, 50.

Sullivan, John L., James Piereson, and George E. Marcus. *Political Tolerance and American Democracy.* Chicago: University of Chicago Press, 1982.

Sullivan, William L. *Reconstructing Political Philosophy.* Berkeley: University of California Press, 1982.

Swidler, Ann. "In Groups We Trust." *New York Times Book Review,* March 20, 1994, 13.

Takaki, Ronald. *A Different Mirror: A History of Multicultural America.* Boston: Little, Brown, 1993.

Talbot, Margaret. "Love, American Style." *New Republic,* April 14, 1997, 30–38.

Taylor, Bob Pepperman. *America's Bachelor Uncle: Thoreau and the American Polity.* Lawrence: University Press of Kansas, 1996.

———. *Our Limits Transgressed: Environmental Political Thought in America.* Lawrence: University Press of Kansas, 1992.

Taylor, Doceta E. "Blacks and the Environment: Toward an Explanation of the Concern and Action Gap Between Blacks and Whites." *Environmental Behavior* 21 (March 1989): 175–205.

Taylor, Paul. *Respect for Nature.* Princeton, N.J.: Princeton University Press, 1986.

Thernstrom, Stephan, and Abigail Thernstrom. *America in Black and White.* New York: Simon and Schuster, 1997.

Thiele, Leslie Paul. *Thinking Politics: Perspectives in Ancient, Modern, and Postmodern Political Theory.* Chatham, N.J.: Chatham House, 1997.

Tinder, Glenn. *Community: Reflections on a Tragic Ideal.* Baton Rouge: Louisiana State University Press, 1980.

Tocqueville, Alexis de. *Democracy in America.* Edited by Richard D. Heffner. New York: Mentor, 1956.

———. *Democracy in America.* 2 vols. Edited by Phillips Bradley. New York: Vintage, 1954, 1957.

Tong, Rosemarie. *Feminist Thought: A Comprehensive Introduction.* Boulder, Colo.: Westview, 1989.

Tronto, Joan C. *Moral Boundaries: A Political Argument for an Ethic of Care.* New York: Routledge, 1993.

Turner, Frederick Jackson. *The Significance of the Frontier in American History.* New York: Unger, 1982.

Twitchell, James B. *For Shame: The Loss of Common Decency in American Culture.* New York: St. Martin's, 1997.

Tyrrell, Ian. "American Exceptionalism in an Age of International History." *American Historical Review* 96 (October 1991): 1031–55.

"The US in Cross-National Perspective." *Public Perspective* 6 (April–May 1995): 20.

Varenne, Herve. *Americans Together: Structural Diversity in a Midwestern Town.* New York: Columbia University Press, 1977.

Vecoli, Rudolph J. "Ethnicity: A Neglected Dimension of American History." In *The State of American History,* edited by Herbert J. Bags, 70–88. Chicago: University of Chicago Press, 1970.

Veith, Gene Edward, Jr. *Postmodern Times: A Christian Guide to Contemporary Thought and Culture.* Wheaton, Ill.: Crossway, 1994.

Verba, Sidney, Kay Lehman Schlozman, and Henry E. Brady, eds. *Voice and Equality: Civic Voluntarism in American Politics.* Cambridge, Mass.: Harvard University Press, 1995.

Vetterli, Richard, and Gary Bryner. *In Search of the Republic: Public Virtue and the Roots of American Government.* Lanham, Md.: Rowman and Littlefield, 1987.

Voegelin, Eric. *The New Science of Politics.* Chicago: University of Chicago Press, 1952.

Wallace, Michael. "The Uses of Violence in American History." *American Scholar* 40 (Winter 1970–71): 81–100.

Wallach, John R. "Liberals, Communitarians, and the Tasks of Political Theory." *Political Theory* 15 (November 1987): 581–611.

Wallerstein, Judith. *The Good Marriage: How and Why Love Lasts.* Boston: Houghton Mifflin, 1995.

Wallerstein, Judith, and Sandra Blakeslee. *Second Chances: Men, Women, and Children After a Decade of Divorce.* New York: Ticknor and Fields, 1989.

Wallis, Jim. *Agenda for a Biblical People.* New York: Harper, 1976.

———. *The Soul of Politics.* Marynoll, N.Y.: Orbis, 1994.

Walvoord, John F. *Armageddon, Oil, and the Middle East Crisis.* Grand Rapids, Mich.: Zondervan, 1990.

Walzer, Michael. *The Company of Critics: Social Criticism and Political Commitment in the Twentieth Century.* New York: Basic Books, 1988.

———. *On Toleration.* New Haven, Conn.: Yale University Press, 1997.

———. *Spheres of Justice: A Defense of Pluralism and Equality.* New York: Basic Books, 1983.

———. *Thick and Thin: Moral Argument at Home and Abroad.* Notre Dame, Ind.: University of Notre Dame Press, 1994.

————, ed. *Toward a Global Civil Society.* Providence, R.I.: Berghahn, 1995.

Wandesforde-Smith, Geoffrey. "Moral Outrage and the Progress of Environmental Policy." In *Environmental Policy in the 1990s,* edited by Norman J. Vig and Michael Kraft, 325–47. Washington, D.C.: Congressional Quarterly, 1990.

Wapner, Paul. *Environmental Activism and World Civic Politics.* Albany: State University of New York Press, 1996.

Washington, Bryan R. *The Politics of Exile: Ideology in Henry James, F. Scott Fitzgerald, and James Baldwin.* Boston: Northeastern University Press, 1995.

Watt, James. *The Courage of a Conservative.* New York: Simon and Schuster, 1985.

Watt, Leilai. *Caught in the Conflict: My Life with James Watt.* Eugene, Ore.: Harvest House, 1984.

Watts, Nicholas, and Geoffrey Wandesforde-Smith. "Postmaterial Values and Environmental Policy Change." In *Environmental Policy Formation,* edited by Dean E. Mann, 29–42. Lexington, Mass.: D. C. Heath, 1981.

Webking, Robert H. *The American Revolution and the Politics of Liberty.* Baton Rouge: Louisiana State University Press, 1988.

Weinstein, Jerome. *The Corporate Ideal in the Liberal State: 1910–1918.* Boston: Beacon, 1968.

Weissbourd, Richard. "Divided Families, Whole Children." *American Prospect* 18 (Summer 1994): 66–72.

Wells, David F. *No Place for Truth, or Whatever Happened to Evangelical Theology?* Grand Rapids, Mich.: Eerdmans, 1993.

Wertheimer, Jack. *A People Divided: Judaism in Contemporary America.* New York: Basic Books, 1993.

West, Cornel. "The Democratic Soul." *Religion and Values in Public Life* 6 (Fall 1997): 6.

Wheat, Ed. *Love Life for Every Married Couple.* Grand Rapids, Mich.: Zondervan, 1987.

White, Lynn. "The Historic Roots of Our Ecologic Crisis." *Science,* March 10, 1967, 1203–7.

Whitehead, Barbara. "Dan Quayle Was Right." *Atlantic Monthly,* April 1993, 47–50.

————. *The Divorce Culture.* New York: Knopf, 1996.

Wideman, John Edgar. *Fatheralong: A Meditation on Fathers and Sons, Race and Society.* New York: Pantheon, 1994.

Wiebe, Robert H. *Self-Rule: A Cultural History of American Democracy.* Chicago: University of Chicago Press, 1995.

Wildavsky, Aaron. "Resolved, That Individualism and Egalitarianism Be Made Compatible in America; Political Cultural Roots of Exceptionalism." In *Is America Different?* edited by Byron E. Shafer, chap. 5. New York: Oxford University Press, 1991.

Wilentz, Sean. *Chants Democratic: New York City and the Rise of the American Working Class, 1788–1850.* New York: Oxford University Press, 1984.

Wilkinson, Loren. What Can We Learn from the New Testament? In *The Environment and the Christian: What Does the New Testament Say About the Environment?* edited by Calvin DeWitt, chap. 1. Grand Rapids, Mich.: Baker, 1991.

Williams, Patricia. *The Alchemy of Race and Rights: Diary of a Law Professor.* Cambridge, Mass.: Harvard University Press, 1991.

Wills, Garry. *Nixon Agonistes: The Crisis of the Self-Made Man.* New York: Signet, 1970.

Wilson, James Q. *Families, Schools, and Delinquency Prevention.* New York: Springer-Verlag, 1987.

————. "Justice vs. Humanity in the Family." In *The Neoconservative Imagination: Essays in Honor of Irving Kristol,* edited by Christopher DeMuth and William Kristol, 291–304. Washington, D.C.: American Enterprise Institute, 1995.

————. *The Moral Sense*. New York: Free Press, 1993.

————. "The Rediscovery of Character: Private Virtue and Public Policy." *Public Interest* 81 (Fall 1985): 3–16.

Wilson, William Julius. *The Truly Disadvantaged*. Chicago: University of Chicago Press, 1990.

————. *When Work Disappears: The World of the New Urban Poor*. New York: Knopf, 1996.

Wise, Gene. *American Historical Explanations*. Homewood, Ill.: Dorsey, 1973.

Witte, John. *Choice in American Education*. Madison: Wisconsin Center for Educational Policy, 1991.

Witte, John, and Mark Rigdon. "Educational Choice Reforms: Will They Change America's Schools?" *Publius* 23 (Summer 1993): 95–114.

Witte, John, Troy D. Sterr, and Christopher A. Thorn. *Fifth Year Report: Milwaukee Choice Program*. Madison: University of Wisconsin, 1995.

Wolf, Naomi. *Fire with Fire: The New Female Power and How to Use It*. New York: Random House, 1993.

Wolfe, Alan. *Marginalized in the Middle*. Chicago: University of Chicago Press, 1996.

————. *One Nation, After All: What Middle-Class Americans Really Think About God, Country, Family, Poverty, Racism, Welfare, Homosexuality, Immigration, the Left, the Right, and Each Other*. New York: Viking, 1998.

————. *Whose Keeper? Social Science and Moral Obligation*. Berkeley: University of California Press, 1989.

Wolfe, Christopher. "Subsidiarity: The 'Other' Ground of Limited Government." In *Catholicism, Liberalism, and Communitarianism*, edited by Kenneth L. Grasso, Gerald V. Bradley, and Robert P. Hunt, 81–96. Lanham, Md..: Rowman and Littlefield, 1995.

Wolff, Robert Paul. *The Poverty of Liberalism*. Boston: Beacon, 1968.

Wolff, Robert Paul, Barrington Moore, Jr., and Herbert Marcuse. *A Critique of Pure Tolerance*. Boston: Beacon, 1965.

Wolin, Sheldon. "Democracy in the Discourse of Postmodernism." *Social Research* 57 (Spring 1990): 5–30.

————. *Politics and Vision*. Boston: Little, Brown, 1960.

Wolin, Sheldon, and John H. Schaar. *The Berkeley Rebellion and Beyond*. New York: Vintage, 1970.

Wood, Gordon. *The Creation of the American Republic, 1776–1787*. New York: Norton, 1972.

————. *The Radicalism of the American Revolution*. New York: Knopf, 1992.

Woodson, Robert L. "Strangers in a Divided House: Race in America," *Washington Times*, November 2, 1997, B8.

Wuthnow, Robert. "Between the State and the Market: Voluntarism and the Difference It Makes." In *Rights and the Common Good: The Communitarian Perspective*, edited by Amitai Etzioni, 209–21. New York: St Martin's, 1995.

————. "How Small Groups Are Transforming Our Lives." *Christianity Today*, February 7, 1994, 19–24.

————. *Sharing the Journey: Support Groups and America's New Quest for Community*. New York: Free Press, 1994.

Yack, Bernard. *The Fetishism of Modernities: Epochal Self-Consciousness in Contemporary Social and Political Thought*. Notre Dame, Ind.: University of Notre Dame Press, 1997.

————. "Liberalism Without Illusions." In *Essays on Liberal Theory and the Political Vision of Judith N. Shklar*, edited by Bernard Yack, 1–13. Chicago: University of Chicago Press, 1996.

Yamane, David. "Secularization on Trial: A Defense of a Neosecularization Paradigm." *Journal for the Scientific Study of Religion* 36 (1997): 109–22.

Yankelovich, Daniel. "How Changes in the Economy Are Reshaping American Values." In *Values and Public Policy,* edited by Henry J. Aaron, Thomas E. Mann, and Timothy Taylor, 16–53. Washington, D.C.: Brookings, 1994.

———. *New Rules: Searching for Self-fulfillment in a World Turned Upside Down.* New York: Random House, 1981.

Yazawa, Melvin. *From Colonies to Commonwealth: Familial Ideology and the Beginnings of the American Republic.* Baltimore, Md.: Johns Hopkins University Press, 1985.

Young, Iris Marion. "The Ideal of Community and the Politics of Difference." In *Feminism/postmodernism,* edited by Linda Nicholson, chap. 12. New York: Routledge, 1990.

———. *Justice and the Politics of Difference.* Princeton, N.J.: Princeton University Press, 1990.

Young, James P. *Reconsidering American Liberalism: The Troubled Odyssey of the Liberal Idea.* Boulder, Colo.: Westview, 1996.

Zakaria, Fareed. "Paris Is Burning." *New Republic,* January 22, 1996, 27–30.

Zaller, John R. *The Nature and Origins of Mass Opinion.* New York: Cambridge University Press, 1992.

Zinn, Howard. *The Politics of History.* Boston: Beacon, 1971.

Zinn, Maxine Baca. "Family, Race, and Poverty in the Eighties." In *Family in Transition,* edited by Arlene Skolnick and Jerome Skolnick, 399–413. New York: HarperCollins, 1992.

Index

Aaron, Daniel, 15
Abolitionists, 32, 74
Abortion, 127–28, 129, 131
Academic feminism, 45, 47–48
*Achieving Our Country: Leftist Thought
in Twentieth-Century America*
(Rorty), 248
Adams, Henry, 14
Adams, John, 15
Affirmative action, 228
African Americans, 40, 81
and employment, 226
family, 136, 224, 225
family and civil society, 223–24
feminists, 47
and government, 226–28
liberal values, 105–6
males, 228, 231, 232–33, 234
middle class, 234
and multiculturalism, 107
public opinion, 62, 63, 64
and racism, 228–34
Agrarian demands, 12–13, 14
*Alchemy of Race and Rights: Diary of a
Law Professor* (Williams), 54
America in Black and White (Thernstrom
and Thernstrom), 227
American culture, 25–26, 27, 30,
100
"American dream," 105
*American Exceptionalism: A Double-
Edged Sword* (Lipset), 62
American Historical Association, 8
American political thought, 251
minor traditions, 84
nineteenth-century interpretations, 2–
11
in Progressive Era, 19, 73

See also Civil society; Community;
Conflict interpretations; Consensus
interpretations; Environmentalism;
Postmodernism
American Political Tradition, The
(Hofstadter), 22–23
*American Politics: The Promise of
Disharmony* (Huntington), 98
American Revolution (1775–1783),
88
Boorstin on, 31–32
and community, 162
Hartz on, 28
and liberalism, 93
and religion, 91–92
*Americans, The: The Democratic
Experience* (Boorstin), 30, 33
Americans, The: The National Experience
(Boorstin), 30
American Scene, The (James), 19
American value consensus, 22, 62, 65,
66–67
and 1960s, 36
American value system, 14, 62–65,
245–46
*America's Bachelor Uncle: Thoreau and the
American Polity* (Taylor), 179
Anarchism, 42, 43
eco-, 192–94
Anderson, Charles W., 60–61
Anti-Communist foreign policy, 120
Anti-Federalists, 94, 95
Anti-institutionalism, 101–2
Antiutopia, 190–91
Appleby, Joyce, 86, 91, 94
Armey, Dick, 119
Asian Americans, 71, 81
Atlantic Monthly, 218

319